BEATLEMANIA!

THE REAL STORY OF
THE BEATLES
UK TOURS
1963-1965

BEATLEMANIA!

THE REAL STORY OF
THE BEATLES
UK TOURS
1963-1965
MARTIN CREASY

OMNIBUS PRESS

London / New York / Paris / Sydney / Copenhagen / Berlin / Madrid / Tokyo

Exclusive Distributors
Music Sales Limited,
14/15 Berners Street,
London, W1T 3LJ.

Music Sales Corporation,
257 Park Avenue South,
New York, NY 10010, USA.

Macmillan Distribution Services,
56 Parkwest Drive
Derrimut, Vic 3030,
Australia.

Every effort has been made to trace the copyright holders of the photographs in this book but one or two were unreachable. We would be grateful if the photographers concerned would contact us.

Printed in the E.U.

A catalogue record for this book is available from the British Library.

Visit Omnibus Press on the web at www.omnibuspress.com

Contents

Author's Note

I WAS just that little bit young to fully appreciate the joyous impact The Beatles had when they burst on to the British pop scene at the beginning of 1963. It was an explosion of verve and vitality that arrived in the wake of a depressingly long, arduous and colourless winter that is recalled by all who remember it as one of the worst on record. In hindsight it seems only fitting that it should have been followed by something as sizzling as The Beatles.

Later that year, however, the first record I ever purchased was 'I Want To Hold Your Hand' which, at 6s 6d, cost me a few weeks' pocket money. I can still remember my disappointment on discovering that 'She Loves You' was not on the B-side. I was eight years old at the time and that meant I wasn't really on the page. You had to be a teenager to appreciate the cultural earthquake that spread out from Liverpool to rock the country and, eventually, the world.

The first tremors occurred at the very beginning of 1963 when the four young men who were to change music forever undertook their first national tour, supporting Helen Shapiro and several other pop favourites of the day. That tour happily coincided with the rapid ascent up the charts of their second single, 'Please Please Me', which, almost overnight, rendered superfluous to requirements the run-of-the-mill American crooners who had previously annexed our pop charts.

But the rest wasn't quite history yet. National newspapers hadn't yet assigned reporters and photographers to record The Beatles' every word, describe every exciting detail of their lives in extravagant prose or capture a thousand pictures of the four young men and the girls who screamed at them. They didn't become aware of The Beatles until about the same time as I did, in the autumn of 1963, when 'She Loves You' was number one and the scenes after their *Sunday Night At The London Palladium* performance gave birth to the title of this book, Beatlemania. By that time The Beatles had undertaken three national tours and there wasn't a teenager in the land who wasn't dancing to a beat that had yet to reach the ears of their parents.

Recent films about the early days of The Beatles have created a distorted picture of these times and developments. The 1994 film *Backbeat*, centring on Stuart Sutcliffe and dealing with the often complex relationships between the key players, came over as dark and depressing, and even 2009's *Nowhere Boy* had a tragic air about it. While both films are worthy expressions of the problems encountered by the pre-fame Beatles, and John Lennon in particular, they hardly do justice to what The Beatles really became. The Beatles in 1963 and for some time beyond were young, and full of energy, optimism and fun. And that fun was infectious. We were all bitten by it. We all caught Beatlemania.

Maybe one day a film will be made that does justice to the rise of The Beatles and to the immense joy their music and presence brought to a Britain still trying to shake off the after-effects of war. Nowhere was that joy more in evidence than in their live performances before they became household names.

In the pages of this book, dozens of fans – many now grandparents – from towns and cities the length of Britain tell their stories, as do the policemen who protected those young fans from themselves, the regional journalists who covered the shows, the staff from the venues and the pop stars who had the pleasure of being on tour with The Beatles. There is even the hotelier's daughter who gave up her bed for the night so a Beatle could get some precious sleep.

Perhaps these incredible tour concert scenes will be recreated for cinema audiences one day – and with the music at the centre of it, what a film that would be. In the meantime, join me on a journey back to this island's golden musical years. Welcome to the early 1960s. Welcome to Beatleland.

INTRODUCTION

Getting Ready To Go National

AT the beginning of 1963 Liverpool was a divided city. This wasn't the perennial rivalry between Liverpool and Everton, the reds and the blues, but between fans of the city's favourite pop group who, having conquered all before them on the local music scene, were now ready for the leaving of Liverpool, and not everyone was happy.

Many of these fans had followed the boys from their humble beginnings at the Casbah and Litherland Town Hall, and had joined the queue along Mathew Street for a lunchtime session at the Cavern Club. Some were hoping that the group's second single, 'Please Please Me', would storm the charts so the rest of the country could share in the magic that had entranced Liverpool; others, equally devoted to the group, felt that once everyone else woke up to them, they would be lost to the city forever.

Little known outside Merseyside, The Beatles were on the cusp of success, and in sharing manager Brian Epstein's ambition to be bigger than Elvis, they knew full well they were never going to achieve this dream by playing only in their own back yard. It's easy to look back now and assume there was an inevitability about their success. Certainly, their music was exciting and vibrant and they had the looks and personalities to match but there were hundreds of young men with electric guitars and drums playing in groups in Liverpool alone, and not all of the early signs were encouraging for The Beatles.

Despite huge support from the city, their debut single, 'Love Me Do', had troubled only the lower regions of the charts, and when they took their show on the road not every Beatle gig ended in screams, cheers . . . or even polite applause. On one notable occasion there were even a few cat-calls and jeers from those as yet unimpressed by Merseyside's finest.

However, that show, starring yodeller Frank Ifield, at the Embassy

1

Cinema in Peterborough on December 2, 1962, though ignominious for the group at the time, was to have happier repercussions. In the audience was the promoter Arthur Howes and his junior secretary Susan Fuller, and they saw the group's potential, even if some of the audience (and the local newspaper critic) didn't.

Howes was there because Epstein had telephoned him at the end of October, and told him – as he told everybody who would listen – that his boys were destined for great things, and Fuller acknowledges the part that Neil Brooks, manager of the Empire Theatre in Liverpool at the time, played in bringing the two together. "Neil telephoned Arthur and raved on about The Beatles," she says. "He asked Arthur if he could give Arthur's telephone number to Brian."

Perhaps surprisingly, on the strength of Neil and Brian's enthusiasm, Howes booked The Beatles on to his Helen Shapiro package the following February. He also told Epstein that in order for him to assess their performance he wanted the group to first play 10-minute spots on Ifield's two Peterborough houses for expenses only.

Their hearts may have sunk as they crept offstage that December night, but Howes and his assistant had a surprise for them. "My memory, along with Arthur and my mother, when they were both alive, was that the Peterborough audience were booing and yelling 'Get off', 'Rubbish' etc," says Fuller, "but we all thought the boys had great talent. I remember drinking with Eppy and Arthur discussing the concert afterwards and we were all most confident of their talent leading to great success." Howes was also impressed with Epstein as a businessman, and this may also have been a factor in his decision.

Not only did The Beatles retain their spot on the Shapiro package, but Howes wasted no time in booking them on to his Chris Montez and Tommy Roe double header that would immediately follow. Epstein, touched by Howe's faith in his boys, responded by giving an undertaking that Howes could have first refusal on all future Beatle UK tours.

Arthur Howes and Susan Fuller weren't the only ones to see something in The Beatles that night. In the audience were 15-year-old Carol Barrett and her Peterborough County Grammar School pals Pauline White and Margaret Cawfield. They liked The Beatles so much that they joined their fan club immediately afterwards.

Reports that The Beatles received a frosty reception are exaggerated, according to Carol. "People were screaming," she says, "Margaret was screaming, too. It was all so unheard of. People just got so wound up about four lads on the stage. I do remember Margaret screaming at that first show. We must have thought they were good because it made us join their fan club that night."

Carol and her friends were typical teenagers and pop music was very much a part of their lives. "I hadn't heard of The Beatles before," admits Carol (now Carol Abell), "but I knew about the scene at the Cavern as I spent my school summer holidays with family in Liverpool.

"We went to all the pop shows at the Embassy – I think the first was Tommy Steele. The Beatles were special though. They were very friendly, just ordinary lads – very jokey. They were quite happy to meet us and sign autographs, but not all pop stars did. Tommy Steele and Adam Faith sent people out to pick up the autograph books, so you couldn't be certain they'd signed them, but The Beatles signed our books and programmes."

Those Beatle signings didn't take place at the Embassy, but across town at the hotel where they were staying. A little local knowledge goes a long way – and Carol and her friends knew that the stars often stayed at the Bull Hotel on Westgate in the city centre. So off they all trundled – and hit the jackpot. "The hotel entrance was in a car park at the side and we gathered there and started yelling, hoping The Beatles would hear us," she recalls. "They must have done because they came downstairs to meet us. I remember they were casually dressed in leather and suede jackets, not the suits they had worn onstage."

The girls were delighted to listen to all four Beatles talking about their first record and their first steps to stardom. "They were just really down-to-earth, sunny and chatty," adds Carol. "We were struck with how normal they all were."

Dougie Wright, drummer of The Ted Taylor Four who were also on the bill that night, watched The Beatles' performance from the wings, and he was another who was impressed.

"The song that stuck in my mind that night was 'A Taste Of Honey'," he says. "Paul McCartney was singing and I just thought this is fantastic. This was a jazz waltz being sung by a pop group and it was beautiful. I remember talking to sax player Jimmy Stead afterwards and telling him that this new group were going to knock The Shadows into a cocked hat, and of course they did. But things were changing rapidly at that moment. Instrumental groups were making way for vocal groups and I sensed The Beatles were going to be huge."

And the reaction of the Peterborough audience? "As far as I recall they gave everybody a good reception."

While the reaction to The Beatles in Peterborough was mixed, it certainly wasn't an all-round disaster. Howes was shrewd enough to realise that those who went to watch Frank Ifield would not necessarily appreciate what The Beatles had to offer. Their place on a national tour – a vital shop window back then – was confirmed.

The countdown to the tour included a handful of concerts, TV and radio dates to plug 'Love Me Do' and a final, not necessarily welcome, two-week stint at the Star Club in Hamburg that climaxed with a marathon session on New Year's Eve. Shaking hands and drinking toasts with friends old and new on the Reeperbahn as 1962 became 1963, The Beatles were chomping at the bit to get home to what certainly had the makings of a prosperous New Year.

It began with a five-day visit to Scotland, but their minds would clearly have been on their upcoming first national tour – how would they grab the fans' attention from their humble spot on the bill? Fortunately, back on Monday, November 26 – just a few days before their appearance on the Frank Ifield Peterborough package – The Beatles had returned to Abbey Road to record their second single. It was a song altogether more exciting than their first – pacy, tuneful and instantly catchy. It laid down a marker for the dazzling hits that were to follow.

The release of 'Please Please Me' on Friday, January 11, just three weeks before the first tour commenced, would change things forever.

CHAPTER ONE

The First Tour
Please Pleasing Iced-up Britain

February 2 – March 3, 1963
Featuring Helen Shapiro, Danny Williams, Kenny Lynch,
The Beatles, The Red Price Band, The Honeys and The Kestrels
Compère: Dave Allen

IT wasn't exactly one giant leap, more one small but significant step for Beatles impatient to cash in on the modest success of their debut disc, 'Love Me Do'. They wouldn't have the spotlight all to themselves and were way down the bill as they started out on their first national tour in the bitter grip of the worst winter in more than 200 years, travelling on a coach with performers who had already enjoyed considerable levels of success.

Bill-topper Helen Shapiro may have been just 16, but she already had five Top 10 hits to her name, including two number ones, 'You Don't Know' and 'Walking Back To Happiness' before she had reached her fifteenth birthday. Born in Bethnal Green, east London, music was in the family blood. Helen's mother and grandfather were both accomplished violinists and she became a pupil of the Maurice Burman School Of Modern Pop Singing, where her extraordinarily mature voice was honed to perfection. She was a celluloid star, too, with a lead role in the film *It's Trad Dad*, starring alongside Craig Douglas, and had also sung a couple of songs in the film *Play It Cool*.

However, Shapiro's pop career had been coasting for a while, her last two singles having failed to take off, but the tour coincided with the release of 'Queen For Tonight' that she hoped would reverse the trend. A review in that week's *Melody Maker* was headlined 'Will This Put Helen Back On Her Feet?'

South African-born singer Danny Williams was also a household name. His recording of 'Moon River' from the film *Breakfast At Tiffany's* had been a huge hit, reaching number one at Christmas 1961 and staying in the UK charts for an impressive 19 weeks. Williams had first come to Britain in 1959 when he was a singer in The Golden City Dixies show which had already been a hit in South Africa. The show toured Britain and Williams was signed to the HMV label by EMI's Norman Newell. He went back to South Africa but, missing England, telephoned Newell who gladly welcomed back his young protégé in August 1960. His chart break-through came with the Russ Conway and Lionel Bart penned 'We Will Never Be As Young As This Again' but he also had a song to plug, an oldie, 'My Own True Love', his latest single.

Kenny Lynch, another high profile singer on the package was also an east ender. The youngest of 13 children, Lynch was approaching his twenty-fifth birthday and had already climbed a few steps on the ladder of life. He had done National Service in the Royal Army Service Corps, where he made a name for himself as a featherweight boxer, and he was already an established singer and songwriter. The pop film *Just For Fun*, about to be released, included four of his compositions. Lynch was enjoy-ing chart success with 'Up On The Roof' which had been released late in 1962 and was still at number nine as the tour was about to get underway.

Nevertheless Lynch, who had already sung with industry heavyweights such as Bob Miller's band and the Phil Moss Band, was uneasy about the state of British pop. On the day the tour commenced he was bemoaning things in a double-page spread in *Melody Maker*, headlined 'We're Brain-washed By The Charts'. Lynch had opened his heart to the newspaper's Ray Coleman, offering his opinion on how record companies were crush-ing the life out of singers by trying to adapt their style to achieve commer-cial success.

On the very same day Lynch was quoted in the rival *Record Mirror* singing the praises of The Beatles. "One reason I think they'll succeed is because they manage to reproduce their record sound onstage. This is why The Shadows succeeded and this is why The Beatles will. Apart from that, their sound is so great they can't miss," he prophesied.

Bristol singing quartet The Kestrels (Geoff Williams, Roger Greenaway, Pete Gullane and Tony Burrows) were also on the package. They were highly professional and polished, and stars such as Billy Fury and Joe

Brown had employed their talents. Despite interruptions for National Service, The Kestrels had been flying high since the 1950s, initially as a skiffle and rock'n'roll trio, but as time wore on they were increasingly influenced by American harmony groups in the mould of The Platters, especially after Geoff Williams joined and expanded their vocal range.

Portsmouth-based blonde singing sisters The Honeys – Vilma, Anita and Pearl Liddell – were also seasoned travellers. Modelled on The Beverley Sisters, they were familiar faces on Southern Television and had toured with some of the biggest names in the pop world, including Cliff Richard, Adam Faith and Bobby Vee.

Backing them and playing in their own slot were The Red Price Band, who were also familiar faces on the touring scene. Red was a tenor sax player from Liverpool who had played in the Ted Heath Band and was later the featured horn player with Lord Rockingham's XI. Red's distinctive tenor sax had backed many a star on tours and on record. Chosen to lead the 15-piece New Orleans Rockers on Larry Parnes' Rock 'n' Trad Spectacular in November 1960, he went on to form The Red Price Combo the following year. Alongside Red were Bernie Sharpe on trumpet, Bill Stark on bass and Andy White on drums, and they had enjoyed tours with Adam Faith and Chubby Checker.

Helen, who went on to tour with them in Australia, Israel and South Africa, as well as the UK, remembers Red and his jazzers with affection. "They were lovely guys, funny and good players, all of them. It was a fluid line-up – they would have guest players – but the regulars were Red on tenor sax, Alan Skidmore also on sax, with Les Dawson (not the famous comedian) on drums, Bill Stark on bass and Jimmy Curry was the guitarist.

"They were older guys – in their forties probably – and of course I was only 16 but they were friendly and they appreciated what I did," says Helen. "I remember they would often start with a piece called 'Four Brothers'. Red would enter from one side of the stage and Alan from the other, like they were duelling. Red was a funny guy. I remember him sitting on the coach eating onions like they were apples because he'd read somewhere they were good for you. He was a gentle giant. I appreciated their musicianship and they saw something in my voice."

The tour's resident wit and Master of Ceremonies was a young Irishman called Dave Allen, who was later to carve his own place in showbiz history. He was born David Tynan O'Mahoney in Dublin in 1936.

7

His father was a highly rated journalist who rose to managing editor of *The Irish Times* and though the boy initially followed his father into the profession he soon became infatuated with the entertainment business, particularly the artistry of the comedian. After trying his luck as a Redcoat at a Butlin's holiday camp in Skegness, he took his stand-up routine on the club circuit where he was spotted by a BBC producer and moved into television. He also became a popular turn at Army bases across the world. Somewhere along the line his agent had reasoned that the name O'Mahoney was difficult to handle and so Dave Allen was born.

He liked to tell tall tales about why part of the index finger of his left hand was missing, but the truth was duller than the stories he told. It had got caught in a cog of a machine in a school accident. It was no surprise that Dave was included as he had compèred some of Helen's early tours and the pair got on very well.

Unlike everyone else, The Beatles were something of an unknown quantity. They had served a tough apprenticeship, with hour upon hour on the dimly lit stages of Hamburg nightclubs having honed an act that had since taken Liverpool by storm. Their sets on this 14-date tour of mainly northern venues, with a break in the middle, would be a doddle in comparison. There were two shows a night (6.15pm and 8.30pm), but as a humble down-the-bill act they would be required to perform just four songs per house – not much more than a quarter of an hour onstage.

Their four songs for the tour were 'Chains', 'Keep Your Hands Off My Baby', 'A Taste Of Honey' and 'Please Please Me'. However, such was their rapid rise that they ended up also playing two further songs – 'Love Me Do' and 'Beautiful Dreamer' (composed in the 1860s by US songwriter Stephen Foster) – which had been listed as substitute numbers. The regional press reported that they also added 'Long Tall Sally' on several occasions.

These were still fairly early days as a Beatle for drummer Ringo Starr. Controversially drafted in as Pete Best's replacement just a few months before, he still appeared insecure around the three Beatles who had been through so much together. Ringo generally roomed with Paul, and John shared with George.

Helen Shapiro can recall the moment she was told by promoter Arthur Howes that The Beatles would be joining her tour. "I'd had a meeting with Arthur and he'd said that for this new tour I'd be accompanied by

Danny Williams and Kenny Lynch and that The Red Price Combo would be my backing band. Dave Allen would be the compère and there would also be this new group called The Beatles.

"He asked if I'd heard of them and of course, I had. I loved their song 'Love Me Do' and I was looking forward to the tour. Dave Allen didn't have a halfpenny to his name in those days, but he was a lovely guy and very funny. I was always touring with Danny and Kenny, and so I knew them well."

The Kestrels, like the others, were old friends, but Helen recalls her first meeting with the Liverpudlian newcomers at a pre-tour rehearsal. "The Beatles were already onstage setting up when I was introduced to them. Paul was the spokesman. He was bright and chirpy and he introduced me to the others. I remember them being very upbeat and excited. After all, this was a national tour and they hadn't done one of those before. They had played the Cavern, Hamburg and the ballrooms, all that stuff, but this was quite different."

If The Beatles were feeling optimistic at the beginning of February 1963 they were pretty much on their own. Most people in the UK would have opted for hibernation. This was the winter from hell. As the party of popsters headed out of London from the bus depot at Allsop Place at the rear of the Planetarium on Marylebone Road for that opening gig at the Gaumont in Bradford they were quite literally heading into the frozen north.

Records show that Yorkshire was covered in several inches of snow that day with a top temperature of minus 1°C, dropping to a biting –9°C by nightfall. The snow was *the* story of the moment. It never lifted through-out the whole tour and attendances were affected as a result. However, The Beatles were not on the coach for that first icy trip north. They had spent the previous evening, February 1, performing at the Assembly Rooms in Tamworth, followed by a quick dash down to Staffordshire to strut their stuff at Maney Hall in Sutton Coldfield. On dates such as these they did not yet have the luxury of being ferried around in a big car. For now they would have crammed into roadie Neil Aspinall's old Commer van, alongside their amps and guitars.

The coach arrived at the Gaumont, welcomed by groups of delighted young fans waiting to greet them and grab an autograph. Not everybody knew who The Beatles were yet. Vilma Liddell (now Harvey) of The

Honeys remembers fans coming up to her and asking if she was a Beatle! Fans, even in those innocent early days, were keen to be one step ahead. That afternoon a group of intrepid girls managed to sneak into the Bradford theatre through a side door in Quebec Street that led on to the stage. Already up there chatting were Helen Shapiro, The Beatles and The Honeys.

One of the cheeky autograph hunters was 13-year-old schoolboy Terry Bostock who managed to get Helen, The Honeys and a Beatle to sign his book before a booming voice from the auditorium told him to kindly leave the stage and he and the girl fans quickly dispersed.

Terry explains: "There is a side door to the stage through Quebec Street that runs alongside the old Gaumont. I saw that it was ajar and just went in. It leads through on to the stage and there they all were, just standing around chatting. It was Helen Shapiro's autograph I wanted really – she was the one I knew. So I made a beeline for her and she signed my autograph book. Then I went to The Honeys and got their signatures.

"I'd left The Beatles because they were surrounded by the girls all wanting their autographs. When it was clear, I went over and one of them signed, but then came this voice from the balcony and that was it. The other Beatles refused to sign. Whoever was yelling must have had some authority with them. I'd like to think it was Brian Epstein who called out, but it could just as easily have been a member of the cinema staff!"

Terry didn't get to see the show that night, but he does still have that precious autograph book. The Beatle who signed it was John Lennon.

Terry wasn't the only intrepid person in Bradford on that historic opening night. Stan Richardson, a freelance photographer, was at the Gaumont with a reporter on behalf of the *Melody Maker* to cover the first of the two performances. The Beatles made quite an impression on Stan so he asked them to pose for a photograph and they duly did. Between shows he nipped home to process the negative and returned during the second house with a 20in by 16in print which he had the good sense to ask the group to sign.

An impressed Brian Epstein asked him if he could do some publicity photos for the band, but Stan declined, saying he had difficulties getting paid by bands. Richardson recalls: "The picture was taken in the foyer. We were trying to get a picture and interview with Helen, but she refused. Then these Liverpool lads piped up 'We'll have our pictures taken.'

His Lordship (Epstein) was there in his white suit and pink carnation and he said, 'Come on, come on, take a picture of my boys.'

"I went home and processed it and returned for the end of the second house. I remember Epstein putting his arm around me and saying, 'Oh darling, I want you to take a whole set of pictures of my boys.' I refused. It sounds crazy now, but I'd taken pictures of pop stars before and you hardly ever got paid. The only time I ever got paid was when I took pictures of Lulu. Her people paid up straight away."

The show was opened by The Red Price Band, followed by The Honeys. Compère Dave Allen then took centre stage to introduce The Beatles. After their set he strode back out again for another gag or two before bringing on Danny Williams to close the first half. The Red Price Band got the second half underway, followed by The Kestrels. Then it was time for Kenny Lynch, and then Dave Allen finally got to introduce the show-closer, Helen Shapiro. This running order would change during the tour. Such were the screams for The Beatles that Arthur Howes felt compelled to change the running order to give them more than their usual 15 minutes or so.

It was a nervous first night onstage. Lack of rehearsals led to a few mishaps – The Red Price Combo and Danny Williams were in different keys at the start of one number, and the same thing happened to Kenny Lynch. Helen was tentative, too, until finding her feet – and powerful voice – to quickly get into her stride.

A fair few of the 3,318 seats were empty for the first house at 6pm. The terrible weather was having its effect. But what of The Beatles?

Epstein, with his taste for the theatrical, had ensured that his "boys" would look, as well as sound, like stars. Their old slicked back Teddy boy haircuts had long ago been ditched in favour of the mop-top fringe. Onstage they wore posh burgundy suits with velvet collars.

Photographer Richardson says that The Beatles, at that point still largely unknown outside Liverpool, made quite an impact. "They brought the house down – they just lit the whole show up. They were vibrant, alive, kicking – and the audience responded to them. They really stole the show."

His view was echoed by the *Yorkshire Post* reporter Reginald Brace who deserves credit for spotting that this as yet largely unknown but feisty young group, was destined for the top. Part of his report read: "Best of all, there were four young men from Liverpool called The Beatles, who, I predict, will go from strength to strength this year. They sing and strum their guitars with enormous, infectious zest."

While The Beatles' star was on the rise, Helen was coming under a little pressure. With her two previous singles stalling, in his column, headed 'Helen Shapiro Keeps Her Poise', Brace wrote that at just 16 she was learning how precarious a pop star's life could be. Helen confessed her worries in a dressing room interview, but Brace reported that Helen gave a professional performance onstage. She sang her current record 'Queen For Tonight' and was keeping everything crossed that it would propel her back up the charts. "She is a game little trouper," wrote Brace. "A petite figure in a frothy pink dress, she sang with poise and confidence as though she had not a care in the world."

Brace described it as one of the best shows of its type that he'd seen – an "entertaining bill illuminated by Danny Williams". He was also impressed by a "cocky, virile newcomer to the Hit Parade" – his description of Kenny Lynch. Then came his inspired comments about The Beatles.

A comprehensive report on the first house by Gordon Sampson in *New Musical Express* nailed down not only most of the set lists, but also the fact that The Beatles sang six numbers on the opening night of their very first national tour. He noted that the "colourfully dressed" Beatles got a great reception, with the audience already calling for them while other artists were onstage. He said their best number was 'A Taste Of Honey', given "an unusual vocal treatment" and "sung by left-handed bass guitarist Paul McCartney, with the others harmonising". Sampson added that they closed with 'Please Please Me' (that week at five in *NME*'s own chart) and that it got the best reception. He also noted that they sang 'Love Me Do', 'Beautiful Dreamer', 'Chains' and 'Keep Your Hands Off My Baby'.

The Red Price band were excellent musicians, but the lack of rehearsal time made it a tricky opening night for Kenny and Danny. Sampson said that Kenny had to struggle with his backing but made a big impact with his five songs, listing 'Up On The Roof', 'Mack The Knife' and 'Things' as among them.

Danny Williams didn't rely on movement for his performance. That voice was enough to hold the attention. The rock was left to the Liverpool boys as Danny serenaded with some classic ballads – 'Jeannie', 'The Wonderful World Of The Young', 'My Own True Love', 'Moon River' and his version of the Elvis number 'Can't Help Falling In Love' (the latter to just a piano accompaniment).

The *NME* report described The Kestrels as "a slick vocal quartet", revealing that their latest single 'Walk Right In' and their knockabout version of 'Blue Moon' were among their set. The Honeys were given four numbers, of which 'Let's Dance' went down best with the reporter.

It was star girl Helen who made the headline 'An Improved Helen' and Sampson announced that her voice had matured and she looked relaxed and confident. Helen had enough hits to enable her to offer them in medleys, opening with a short version of 'You Don't Know' followed by 'Little Miss Lonely', 'Don't Treat Me Like A Child', 'Tell Me What He Said', 'Walking Back To Happiness' and a reprise of 'You Don't Know'.

She demonstrated the versatility of her voice with 'The Birth Of The Blues' and then sang her latest 'A Queen For Tonight' which she hoped would re-ignite her chart career. Her second medley was pure music hall; accompanying herself on the tenor banjo in what Sampson described as "full blooded performances" of 'Some Of These Days', 'Baby Face', 'Toot Toot Tootsie' and 'If You Were The Only Boy In The World'. There was even time for a two-song encore with 'Goody Goody' and then 'I Want To Be Happy' in which Helen repeated the dance routines from her recent performance at The Palladium.

The listing of so many of the songs gives a fascinating insight into a remarkable collection of talented performers presenting a wide variety of music. The Beatles were positioning themselves right at the very heart of British show business and they looked perfectly at home sharing (and almost stealing) the limelight from some of the biggest names in pop.

Looking back in 2010, Sampson said he still has a letter from *NME* news editor Don Wedge with some important instructions. "He told me to look out for this new band called The Beatles. He said it would be worth giving them a mention in my report."

Sampson knows that his report was well received, not only by *NME* but by The Beatles themselves. "When I went to see them at Sheffield shortly afterwards they thanked me for it and they all signed a picture and gave it to me." He also remembers the cramped conditions of The Beatles' dressing room in Bradford. "Helen had the star dressing room downstairs, but you had to go up the steps to the small room The Beatles were in that night. You couldn't swing the proverbial cat in it. As I recall, we were all stood up. They were sort of propped up by the small mirror – two at one end and two at the other, with Brian in the background. We were the only people in the room.

"We would just have talked about the usual things – their recording plans, what it was like to be on a national tour in the spotlight, that kind of thing. They were very friendly and a bit of a laugh, but there was no mickey-taking or anything like that. They were very polite."

Possession of the treasured *NME* pass not only got you a welcome back-stage, but it got you the respect of performers who knew that what was printed in it – and the other respected music papers – was important to your career prospects. Sampson also interviewed Helen and Kenny that night. He covered many shows for *NME*, but he regarded it as a bonus. His day job was as a reporter on the *Halifax Evening Courier*.

But it was an unusual start to a tour. Having blitzed their way through that opening Saturday night in Bradford, The Beatles and the rest didn't play the second date until the Tuesday. An immediate mini-break in the tour it may have been, but they weren't days off for The Beatles. They had dates at the Cavern on the Sunday evening and Monday lunchtime before the tour resumed at the Gaumont at Hallgate in Doncaster, still in the chill of winter, on Tuesday, February 5.

After their brief trip home, The Beatles rejoined the rest of the crew for the two shows at the Doncaster Gaumont. They checked into the Regent Hotel, which was very handy as the venue was just about next door to the cinema. Fifteen-year-old Mick Longworth, the son of the hotel's owner, couldn't believe his luck. "Like all good teenagers I had a paper round," he says. "But when I got home from school that day there were six or seven girls outside the hotel. I asked my mum what was going on and she said 'Oh it's nothing. There's this group playing at the Gaumont tonight and they're staying here.'

"I already had tickets for the show but when mum said The Beatles were staying here I was very excited about it. After a few minutes I went upstairs. The TV lounge was up there and The Beatles were inside strum-ming their guitars. I didn't go in – that was not done, you didn't disturb guests. But I went near the glass doors and heard them. I've often won-dered if they were working on one of their early hits that day.

"I immediately called in to cancel my paper round the next morning so I could join my brother Dave in taking their tea up to their two twin rooms in the morning. Unfortunately, when we took the tea up they were all asleep. We went off to school, which was also very close by, but we both returned home fairly soon after, feeling unwell. It was probably the excitement and knowing The Beatles were probably still in the hotel. Anyway, when we got back there were The Beatles – all four of them in the restaurant finishing off their breakfast. They signed Parlophone promotion cards for us – and for some of the waitresses and kitchen staff.

"They had all signed the hotel register. There was a space for a name, date and nationality. George wrote George Harrison, British, February 5, 1963. But Ringo got the year wrong. He put Ringo Starr, British, February 5, 1962. The others also put the wrong year. John Lennon signed his name but under nationality wrote "white man" and Paul put "green man". Both followed Ringo in putting 1962. The funny thing was the next six people staying also put 1962 until one of them realised it was wrong and corrected it to 1963.

"I remember later saying to my dad and mum, who jointly owned the hotel, that we needed to put the beds up for sale. Everything to do with The Beatles was wanted – sheets they'd slept in, etc. 'Don't be so bloody stupid,' my dad said. The register they signed is in a bank vault now, but we have copies displayed."

As for the show, it made only a few paragraphs in the local paper, but those few paragraphs were complimentary. Under the heading 'Gaumont Show A Star-Studded Hit' it name-checked all the artists and said that "impresario" Arthur Howes congratulated recently appointed cinema manager J. Gaukrodger on a "marvellous show".

Unfortunately, for anyone interested in hearing music, the screaming had already started. Longworth recalls: "A lot of girls were hysterical during The Beatles' performance on the Shapiro bill. You couldn't hear very much. I was downstairs 20 rows back. I remember thinking I wish these bloody girls would shut up. The Beatles were fantastic, though. I have to say the PAs in those days were useless. They were probably singing through the cinema's PA, but the way they played their guitars – this was something you'd not heard before. John Lennon's voice, too. You listened to their harmonies – they were great. They started with something pacey, so it was probably 'Please Please Me'. The funny thing was bands were starting to go out of fashion at the time . . ."

Photographer Charlie Worsdale is more of a jazz fan than a pop fan, but he can look back on that night with pride as he spent some precious time with The Beatles in their dressing room and was accorded the reasonably rare privilege of being allowed to photograph the boys from the stage. Worsdale worked for the Foto News agency run by Bill Anderson and Ron Cookson and he was there with local girl Carol Roope whose happy duty it was to interview the pop stars for the agency.

He recalls what was happening when he went into their dressing room. "They were playing Ray Charles records on a portable player, and tracks by people like Chuck Berry and Bo Diddley. I was particularly chuffed they were listening to Ray Charles because I was quite a fan. I remember them joking among themselves about how audiences were reacting to them. They were poking fun at an audience which was now largely screaming girls who practically drowned out their music.

"I took my pictures from the wings while they were playing, but you couldn't hear that much. What was obvious was the excitement they were creating in the audience – it was obvious that they were going to be big. The music was largely drowned out, though.

"I also took pictures of Helen in the dressing room. I was quite an inexperienced photographer at the time. I shot them on 400asa speed – so they were experimental shots that night. You couldn't use flash. You just did the best you could, but I think the pictures are quite atmospheric."

The screaming at Doncaster on that first tour was not yet par for the course at a Beatles gig. Helen Shapiro recalls: "It sort of gradually built up really. After 'Please Please Me' hit the charts, that's what started things. It wasn't out of hand yet. Beatlemania hadn't started, but there was screaming for The Beatles. But they weren't screaming over them, during the songs. They would finish a number and that's when they screamed."

The look as well as the sound was all important for the group, and an onstage presence was key. The boys were quick learners. They prided themselves on steering clear of the stiff dance routines of The Shadows, preferring a cooler stage persona. They perfected the head-shaking on this tour and emphasised the falsetto oohs that were later to drive girls into such a frenzy.

The touring party left Doncaster the next morning to head down to Bedfordshire for two houses at the Granada Cinema in Bedford, the first starting at 7pm and the second at 9.10pm. The cinema in St Peter's Street had, like many others, been built during the 1930s boom of picture houses, but pop music was now gaining a foothold. The front of the building that night boldly proclaimed the "Helen Shapiro Show", and up in lights with her were The Beatles and Danny Williams, evidence that John, Paul, George and Ringo were already getting noticed.

The cinema was also prominently advertising the forthcoming visit of Bryan Hyland who was due there three weeks later.

Photographs of the crowds gathering show plenty of young faces – there were boys as well as girls – and there were signs that the teenage jungle drums were beating. The Bedford Granada's general manager may not have heard much about The Beatles before that night, but he pretty soon got the message. In fact, Ivan Morgan found himself making a very unusual request.

"The cinema was packed for both houses and The Beatles got such a reception when they closed the first half of the first house that I went up to Helen in between the shows and asked her if they could take her spot and close the show for the second house. She said OK. She was getting well paid and didn't seem to mind about it. They brought the house down. Of course we didn't know they were going to be that big, but they were certainly popular here."

Granada managers had more power than other cinema bosses at the time, with total control of everything that went on within the four walls of their buildings. This meant that Morgan had a say on how performers looked on the stage, as well as what they sounded like. Scruffy tops and torn jeans were out – no problem for the suited Beatles, of course – and Ivan got to oversee the Band Call – the rehearsals – to make sure the sound was right. "This was crucial. The sound level could make or break a show. Everything had to be right – the look and the sound and presentation," he said.

First houses were scrutinised by what Morgan called his Watch Committee, who reported anything unacceptable that would have to be put right for the second house. He had been staging pop shows since the notorious Bill Haley days when cinema audiences, as well as rocking it up became partial to ripping it up . . . including the seats. His answer was to employ the services of Bedford Rugby Club players to help keep order by protecting the stage and patrolling the aisles to make sure nothing got out of hand. Morgan recalls their services not being over-stretched that night, despite the excitement. The girls may have screamed, but they stayed in their seats to do it. "There was never any trouble here," he said, "and those Beatles shows went remarkably well."

The tour was now properly underway and the evidence suggests that everyone was rubbing along well. Helen, or Helly as she was dubbed by the boys, has spoken of the coach sing-alongs, with rousing renditions of favourite songs – and all backed by Beatle guitars. "The Beatles would be strumming away and sometimes I would take the lead, with them harmonising, and sometimes other people would be singing," she said. "We were all on the coach and we all used to sing together. The Beatles used to sing all sorts. They introduced us to all that Tamla Motown stuff that they loved. None of us had heard it before, but I guess Brian Epstein had first dibs on it all because he had run the record shop (NEMS). I would probably be singing Little Eva songs too – stuff like that."

Kenny Lynch also remembers the sing-alongs: "We would always do that – but it all depended on how hoarse we were from the show. I mean, if you think of the sound we have now and the sound we had then, it was a joke. We used to sing out of two bass amps or something, or the local place's speakers. And now they go out with a wall of sound and 14 lorry-loads."

Kenny had struck up a friendship with Paul and he certainly shared John's habit of straight talking. He recalled in 2010: "The first time I ever met The Beatles I asked them what they wanted out of the business. To be millionaires, they said. I just laughed and said you've got some chance. I've been in the business for years and haven't got two halfpennies to rub together! Shows what a judge I am. It's a good job I'm not at the Old Bailey – you'd get five years for parking!"

From Bedford on the Wednesday it was eyes down for another show in Yorkshire.

Wakefield Regal projectionists Gerald Parkes, who was still a teenager, and Donald Issatt found themselves on lighting duties when the tour hit their town the next day, Thursday, February 7. Parkes, who was working the spotlight, remembers The Beatles not being on the coach, but turning up separately. He said they worked through an enthusiastic soundcheck to prepare for the show and were quite particular about how they looked and sounded.

"Both shows were sell-outs and The Beatles were brilliant. The audiences knew of them all right. There was huge excitement. The kids were waiting for them before the show and pretty soon found out where the dressing rooms were. The Beatles went down exceedingly well. There was screaming and shouting – there always was for these shows. It wasn't so bad while they were singing, but the kids screamed between the songs.

"We had two spots and I was working the dimmer board. Helen was on good form, but she changed her dress for the second show and nobody told us. She had a frothy pink dress for the first show and we put a magenta spotlight on it and it looked great, but the colours really clashed for the second house."

Helen made quite an impact on him. "She was my age and I fell in love with her. Her performance to me was really an impersonation of Alma Cogan – until she developed her own style."

Parkes believes he may have played a part in the ABC organisation investing in these cinema pop shows. "I wrote to them, pretending to be a customer, and said they should put on live shows. It was pretty soon after that they started. When these cinemas were built in the 1930s they had variety in mind, but the Regal at Wakefield hadn't been used for live shows since before the war so we had to work for months to clean everything up and prepare for the concerts. We had 1,500 seats – balcony and stalls – and it was perfect for live shows."

Parkes loved the excitement of the shows, especially that Beatles show. "Our projection room at the back was soundproofed, so technically we shouldn't have heard anything. But it got picked up through the intercom on the stage and you could hear the music and the screaming. In fact, it wasn't just from the stage, you could hear it anyway so it must have been pretty loud."

Danny Williams entranced the audience and Kenny Lynch was "full of bounce", cracking gags and holding his own as a singer.

Donald Issatt said: "The Beatles closed the first half as far as I can remember. We had a monitor up in the projection room so you could hear them, too. They did their soundcheck in the afternoon and then sent someone out for fish and chips – there was a chippie called Sam Herbert's on the other side of the road. It's still a fish shop today, but under a different name.

"I don't think the kids over-reacted to them because most would have come to see Helen, as she was the star. I think Helen had a chaperone and I remember the pink spotlight on Helen's dress."

On tour there was never much time to reflect on the previous night's glory. It was all aboard for another town and another two shows the next night. The snow was still lying thick on the ground as the tour bus battled its way up from Wakefield to Carlisle for the two houses at the town's ABC Cinema on the Friday.

And while the support for Helen was noted at Wakefield, it couldn't be heard above the screams for The Beatles throughout both houses at Carlisle. There's no getting away from the fact that Helen was under pressure at this point. The Beatles' star was rapidly rising and hers appeared to be fading. As if to hammer home the point, she was confronted that morning with the headline 'Is Helen Shapiro A Has-Been At 16?' in the *Melody Maker*.

The concept appears ludicrous, but the music business has its own logic and Helen acknowledged the problem in her 1993 autobiography *Walking Back To Happiness*, in which she conceded: "I was still getting in the charts, but not necessarily the top five, or even the top ten. I'd been a novelty at 14, but I suffered from the Shirley Temple syndrome. I'd grown up. Suddenly I was beginning to look a little bit passé, in spite of topping the bill."

John, infamously the most cutting Beatle, could also be the most sensitive. And it was John who tapped Helen on the shoulder on the coach and told her not to let the "swine" get her down, adding, "You don't want to be bothered with that rubbish. You're all right. You'll be going on for years."

John's kindness would have been some comfort to Helen. She had an enormous crush on him, without realising, of course, that he was already the married Beatle and that his wife was to give birth to their son Julian on April 8, little more than a month after the end of the tour.

Calum Scott-Buccleuch, whose father Norman was the cinema manager, was working as a stage hand that night in Carlisle, and he had already heard of The Beatles. "I quite liked them. I was 24 at the time and kept up with it all and I thought 'Love Me Do' and 'Please Please Me' were good, but if you ask me did I think they were going to be as big as they became, I would have to say no.

"I don't remember much of any of the performances because of course I was doing a job of work, but I could at least hear the music because I was on the right hand side of the stage working the tabs [curtains]."

Helen was not the only performer discomfited by the growing attention

The Beatles were receiving. The baying for The Beatles continued through the performances of all the other acts.

In the audience that night was 20-year-old Andy Park who had a weekly column – Andy's Pop Talk – in the *Carlisle Journal*. "Don't ask me what they were like – the screaming was too much for me to hear their music," he recalls. "I would have been standing at the side probably as I got in on my press pass, but it didn't help me hear anything. When the compère Dave Allen, who was fantastic, said 'The Beatles' that was it. You couldn't hear anything else. It was absolute bedlam. It wasn't just The Beatles. They would have these pop package shows every four to six weeks at that time and there was always screaming. There wasn't much I could write about The Beatles' performance because of it, but I did get to interview them afterwards. They were very nice, but their biggest concern was where they could go on to after the show."

And on this night in Carlisle it was not performances onstage that made the headlines but events after the shows, and it was to leave 16-year-old Helen, in particular, red-faced.

The Beatles, with Helen and Kenny in tow, travelled a few hundred yards through the city centre to the upmarket Crown & Mitre Hotel where they were staying that night. The members and guests of Carlisle Golf Club were holding their annual dinner and dance there at the hotel that night – The Beatles decided to join them. Club chairman Bill Berry, however, took exception to a bunch of leather jacketed young rockers strolling into the dance and merrily tucking into the buffet. A word was had and the unwelcome guests were turfed out.

It might not sound like much of an incident but this was 1963, and the fact that this made a story in the *Daily Express* the next day was potentially disastrous for Helen. She recalls: "We were in the lobby area. Kenny and The Beatles were having a drink and I was having a cup of tea. This fellow was going into the banqueting suite when he saw us. He was really chuffed and asked us to go in. We weren't interested. They were all dressed up and it wasn't our kind of thing. We were just having a quiet drink, but he was really insistent. They had a buffet in there and that probably swung it. We never seemed to get much to eat on tour.

"We went to the buffet table and had something to eat. Ringo was particularly enjoying the food. Then we went on the dance floor – we may have still been eating. I think I was twisting with Ringo. There were these ladies with their long gowns who made a beeline for The Beatles in their leather gear. Then suddenly this guy came over, a much older man, and he was huffing and puffing, getting red in the face. He ordered us to leave. 'Who invited you?' he asked. It was a shame really because nobody seemed to have a problem with us, apart from the one bloke."

Helen's misery was complete when the story got out. "The *Daily Express* headline was something like 'Helen Shapiro Asked To Leave Golf Club Dance'. It referred to Helen Shapiro and 'The instrumental group the Four Beatles' being asked to leave.

"I was mortified. I thought that would be the end of me. I was only 16 and that sort of thing was not something to be proud of then. I never found out for certain who tipped off the press."

Dr George Jolly, a GP in Carlisle for many years and a long-time member of the golf club, was at the Crown & Mitre that night. Dr Jolly died in 2006 at the age of 91, but he had spoken about that evening to the local newspaper, the *News & Star*.

"The annual dance was a dinner-jacket affair in those days. I was the golf club's vice-captain that year. The captain was a bluff Yorkshireman called Bill Berry. I was having a meal with Bill and his wife and my wife. Somebody had introduced four rather scruffy young men into the dance. They were leather-jacketed and all the rest.

"We saw them across the room and Bill said to me, 'I think we should ask them to leave. What do you think?' I said, 'Yes, I think maybe we should.' I didn't recognise them and neither did Bill. They (The Beatles) were just coming into their fame. Bill went across to have a word with them. They left without any ill-feeling."

Word seemed to spread and pop columnist Andy Park was quick to hear the gossip. "I was in the 101 Club on Botchergate a couple of hours afterwards and people were talking about it. I'm a golf fanatic – but it was a bit of an elite sport in those days. These pop stars weren't good enough to mix with golf people. Pop had just started – they were five-minute wonders. A few would have known about Helen because she had hits in the charts, but they wouldn't have known about The Beatles. Nobody knew that The Beatles were going to be so big, or last so long."

So the chastened Fabs discovered that their rising popularity wasn't an automatic ticket to everywhere just yet.

However, there was good news that weekend. The national music press was beginning to sit up and take notice. *Melody Maker* carried an upbeat piece entitled It's All Happening Beatlewise by reporter Chris Roberts, along with individual head-and-shoulders pictures of each Beatle.

From Carlisle the tour headed off the next day, Saturday, February 9, for two houses at the Empire Theatre in Sunderland. Budding young photographer Ian Wright, the darkroom boy at the *Northern Echo*, under the editorship of Harold Evans, was a very interested observer of both, having been given the opportunity to photograph visiting pop groups for the newspaper's new supplement *The Teenage Special*. Not yet old enough to drive, Ian somehow had to manage carrying his heavy photographic equipment on his bicycle, or if he was really lucky he might get the bus.

His reward on this particular night was to be able to photograph the stars onstage and relaxing at the theatre. This was quite a privilege – pictures from this tour are relatively rare – and his book *On The Brink Of Fame*, published in 2009, includes a photo of Helen Shapiro on a sofa, Danny Williams on Ringo's drums and shots of The Beatles onstage and in a lift "to signify their song 'Please Please Me' was on its way up the charts".

"There was little screaming or shouting while they were singing," he recalls. "There was applause and the odd shout and scream between the songs. They were just so different from most groups at that time. It wasn't just their sound and look. So many groups back then would just stand still, but The Beatles had movement. All of a sudden they would shake their heads and two would gather around one mike to sing. And it was also that they were so obviously enjoying themselves – they were so happy and were obviously enjoying every second.

"The pictures were just what I could get. This was all new. There was no formula – no set pattern. Nobody had done this before."

The photographer they affectionately referred to as Wrighty was to return to take photos of the group whenever they played in the north-east. Ian, who now lives in Las Vegas, remembers the bleakness of that February evening in Sunderland in 1963. "This was the worst winter in living memory and the Empire was only half full that night. It was only the bravest who ventured out. It was the year the sea froze over (Herne Bay) and there were 20ft snowdrifts in Kent, which was completely cut off.

"I remember the tour bus with the windows frozen inside and out and people huddled together shivering, with overcoats and balaclavas trying to do anything to fend off the cold. And isn't it ironic that not much more than 500 saw them that night, but when they returned to Sunderland a few months later (November 30) there were 50,000 people in the streets just hoping to catch a mere glimpse of them arriving. And one year to the day, on February 9, 1964, they were watched by 73 million people on *The Ed Sullivan Show*."

Another to meet the boys that bitter February afternoon was *Sunderland Echo* photographer Tony Colling at a photocall at the Empire. He remembers them as "four happy-go-lucky musicians, friendly and chatty".

Star of the show Helen made a good impression on the *Echo's* teenage reporter Carol Anderson who was covering the show. But Carol (the now-retired Carol Roberton), was not so enamoured with the Liverpudlians with the funny haircuts. Carol has put up with some good natured ribbing from colleagues down the years due to her review of the Sunderland concerts that night, which would have earned her fully paid-up membership of the 'Beatles Are Overrated' club. She didn't hold back.

"Mention must be made of the scream-evoking group The Beatles, three of whom plucked on their electric guitars while a fourth played the drums. Identically dressed and with the same strange haircut, they pleased most of the audience with similar-sounding numbers, such as 'Please Please Me' and 'Love Me Do'. Their instrumental qualifications certainly did not measure up to the high standard of The Red Price Band, who provided the backing to most of the stars, as well as entertaining in two spots of their own."

Carol, while conceding that The Beatles went down well with the teen audience, was also quite justified in paying tribute to Helen's talent. "The deep powerful voice of Helen Shapiro has proved more than a match for the high-pitched girlish notes of youth who have dominated the hit parade for so long.

"In her own show at the Sunderland Empire on Saturday night, the petite 16-year-old sang a selection of the songs which first established this fact and demonstrated the ability she has acquired in two years of show business to command a packed audience. She showed versatility in switching from the classic 'The Birth Of The Blues' to her latest recording 'Queen For Tonight' but her attempt at banjo playing added nothing to her performance.

"Danny Williams, of 'Moon River' fame, and Kenny Lynch, who looks like becoming a firm favourite with 'Up On The Roof', presented variety with both slow ballads and swinging rhythm – a relief from the noisier efforts of most of the rest of the supporting programme."

After Sunderland, the first leg of the tour was to finish the next evening with two shows in Peterborough, but The Beatles were replaced that night by Peter Jay & The Jaywalkers. The Beatles had other business to attend to: a recording session booked early on February 11 at the Abbey Road studios in London to complete their first album. A short story in *NME* on February 8 suggested that the title of the LP was to be *Off The Beatle Track*. But the following week's edition confirmed that the album was instead going to be named after the current hit single.

In the modern era groups like U2 and Coldplay can take weeks, months, even years to record an album but in 1963 The Beatles were allowed just one day. It took three gruelling back-to-back sessions to record the final 10 tracks for *Please Please Me*, even though John was suffering from a cold which made his performance in 'Twist And Shout', the throat-tearing final track, even more remarkable.

At least there was now a two-week break from the tour, but there was no rest for the busy Beatles. They played gigs on every day bar two – February 17, when they recorded a performance of 'Please Please Me' for *Thank Your Lucky Stars*, and February 20 when they played 'Love Me Do' and 'Please Please Me' in a live performance on BBC radio's *Parade Of The Pops*.

One of those gigs – at the Astoria Ballroom in King Street, Oldham, on Tuesday, February 12 – the night following that marathon stint at Abbey Road – was the subject of a book called *It Won't Be Long* by Michael Turner. The pictures and reports of that night paint a vivid picture of the excitement the group was beginning to generate.

The ballroom was packed, with girls right up against the stage, and the small, nervous security team had to work hard to make sure things didn't get out of hand.

The local paper, *The Oldham Evening Chronicle,* reported the next day that "nearly 2,000 teenagers stormed" the ballroom "to see the current top rock group The Beatles" and that a guard rail collapsed outside under the weight of the gathering girls.

The *Chronicle* report stated that the queue stretched back to Wellington Street, blocking the pavement. More than 800 were admitted and many of those turned away remained outside the ballroom for two hours. "Those who got inside to see the Liverpool vocal-instrumental group started a screaming riot," the paper told its readers. "Protected by a bodyguard of attendants, The Beatles began their act, but excited fans swarmed towards the stage, stood on chairs, sat on each other's shoulders and struggled to get on the bandstand. One shrieking teenage girl was handled off the stage with her dress almost torn from her back," the report continued.

The boys included 'Love Me Do' and 'Please Please Me' in their two half-hour sets that night, and it was the success of these first two singles that changed their fortunes almost overnight.

Michael Turner: "I was only eight at the time but I had heard 'Love Me Do' on the radio in 1962 and word was getting around about these wild boys with their long hair and pop songs. They were already making an impression here. Perhaps it was a northern thing because they were playing these dances in places like Oldham and Manchester, as well as all the Liverpool gigs. People in Lancashire and Cheshire were aware of them at that early stage."

A week later, on the evening of Tuesday, February 19, Bob Wooler, the Cavern DJ, announced that The Beatles had received news by telegram that 'Please Please Me' was at number one in *NME*'s charts. The Beatles were about to take the stage, but the reaction of the cave dwellers was reportedly stunned silence.

The night before the tour resumed, the group played the Oasis Club in Manchester. The place was packed and yet it was an intimate venue and a relatively calm atmosphere. This was to become a rarity – you could hear as well as see them that night and Paul was even able to sit on the stage afterwards and sign autographs and chat to fans.

However, the dramatic rise of 'Please Please Me' up the charts during the fortnight break prompted even more excitement when the tour resumed at the Granada in Mansfield on Saturday, February 23. By now that excitement was almost exclusively for The Beatles, and that afternoon the fans were eagerly awaiting the arrival of their heroes. Their heroes, meanwhile, were facing the usual problem of how to while away a few humdrum hours before they got down to work.

Kestrel Geoff Williams, a rugby fan who later went on to become a referee for nearly 30 years, had the perfect solution. Right next to the Granada Cinema in West Gate was a Granada television shop and England were playing France in an international at Twickenham. Geoff recalls:

"We knew the rugby was on so about 10 of us – including The Beatles – went into the TV shop and explained that we were due to put on a show at the cinema that evening and asked if we could watch the game on a TV at the back of the shop. They said it was fine, so we watched the match.

"The Beatles weren't known for their love of sport, but you had around five hours to kill before these shows and it could be pretty boring. Normally, you'd just sit in the theatre or go for a walk, but with the game on next door it was ideal."

There was something to cheer as England won 6–5 and then there was time for a bite to eat before heading back to the cinema.

There was another, even more memorable, incident that Geoff recalls from the Mansfield Granada that night. "I don't think it was a particularly big place and apart from Helen, we all shared a dressing room. I remember there was a fire escape leading up to it and a door at the back. Well there was this knocking on the door and a girl kept asking if she could come in. Lennon, in his usual way, told her to fuck off, but she kept knocking and asking to come in.

"Lennon said, 'Well you can come in if you take all your clothes off.' So John let her in and she stood there all shy and then he said, 'Well get your clothes off then.' The poor girl – she was a trainee nurse – duly stripped off and she was stark naked when the theatre manager walked in – and then promptly walked out again. It was typical John. He could be as crude and as coarse as they come."

Williams recalls that Shane Fenton (later Alvin Stardust), who came from Mansfield, was also in the backstage dressing room with them that night.

Dave Spalding, 16, of Kirkby-in-Ashfield, was there with his pal Nobby Clark to see star turn Helen Shapiro. But it was The Beatles who were holding court behind the cinema when they turned up. Dave had been working in the pits in Kirkby for at least a year but he was shocked by their language. "They were effing and jeffing and I said, 'There's no need for that, lads. We don't use language like that down the pit.' They said, 'If you don't like it, you know what you can do.'

"We were seated downstairs and I said to Nobby, 'I don't think this lot will be much good with a name like that.' They were brilliant, though. There was plenty of screaming but you could hear them all right so most of it was between the songs. We'd never heard anything like them before.

They made it look so easy. But the girls were gathering in the aisles and heading towards the front and I thought someone could get hurt here."

Onstage, to a backdrop of rising screams, The Beatles and the other acts were having to battle harder to be heard than they had just a couple of weeks before. While more and more of the spotlight was falling on The Beatles, at least in Kenny Lynch the tour possessed a performer who had no problems with his ego. If the growing attention on The Beatles meant less time for him onstage, he was quite happy with that.

Could Kenny put his finger on how these young upstarts were doing it? He noted that The Beatles, perhaps unwittingly, had that knack of making every girl in the place believe they were singing just to her. Every boy saw himself up on the stage in their place.

The following 24 hours were to be hugely significant – even by the standards of The Beatles. 'Please Please Me' was now in the running for being named number one on BBC radio's *Pick Of The Pops* listings.

Kenny Lynch recalls that the day after the Mansfield shows, John, Paul and George had taken up an offer of Kenny's to ride with him in a car he'd hired to follow the coach for the Sunday night shows at the Coventry Theatre. He recalls they had been to look around the cathedral but were back in the car behind Coventry's Lucien Theatre to pick up the count-down on the radio. It was a two-way fight. 'Please Please Me' and Frank Ifield's 'The Wayward Wind' were the two singles selling by the bucket-load that week. John, Paul and George sat transfixed staring at that car radio. Eventually came the words they had been longing to hear.

Kenny: "When it came over that they were number one a big 'Yeah' went up and they were whooping – probably a few expletives thrown in, too."

The good people of Coventry would be the first to welcome The Beatles as BBC radio chart toppers. Ironically, The Beatles' tussle was with a local man as Ifield was born in the city. The screaming seemed to be turned up yet another notch, as if in tribute. It also marked a distinct shift of power. As George Harrison noted in the *Anthology* book, from now on the crowds were all gathering for them.

Journalist and broadcaster Pete Chambers was in the audience that night and he recalls in his book *The Beatles – Sent To Coventry* that the band and the audience were in good spirits. He writes: "Despite Beatlemania not fully being on the agenda, the crowd were already screaming and making the concert a noisy affair (as all subsequent Beatles concerts would be)." Pete recalls the crowd shouting out for The Beatles while the other acts were on, and the PA sound being particularly bad.

But there was good news for one cheeky chappie. "Nuneaton guy Neil Batchelor got in for free, met all the acts (including The Beatles) and got a full set of autographs, apart from Danny Williams who was onstage at the time. Neil had found a way into the theatre through the costume department. Shortly after getting his autographs he was rumbled and got thrown out, though he still has the autographs," wrote Pete.

He goes on to describe The Beatles setting up their equipment and Kenny testing the mikes and then Helen trying her best to give an interview over the sound of Beatles voices, guitars and drums during their soundcheck.

There was finally respite for Helen when Kenny and the boys were taken up to the circle for a photo shoot as Kenny revealed he was about to record John and Paul's song 'Misery'. Onstage later The Beatles performed their songs over the screams at both houses, starting at 6pm and 8.30pm.

The tour took a one-day break after Coventry, but there was no such thing as a day off for The Beatles in those days. They jumped in their van and headed back up to Lancashire for what was billed as a NEMS Enterprises dance at the Casino Ballroom in Lord Street, Leigh.

In the audience that night was Georgie Fame, who said in 2003: "I went home to Leigh in 1963 and one of my friends, who I used to play with in The Dominoes, said you've got to come around to the Casino because there's this band from Liverpool and they're tearing the place apart. I went in and there were The Beatles, and all these girls were screaming . . . in my home town! I went back to London, and nobody had ever heard of them."

There were reports of coaches parked up along Lord Street, where the club was based, and nearby Silk Street in front of the entrance. The place was packed and there were plenty of girls without tickets, presenting a headache for doormen Peter Hume and Vinnie Hilton.

Inside, fans were hanging over the balcony and packing the dance floor. The Beatles' amplifiers were up to the max so they could be heard over the screams. Paul was heard to thank everyone for getting 'Please Please Me' to number one as the boys launched into it.

The tour resumed the next night with The Beatles heading south-west to the picturesque town of Taunton in Somerset where two houses were due to take place at the local Gaumont Cinema. These Taunton shows, however, were minus the star turn as Helen had succumbed to a cold. Singer Billie Davis, in the charts with 'Tell Him', was drafted in to replace her.

We know – thanks to reports in Taunton's two busy weekly newspapers, the *Somerset County Gazette* and the *County Herald* – that The Beatles, with their new-found status as a number one act, played at least six songs to the enraptured teenagers who packed both houses. We also know that Danny Williams – elevated to star of the show in the absence of Helen – appeared slightly irritated by the level of screams from the audience, rather than the polite applause he preferred.

The two reports indicate that The Beatles performed the four songs they prepared for the tour – 'Chains', 'Keep Your Hands Off My Baby', 'A Taste Of Honey' and 'Please Please Me' – but one refers to them playing substitute song 'Beautiful Dreamer' that night and both mention them playing 'Long Tall Sally', which was not on their tour set list. It is also highly likely that they performed 'Love Me Do' although it isn't mentioned in either report. The extra songs are evidence of their instant star status on the back of the success of 'Please Please Me' and that the screams they were drawing had earned them more time as well as a higher profile onstage.

There are only initials as clues to the identity of the reporters – M.G. in the *Gazette* and H.A. in the *Herald* – but the betting is on them being veteran rather than junior reporters, judging by their comments on the latest chart sensations.

Both were underwhelmed by the soon-to-be Fab Four and both indicated in their reports that The Beatles made a bit of a hash of 'A Taste Of Honey'. M.G. went so far as to add the harsh rider that "in parts, their act was rather amateurish".

The kids, though, as both reporters make clear, saw things rather differently.

The *Gazette* report was headlined 'Danny Williams Made Taunton Show – Without Helen Shapiro – A Winner'.

It started by referring to Helen's replacement: "Billie Davis, a newcomer to the record charts, who has hit the high spots with a recording of 'Tell Him', had only a few hours' notice to deputise for Helen. Because of the lack of music and a chance for a rehearsal the Red Price Band's backing of her songs was not as good as it could have been. She opened with a ballad version of the standard 'If You Were The Only Boy In The World' and then increased the tempo for the Buddy Holly (and Elvis) recording 'Baby I Don't Care' including, of course, the popular song 'Tell Him'."

The reporter certainly appreciated Danny's efforts, writing: "No one could fault the professional and polished performance by South African Danny Williams. The tonal quality and perfection of presentation of this coloured singer in his first visit to the town were unmistakable.

"He sounds exactly the same onstage as on record – a claim few popular singers can make without the aid of echo chambers and trick recording facilities.

Although he is better known for his slow ballads, he gave laudable performances of 'beat ballad' numbers, such as 'Up A Lazy River', but reverted to the gentle easy pace for his latest recording, 'My Own True Love'."

MG was allowed a precious few minutes with Danny that evening. His report continued: "Backstage between the two shows his reaction to the audience was 'too much screaming'. He likes his public to show appreciation of the numbers, but prefers a good, solid round of applause to a short, sharp burst of frustrated screams – and then silence. As it was his first show at Taunton he was not to know that the audience was being very moderate and that, in fact, he escaped lightly!"

Then MG comes to The Beatles: "The Beatles, a vocal-instrumental quartet whose style is reminiscent of the Tex/Mex originals, the long-standing Crickets, came over well aurally, but in parts their act was rather amateurish. Their 'Beautiful Dreamer' and 'Please Please Me' did them justice, as did most of their punchy numbers, such as 'Long Tall Sally' and a Cookies' original 'Chains'. But as soon as they relaxed the pace to vocalise Acker Bilk's 'A Taste Of Honey' their co-ordination fell to pieces."

As The Beatles left the stage during that first house, enter another of the singers. "Kenny Lynch bounced onstage with a rendering of the Bobby Darin record 'Things', following it up with a powerful version of 'Like I Do', but with a slight alteration of the words from the Maureen Evans' original, and 'Crazy Crazy' which is one of the numbers from the film *Just For Fun*, in which he appears. Needless to say, 'Up On The Roof' was well, if a little noisily, received."

Next onstage were the Bristol boys – virtual neighbours to Taunton – and the *Gazette*'s MG was impressed. "The Kestrels made great play with the dropping of handkerchiefs and false moustaches, which gave their act an amusing side to make them that little bit different from the more run-of-the-mill quartets."

The Liddell triplets got a mention, too. "The blonde trio The Honeys were too harsh to be completely pleasing, but they managed, with the aid of The Red Price Band, to put plenty of swing into the calypso number 'Manana'. Yes," the report concludes, "despite Miss Shapiro's absence, Billie Davis did not let the other performers down and the appearance of Danny Williams made the show quite a winner."

Over at the *Herald*, reporter H.A. was also having a say. Under the headline 'Shapiro Show, But No Helen', the report gave all the acts a mention, but Danny Williams again fared best. Clearly, local entertainment reporters were as yet having trouble working out the appeal of John, Paul, George and Ringo.

"The audience received with most enthusiasm an orgy of dissonant electronic noises from The Beatles, who have crashed the Top Twenty like a spaceship to the moon with 'Please Please Me'," read the report. "Vocally nasal and instrumentally catarrhal-sounding, these four Liverpudlians made heavy weather of 'A Taste Of Honey' but blew up a storm of excitement with 'Long Tall Sally' and 'Keep Your Hands Off My Baby'.

"Danny Williams, who headed the bill, was rather more pleasant to listen to than some of these 'rockers'. He has a voice and knows how to sing a romantic song."

Billie and The Honeys were clearly not to the writer's taste. "Billie Davis, who replaced Helen Shapiro, bawled 'Tell Him' and others. Her brand of hysteria is not everyone's choice. The Honeys provided inconsequential teenage stuff, but sang 'This Could Be The Start Of Something' with enthusiasm, as well they might, for it is a good song. Then there was Kenny Lynch who sounded best in his ballads. He might be any other noisy young man in the other numbers. The Kestrels specialised in novelty numbers and were quite funny."

Looking back, Kestrel Geoff Williams says comedy was a key part of his group's act. "You had to be different in those days," he says. "The moustaches and the draping of the towels over our arms was during 'Blue

Moon', and that was one of our main numbers. We'd sing it in four stages. We'd start off singing it normally, then we'd go into barbershop harmony with the false moustaches and the towels over our arms as waiters used to do, then we'd do eight bars still in barbershop harmony, but humphy humphy Temperance Seven style, and then finish up doing it in the style of the originals, The Marcels. It was our pièce de résistance if you like. We sang 'Blue Moon' wherever we went."

Geoff recalls that for the Helen tour The Kestrels started with a close harmony version of 'Who Put The Bomp (In The Bomp Bomp Bomp)', followed by 'Once In A While', 'Blue Moon' and either 'Hit The Road Jack' or 'Michael Row The Boat Ashore'. They would finish each night with 'Speedy Gonzales'.

The comedy was popular – with fans as well as reporters – but it wasn't at the expense of the music. "We could sing, you see," said Geoff. "Just look at the songs we were performing. We could do an hour if we needed to, but of course you got nothing like that amount of time onstage during these tours."

Taunton's *Gazette* and *Herald* were both Saturday weeklies at the time and as was common with these tours, they ran small advertisements in the preceding weeks. The *Herald* also ran a four paragraph preview the Saturday before the show. The reviews may have been somewhat mixed, with only Danny earning universal praise, but the performers would in any case have been blissfully unaware as they boarded the coach for the long trip to York the next morning, several days before the reports were published. The Beatles, the new chart-toppers, were still travelling with the ordinary mortals.

"They were definitely on the coach heading off from Taunton to York the next day – it made sense," says Williams. "Of course us Kestrels lived in nearby Bristol so we had gone home that night while the others stayed somewhere locally. The coach picked us up in Bristol for the trip north. The Beatles didn't make a fuss out of being number one either. If it was me I would have been shouting about it for weeks, but they just took everything in their stride. They just seemed interested in what they were doing next."

What they were doing next was heading back up north, still without cold victim Helen, for two shows at the Rialto in York. It meant leaving the dry roads of the West Country and heading straight back into the snow-laden north where records show that two inches of snow lay on the ground and temperatures were down to −3°C.

York's teenagers may have been eagerly awaiting the stars, but the York press didn't cover the show. However, Steve Cassidy, singer with York group The Escorts, was in the Rialto that night. "They put on a great show," he says, "and I've memories of them closing the show and of Paul doing a great version of Little Richard's 'Long Tall Sally'. Not many people made a fist of a Little Richard song, but Paul did. There was screaming – there was screaming at the Rialto dating back to when Tommy Steele played there – but you could hear The Beatles over it. The Beatles were a rock'n'roll band and people were excited by what they did."

Steve recalls that poet and journalist Peter Morgan, who edited York's *Ouse Beat* newspaper at the time, had sent along a reporter and photographer to cover the show. "It was a monthly newspaper and a picture of Paul McCartney taken that night appeared on the front of the next edition."

Colin Carr, drummer with local band The Clubmen, was lucky enough to catch all four Beatle appearances at the York Rialto in 1963. "Of course the memories start to roll into one after all these years, but when I first heard them sing 'Please Please Me', which would have been on that first tour, the excitement of the sound was so different from everything else around at the time. It was magic. The girls were going mad for them every time they played here," he says.

One of the girls who went mad for them at every York show was 13-year-old Christine Woodcock who saw The Beatles with her cousin Angela Long and her friend Susan Blackburn. She went out of the theatre during the interval of the first show to stand in the street under the dressing room window.

"Although it was early days, we were already big fans of The Beatles," she says. "It was The Beatles we had gone to see. Susan's dad had queued for hours to get us the tickets so that we wouldn't skip school. We went round the side during the break and were shouting up at them. One of them shouted back 'What?' but they fluttered down some pictures for us and then several of them came down. It was Paul who spoke to us and we wrote to him afterwards – we were in the fan club even then – and he wrote back. But as for the performance, we just screamed and cried. You could still hear them singing at that stage though. Of course the detail fades after all these years, but I can still remember the liveliness of it – the sense and smell of it. We thought 'Love Me Do' was great – we were sold on them from then."

The Beatles were on the bus as it headed out of York next day to Shrewsbury for the shows that night at the town's striking Granada Cinema in Castle Gates. Apart from the usual jocularity on the bus we know that they also wrote what turned out to be their next big hit on that trip. There was an exclusive for Yorkshire reporter Stacey Brewer of the *Evening Press* as George Harrison told him that they wrote 'From Me To You' on the bus heading off to Shrewsbury.

The song had been inspired by the letters section of the *New Musical Express* which was called From You To Us.

In the *Anthology* book, John was quoted: "We weren't taking ourselves seriously – just fooling around on the guitar – when we began to get a good melody line, and we really started to work at it. Before that journey was over, we'd completed the lyric, everything. I think the first line was mine and we took it from there."

The song was to hit number one in April and stay there for an impressive seven weeks, but at least one celebrity on the tour bus was distinctly unimpressed as John and Paul got down to work. Kenny Lynch had already dipped a toe in the songwriting waters and on the back of his recent hit 'Up On The Roof' was confident enough to pass on a few tips to these newcomers, so he sauntered up to the back of the coach to give The Beatles' inbuilt tunesmith team the benefit of his experience.

What happened next was observed by Kestrel Roger Greenaway who, inspired by John and Paul's work, went on to write some huge hits himself, in partnership with Roger Cook. He recalls Kenny advising the boys that their high pitched vocals would "make them sound like a bunch of fairies". Kenny's input wasn't welcomed – particularly by John – and Kenny duly drifted back to his seat pronouncing them idiots, their efforts rubbish and that they "didn't know music from their backsides".

Kenny claims to have helped The Beatles write a line of the song that was to end up as the B-side. "We were on the coach and they were driving me mad. I could hear them behind me and I was trying to have a sleep and they sang 'Thank You Girl' and I said, 'Thank you girl for loving me the way that you do. Can I go to sleep?' and he [John] said he'd use it in the song and they did."

Helen remembers John and Paul coming up to her (probably at the

Shrewsbury Granada) and asking a favour. Paul sat down at a piano, with John standing by the side, and they sang 'From Me To You' and 'Thank You Girl' and asked her opinion. Helen said she preferred 'From Me To You'.

The old Granada Cinema had been hosting shows in Shrewsbury for the best part of a decade, but there was growing excitement that pop's hottest new properties were coming to town. Terry Walmsley, one of the cinema's projectionists, had seen most of those showbiz stars strutting their stuff at the Granada and he recalls the build-up to The Beatles and Helen show. "There were some girls in there one day in the run-up to The Beatles and Helen show and they must have overheard us talking because the news was suddenly all over town. I know that it was a packed house that night and the girls were all screaming their heads off."

Walmsley had worked there since 1955, operating a spotlight in the early days. Ruby Murray was the first star illuminated by that spotlight, but he was working the lighting board on the stage when The Beatles came to town.

"I remember The Beatles being a good set of lads. They would probably have arrived about 11am and set up their gear and run through their set – that's what most of them did. They were good to work with – no airs and graces – just normal people really. We would have talked about the lighting and how that was going to work, things like that. Of course, Helen was the star name at the time. The Beatles were only just making their name, but it was a good show that went down very well." In the Granada audience that night was Jim Burgess, singer of local band Andre & The Electrons, and his over-riding memory is of the screaming that greeted the new chart-toppers. "The screaming was so loud that it was difficult to make out much of The Beatles' performance. I remember leaving the cinema and feeling distinctly peeved about it.

"Of course, The Beatles were still using their little Vox AC30 amps – and the cinema sound system was appalling. We must have queued for a couple of hours that night – we already had our tickets and knew where we were sitting – but such was the excitement they generated."

With Jim that night was his girlfriend Chris – now his wife of 40 years.

"Chris was quite a fan of Helen's and I liked The Beatles – and I think she at least got to hear Helen that night as the screams were nowhere near as bad for the other acts."

Jim, who now lives in St Albans, and his Electrons got to share a stage with The Beatles when they returned to Shrewsbury a few weeks' later for a performance at the town's much vaunted Music Hall for promoter Lewis Buckley.

"They were good guys," he said. "I particularly liked Ringo. John was remote and George was the quiet one and Paul certainly had an eye for the ladies, let's say that!"

Back on the tour, all the young guns were having fun. The Liddell sisters who made up The Honeys were naturally the centre of attention. Kestrel Geoff Williams had a suspicion that smoothie Danny Williams was smoking cannabis – but The Beatles were not. Kenny Lynch recalls that drink and drugs were never an issue.

The Beatles were getting all the kicks they needed by playing before big houses on a national tour. Egg and chips, fizzy drinks and milk kept them fortified, although there was always time for a scotch and coke when they got back to their digs.

Coach driver Ron King has recalled John as the serious Beatle with his head buried in the newspapers. It wasn't just to keep up with the news. John gained inspiration from all sorts of sources for his songs. A phrase from a newspaper or book, a snippet from the television or something said in conversation – they were all fair game to John. It was an early indication – even in the days when every Beatle song seemed to have an I, Me, You and Love in the title, never mind the lyrics – that Lennon was not solely interested in writing about teenage love.

The Shrewsbury houses over, the touring party were on their travels again and from The Beatles' point of view they were homeward bound. There was a taste of things to come for them as the press and fans were waiting for them when they arrived in Southport, around 20 miles north of Liverpool, for the two Friday evening houses (6.25pm and 8.40pm) at the Odeon on Friday, March 1.

It was a case of the weekend starts here as a sell-out crowd of screaming teenagers cried their way through both houses. Cinema manager Ken Lloyd, who also booked the group for a week that August, was delighted with his night's work as The Beatles show came to town. By now, and especially in Southport, it really was The Beatles show.

Plum Connolly, wife of journalist, author and Beatle chronicler Ray Connolly, was in the Odeon audience in Southport and the over-riding memory all these years later is of the hysterical reaction to The Beatles – and of how upsetting it must have been for Shapiro. "Everybody was just screaming for The Beatles and it must have been so difficult for Helen. She was supposed to be the star but by then people were just interested in them. I was 18 at the time and in the sixth form so I was probably there with some school friends, but you just couldn't hear anything The Beatles were singing because of the screaming – and yes, I was screaming, too," she recalls.

It wasn't the first time Plum had seen the group. Already the proud owner of their 'Love Me Do' debut single, she had been in the audience on December 6, 1962, when The Beatles played at the Club Django at the Queen's Hotel in Southport.

"There was a big difference from when I first saw them. At the Club Django you could hear them. People were cheering that first time, but they weren't screaming over them. It was totally different by the time I saw them with Helen. You just couldn't hear a thing."

Although husband Ray would become a celebrated admirer of the Fab Four, it was Plum who got there first. "I told him how great The Beatles were, but he wasn't interested in hearing them. He was an Elvis fan and away in London at university at the time so he completely missed the release of 'Love Me Do'. But then he heard 'Please Please Me' on the day it was released and he was instantly converted. Later he became a journalist on the *Evening Standard* in London and became very involved with them."

Plum was mildly surprised to be reminded of the other household names on the stage with The Beatles and Helen on that March 1963 night at the Odeon.

"At the time it really just was all about The Beatles," she said. "We didn't really take much notice of anyone else. My memory is that people were just screaming 'We want The Beatles' for most of the night."

It also proved a memorable night for John Daly – then a raw, 16-year-old trainee photographer with local paper the *Southport Visiter*. Daly had managed to get himself onto the stage, right at the back by the curtains, as The Beatles were waiting to be introduced for their slot in the first house, and he took a quick photo of the group.

Unfortunately, his triumph was to be very short-lived and ended in rather humiliating fashion. Daly recalls: "It all happened so quickly. A policeman asked John Lennon for his autograph and he proffered a piece of paper or an autograph book but he had nothing to write with and John responded in typical fashion. He said, "Ho, ho ho, a hofficer without a pencil". Someone came up with one and John signed and I took my picture.

"I wasn't 100 per cent happy with it and was preparing to take a second shot when these two security guys grabbed me and threw me off the stage at the front and I landed in the area between the organ and the seats. The security guys were with The Beatles I think, and they said I wouldn't work at the Odeon again, or with The Beatles.

"I was staring up at the stage from where I landed and I remember the kids jumping up and down and screaming. I lived 22 miles away in Litherland and there was enthusiasm in the office for the show because The Beatles were on. I left pretty soon after – perhaps after one Beatles song – because I wanted to get back to the darkroom to process the picture. My mentor Peter Hutchinson was there with his camera and I think there were a couple of *Visiter* reporters there and one of them was taking pictures with his own camera."

It's worth noting also that the lucky fans got to see all those stars onstage at what were bargain basement prices. Southport prices were set at 8s 6d, 6s 6d and 4s 6d – in today's money about 42p, 32p and 22p, and taking inflation into account £6.67, £5.10 and £3.53, which demonstrates how the cost of concert tickets has risen way above the rate of inflation during the past half-century.

The old Southport cinema, like so many across the country, has long since gone – in this case replaced by a Sainsbury's supermarket – but the response they attracted there was equalled when they arrived in Sheffield the next day for two Saturday night shows at the City Hall.

While the reporters down in Taunton just a few days earlier had been somewhat underwhelmed by the group, the *Sheffield Star* was far more in tune with the times. Its report of the shows, complete with a charming portrait photo of Helen, was headlined 'Beatles Deserve The Top Billing'. Enough said. Less than a week after the group had notched up their first big hit, reporters in the regional press were beginning to note not just the reaction of the young audiences, but the sheer star quality of the young men on the stage who were triggering it.

The history books record that Beatlemania began in the autumn of 1963. The evidence suggests that the mania – teens gathering in their hordes and screaming for all their worth at the group – was building up much earlier. It's just that the national press was surprisingly slow to pick up on it. In those days pop shows rarely made front page news. That Sheffield report – initialled C.N. – was inspired in acknowledging who were the true stars of the show.

It opened: "Halfway down the bill – in small letters – are a group called The Beatles. But don't let the fact that they are not top of the bill mislead you. The Beatles are NEWS." After pointing out that when the tour began, the group was largely unknown outside of "Liverpool's clubland" and had made only a brief appearance in the Top 20 courtesy of "a rather unusual number called 'Love Me Do', the report continued: "Now their latest disc 'Please Please Me' stands at the top of the hit parade and they are currently the hottest new property on the pop scene.

"And although this is their first stage tour, they proved that they deserve every bit of praise heaped upon them. They write most of their own tunes and are first-class instrumentalists and sing extremely well. They were the hit of the show with such numbers as 'Please Please Me', 'Love Me Do' and 'A Taste Of Honey'."

The world of pop music has always been a harsh business, and the reporter's comment on top-of-the-bill Helen Shapiro summed up her predicament. "Helen Shapiro has a wonderful voice and is developing a good blues style, but she doesn't have the personality and showmanship of many of her female contemporaries, such as Susan Maughan and Brenda Lee. And instead of introducing new material we got a potted history of her hits, beginning as far back as 'Don't Treat Me Like A Child'."

And Danny Williams, so beloved of the Taunton set, was this time put in a more realistic context compared with the rising Beatles: "Danny Williams is an excellent performer, but more suited to intimate cabaret, as he showed with a highly individual rendering of 'This Must Be Love'." Kenny Lynch had a good night in Sheffield as his performance "showed that he is gradually climbing to the forefront among British ballad singers. He has a strong voice and easy, polished style." The Kestrels and The Honeys got a mention, as did The Red Price Band who "did a good backing job throughout the show".

In the Sheffield audience that night were young parents Shirley and Bryan Grocutt. They didn't have much money to throw around at the beginning of 1963, Shirley having given up the job she had held for

10 years as a wages clerk at Sheffield toolmakers Moore & Wright when her daughter Lindsay was born. Lindsay was now four years old and fast approaching school age.

A night out at a pop concert was an unlikely luxury for the couple – but as good luck would have it, Shirley's birthday fell in February, just before the Helen Shapiro tour, with this unknown group called The Beatles, stopped off at the City Hall in Sheffield on March 2. "Bryan saw that the show was on and got the tickets as a birthday treat for me," recalled Shirley. "It was a real treat, too, as we both liked all sorts of music."

So little Lindsay was packed off to her grandmother Ida's that Saturday evening as mum and dad boarded the double-decker Gleadless bus and set off for the City Hall in search of the stars. "We went to see Helen, to be honest. We didn't really know about The Beatles, but Helen was really well known at the time," recalls Shirley. "Being so broke we ended up in the cheapest seats in the house. For anyone who remembers the City Hall as it was in those days, there were two statues of lions lying down on the stage looking out at the audience and we were at their feet. They were the cheapest seats because we were on the stage – but behind the stars looking at the backs of their heads!

"Between the lions on the stage were stairs that led to the dressing rooms and this is how the stars got on and off. Bryan and I were on either side of the lions peering out. I can remember that Helen Shapiro had very short, black hair. The other thing I remember is that The Beatles were incredible. The minute they started to play the place was electric. And what was so nice about those boys was they were so delighted that people were there to see them that they kept turning towards us. It was wonderful."

The timing was perfect. 'Please Please Me' had also reached number one in the *Disc* music paper chart the previous week. Shirley may not have known much about The Beatles – she was a married mum of 28 – but those teens in the audience certainly had got the message.

"They must have played well because there was so much cheering and shouting and people half standing up, clapping and happy. There was such an atmosphere. It was magic. Absolutely magic – people getting up and dancing or tapping their feet. It was the fact that there all these stars were – live – this wasn't a film. They were appearing there live for us. People didn't want them to go off. It must have been difficult for whoever had to follow them."

Less impressive in Shirley's memory were the Fabs' stage suits. "They were diabolical," she says. "They were burgundy, full draped suits which they wore with a shoestring tie and brothel creepers. But it looked like they'd slept, ate, gone on holiday and lived in those suits. I was astounded that they would appear at the City Hall like that. They were the most awful suits I'd ever seen. But to be fair, they were fashionable at the time."

Amazingly, despite those two tumultuous performances, The Beatles' night was not done. As soon as they were offstage they faced a 38-mile dash to Manchester for a live interview for the *ABC At Large* TV show, which was screened from 11pm–11.50pm in the Midlands and the north. Posing the questions was David Hamilton – later to become a household name as DJ "Diddy" David Hamilton. An earlier mimed performance of 'Please Please Me' for *Thank Your Lucky Stars* was screened, so at least they didn't have to perform, but they were joined by Brian Epstein for a debate about their growing success.

Later, back at their Sheffield hotel, there was still no rest for The Beatles, as Helen recalls. "The kids found out where we were. They were outside screaming and shouting for The Beatles and me, and we were throwing photos from a hotel lounge window. George used to practise signing his autograph – on cigarette packets, anything he could find, even other people's pictures. I just loved everything about those coach tours back then. Of course, the novelty wore off a bit later on when I realised what blooming hard work they were!"

At some point they all finally managed to get some sleep and then it was back on the road the next day for the final night of the tour at Hanley in Staffordshire, with the two performances at the Gaumont Cinema. Such was the response of the Hanley public that night that Dave Allen had a hard job keeping order. More than 2,000 teenagers packed into each house and afterwards hundreds gathered outside the stage door hoping for a glimpse of the stars. Cinema manager Mr J. A. E. Ramsden was pretty pleased with it all, declaring it "one of the most successful shows ever held at the theatre".

There to record proceedings for the *Evening Sentinel*'s Out And About section was junior reporter Derek Adams who was to spend a few hours in the company of the Fab Four. Some of the profession's most senior and respected figures would soon have gladly given up a year's expenses to have swapped places with him that night. Derek got a great view of both houses from the wings, spoke at length to the group during the break, and witnessed The Beatles at play before sharing a fish supper with them at the end.

He confesses to only vaguely knowing who they were before the show, but he took to them as he witnessed them larking about and pushing each other around before stepping out onto the stage to try to sing over the screams during both packed houses. He was there to witness a sweaty John and Paul dunking themselves under a cold tap in the dressing room between shows. He interviewed them in the dressing room as baying girls gathered by the window on the pavement outside, and watched as Ringo threw a glass of water from the open window, much to the delight of the screamers.

"There must have been 100 girls at their dressing room window that night, but they took it all in their stride," says Adams. "I said to John – how do you deal with all this screaming? He said, 'We're used to it – it happens all the time.' It must have been hard for the others on that tour as by then all the screams were for The Beatles. The other acts were okay, but really everyone was there for The Beatles."

Derek recalls the other Beatles pressing George into doing the interviews and that John came over as quite shy, despite his brash image. He was preparing to leave the theatre after the second house when John Lennon asked if there was a chippie they could drive to out of the clutches of the fans. "I knew of a fish and chip shop in an area known as Etruria, near Hanley, where you could sit at tables in the back of the shop," says Derek. "It also served bread and butter and tea. It was arranged that The Beatles would follow my car in their Transit van and that we would all dine together. The meal lasted about an hour amid much laughter and joking and the occasional chip being rescued from someone's tea."

"John made his chip butties, Paul squeezed tomato sauce all over his grub, George drank his tea from a saucer and Ringo mistakenly shook sugar on his chips instead of salt. They argued over the bill – with Ringo eventually losing out."

After they finished eating, the group had a favour to ask. "John said to me, 'Hey Wack, do you know how we get to our digs from here?' Etruria is a mile and a half or two miles out of Hanley and they didn't know their way, so I said follow me and they jumped into the van and I got into my car and led them there. I vaguely remember them borrowing the van from a roadie. Then I returned to my lonely bedsitter in an area known as Basford."

The Beatles stayed that night at 6 Adventure Place, Hanley, with a landlady who regularly looked after showbiz people. The property is still there today.

But what of Derek's review? He recalls referring to The Beatles as "a pleasant boy band, typical of many others of this time, but who could just make the very competitive pop scene if only they could make another hit record.

"When I look back now they are such fond memories. The Beatles weren't hotshots, they were modest – there was no edge to them. They were just saying the usual things, like 'Make sure you give us a good write-up.' We were like just five lads together that night."

A Hanley teenager known only as Dawn also had happy memories of that night. She was so impressed by The Beatles' performance that she wrote to them asking about whether they had a Stoke fan club. The bad news was they didn't . . . but the good news was that the bad news was delivered in a hand-written letter by John from his home in Woolton, Liverpool. The letter emerged a few years ago and experts date it to March, 1963.

John put his full address – 251 Menlove Avenue, Woolton, Liverpool 25 – at the top right of his letter and wrote: *"Dear Dawn, Thank you for your letter, glad you liked the show. For fan club information, I can't tell you about opening a Stoke-on-Trent branch, but I suggest you get in touch with the northern branch here in Liverpool and they can let you know all about it. The address is NEMS, 12–14 Whitechapel, Liverpool 1, Lancs. Thanks again, hope to be in Hanley again soon. Cheerio, love John Lennon x."*

This letter may have taken The Beatle only a few minutes to compose, but it would have been very special for Dawn and it underlines just how generous The Beatles could be while they had the space to take a breath. This letter is believed to be one of the last that John would have sent from Mendips.

And so The Beatles' first national tour was over. A total of 14 dates – with a break in the middle – a gentle introduction to the "whirling world of one-nighters". If you were lucky enough to have been at one of these shows you would have seen the world's greatest group going full throttle, having fun and enjoying themselves on the very brink of achieving their dream.

Of course, the cinemas weren't designed as concert venues. The sound systems were archaic, with most venues only set up for one microphone, and staff not trained to deal with the complexities of live shows. Spotlights would sometimes be shone on John instead of George, or Ringo instead of Paul, by the harassed and under-trained cinema staff. Some of The Beatles' own equipment wasn't up to scratch either and it proved to be a baptism of fire for Neil Aspinall, their long standing friend who was by now their roadie. It would probably have been Neil driving the van with their amps and guitars that followed The Beatles and the rest in the coach.

But these were the days when you could still hear something – and The Beatles were performing raw rock'n'roll from their Cavern sets, too.

The Beatles had enjoyed an amount of freedom on this tour. Even the humble boarding houses where they wound down with their scotch and cokes after the shows were like small palaces compared with where they had been staying just a few months before.

The Beatles were not alone in enjoying themselves. Looking back in late May 2010, Kenny Lynch had good memories. "They were fantastic days. Everybody got on together. I don't remember anybody being an arsehole on the tour. [The Beatles] were fun guys. They were Liverpool working-class lads. Especially with me being the same – working class, but out of the East End. We never stopped laughing. Eighteen hours a day we were laughing. We weren't sleeping – we were laughing or singing."

Even the tour's elder statesmen were up for having fun. The Red Price Band were the key musicians providing the backing for the singers. They were professional, but let their hair down, too. Kenny says: "Well they were jazzers – so they were always in the pub. A couple of them were session boys, I think, and all good players, because they played all the time – out on the tours as well."

The screaming for The Beatles didn't create jealousy – but it did create problems for several of the star names. The Taunton reporter noted that Danny Williams was uncomfortable with it. Kenny confirms it. "Danny completely hated it. He hated the screaming. He wasn't too keen on The Beatles either. He thought they were noisy. 'Oh Kenny, they are so noisy,' he would say. They were good lads, but Danny was very quiet. He'd just come out of the middle of apartheid and he used to walk behind me all the time. I used to keep looking round for him. He would always be with me – perhaps because I was black as well. I would say 'For Christ's sake!' And he wouldn't talk to some people, but after about two or three years, he got out of it, but he was very nervous of everybody. He thought somebody was going to give him a bollocking every moment. Shame, because he was a lovely kid."

Helen, despite being under a little pressure at the time, looks back fondly on the tour. As the star turn, she had been offered a car for the tour by Arthur Howes, but rarely used it because she was enjoying the camaraderie of the tour bus – particularly the company of her cheeky new Beatle friends. She later told the *Beatles Book* fan monthly of how they would strum away at the back of the coach, sometimes working hard on their harmonies or new songs, and at others belting out some early Tamla Motown favourites or raucously singing some rude ditty. Everybody would join in these sing-alongs, and not just the pop stars. Dave Allen enjoyed music as well as gags and he was happy to be at the centre of it all.

Helen remembers: "Dave loved The Beatles and he loved John Lennon because they had the same sardonic wit and Liverpool and Irish humour is naturally intertwined anyway. So he got on with them well and he was someone who was fascinated with any kind of phenomenon like that – whether it was screaming fans, or pop music or the music industry, and it made him ideally placed to observe the admirable aspects and the absurd ones as well."

At quieter moments the coach travellers would play cards, particularly George and Ringo if John and Paul were working on another new song.

Helen's verdict on each Beatle was pretty much typical – Paul was the charming one, George was sincere, intelligent and keen to learn everything about the music business. Ringo was the Beatle with the dry wit who would often prompt a burst of the giggles. John was the dangerous one, with a gathering reputation for being aggressive and cutting. But to Helen he was protective and kind, and he was The Beatle she fell for.

In reality, The Beatles only did half the tour, though. It wasn't the end of the road for the rest of the performers who, after a 13-night break, resumed with Jet Harris & Tony Meehan, who had both just left The Shadows, taking the place of The Beatles for seven shows from Saturday, March 16 at Birmingham, and on to Derby, Maidstone, Aylesbury, Cheltenham, Plymouth and Cardiff.

The Beatles, meanwhile, had a mere five days before the start of their second tour and they were kept busy. There was time for an EMI recording session on March 5 (which produced 'From Me To You' and 'Thank You Girl'), their first £100 booking, their final recordings for the *Here We Go* radio show in Manchester and further performances in Nottingham and Harrogate before their second trek across the country.

This time it would be two big stars from across the pond who would be caught in the path of the gathering Beatle storm.

CHAPTER TWO

The Second Tour
Thanks To The Yanks

March 9 – March 31, 1963
Featuring Chris Montez, Tommy Roe, The Beatles, The Viscounts,
Debbie Lee, The Terry Young Six
Compère: Tony Marsh

BARELY had The Beatles got their breath back from their first national tour than they were off on their travels again – this time with two big American stars as joint bill-toppers. The 21-date tour with Chris Montez and Tommy Roe was another Arthur Howes promotion, in association with Eve Taylor, the formidable agent who represented Adam Faith (and later Sandie Shaw). It opened at the Granada Cinema in East Ham on Saturday, March 9, 1963, just six days after The Beatles had finished their stint on the Shapiro package.

Fortunately a thaw had set in and the ice that had gripped Britain for months was at last at an end. March 6 was the first morning of 1963 without any frost anywhere in Britain. The temperatures were soon soaring up to 17°C (62.6°F) and the snow that had so stubbornly refused to budge was now disappearing. This was a welcome relief – not least because the night before the tour commenced in east London, The Beatles were more than 200 miles away at the Royal Hall in Harrogate, north Yorkshire, on a bill that included local bands Ricky Fenton & The Apaches, plus Barry Corbett & The Mustangs.

Montez and Roe had both already made their mark on the UK charts. In late 1962 Chris had enjoyed a number two hit with 'Let's Dance' and Tommy a number three with 'Sheila'. Roe's latest song, 'The Folk Singer', was to hit the charts in the middle of the tour and reach a creditable four. All of this, however, couldn't stop the Americans getting the shock of their professional lives when teenage girls descended on venue after venue to demonstrate their love of the English upstarts by screaming their heads off.

The riveting sound of 'Please Please Me', combined with the energy, charisma and pure cool factor of the Liverpool boys singing it, rendered the transatlantic battle for attention a no-contest. This is not to say the Americans didn't receive a warm and polite welcome from English audiences, but there was nothing polite about the reception The Beatles received. It started at the first house of that first show at East Ham and there was no let-up right through the tour to the final house at the De Montfort Hall in Leicester on Sunday, March 31.

Montez was singularly unprepared for what was about to hit him. He was reported as saying: "Who are these guys The Beatles? I try to keep up with the British scene, but I don't know their work."

Ezekiel Christopher Montanez was born on January 17, 1943, in California to Mexican parents. He had many siblings, but his father Isaac had died in 1957. Influenced and inspired by the music of Ritchie Valens, his first single, 'She's My Rockin' Baby', had been released back in 1958, and he had already toured with Sam Cooke and Smokey Robinson. Tommy Roe, 21, was from Atlanta, Georgia. His repertoire included ballads and rockers, and he was a fan of and had been influenced by Buddy Holly. Both hoped the tour would build a big UK fan base and cement them as chart stars in Britain. Both were destined to suffer some unexpected competition in the shape of some very exciting home-grown talent, and it wasn't just from The Beatles.

The Viscounts comprised three singers – Don Paul, Ronnie Wells and Gordon Mills – and all three had previously been members of Morton Fraser's Harmonica Gang, but they left in 1958 to form their own band and caught the eye of impressario Larry Parnes. Signed to Pye Records in 1960, they recorded a song called 'Rockin' Little Angel' and then 'Shortnin' Bread', which reached 16 in the charts. Their 1961 version of 'Who Put the Bomp (In The Bomp, Bomp, Bomp)' reached 21 and they had already toured with such rock'n'roll greats as Gene Vincent and Eddie Cochran.

There was also a young female singer on the tour. Debbie Lee was an attractive, blonde 22-year-old, whom Ronnie Wells remembers as a typical female pop singer of the period. "She was with the same agency as us, Eden Kane and The Kestrels. I remember Debbie as having a pleasant voice, with a pleasant personality to match." She was also a dab hand as an impressionist and she had already made her first TV appearance – as a guest of loveable East End piano queen Mrs Mills on her sing-along TV show. By the end of the year Debbie was a regular on *Stars And Garters*, a variety themed pub sing-along TV show that was a launching pad for Kathy Kirby.

The tour band backing the singers were the Terry Young Six who, along with Terry, comprised Barry Daniel (Terry's brother) on drums, John Rostill (bass), Barry Booth (keyboards), John Lord and Kevin Peake (saxophonists) and Bruce Baxter (guitar). A proficient working band, they had already toured with Phil Everly and Frank Ifield.

Compère Tony Marsh was also a familiar face on the circuit. He was a hard-bitten professional, known for his love of a prank and straight talking. He could also stand a drink. Peter Moore of Smokey Robinson's Miracles remembers Marsh on a later tour taking him to pubs the length and breadth of Britain and the bus once being held up by three "gunmen" – another Marsh prank.

Ronnie Wells recalls: "We used to come across him now and again, because there would be two or three tours going and you would some-times use the same meeting places on the road. He was a bit rough around the edges – a bit of a Jack the Lad. I suppose that's how you had to be if you were a comic. He did a lot of these tours."

The action got underway at the Granada Cinema in Barking Road, East Ham on Saturday, March 9. The plan had been for Montez and Roe to share the top honours, one closing the first half and the other the second. The roles would be reversed in the second house. Neither had bargained for the rise of The Beatles.

George Harrison later recalled a huddled meeting which ended with Howes suggesting The Beatles close the first half. George said Tommy Roe found this unacceptable, maintaining he had a contract and would walk out if that happened. Rusty Douch, rhythm guitar and vocals of East End band The Foresters, claims to have overheard an exchange between Chris Montez's manager and Howes that led to Chris also making a protest.

"The Beatles closed the first half of the first show and either Roe or

Montez closed the show, but during the break the tour manager said I want these guys, The Beatles, to close the second show," he says. "There was a bit of an argument and Montez's manager said he wasn't going to do it and that was it. He pulled him (Montez) out of the second show, and Tommy closed the first half and The Beatles closed the second. My brother Bob played drums for us and he was there that night and also remembers Chris not doing that second house."

A report in that weekend's *Melody Maker* confirms that The Beatles did close the show on the second house on this very first night of the tour. "The Beatles' storming act broke up the show – literally – at East Ham Granada," it read. Describing them as "the Merseyside marvels" it stated that they were "moved into the star spot for the second house after disappointing performances from the two Americans".

The reporter didn't mention Montez walking out, but he did note triumphantly: "The Beatles could take it to the Americans, and that's about the highest compliment you could pay a British R&B style group."

The Beatles were stealing the Americans' thunder from the very start and neither was happy about it. Chris and Tommy would have been quite justified in feeling let down. From their point of view, they had signed contracts to top the bill on a UK tour and almost before the show got rolling they faced the prospect of being upstaged for the next three weeks by a bunch of Brits they had never heard of. Bruised egos and disputes over starring roles were a common part of touring life with promoters concerned only with putting bums on seats and record companies using tours to sell records. With 'Please Please Me' rapidly ascending the charts, The Beatles were quite simply what was happening at that moment, and the reaction of the screaming girls merely confirmed it. There was no room for sentiment.

Howes wouldn't have enjoyed upsetting Montez and Roe, but there was no sense in ignoring what was blindingly obvious – audiences were appreciative of the Americans, but they were wildly excited about The Beatles. Some compromises were made, with The Beatles generally closing the first half on this tour, and Montez the second, but it was a hollow victory. The fans made it abundantly clear who they had come to see.

The Beatles were accorded the honour of topping the bill when the tour reached Liverpool and played to two packed houses at the Empire

Theatre. More and more attention was to fall on them, and the two Americans adopted wildly different tactics for dealing with their dilemma. Chris Montez went for full-on showmanship, cavorting around the stage, sometimes falling to his knees to weep down the mike as he attempted to work the girls into a frenzy. This was early 1963, and it earned him some hostile reviews. Tommy Roe, by contrast, refused to abandon his laid-back style. He would trade on the strength of his voice and the quality of his songs.

A newspaper report from Leicester, the final show of the tour, confirmed that Tommy and Chris retained their closing spots on this night – but the biggest screams were for The Beatles who, restricted to just four songs at the start of their previous tour a little over a month before, were now given sufficient time to sing six. Their selected numbers for the tour were 'Love Me Do', 'Misery', 'A Taste Of Honey', 'Do You Want To Know A Secret', 'Please Please Me' and 'I Saw Her Standing There'.

All six were from their debut *Please Please Me* LP recorded the previous month and released on March 22 on the day the tour was heading into Doncaster. As we shall discover, by the time they reached Doncaster The Beatles were allotted enough time to squeeze in more songs, with 'Ask Me Why' and what a fan in his notes describes as "a rocker" added. In fact, a press report confirms The Beatles sang seven songs on the opening night's two shows, their first live gigs in London.

Rusty Douch continues: "What sticks in my mind all these years later was trying to leave the cinema by the back doors after the shows. We couldn't get out. It was chaos. There were thousands of screaming kids. As we opened the doors the whole area seemed filled with people screaming. We thought, 'What the hell's going on here?' They obviously thought The Beatles might be leaving out the back, so they gathered outside. We were locked in. We had to go back inside and try to wait it out.

"I vaguely remember someone being sent out the front to get sandwiches from this little Italian place over the road and us being stuck in the cinema until 2am or 3am. Whatever, there was definitely mania there that night."

Douch and his pals witnessed The Beatles' soundcheck plus both shows, and they were able to chat with them. Starting out as a skiffle player in 1958, he was still playing in 2010, and now lives in New Milton, Hampshire. "We regularly played the cinema for the manager Jock

Livingstone and we were booked that night to play in the foyer as the crowds went in." He remembers The Beatles as friendly and talented. "I thought they were excellent. 'Love Me Do' sticks in the mind and 'Do You Want To Know A Secret' was excellent. You got used to seeing bands in all the towns and villages, but The Beatles came along and they were totally different. It was an excellent sound, and it all looked so easy. Also, they looked different, with Paul playing left-handed and George coming to join him around the mike for the harmonies. It was all part of it. They just rocked the place. They could have taken the wallpaper off by the end."

Douch said Jock Livingstone's verdict was that they were either brilliant or very cocky, but he found them easy to talk to. "Brian Epstein was there and we shook hands, but he was a bit aloof. But The Beatles were great guys – just ordinary people to talk to. Of course, if we'd known then . . . we'd have taken photos and got autographs – the works – but they were just another band at the time, like we were."

Fan Jim Rollinson must have seen the second house that night, because he also recalls The Beatles closing the show. "My girlfriend [now wife] and I saw that show at East Ham that night and I still have the ticket stubs," he says. "We originally booked as fans of Chris Montez and Tommy Roe, but The Beatles ended up topping the bill and it was clear they were destined for greater things. We became instant fans. There wasn't quite Beatlemania at that stage, but we saw them later that year and couldn't hear them for the screaming."

The *Melody Maker* gave worthy mentions to the performances of The Terry Young Six, The Viscounts and Debbie Lee, who all "performed smoothly", and praised compère Tony Marsh for his "non blue" gags . . . and also for his "swinging singing spot". Quite the all-round entertainer.

Another press report from East Ham lists seven Beatle songs, stating that they "crashed into their act with a fast rocker ['I Saw Her Standing There']" then drifted into a harmonica-accented 'Love Me Do' and 'Misery' "which led into some good comedy". This is presumably some Beatle banter before continuing with 'A Taste Of Honey' then, "George Harrison is tops in 'Do You Want To Know A Secret'," and "'Please Please Me' brought screams throughout as The Beatles brewed up a torrid storm."

The report, covering the first house that night, states that The Beatles concluded with "a fast, rocking gospel song with Paul McCartney soloing" – probably his description of 'Long Tall Sally'. It "brought the breathtaking act to a tremendous, and too early, close," concluded reporter Andy Gray.

His article opened by referring to the scream-filled reception for the stars "but The Beatles stole top honours for entertainment and audience reaction". He was clearly impressed by their act . . . but he had a few tips on how they might improve their presentation. "This all-action quartet from Liverpool has everything – exciting new sound, terrific instrumental attack, exhilarating solo and group vocal effects and a fresh energy that leaves them (they told me later) limp at the end of each act," he wrote. Then came the advice: "Admitted, they still need better production, and a good choreographer, tailor and barber, but this apart, they are the most exciting newcomers in Britain today."

Roe was onstage before Montez, looking smart and slim in a grey jacket and black trousers. He started with 'Whole Lotta Shakin'', followed by 'Count On Me', 'The Folk Singer' and 'Maybellene'. He injected some pace with 'Good Good Lovin'' and received his best response for 'Sheila' before ending on a high with a rousing version of the hand-clapping spiritual 'There's A Great Day Coming'.

His approach was markedly different from Montez. Roe's twisting during his final number brought screams from the girls – so he promptly stopped doing it. Montez, however, was quite prepared to flaunt himself. He crashed through 'Bony Moronie' and his big hit 'Let's Dance' and threw in his own version of a striptease, removing his jacket and tie and unbuttoning his shirt to the waist as he added 'Some Kinda Fun' to the party. He got the crowd going with 'La Bamba', before his one slow number, 'You're The One'. If he was going down on this tour, he was going down fighting.

The Viscounts were destined to be warmly welcomed by critics and fans as the tour progressed – quite a compliment in such esteemed company. The band had been on the touring circuit for years, so it is no surprise that they could look after themselves onstage, although they had only a couple of hits. They sang their latest single, 'Don't Let Me Cross Over' at East Ham and left an impression . . . with their impressions. Helen Shapiro, The Vernons Girls, Frank Ifield and Karl Denver all had the backhanded compliment of being taken off by The Viscounts on this tour.

Debbie Lee, in the opening spot, was a decent singer – but one destined to struggle on a tour like this. Compère Tony Marsh — a dab hand at working a crowd — was even given his own song to sing.

Just to underline the audience reaction to The Beatles on this opening night — this from Tommy Roe in an interview with the photographer and journalist Ian Wright: "It was complete mayhem, with hundreds of screaming girls rushing the stage like lemmings. They were completely out of control, with only a few theatre staff and usherettes trying to keep some sort of order. How could you possibly follow that?"

Roe recalled that it wasn't just the honour of closing the show that went to the bill-topper. He said that with the M1 being the only motorway in 1963 (and then only between Watford and Rugby), the tour bus sometimes had to travel through the night, but there was a special privilege for the "star". "The long back seat of the bus became a bed for the exclusive use of the star. On this occasion, there were two headliners, so Montez and I took turns with the bed."

Incidentally, the old cinema in Barking Road still stands, but like most of the few that remain, it is now a Gala bingo hall.

The opening night dramas over, the party headed up to the Midlands to play the grand old Hippodrome Theatre in Hurst Street, Birmingham, on the Sunday. The city's fans gave an enthusiastic welcome to pop shows and the storm of the opening night seemed to have abated.

The hurt, however, had not gone away. Montez knew his spot was under threat and once again the Brits received the hottest reception. He knew he was going to have to work his socks off — or at least his jacket, tie and shirt — most nights to keep pace. The Beatles, as we shall see, barely had to shake their mop-topped heads to drive up the screams.

But the compromise had been worked out — with The Beatles now promoted to closing the first half and Chris Montez retaining his prized spot. It wasn't set in stone, though. Montez was going to have to earn it. For a start, he would have to develop a stage act, something that had reportedly been lacking in the first house of the opening night. His response was to put some raw emotion, raunchiness and showmanship into his routine. He now knew that it wasn't enough to have a hit record and be able to hold a microphone.

Montez and Roe may not have known it, but the Birmingham Hippodrome, even back then, was already one of the proudest old entertainment venues in England. There had been a theatre of some sort on the site since

1895 and the Hippodrome had been in existence in its own right since 1903. The Birmingham public were used to seeing star performers from all of the arts in their city and they weren't over-awed by them . . . yet. It was an enthusiastic, but relatively polite reception for The Beatles and their touring buddies for the two houses.

There was a day off the next day, but The Beatles spent the evening in a small studio at EMI House in London recording a fourth and final appearance for Radio Luxembourg's *The Friday Spectacular*, transmitted just a few days later. It involved some light chat and both sides of their single – 'Please Please Me' and 'Ask Me Why' – being broadcast. A day off was something of a rarity. Their only other day off for three weeks was on Monday, March 25, and even that wasn't a real day off as photographer Dezo Hoffmann grabbed them for a picture and filming session.

It was back on the road again on Tuesday, March 12 with the tour heading into Bedford for two shows at the town's Granada Cinema. They left without John, who had gone down with a heavy cold, and so the two packed houses that evening witnessed The Beatles performing as a trio. Their repertoire was adapted and the group carried on regardless. Even pop stars couldn't avoid picking up colds, and groups got used to battling on without key members rather than face the problem of thousands of disappointed fans – or worse, the prospect of being sued for not fulfilling an engagement.

In this case, George and Paul worked overtime to cover John's absence in a re-arranged set. This was an added benefit of their not having to rely on just one lead singer, as John once recalled: "It's quite a strain, singing numbers like 'Twist And Shout' night after night. I lose my voice for days on end sometimes. Thankfully, it doesn't affect our act. We've got such a big repertoire of songs. We just arrange it that the others fill in."

Cinema manager Ivan Morgan, who had been so knocked out by the group just a few weeks before during the Shapiro tour, remembers that despite John's absence it was The Beatles, rather than Montez and Roe, who got all the attention. "The shows went remarkably well again," he recalls. "This time we had a job getting The Beatles out to a car that was waiting for them. It was down in Midland Road and we had to smuggle them away.

"There was one incident that night. A girl contacted me to say her wallet had been stolen and with it she had lost her tickets to see The

The first tour, February/March 1963. *(Courtesy Peter Nash)*

Helen Shapiro, who topped the bill on
The Beatles' first UK tour. (*Ian Wright*)

The South African born singer Danny Williams was one
of the leading lights on The Beatles' first tour. (*Ian Wright*)

Portsmouth-based singing sisters The Honeys
who opened the show on the first tour.

East ender Kenny Lynch was already a
household name when he toured with The Beatles
in February, 1963. (*Dezo Hoffmann/Rex Features*)

Empire Theatre, Sunderland, February 9, 1963. (*Ian Wright*)

The weekend starts here… Helen Shapiro with Keith Fordyce, Dusty Springfield
and The Beatles on ITV's *Ready Steady Go!* (*Mail On Sunday/Rex Features*)

Hold Me Tight… Helen Shapiro gets up close with John Lennon during a break in filming *Ready Steady Go!* But did the Beatle know that Helen had an enormous crush on him? *(David Redfern/Redferns)*

In their collarless suits, the four boys from Liverpool were already on the way to achieving their dream of being "bigger than Elvis". *(Harry Hammond/V&A Images)*

CHRIS MONTEZ

RIALTO · YORK

Manager : D. J. McCALLION   Phone : 22119

6.40 — WED., 13th MARCH, 1963 — 8.45

TWO PERFORMANCES ONLY

ONE NIGHT ONLY

ARTHUR HOWES presents (in association with EVELYN TAYLOR)

AMERICA'S EXCITING
CHRIS MONTEZ
'LET'S DANCE'   'SOME KINDA FUN'

AMERICA'S FABULOUS
TOMMY ROE
'SHEILA'

The **TERRY YOUNG SIX**

GLAMOROUS **DEBBIE LEE** PARLOPHONE

The **VISCOUNTS** PYE RECORDING STARS

YOUR 208 D.J. **TONY MARSH**

BRITAIN'S DYNAMIC
BEATLES
'LOVE ME DO'   'PLEASE, PLEASE ME'

PRICES: 8/6   6/6   4/6

BOX OFFICE
RIALTO
YORK

POSTAL BOOKING FORM
Wednesday, 13th March, 1963
Chris Montez/Tommy Roe Show   Date...........

Please forward ....

...ily EVENING 6.40 / 8.45 performance

...e stamped addressed envelope and ...
(Please del...

...SS
Use this form if inconvenient to call at the ...
Printed by Electric (Mo...

your prog...

g Six
...unts
...rsh
...TEZ

The second tour, March 1963.

Chris 'Let's Dance' Montez. *(Michael Ochs Archives/Getty Images)*

Tommy 'Sheila' Roe. *(Michael Ochs Archives/Getty Images)*

On their second UK tour The Beatles were outbilled by Chris Montez and
Tommy Roe but the fans made it clear who they really wanted to see.

The Viscounts singing trio – Ronnie Wells, Gordon Mills and Don Paul – enjoyed some rave reviews on the Montez and Roe tour in March 1963. *(Paul Naylor/Redferns)*

Ready to rock: John, Ringo, George and Paul with Chris Montez and Tommy Roe during their tour. *(Harry Hammond/V&A Images)*

Beatles. She knew the seat numbers so I telephoned the police and some-body from CID came down just in case the thief had the audacity to come to the show. Sure enough he did and I stopped the bloke at the entrance and he ran off. I helped to give chase – I was young and fit then – and we caught the guy and waited for the uniformed officers to pick him up. The girl and her friend got to see the show."

In the audience in the first house that night was 20-year-old Stuart O'Dell who had just about the ideal job for someone interested in seeing pop shows at the Granada. "I used to print the tickets," he said. "I was an apprentice at Stonebridges Printers in Brereton Road, Bedford, and the job of printing the tickets for these shows fell to me. I used to get complimentaries, but sometimes I did have to pay. I remember there were only three Beatles that night, but they played very well. They covered the vocals and still managed to put the music over well. I don't think anyone went home disappointed.

"There was the odd bit of screaming and shouting but you could hear the music and it was enjoyable. I wasn't so bothered about seeing Chris Montez or Tommy Roe, but 'Please Please Me' had been quite a hit so it was good to see The Beatles."

Stuart lived a couple of miles from the Granada but his job in the town centre meant only a quick stroll down the road to take his seat for the first house. "I saw a few pop shows there," he said. "It was not a terrifically big place and the acoustics were good. It was sad that they decided to pull it down."

Due to the magic of radio, while The Beatles were preparing for the Bedford shows at 5pm, pop fans tuning into *Teenager's Turn (Here We Go)* on the Light Programme heard them playing 'Misery', 'Please Please Me' and 'Do You Want To Know A Secret' live. In fact, the songs had been recorded the previous Wednesday in front of a live audience at the Playhouse Theatre in Manchester, the group's fifth and final appearance on the programme.

The tour coach left Bedford the next day for the long trip north for per-formances at the Rialto Theatre in the ancient cathedral city of York, but there were no Beatles on board. They travelled under their own steam as they had first to attend a session at EMI's Abbey Road studios in London for some overdubbing work on 'Thank You Girl', the song destined to become the B-side of their next single.

It was lunchtime when they set off on the 208-mile journey to York, again as a trio, as John was still struggling with his cold. The pouring rain and the absence of John didn't dampen the enthusiasm of the fans waiting outside the York Rialto. In fact, theatre manager Don McCallion decided to put his foot down with a firm hand when Montez, Roe and The Beatles were mobbed by their admirers.

He called a halt to an autograph signing session after 25 minutes as girls who had been patiently queuing in the rain suddenly tried to storm the stage door to get at the stars. "I've had enough. I warned them that if they didn't behave and form orderly queues I'd stop the session. Well they wouldn't play fair, so I'm having no more. I can't spare the staff to control them," he told local newspaper the *Evening Press*.

Despite this, hundreds did manage to get autographs that night, with the stars putting pen to paper before, during and after the two houses. Dozens of girls jostled to get near them after the show.

John was not the only absentee. The Terry Young Six were a man down, not that the excited fans seemed to care.

In fairness, this show wasn't just about The Beatles. Montez and Roe both put on a good show for their fans, and were well received for their efforts. Montez, in what appeared to be bright red slippers, hit them with 'Let's Dance' and 'Some Kinda Fun' among a collection of upbeat numbers. During the second number he again flung his jacket into the wings, with his tie following a few bars later, as he twisted and gyrated through the rest of the song. He even left the stage to join the audience at one point, such was his determination to make an impact.

Roe received generous encores after running through his top ten hit 'Sheila' and 'The Folk Singer', and the crowd went wild when he launched into Chubby Checker's 'Good Good Lovin''.

Reporter Stacey Brewer contended that The Beatles "coped wonderfully" without John. "Despite having no lead singer," he wrote, "the boys struggled admirably with their hit number 'Please Please Me'. The rest of their programme was re-jigged for two-part singing. It included 'Misery', 'Till There Was You' and 'Do You Want To Know A Secret'." The fact that Paul sang 'Till There Was You' was unusual in that it wasn't among the six songs prepared for the tour and would not be heard on a Beatles record until November when it was included on their second album, *With The Beatles*. However, it was a song famously thrown in by Paul from time to time – particularly when their amps packed up at the Cavern – and was ideal for this night as John didn't sing on it.

The Terry Young Six opened the show, followed by Debbie Lee who included 'Fly Me To The Moon', 'Bossa Nova', 'The Wayward Wind' and 'Like I Do' in her set. Stacey Brewer was particularly taken with The Viscounts, both visually and vocally. "They took the honours, particularly in their lively medley of star take-offs, including 'Don't Treat Me Like A Child' and 'I Remember You'," he wrote.

With John again out of action it was still a case of the three-tles appearing at the Gaumont in Wolverhampton the next night. Being a man light didn't warrant a comment in a brief Wolverhampton *Express & Star* report which simply stated that: "The Beatles, with their unusual haircuts, did well to emerge from a particularly ill-mannered audience buffeting with credit."

Of course, the group were glad of their "buffeting" – it would be some months before they were to tire of such treatment. For now, it simply meant that audiences were lapping them up, and The Beatles were lapping up the attention. Their comparatively raucous sets – in contrast to so many lightweight acts of the period – gave them credibility with the boys, as well as thrilling their rapidly growing numbers of female admirers.

Wolverhampton locals knew a thing or two about genuine rock'n'roll, and they appreciated that they were witnessing something special. In the audience that night was fifth form grammar school boy and music fan Keith Farley, who went on to become a respected Wolverhampton historian. Farley has a connection with Liverpool, too. His father was born there and young Keith would sometimes travel up to watch Everton and maybe catch a session at the Cavern. He hadn't been overly impressed when he first saw The Beatles, but they had since risen considerably in his estimation.

"I must have seen them seven or eight times in all," he recalls. "One night I remember was when they played the Plaza Ballroom in Old Hill near Dudley [January 11, 1963]. The Plaza had a revolving stage and when it turned round and they came on, it was quite something. Everyone that night just listened because the sound they made was so great. Ma Regan ran the Plaza and four or five venues and it was her powerful personality that persuaded them to come back and do a second gig there.

"What I liked about The Beatles was that they played what I called authentic rock'n'roll – songs by people like Eddie Cochran, Little Richard and Gene Vincent. At the Gaumont of course they played their own songs, but it didn't matter. They were great. I'd primarily gone along because I loved Chris Montez's 'Let's Dance'. My mate was there to see Tommy Roe. But we both agreed at the end that The Beatles were the best. They were superb, even as a trio. Paul McCartney's voice was fabulous. The kids who were there thought they were great. The next day I went out and bought 'Please Please Me'. I bet the local 'Please Please Me' sales quadrupled after that show.

"As I recall it, The Beatles closed the first half. There was noise from the girls that night, but it wasn't too bad. You could hear The Beatles. We were downstairs and it's interesting that they played 'I Saw Her Standing There' as it's always been my favourite Beatles record. We were at the second house because I remember all the girls later waiting for The Beatles to come out."

That short report in the *Express & Star* mentioned not only that Beatle buffeting, but also that tour headliner Montez enjoyed a "vastly enthusiastic" reception from the audience. The writer (revealed only as D.W.) also commented that Roe "whose forte until now has been vocal imitation of the late Buddy Holly, displayed last night a pleasing talent of his own". Roe reportedly drew warm applause for 'The Folk Singer' which was described as "a lightweight country and western ballad".

By now the tour was in full swing and The Beatles and the rest were heading down to Bristol on the Friday for two shows at the Colston Hall – one of the 1960s pop package venues that is still standing. There was great relief that John had recovered from his cold and was able to join the other Beatles for these shows. His distinctive vocals and harmonica work restored the group's unique sound for their performances of 'Please Please Me' and 'Love Me Do'. 'Misery' benefited from John's matchless delivery and Paul's emergency song 'Till There Was You' was dropped.

Team Beatles knew that these shows in front of large audiences up and down the country were important and John was a key element in the pure excitement of their sound. There was also a growing momentum behind young British acts, with a feeling among teenagers that American pretty boys had been dominating our charts for too long. But it wasn't just The Beatles who earned the cheers. The Viscounts, so adeptly backed by Terry Young and his crew, were enjoyed at the Colston Hall (and at other venues) for their vocal talents and their ability to entertain by mimicking the stars of the day. Montez and Roe were the star names – still filling a fair percentage of seats with their fans – but plenty were going home talking about the home-grown talent on the bill. Montez and Roe were getting applause, but there were still Teds at some of these gigs and they made it clear they didn't appreciate the ballads thrown in for the girls.

But The Beatles' bandwagon was rolling – and it left the West Country with yet more converts on board. There was, of course, nothing straightforward in a Beatles schedule. They set off from Bristol the next morning (Saturday, March 16), but it wasn't in the direction of Sheffield for the two houses that evening at the City Hall. Before they could even contemplate that there was a drive from Bristol to London for a live morning BBC radio performance on Brian Matthew's *Saturday Club*.

They performed six songs for the radio show – three of their own and three covers, kicking off with 'I Saw Her Standing There' and 'Misery' followed by John belting out two Chuck Berry songs, 'Too Much Monkey Business' and 'I'm Talking About You'. Then it was 'Please Please Me' before closing with a Cavern favourite, 'The Hippy Hippy Shake'. There was the usual playful banter with Matthew, by now no stranger to The Beatles, playing the good-natured and benevolent teacher keeping his unruly but talented pupils in line.

He commented on John's recovery from his "dodgy throat" and asked him why they had given 'Misery' to Kenny Lynch. John explained that Kenny was a friend from the Helen tour and he hoped the public would buy the record. He also mentioned that it was on The Beatles LP that was coming out next week. The high profile radio coverage was a big boost to the group at that time, and their *Saturday Club* appearance was advertised in that week's *Radio Times*, complete with a picture of them.

The show completed, they dashed up to Sheffield to rejoin the package for the two City Hall shows. Both were packed and the kids gave The Beatles and their American cousins a rapturous welcome. The concert merited a few paragraphs in the *Daily Telegraph* which mentioned The Beatles' dash up from the *Saturday Club* appearance in London to get to Sheffield in time. Referring to them as "Britain's newest singing, swinging group", the reporter commented that "The Beatles have built up a good reputation for good-sounding music and appealing singing."

The group attracted screams and cheers at both houses, but the audience also appreciated Montez and Roe. Chris was relaxing backstage in his red slippers but was full of energy onstage, gyrating and twisting to the music, which clearly went down well in Sheffield. There can be no question that the competition between artists – each with such a limited amount of time onstage to make an impact – played a key part of the success of these pop package tours. The battle for the headlines guaranteed that all the performers put in the maximum effort and the winners were the fans.

Some fans were particularly fortunate. Teenager Julie Allman (now Barnett) was the envy of her mates after being sneaked backstage by a friend who worked for Sheffield Council. She bumped into some of the stars and was bold enough to ask them to autograph her programme. Her reward – the signatures of Beatles Paul and George, plus Montez and Roe.

Julie recalls: "We originally booked to see Chris Montez, but by the time the show arrived everyone was excited about The Beatles. I got Chris's autograph in his dressing room and I bumped into George and Paul in a corridor, so I got them to sign as well."

The autographed programme was to remain in a suitcase in the attic of Julie's Worksop home for 45 years until she decided to auction it in 2008. "I'm not entirely sure why I held on to it. Perhaps it was just a momento of a really good evening," she says.

Tommy Roe preferred the girls not to scream while he was singing, but he wasn't to totally get his way this night, as local teenager Mike Lawton, another in the audience, recalls. And according to Lawton, there were still people who weren't aware of The Beatles. A 16-year-old apprentice bricklayer for local building firm Ackroyd & Abbott, he was into pop music and the cinema, and he recalls: "I was looking forward to seeing Montez and Roe, but I was also keen to see The Beatles, unlike some others in the audience, who weren't really aware of them. I enjoyed their short set, but not as much as the record, or as Tommy and Chris that night. The only thing that spoiled the show for me was the screaming by girls when Tommy was singing."

The Beatles were back on the scene of their December setback on the Frank Ifield show when they returned to the Embassy Cinema in Peterborough the next day (Sunday). And what a difference three months can make. This time the *Evening Telegraph* reviewer was neither withering nor dismissive of the talent of the rising stars from Liverpool. "As far as musical ability goes, their act gave them little chance to display any. But presentation wise, they are home and dry. The Beatles are right at the top – and they deserve to be there," he wrote.

This wasn't just any old gig on the tour. Peterborough was the home town of promoter Arthur Howes and he believed in giving young hopefuls a chance. So added to the bill, for this night only, were Peterborough's finest – The Dynatones. For them it was an opportunity to play a major date with the stars and then settle back in their seats to watch the rest of the show. The Beatles made an immediate impact on them.

Dynatones keyboard player Adrian Titman-King, who now lives in Dallas, Texas, has clear memories of that St Patrick's night gig and of sitting upstairs at the Embassy to see the Fab Four bring the house down little more than three months after Peterborough had given them such a mixed reception. "The timing for Montez and Roe was terrible," he recalls. "They had nothing to offer. It wasn't so bad for Roe, who played about 20 minutes, but Montez, who closed the show that night, had a hard time. As I recall he did about 40 minutes and it was far too long. I watched from on high and the kids were crying out for The Beatles while he was singing."

Adrian says The Dynatones won their spot because Howes already knew how good they were. "He billed us as the number one band in East Anglia, and we were. Nobody was left off the bill, but a few of the acts, like The Viscounts and Debbie Lee, had their slots cut to 10 minutes to fit us in. John Lennon came up to me at the side of the stage between the shows and said, 'You're great players, but get off The Shadows' shit!' I told him that me and the bass player were already playing jazz and blues stuff and he said that's what we should be doing."

What was it about The Beatles that was making the audiences so wild and making the Americans look pale in comparison? "They just had everything. They were so refreshing. They had the Beatle suits, the Beatle boots and those haircuts – their look and their sound were so different and so natural, and yet they were ordinary people – like the guys next door. And what great showmen. They put on a show. The sound – those harmonies – and the guitar sound. Don't forget, everyone was using Fender Strats and Precision bass guitars at the time, but they were different. Lennon on his Rickenbacker and Paul with the Hofner violin bass – it gave them a different sound. The audience went wild when they played 'Please Please Me'."

Adrian also recalls having a two-minute jam with two Beatles that night. "I was always wanting to play the Steinway piano at the Embassy and I got on it that night and was beginning to swing – Macca was tuning up and Ringo was setting up and then they joined in and we played for a couple of minutes until the rest of the lads arrived with their gear."

The Dynatones were the most popular band around Peterborough at the time and bass player Colin Hodgkinson believes that is why Howes rewarded them with the spot. "I remember Chris Montez being on the bill and of course we were delighted to be able to take part. We were probably a bit nervous beforehand because we were used to playing local dances, not a big stage show like that. Because we opened, we were free to watch The Beatles onstage later and my memory is of how incredibly tight they were as a band – such a fresh and tight sound. There was some screaming, but nowhere near as bad as it got later on. I'm sure Montez and Tommy Roe would have gone down well, but the kids were there to see The Beatles – you could tell that."

Colin had just bought a Fender bass and, like McCartney, he was left-handed. "The Beatles were very friendly and approachable. We chatted to them afterwards and I remember talking to Paul about my new left-handed Fender bass. He said he hadn't played a Fender, so he had a go. They were just down-to-earth guys."

Dynatones guitarist Richard Austin, who has lived in Queensland, Australia, since 1968, also has fond memories. "At that time we were more of an instrumental band and we played the old classic 'Donkey Serenade' and the 'Can Can' – plus The Shadows [as John mentioned], and Cliff's 'Dancing Shoes'. We went upstairs to watch the show after our spot. The guys [Beatles] were really excellent, on and offstage. They just had this charisma onstage – this confidence in the way they performed. They knew everything they played so well. As musicians you sometimes listened out for mistakes, but they were so tight. All those hours in Hamburg I suppose – being away from the British pop scene and doing their own thing. There must have been screaming, but it's not a big memory of the night. It was just like a recognition of the songs they played, that was all."

Austin also had his moment with a Beatle. "I remember having a bit of a yarn with Paul while John was practising and George was setting up. Just the usual thing about instruments, but we also discussed how they all came together and a little about their songwriting."

The other three members of the Dynatones, rhythm guitarist Mick Lemmon, drummer Trevor Wright and singer Tony Benham, are now dead.

Carol Barrett and her Peterborough County Grammar School pals Pauline White and Margaret Cawfield, who had met The Beatles at the Embassy gig in December, were back in the audience again. Although the group had moved on since then, security was quite lax and the girls were able to get backstage after the first house to meet them again.

"We just knocked on the door and somebody let us in. It was as simple as that," says Carol. "There were only about 10 or 15 of us. I remember The Beatles had these odd comics – things we hadn't heard of or seen before. Perhaps they were American? But they were laughing about them."

The Beatles had a record player – but for some reason no records to play on it to while away the spare time that day, so they paid for Carol to get a taxi home to bring along some of her favourites. She had the wonderful bonus of having Beatle signatures on those precious Beatle records – but her sister took them in for a teacher and that was the last she saw of them. "That's little sisters for you!" says Carol.

Had The Beatles changed in the short time since December? "Not really," says Carol, who was living with her family at Midland Road then and is still in Peterborough today. "They had no pretensions. They were still the same down-to-earth, friendly lads. George didn't say too much, but then he was always quieter. John went off pretty quickly, saying he wanted a practice. I recall him going up on the stage and playing a piano."

The Peterborough fun and games over, it was straight back on the road to Gloucester the following morning. Pop stars became used to having objects of affection hurled at them during a performance, and Chris Montez was duly struck on the shoulder at The Regal in Gloucester that night, ironically as he was singing 'You're The One'. The hurler of the object was schoolgirl Sally Burge of Leighterton, Tetbury, who had raced down the aisle to lob the neatly wrapped package over the footlights onto the stage, to the astonishment of the audience and the singer. And while Montez picked up the parcel and placed it at the side of the stage to open later, love-struck Sally ended up toppling into the orchestra pit and was carried out of the theatre.

Montez discovered a box of chocolates and a letter inside the parcel and he was clearly moved when he spoke to local reporter Hugh Worsnip of the *Gloucester Citizen* later while dining at the New County Hotel in nearby Southgate Street, where the touring party were staying. Montez said he saw the package flying over the lights but couldn't see who had thrown it. In the letter Sally said she had given up three school lunches to pay for the chocolates and that she had also travelled to Bristol the previous Friday to see the show at the Colston Hall. "That shows such great loyalty that I'm gonna get in touch with her real soon. I only wish I could have met her tonight," Chris told the reporter. Whether he did or not remains unrecorded.

The 1,000 or so in the audiences that night lapped up the performances, and there was an excited reaction to the Americans and the Brits. The *Citizen* had carried a brief preview (on the same page as a paid advertisement for the show) just a few days before, and had questioned whether Montez and Roe's thunder was about to be stolen by the young newcomers.

However, there was no mention of John, Paul, George or Ringo in the *Citizen* review of the show the next day – but plenty about the plight of poor Sally. "That would be down to the subeditors because I definitely included them in my report," recalls Worsnip, now retired after more than 40 years on the paper. "I was 20 at the time and played in a local band called The Beatniks. Our manager Paul Davies, who also worked on the *Citizen*, was with me that night. We were on the left hand side in the stalls about halfway down. The Beatles were absolutely terrific. They closed the first half and there was just so much screaming. I wrote something along the lines that they were great and judging by the reaction of the audience they were destined to go places, but the paper only included the story about Sally.

"My memory is that Sally ended up in the orchestra pit when she threw her parcel and was injured. She was carried out by St John's volunteers. Chris made some remark from the stage that he hoped she would be OK. After the show I went back to the office, which was only a couple of hundred yards from the Regal, to do the report but then decided to pop along to the hotel to talk to Chris Montez and see if he was going to send her a bunch of flowers or something. He was dining in the restaurant when I arrived so I joined him and we were in conversation when two of The Beatles – John and Paul – came over. They were saying things like they were an up-and-coming band and were going to be big and I gave them my notebook and said why don't you write your names down to make sure they're all spelt correctly. We held on to our notebooks for six months for legal reasons – then they were thrown out. I never thought to keep it."

Hugh recalls that the *Citizen*'s receptionist fared a little better. She had a relative who worked at the Regal and ended up with the autographs of all four Beatles. The cinema closed in 1990, but the building survives as a J. D. Wetherspoon pub.

Having travelled east to west from Peterborough to Gloucester, the tour was now headed back east for two houses at the Regal Cinema in Cambridge on the Tuesday. The evidence suggests that you could still hear a decent amount above the screams – provided you had a seat in the right place.

However, even an esteemed position such as President of the Cambridge Union wasn't enough to guarantee you a top seat at The Beatles show. Peterhouse Cambridge student Michael Howard, who held that proud title in March 1963, was already a Beatles fan. But the man who went on to lead the Conservative Party didn't hear much music that night. He says: "I was present at the performance given by The Beatles at the Regal Cinema in Cambridge on March 19, 1963. I also saw them at Carnegie Hall in early 1964 and on at least one occasion at Hammersmith Odeon.

"My most abiding memory of the concert at the Regal was that it was impossible to hear any of the music because of the screaming of the fans. I don't suppose that was unique later on, but I imagine that was one of the earliest examples of that phenomenon. A little while later I bought The Beatles' first album *Please Please Me*, and you will recall that the sleeve contains the immortal message that The Beatles are the biggest thing to hit showbusiness since The Shadows."

Another in the crowd that night was 19-year-old Jean Chainey who was there with her pals from the GPO telephone exchange. "We used to go to all the pop shows at the Regal. I remember seeing Cliff there, among others, but this night I was more interested in The Beatles than the Americans. We all loved 'Please Please Me' – even my mother was fond of them. What I remember now is that we queued for such a long time to get the tickets and then again to get in. Other than that, at the show everybody was screaming!"

However, the screaming at the Regal wasn't unbearable if you were near the stage. Tommy Roe fan Mick Oates, who still lives in Cambridge, must have had a good seat. He recalls: "In contrast to Michael Howard, I remember hearing The Beatles' songs very clearly. There was no 'wall of noise' such as I encountered a couple of years later when a crowd of us went to see them perform at a venue in London when they were top of the bill. On that occasion I couldn't hear a word they were singing and we were seated so far back that one of the girls in our group said they looked like puppets because they were so far away!

"But at the Regal I could hear them very well. They hadn't yet got a tremendous fan base. People were just going along to listen to see who this new group were. I was there with my girlfriend who was also a Tommy Roe fan and I suspect that I got fairly good seats near the stage to impress her. We saw Cliff and everyone else at the Regal and the screaming for The Beatles was at about the same level."

Helping to keep everything under control were members of Great Shelford Football Club who patrolled the aisles and protected the stage from the over-excited fans. Football club secretary Jim Dean worked at the cinema as a floor layer so it made good sense to ask him if he had any burly mates who fancied earning 10 bob for the night, protecting pop stars from their fans. "We did this for all the pop shows, but we had more lads drafted in when The Beatles or The Rolling Stones were playing. It was brilliant. I was there for the music really. I loved it all.

"On the Montez night they arrived in the mid afternoon and I remember John Lennon taking his shirt off in the dressing room and discovering he had a dirty collar. I said I could sort that out for him, so I gave it a bit of a scrub in the boiler room and he was well pleased. I did occasionally get autographs for people but you had to respect them and not stay too long. They needed to get some peace in their dressing room."

Dean remembers the audience reaction that night, from his privileged position in front of the stage. "There was a lot of excitement. There was screaming, but when they played you could hear a pin drop."

Well it must have helped you to hear The Beatles that night if you weren't screaming yourself. That was not the case with 15-year-old Kathy Elliott. "I was living in Soham, about 15 miles from Cambridge, and attending Soham Village College. My friends and I were absolutely Beatles mad and when we heard that they were coming to the Regal we managed to get tickets. I can't remember how, but it was probably with the help of a parent, a minibus was organised to take us to Cambridge because not many of our parents had cars. We felt so grown up and cool, but when we arrived in Cambridge and got off the bus we noticed a big sign on the back saying School Bus, which brought us back to earth a bit!

"My main recollection is that we didn't really hear much of the music because we, along with most of the other girls in the audience, were screaming our heads off! After the concert we tried to get across to the University Arms where we thought The Beatles would be staying, but it was difficult to get through the crowds of girls who had the same idea, and also our bus was waiting to take us home."

And what did the local paper, the *Cambridge News*, make of it all? Their reporter's verdict was: "The fast moving show was not the best Cambridge audiences have seen."

From Cambridge the show hit the road south for two performances at the ABC in Romford the next day. But The Beatles had a personal appointment to keep before heading to the cinema in South Street to carry out their professional duties – a meeting with James and Louisa Graves at the couple's home in nearby George Street, Romford. James and Louisa were the parents of Ringo's stepfather Harry Graves. Harry had moved from Romford to Liverpool in the early 1950s where he met and later married Ringo's divorced mum Elsie. Harry and Ringo grew close and Harry encouraged his stepson's love of music. James is credited with buying Ringo's first full drum kit which Harry faithfully transported from Euston up to Liverpool in the guard's compartment of a train.

Ringo's uncle Alf joined the gathering and all parties clearly enjoyed themselves. The Graves family were always content to stay out of the limelight, but grandfather James, in his one and only interview the following year, referred to this day, deeming The Beatles "a wonderful bunch of boys, not at all big-headed about their success".

The niceties over, The Beatles joined up with the rest of the cast and crew at the ABC. This was a very enjoyable period in their progress. Their stock seemed to be rising by the day. The all-star appeal of the bill saw every ticket sold within a few hours of them going on sale a week before the show. Even ticketless fans travelled in from all over Essex and from London on the day in the hope of sneaking in. But their only reward (if they were lucky) was to catch a glimpse of the stars as they entered by the stage door.

As for The Beatles' local school-age fans, some were already devoted enough to give up their dinner money to pay for their precious seats – and of course, every one of them would have deemed it well worth giving up the odd meal for.

Chris Montez again closed the show ahead of Tommy Roe, and The Beatles grabbed their now regular spot of closing the first half. The ABC, opened at the height of the cinema boom in 1938, seated 2,000, and both houses were in good voice. The cinema was an occasional venue for these pop package tours but rarely did they contain such a collection of stars from both sides of the Atlantic.

The Beatles' vibrant set – particularly 'I Saw Her Standing There' and 'Please Please Me' – got the crowds stomping and both houses were royally entertained. This was their only appearance at this venue, but they did return to Romford to play the Odeon, which was also in South Street, a few months later, on June 16, on a Merseybeat show with Gerry & The Pacemakers and Billy J. Kramer & The Dakotas. That concert ended up as quite a coup since those three acts held the top three positions in the charts that week. The Beatles again took the opportunity to visit James and Louisa, whose home was just a five minute stroll away. But by that time the crowds were so great that they had to scramble into a van in Eastern Road to be able to get back to the cinema.

The ABC closed in 1999 and has been demolished. The site is now occupied by flats, known as Gibson Court.

The Beatles had more radio work to do the next day before they could think about that night's two houses at the ABC Cinema in West Croydon. There was an early morning trip into the BBC's studios in Piccadilly, London, to record three songs to be broadcast on the radio show *On The Scene* on the Light Programme a week later. 'Misery', 'Do You Want To Know A Secret' and 'Please Please Me' were recorded between 1pm and 2pm, following a 10am rehearsal. The show was to be presented by Craig Douglas, with Mike Berry and Shane Fenton among the other performers.

Then came the drive to West Croydon, and this was one night when all the major artists faced the same dilemma. Just how do you solve the problem of performing in a rock'n'roll show to a packed out audience that can't hear a single word you're singing because of their non-stop screaming?

At some venues Chris Montez had a clear run until the end of each song, which was greeted with polite applause, but at the ABC in West

Croydon Montez was getting the scream treatment throughout and struggling to make himself heard over it. He was still only 20, but he'd been around long enough to let instinct take over. He wasn't complaining about the screams. In fact, he worked his act around building them up. He concentrated on sight rather than sound. The discarding of the jacket of his black suit at the end of the first song, the casual tossing away of his bright red neckerchief across the stage, the kisses blown to the girls, the shirt being dramatically unbuttoned to the waist and the sexy drawling into the microphone – all were thrown in to give the girls a show, even if they couldn't hear anything.

But how do you review a concert when you can't hear a note of it? Reporters for *The Croydon Advertiser* and *The Croydon Times* were united in their frustration. Their reports, published eight days later due to the deadlines they faced, reflected the pointlessness of staging a concert with little audible music.

For Montez, though, this was a good night. He was getting the attention he craved and he was right there in the limelight. Those newspaper reports confirm that it was he who closed the shows that night and he was revelling in it, even if the reviewers weren't impressed. He had seen The Beatles pump up the screams on other nights with little more effort than shaking their heads, and he was determined not to be outdone, his assumption being that if the crowd could hear you, it was a sign they didn't care much.

That was the fate suffered by Debbie Lee, who opened the show, but to little response. This was in no way a reflection on Debbie's performance. Viscount Ronnie Wells remembers Debbie as a pleasant girl with a voice to match, a view shared by those who worked with Debbie on TV shows at that time. But these pop package shows were mainly for teenage girls – and they came to scream at boys. Especially when The Beatles were in town.

The Terry Young Six (again a man short due to that dastardly flu) provided solid backing, and at least The Viscounts could be heard. They again impressed the critics. *Croydon Times* reviewer Peter Watson noted: "They were good. Very good. They displayed talent, which doesn't go down well with the screamers of course, but I thoroughly enjoyed them."

Watson confirms the act The Viscounts used on the tour, remarking on their impressions of Karl Denver, Frank Ifield and Helen Shapiro, adding:

"and they blended well together in their more serious numbers". He was disappointed with The Beatles, but admitted it was "probably because I was able to hear very little of them". He was particularly cutting about Chris Montez, saying he was last on the bill and he liked him the least. He listed the singer's stage antics and concluded: "His 20-minute act seemed like a whole evening to me. Still, I hadn't come to see his chest."

This kind of criticism from reporters was to resurface, though Watson was grateful for compère Tony Marsh's efforts to quiet the girls, even if he did imply it was too little, too late.

The *Advertiser* reviewer (initialled J.T.S.) was withering as he noted what a "great pleasure and privilege it was to come to the ABC to hear Montez and Roe say what a pleasure and privilege it was 'to be there'", as he heard little else from them. The exception to the rule was Roe's 'The Folk Singer', which clearly awed the screamers to silence for a while – at least until Roe bent on to one knee and set them off again.

As the tour headed up north the next morning for two houses at Doncaster's Gaumont Cinema it was another momentous day for The Beatles. Their first LP, *Please Please Me*, was released in the UK. With 14 vibrant songs that so perfectly captured the group's appeal as a live act at that time it did, indeed, have all the feel of a genuine live album – a barnstorming, high energy, let's do the show right here performance of songs their Liverpool fans had grown to love. Included, of course, were 'Love Me Do' and 'Please Please Me' – by now regular numbers in their stage act – and fêted as the songs that had handed John, Paul, George and Ringo their national breakthrough, but it was the all out rock numbers, 'I Saw Her Standing There' and 'Twist And Shout', which opened and closed the LP, that showcased The Beatles' real strength and proved to be the enduring highlights.

Policeman's son Martyn Vickers, an 18-year-old lab assistant with British Nylon Spinners, was at the show with some of his workmates. They shared an enthusiasm for The Beatles. Vickers retained his ticket stub, programme and an *NME* report of the show – together with a list of the songs they played. "I saw them twice at the Gaumont," he says. "The second time, in December 1963, you could hardly hear a thing, but my father, Inspector Cyril Vickers, was part of the team getting The Beatles out that night and he managed to get my programme signed by them. I still have it.

"But the Montez show was better because you could hear them. I saw the later, 8.30pm show, and The Beatles were great. They closed the first half. I bought the *Please Please Me* LP shortly afterwards and that was quite something for me to do because it was the first album I'd ever bought. I was strictly a singles man."

Vickers is a little embarrassed that he noted down the songs performed at The Gaumont that night – by all the performers. But we should be grateful to him, for it offers an accurate record of the music put on for the Doncaster teens that night. He has even listed the order in which everybody appeared – confirming that The Beatles closed the first half and that Montez had the star spot of closing the show.

The Terry Young Six opened the show with 'Let's Go' and then welcomed Debbie Lee who sang four songs – 'Bill Bailey', 'Like I Do', then a bossa nova beat for 'Fly Me To The Moon' and finally 'Loop De Loop'. Tommy Roe was onstage next, kicking off with 'Oh Boy' and 'Susie Darlin'' to his own guitar accompaniment. 'A Whole Lotta Shakin'', 'The Folk Singer', 'Maybellene' and 'Sheila' followed, before his closing song 'There's A Great Day Coming'.

Then it was time to close the first half with a rousing eight-song set from The Beatles. Vickers describes the first song as "a rocker". It is almost certainly 'I Saw Her Standing There', as he doesn't list that song in the set and we know it was a tour song for them. He does list the rest of the set, though – 'Love Me Do', 'Ask Me Why', 'Misery', 'A Taste Of Honey', 'Do You Want To Know A Secret', 'Please Please Me' and 'Long Tall Sally'.

The second half began, as it did every other night, with the Terry Young Six (still a man light, though) and they stayed on to back The Viscounts, who performed 'Mr Bass Man' and 'Blame It On The Bossa Nova' before their doffed-hat tributes to Shapiro, The Vernons Girls, Ifield and Denver. Compère Tony Marsh then got to sing his song – 'My Kind Of Girl' – before introducing bill-topper Chris Montez. Chris is listed as singing six songs – 'Rockin' Blues', 'Let's Dance', 'Bony Moronie', 'La Bamba', 'You're The One' and 'Some Kinda Fun'.

It was all aboard the coach the next morning for the ride to Newcastle. The pace of the tour was relentless. It had now been going full out for two weeks with just a single day off 12 days previous. This proved to be the day from hell for poor Chris Montez. Tommy Roe recalls Lennon giving Chris some grief on the coach on the way to Newcastle . . . and then soaking Chris with a pint of beer after the show.

Bruce Baxter, of the Terry Young Six, who were backing Chris, recalls even more grief for Montez when his tactic of firing up the crowd backfired spectacularly in the second house. Chris ended up being dragged off the stage and hurt. Baxter recalls: "Chris was singing 'Let's Dance' – it was maybe the third or fourth number – and the crowd were getting quite excited, so he took his shirt off and threw it across the stage. He went to the edge of the stage and the girls had got over the choir seats at the back and he put out his hand and this girl grabbed him and dragged him down. He was buried in a heap of bodies.

"His manager was screaming 'Get that whiteback out of there!' The tour manager came on and told us to play 'God Save The Queen' to close the show early. By this time some blokes had got up on the stage and they were looking at us quite menacingly. Chris eventually emerged battered and bleeding and he was crying, 'I've lost my St Christopher.' It was chaos. We had to slink off the stage. I unplugged my guitar and took it with me but we had to leave the amps."

The trouble on the coach beforehand was recalled by Tommy Roe when he was interviewed by Ian Wright. According to Roe, The Beatles had tired of Chris pestering them with questions about how they wrote songs and why they were so popular. "John had enough of Montez's constant questions and roughed him up a bit – nothing violent, just letting off steam – part of the inevitable arguments during touring," he said. "After the Newcastle gig everyone was in the City Hall bar for sandwiches and drinks when John threw a beer at Montez, soaking the side of his head and jacket. George asked, 'What did you do that for?' and Lennon responded, 'Bloody hell, I haven't got the price for another pint!'"

Ironically, Chris had done pretty well onstage this night, before he went too far in the second show. He had worked hard to bring the audience to its feet. It was his first visit to the city, and the first house, which included quite a few young mums and dads, had given no hint of the trouble that was to follow. He threw himself around the stage in his usual high energy act that had appeared more an act of desperation at some venues. But at the City Hall he was getting the required response . . . until it got out of control when he removed his jacket and shirt during 'Let's Dance' in the second house. Roe, for his part, received generous applause when he sang 'Sheila' to the Geordie nation.

Although the momentum was with The Beatles, there were still a fair number of fans who had bought their tickets to see Roe and Montez. Roe's fans in particular were more likely to register their approval with applause at the end of a song, something which we know he preferred. The screams for the Merseysiders were at least as loud as for the American show-closer.

The Beatles, who closed the first half this night and lit the place up with 'Please Please Me', were described as "the exciting new group" by the Newcastle *Journal* which ventured that they and The Viscounts deserved a higher profile on the bill.

It wasn't just every seat in the house that went at Beatles shows, even this early in their career. Sometimes theatres were creative in accommodating people desperate to see the show. Half a crown each this night bought around 100 people an unusual view from the choir seats at the back of the stage at the City Hall. Those fans got a fairly close-up view of the four Beatle mop-tops from the rear as they serenaded their growing north-east fan base. However, being Beatles they were determined to put on a show, even for the 100. So bang on cue they turned around in one song and serenaded them face to face as the screams continued around the arena.

In the audience that night – and trying desperately to listen above the screams – was teenager Sheelagh Davies. She recalls: "There was so much noise and screaming. I remember these young men with funny haircuts and suits came on. They were a breath of fresh air, but the girls just screamed louder! I've never been one to scream and remember being a bit annoyed that I couldn't hear the music properly. I was also a bit disappointed with Chris Montez. The crush of girls rushing to the stage door afterwards was amazing – autograph books to hand. Unfortunately, I didn't get close enough."

Newcastle on the Saturday was to be followed by Liverpool on the Sunday. It had been more than a month since The Beatles had appeared in their home city, and while teenagers up and down the country were getting their first glimpse of the group on these early national tours, their Liverpool fans were more than ready to reacquaint themselves with the band they once regarded as their own. But instead of the raucous late-night Tower Ballroom dances, or the faithful gathered at the Cavern, the Casbah club in West Derby or Litherland Town Hall, here were their Beatles at the Empire, proudly taking their place on a national tour alongside (and upstaging) two American chart stars.

Bowing to the inevitable, Montez stepped aside on this night to allow The Beatles to close the show and the screams they received ended any doubts over how the fans would react. Pop's new royal family were on home ground and the city was rejoicing.

The Viscounts, who were earning rave reviews for their own performances up and down the country, witnessed the city renewing its love affair with The Beatles. Singer Ronnie Wells recalls: "I can remember looking out of the dressing room window and it was packed with kids screaming their heads off. Mainly girls, obviously. There was an absolute sea of faces outside the front. It was one of those nights where anybody who stuck their head out of the window was going to get a scream, but obviously the biggest screams were reserved for the Fab Four. They returned home in triumph that night."

Being Liverpool, the crowds gave a decent welcome to the other performers. Even here, there were some who had bought their tickets to see Roe or Montez. They got a generous welcome and The Viscounts – such professional performers – were appreciated for their style and wit.

But the real screams and excitement occurred when the suited and booted Beatles hit the stage to close the show. Liverpool's younger citizens were well aware of the great songs that John and Paul already had at their command and the Empire crowd included friends and family who joined in the stomping for show-opener 'I Saw Her Standing There'. The cheers went up a notch for 'Love Me Do' and 'Please Please Me', the songs that had ironically loosened the city's grasp on its favourite sons, and reached a crescendo for the raucous 'Long Tall Sally'.

There were those in Liverpool, and doubtless in the Empire that night, who preferred the rough, rule-breaking Beatles who returned from Hamburg almost three years earlier, all high energy, leather jackets and unfettered rock'n'roll. Some of those may have been more interested in Montez or Roe at this moment than the cleaned-up Epstein pop stars. But for every one of them there were hundreds of new fans – teenage girls rather than boys – who not only outnumbered the old fans but let it be known that The Beatles may have moved on, but their home city still loved them.

A triumphant night's work done, The Beatles could escape to spend the night with their families in the knowledge they could sleep in and at last enjoy a day off on the Monday. Well, not quite. Photographer Dezo

Hoffmann collared them for a series of photo shoots across the city, at The Cavern, at Horne Brothers barbershop (where Ringo got his first fully fledged Beatle cut), on the Allerton golf course and finally Paul's home in Forthlin Road, ensuring there was really no such thing as a complete day of rest for a Beatle. Hoffman also filmed some colour (but silent) footage of the group on this day. It was the first colour footage with Ringo in the band.*

The following day, Tuesday, the tour visited the mining town of Mansfield for two houses at the Granada Cinema. Schoolgirl Hilary Parsons didn't know the unshaven young man with nicotine stained fingers she met in the alley alongside the stage door at the side of the Granada that afternoon – but she knew by the cut of his expensive, long suede coat that he was one of the pop stars who was going to be onstage later. He was happy to chat with her and her friend Diane Bradley (now Hibbert) while his equally unshaven mates were busy in the local chippie. Fortunately, Hilary (15) and Diane both kept their school magazines that the young man signed for them – "Beatles, Ringo Starr" – with a collection of stars underneath.

"I was so impressed with Ringo. He was very friendly and approachable," says Hilary, who now works at the town's library, "and I've had a soft spot for him ever since. John was still in the chip shop and Paul and George were walking in the alley, but some distance behind Ringo. John caught them up and they were talking, but the rest of them never said anything to us. It was probably a good few weeks before I realised who they were!

"The alley was a short cut that we took on the way home from school, so it would have been around 4pm when we saw them. The school magazine was from a nearby boys' school."

Diane, now a retired teacher, recalls that The Beatles had Marks & Spencer bags, but Ringo nearly made another acquisition at her expense. "I handed my pen to Ringo for him to sign my magazine and he absent-mindedly put it in his inside pocket afterwards. I asked him for it back and he said 'Oh' and handed it to me," she remembers. "The autographs were signed in red biro. That was my 'underlining biro' that I had

* TheBeatleSource website (http://www.beatlesource.com) has a number of these photos on display.

to have for school and I'd have been in dead trouble if I'd lost it. That's why I was so keen to get it back from Ringo. There was a detention at stake!

"Ringo was the chatty one, but I'm not sure we knew who they were. They weren't very well known at that point. But we would have realised they were pop stars because they just looked different. I've often wondered what The Beatles had in those Marks & Spencer bags. I don't think M&S did food back then, so it probably was clothing. That alley was our regular route home. We weren't allowed to be seen eating in the street and by 4pm we were always starving so we used to pop into Woolworths and buy cakes and eat them in the alley – although I don't think we were eating that day."

From Mansfield the coach rumbled south the next day, headed for Northampton. The audiences for the two houses at Northampton's ABC Cinema were typical of this tour. There were those there to see Roe, others to see Montez, but the memories that linger are for the excited reaction to The Beatles who had that happy knack of getting the maximum reaction with very little apparent effort. There was something infectious about these bright new lads, with their smart suits and funny haircuts, who just seemed to be having a whale of a time and the screams increased – even during the course of their 20-minute slots. They were the very epitome of cool and people went away remembering them – even if they had come to see somebody else.

Peter Malpas, who now lives in Duston, was living at the family home in Northampton, but at 16 he was already working and had enough money to get a ticket. "I went along with my mate Dick Kendal, who was a couple of years older than me. It was a night out, rather than just spending the night down the pub. I was in the shoe trade at the time and worked at the Mounts factory. I was looking forward to seeing Tommy Roe because I liked his song 'Sheila' which was a catchy tune, and he certainly did OK.

"It was a good show and it was the main topic of conversation among the girl machinists for a while. You could hear The Beatles initially, but the screams seemed to get louder as they went on and you could hardly hear them by the end. I was certainly impressed by The Beatles. The audience were going mad – more for them than the other acts, as I recall."

It was to be several years before Peter met his wife Elizabeth (York) but she was also there that night along with her pal Lyn Marlow (now Hayhoe). Elizabeth, who lived in Kingsthorpe at the time, says: "We mainly went to see Tommy Roe. We were both fans of his, but we weren't as mad on The Beatles yet. The Beatles went down well. They closed the first half and there were screams and applause, but you could hear them."

Lyn added: "We waited outside the stage door that night in the old car park. Queues used to form there. I managed to get Chris Montez's autograph, but none of The Beatles. But Paul gave us a wave through the window. The Beatles were good but we were not too impressed at the time – we were big Shadows fans. I remember reading afterwards that The Beatles were going to take over from The Shadows, but I doubted that! Tommy, Chris and The Beatles all did well. They could all perform live. There were no enhancements like today. You had to really be able to sing."

Another in the audience that night was 18-year-old Roger Frisby of Northampton, a clerk in an engineering company. But he has as many memories of what happened before the show as during it. "I was having a drink in the pub next door – then called the Bantam Cock – with a friend. There was a large lounge bar at the back which I didn't realise led into the back of the cinema. The lounge bar was closed off this night so the artists could have a quiet drink. As I left to go to the show with my mate three or four girls accosted us and said, 'Are you The Beatles?' Of course, The Beatles weren't quite instantly recognisable yet!

"Chris Montez and Tommy Roe were pretty well known at the time, but you could tell – 'Please Please Me' had just come out – that The Beatles were something different. They harmonised for a start. You didn't see rock groups that could harmonise. The cinema wasn't full. It was about two-thirds full, so there were spare seats. Tommy was very professional and I think he may have closed the show."

The old art deco cinema on the corner of Lower Mounts was in a sad state when the Jesus Army bought it in 2000. A Grade Two Listed building, it had been empty since films were last shown there in 1995. The leaking roofs and moving foundations have now been repaired, the pigeons – which were nesting inside the auditorium – have been removed and the distinctive interior has been restored to something like it originally was in the 1930s. The project has cost the Jesus Army nearly £6 million. Part of the property is already being used by the Jesus Army as a church, but the main cinema has been turned into a 900-seat auditorium with a stage. The two smaller cinemas are now conference suites called the Doré and The Glen. The Jesus Army hope to recoup some of their redevelopment costs by hosting conferences and entertainment shows.

From Northampton the tour moved west to Devon for two houses at the ABC Cinema in Exeter. Fans were waiting for the bus as it approached the city centre on the Thursday afternoon and Paul McCartney was in a playful mood. Terry Young guitarist Bruce Baxter recalls Paul playing a dangerous game. "The girls were waiting just a few yards away when Paul suddenly got up, opened the bus door, got out and ran down the road. They nearly caught him. He got back on by the skin of his teeth. We all thought he was mad."

In fact, The Beatles still felt safe enough to wander the streets after the soundcheck if they had arrived in town early enough. It wasn't just a matter of getting something to eat and drink. In Exeter one fan remembers seeing them pop into a record store opposite the cinema in London Inn Square, where Paul asked if the shop stocked their new LP. The fan recognised them, and got their autographs before they left. With nothing better handy, he produced a paper bag for the group to sign.

The show was an opportunity for local bobby Peter Hinchliffe to earn some overtime pay. The uniformed PC was among those drafted in by cinema manager Bob Parker to beef up security and protect the stars from over-excited fans, and Peter confesses that he also undertook another duty for Mr Parker. "Bob would gather up autograph books from the fans and pass them through to be signed and I have to confess that quite a few fans will have items signed by me, rather than John, Paul, George or Ringo. It wasn't just this show – the cinema staged plenty of these nights and it was something I was asked to do," he recalls.

The keenest fans would already have bought the *Please Please Me* LP by now, so the longer the tour went on the more fans were familiar with more of their songs. On the LP's sleeve notes their PR Tony Barrow points out that the mere mention of two Beatle Christian names had been enough for the audience to drown out Radio Luxembourg DJ (and later children's TV presenter) Muriel Young when she introduced them on EMI's *Friday Spectacular*. Amidst the ensuing din The Beatles mimed to 'Please Please Me' in front of a live London audience at EMI House in Manchester Square near Oxford Street.

The screaming at Exeter, as just about everywhere else on this tour, again started from the moment they were introduced, as Muriel Young and others had already discovered.

Anyone who missed this show first time around had an opportunity to make up for it 40 years later to the day. Tribute band The Fab Beatles put on an anniversary show recreating those two Exeter shows, wearing the same suits, playing the same instruments and singing the same songs as the originals did all those years before. Sadly, the ABC Cinema had gone the way of many others (it was demolished in 1987) so the show went on at the nearby Barnfield Theatre. Kev Day, who plays John, said: "We were elated. It was such a buzz. We were looking forward to it for months and so many people wanted to come along. We could have sold the show out four or five times over."

Snippets of five songs from the set – 'I Saw Her Standing There', 'Do You Want To Know A Secret', 'A Taste Of Honey', 'Love Me Do' and 'Please Please Me' – performed by The Fab Beatles (but sounding remarkably like the real thing) were posted on YouTube to give fans who weren't lucky enough to see The Beatles early in 1963 a taste of what it was like. There's a bonus, too. You can hear the music over the screams. It was the last West Country visit of the tour.

The following day, Friday, the touring party drove to south-east London for two houses at the Odeon Cinema in Lewisham, a distance of 206 miles. They arrived late – at 4.30pm – leaving little time for niceties before doing soundchecks. Nevertheless, The Beatles made time for local reporter Paula Gracey backstage and surprised her with a few "revelations", admitting that they enjoyed classical music and modern jazz. More seriously, George spoke of the recent tour with Helen Shapiro, describing her as one of his favourite singers.

Paula told *Lewisham Borough News* readers that she agreed with radio presenter Brian Matthews' recent comment (quoted on the back of the *Please Please Me* LP) that they were "visually and musically the most exciting and accomplished group to emerge since The Shadows". Paula wrote: "I was somewhat surprised to find them easy to talk to, with plenty of individual personality." They name-checked Ray Charles and Frank Ifield among their favourite singers and Liverpudlian mates The Vernons Girls and Gerry & The Pacemakers among their favourite bands.

Paula also interviewed Chris Montez, who revealed a passion for clothes, especially those made in Britain, as he added that he had bought five suits while over here. He told Paula that his "lucky break" came after he made a demo record back home. Tommy Roe revealed that his father had taught him to play guitar and that Brit crowds were much noisier than their American counterparts.

Here in London there were tangible signs that the success of 'Please Please Me' and a glut of appearances on the radio were thrusting John, Paul, George and Ringo further into the limelight. Girls in the noisy packed houses showered them with toys, chocolates and gifts (including a handmade beetle) as they screamed and cheered them on. One of those making all the noise in the first house was Christine Pilbeam, who was still some weeks away from her thirteenth birthday. "My older sister Annette, who was 14, was going with her friend Joan Bullion so I pestered Mum and Dad to let me go, too. They only agreed because Annette was going and the condition was that I revised so I didn't flunk my Latin exam the next day, but I did. I finished bottom of the class!

"I was already a Beatles fan. I saw them three times that year, but this was the most exciting. They were so new. By the time I saw them at Woolwich on the Roy Orbison tour and at Lewisham again at the end of the year they were such big news, but on this show it was like they were playing for me. They got a really good reception. There was a lot of screaming, but you could hear them – and I wasn't that near the stage. The noise was towards the end of the songs."

Christine, who lived in New Eltham and attended Haberdashers' Aske's Hatcham Girls' School in New Cross, adds: "The other thing I remember about that night was Chris Montez was wearing red shoes. You just didn't see men wearing red shoes – well not in those days anyway! He did move around a lot during his act, but Tommy Roe didn't. But Tommy sang 'Sheila', which I liked."

Christine, who had travelled into Lewisham on the train, didn't head straight home after that first house. Instead, she joined Annette and Joan in the big crowd at the back of the venue screaming up at the window and hoping for a wave from their idols. They were rewarded, as fans often were on these tours. "The window opened and Tommy Roe dropped some stuff down for us – just cards and pictures, things like that. They were all joining in sticking their heads out and waving and everyone was screaming and shouting."

Christine, now Vela-Castro, still lives in London. Her sister Annette, now Saunders and living in Cumbria, was in the right place under that window to clutch a signed photo of Tommy Roe. "Sadly, I haven't still got it," she said. "My memory of that night is of being rather annoyed because I wanted to hear the music, but the girls were screaming. But in the end I joined in and was a screamer at every concert after that!"

The Beatles, diplomatic as ever, remarked afterwards that they enjoyed the reception, and that they considered the people of Lewisham "a real nice crowd".

What this tour was really about was judging the state of popular music on both sides of the Atlantic – that was the line taken by *The Portsmouth Evening News* following the two shows at the city's Guildhall on the Saturday night. And there was an obvious conclusion, according to the newspaper. This was a case of us getting one over on our American cousins. There was no doubt about the winners of this Top 20 tussle, was the newspaper's comment, and those victors were four young men from Liverpool, England.

The Beatles, described by the *Evening News* as "a fiercely swinging group from Liverpool", brought the audience to its feet with 'Please Please Me' and 'Love Me Do', predictably generating maximum excitement. As on other nights, 'I Saw Her Standing There' had the crowd going from the moment The Beatles hit the stage.

Montez and Roe were overshadowed not only by The Beatles but also by The Viscounts who were increasingly winning over fans (and reporters) with their entertaining mix of comic impressions, tight harmony singing and poised, professional delivery. While the English boys were bringing fans to the boil with so little effort, the Americans seemed to be trying everything they knew, but on this night to no avail.

Montez, described as "a wild, energetic rock'n'roller in a bright red suit", was by now beginning to look far from happy. 'Let's Dance', his biggest selling song, seemed to lose much of its impact on the big Portsmouth stage. The quieter numbers were having little effect and the rock'n'roll songs were, well, not rocky enough. Roe fared at least a little better. He was deemed a more polished singer "in the Buddy Holly idiom" and 'Sheila' and 'The Folk Singer' earned some screams.

The Terry Young Six provided quality backing for The Viscounts and Debbie Lee, and compère Tony Marsh drove up the screams where he could. We were not yet at the point where the most arduous task for a Beatle compère was quieting the girls, at least not in the south of the country.

The next port of call, the final date on the tour, was Leicester. Three weeks on the road had seen The Beatles' stock rise considerably, though 'Please Please Me' had by now slipped from the top of the charts. This didn't stop the screams from ringing out at Leicester's De Montfort Hall where only snatches of 'A Taste Of Honey' were discernable, according to the *Leicester Mercury* reporter.

On this final night, despite the Mersey charge, Montez and Roe were back as joint top-of-the-bill artists, but such were the screams for The Beatles that Montez had to work hard to maintain his position and his eye-catching stage performance wasn't to everybody's taste. The girls were beside themselves with excitement in Leicester as he undid first his jacket and then tie and shirt and cast them to the wings, as he had done every other night, and then clutched the microphone to sing. However, it was a step too far for the *Mercury* reporter (initialled M.L.) who labelled it "an ugly demonstration of exhibitionism".

"I'm all for originality in stage shows, but this was just ridiculous," he added. Maybe, but it was an exhibition that did what it was meant to do – capture just enough audience attention and newspaper headlines to allow Montez to at least hang onto the coat-tails of The Beatles.

Roe simply did what he did best, offering a polished performance of steady singing, including 'The Folk Singer', which was now sitting at number 20 in the charts. Debbie Lee had held her own in the singing stakes – being compared to Cleo Laine by some, including M.L. who remarked that she was wasted on this show and was "a newcomer who should certainly go places" – but in concerts dominated by teenage girls screaming at young male pop stars, it was always going to be an uphill battle for her.

Richard Buxton, then a 16-year-old pupil at Wyggeston Grammar School, went on to become music librarian at Huddersfield University. He was in the audience at Leicester – the first of three occasions that he saw The Beatles at the De Montfort. "I remember that *Mercury* review criticising Chris Montez over his shirt removal, but to be fair there was a letter from a lady in the newspaper a few days afterwards saying she didn't mind – he had quite a nice torso!

"Of the three times I saw The Beatles, this was the one when I could hear them best. I was fairly near the front of the circle. My mother had bought the ticket for me. I can't remember too much screaming from this show. Chris Montez had been the chart topper, but my sister and I had the 'Please Please Me' single and I kept up with all the pop news in the *Record Mirror*, so I was well aware of The Beatles."

At the end of it all, how had Montez got along with The Beatles? He has spoken of hanging out with them and that he was knocked out by their music. But there remains the incident that won't go away – of Lennon roughing him up and emptying that beer over him in Newcastle. Montez remains mystified over why he did it. In an interview with Gary James, he stated: "I had just finished doing a gig. I was tired, wiped out. John came in, walked by and poured a beer on my head. That started an argument between us. I got up and called him a name and said, 'What the hell?' And that was it. For a while, I wouldn't talk to John and them guys. I was really perturbed. Maybe he was joking. Maybe he was in a bad mood. I don't know where his mind was, but we became friends again."

The incident was recalled in 2010 by Ronnie Wells of The Viscounts. "I remember John having that spat with Chris Montez on the coach. I don't know what happened, but one of them said something and they squared up to each other. Two people had to pull them apart. We were all on that coach together and we were aware of a lot of animosity between John and Chris. There was no love lost between them. We were all aware of it. John once said to him, 'Go home, Spic, and practice.'"

Another who witnessed the unpleasantness was Bruce Baxter of the Terry Young Six. "John was bullying him. Chris Montez was only a small guy. I wasn't very impressed. Tommy Roe got to his feet. John could be like that. He didn't rate him. Chris was a lucky kid. He just had the one hit and his set wasn't that good. Tommy, by comparison, was very professional. He was a pretty conservative sort of person – a nice man. But The Beatles were great – just ordinary guys really. I got to watch them from the wings and they were great. There was nobody like them – to have three lead singers who could all do backing singing as well. But it was their songs. You knew they were special."

Tommy Roe has fond memories of the tour. He remembers John telling him that The Beatles had included 'Sheila' in their Hamburg sets. In an interview that was included in a tribute to Lennon, he said: "My first record, 'Sheila', was a hit in 1962 but I had no real experience as a performer, while The Beatles had a lot of stage experience. John was inquisitive about the States, asking about my home town, Atlanta, and everywhere else. He was a bundle of energy, always talking, always clowning. I have a photo of him backstage during the tour, and he's coming at me with his hands up like a claw, his glasses on crooked. My memories of being on the bus with The Beatles will be with me forever. On the coach John loaned me his Gibson acoustic to write songs with and I wrote my hit 'Everybody' on the bus with that guitar."

Ronnie Wells feels privileged to have seen The Beatles in action night after night – sometimes from the wings and sometimes from a seat in the auditorium as they pounded out their soon-to-be-famous songs. "We thought we'd seen it all before," he says. "We were a Larry Parnes act so we'd toured with Eddie Cochran, Gene Vincent, Billy Fury, Marty Wilde – all of those. We thought The Beatles were great, but they were part of our downfall really. We'd just got some award from *NME* – us and The Springfields and a couple of other groups. We were doing all right, but then The Beatles came along and they put us all out of business really. They just blew everybody away. I remember they would let us into their dressing room to let us hear the songs they were working on. We couldn't believe they were writing their own songs. They would be at the back of the coach with a guitar – practising or writing. They were doing it all the time. We were very impressed. It was different from anyone else we'd seen. It was almost unheard of. Up until then people were just singing the American stuff – the rock'n'roll records by people like Elvis and Chuck Berry.

"We got on extremely well with The Beatles. They knew about us, too. We had had a couple of hits and I can remember Paul McCartney saying they used to listen to us. They were into the harmony singing, too. It was quite flattering that they were aware of us. Looking back, it was quite a privilege to be on that tour. At the time, we took it in our stride. It was just another rock'n'roll tour. We didn't realise that it would be part of history. We did think this group were going to be big – but we had no idea how big. Nobody would have. But it just got out of control."

Fellow Viscount Don Paul went on to become a record producer and the third Viscount – Gordon Mills – made his own considerable mark in the music business, managing Tom Jones, Engelbert Humperdinck and

Gilbert O'Sullivan and guiding all three to stardom, and writing hit songs, among them co-writing Tom's 'It's Not Unusual'.

But although The Viscounts had won new friends, as Ronnie acknowledged, this tour was all about The Beatles. They had put in a typically energetic performance at Leicester for the tour's grand farewell, but their fans were already competing with them in the noise stakes. The excitement was growing, and before long it would simply explode.

Tommy Roe, in his interview with Ian Wright, revealed that he returned to London as a guest of Brian Epstein who inquired about becoming his manager. Tommy's record producer, Felton Jarvis, who had accompanied Tommy on the tour, told Brian that they would think about it on the six-day QE2 trip back to New York.

Tommy actually tried to do Epstein and The Beatles a favour by returning to America with a copy of the *Please Please Me* LP in his guitar case to play for an important A&R man back home. "Epstein, always persuasive and persistent, asked us to introduce *Please Please Me* to our record company in America. Felton thought it a great idea and within seconds, Epstein produced the full promo pack – album, press releases, bios and photos – the works.

"On Thursday, April 4, we sailed from Southampton aboard the Queen Elizabeth. I didn't realise it at the time, but I was the first person to bring a Beatles LP into the United States. We disembarked at Pier 90 in New York on the morning of April 9 and took a cab to ABC-Paramount, where company president Samuel Clark greeted us like the returning prodigals. We were, in fact, bringing him the tour accounts!

"We had coffee in Sam's office with national sales manager Larry Newton and the company's A&R man, Don Costa. After the usual pleasantries, we enthusiastically presented Epstein's promo pack to the assembled executives. Sam gave the package the once-over, then put the vinyl on the turntable. Side one, track one, 'I Saw Her Standing There', filled the room with that unmistakable Beatles sound. After a few minutes and less than complimentary looks passing between the execs, Sam suddenly snatched up the record and frisbeed it into the trash bin saying, 'Gentlemen, that was crap!'

"In that instant, Samuel Clark made the second biggest mistake in the history of the record business, the first being Decca's rejection of The Beatles. Clark admonished: 'Now Tommy, you just get on with touring, writing and singing your songs and leave all the business decisions to us. Nice to see you, son. Have a nice day.'"

Now retired from performing and living in Beverly Hills with his wife, French actress Josette Banzet, Tommy Roe is concentrating on his golf handicap, photography and travel and planning an autobiography.

The Beatles would have to wait a little longer to kick-start their American campaign, but their progress in the UK was startling. 'From Me To You' – recorded just days before the tour got under way – was to be released less than a fortnight after its finish. Three weeks after that it went to number one in the charts, staying there for seven weeks.

So by the time The Beatles' third national tour got underway on May 18, they were firmly at number one in the charts – yet still they were not bill toppers in their own right. Another American – Roy Orbison – was booked as the star of the show. John, Paul, George and Ringo would also be joined by their Merseyside mates Gerry & The Pacemakers for this jaunt around the UK – on which the screams would rise another notch.

The seven weeks in between the Montez/Roe tour and the Orbison tour saw The Beatles kept busy with concerts, radio and television. Among the highlights was an appearance at the Royal Albert Hall in a show entitled Swinging Sound '63, along with stars like Del Shannon, The Springfields and their old touring buddy Kenny Lynch. Another was their first appearance at an *NME* Poll Winners concert in front of 10,000 screaming pop fans at the Empire Pool, Wembley, on Sunday, April 21, on a 14-act bill headed by Cliff Richard & The Shadows. They squeezed in a night-time appearance at the Cavern and even managed a 12-day holiday.

Not that they spent this holiday together. John and Cynthia's son Julian was born on April 8, but on April 28 John left his family behind for what was to become a much discussed holiday with Brian Epstein in Barcelona. Meanwhile, Paul, George and Ringo headed for Tenerife and a break at a property owned by the family of their old Hamburg friend Klaus Voorman.

Once back in the UK The Beatles got straight back to work with two TV appearances and a slew of concerts before sucking in a collective breath ready for a tour alongside the biggest names yet. The Big O – already a big star – and Gerry, who had enjoyed three weeks at number one with 'How Do You Do It', were serious competition for The Beatles. But there was no turning back once 'From Me To You' toppled Gerry from the top spot. The Beatles were number one now and it wasn't long before those Roy Orbison tour programmes were being reprinted with the words 'The Beatles' at the top.

CHAPTER THREE

The Third Tour
From Us To You . . . Beatling Around
Britain With The Big O And Gerry

May 18 – June 9, 1963

Featuring Roy Orbison, The Beatles, Gerry & The Pacemakers,
The Terry Young Six, Erkey Grant, Ian Crawford, David Macbeth
and Louise Cordet

Compère: Tony Marsh

THERE has always been some debate about the fate of 'Please Please Me', the breakthrough song for The Beatles. It hit number one in three of the four important charts operating in early 1963, those published by *Melody Maker*, *New Musical Express* and the BBC's *Pick Of The Pops*. But it was stuck on two in the *Record Retailer* chart, and this was this chart that evolved into the 'official' UK singles chart. The *Record Retailer* chart, however, was the least regarded of the big four at the time . . . plus the song was also number one in listings published by *Disc* and *Pop Weekly*.

But there is no debate about their third single, 'From Me To You', which hit number one in the *Record Retailer* chart and stayed there for seven weeks. In doing so it ensured that the top spot was held by either The Beatles or Gerry & The Pacemakers for 14 straight weeks from spring to summer 1963. Gerry's debut single 'How Do You Do It', a song initially offered to The Beatles, topped the charts for three weeks from April 11, only to be toppled by 'From Me To You' on May 2, which in turn was toppled by Gerry's second single, 'I Like It', which topped the charts for another four weeks from June 22.

Despite all of this chart success, neither The Beatles nor Gerry were due to take star billing on a UK tour that headed out from the Adelphi Cinema in Slough on Saturday, May 18. That honour was supposed to go to the American singer Roy Orbison. How come? When the tour was planned in March The Beatles had only one big hit to their name and Gerry was virtually unknown outside Merseyside, but the Big O, as Orbison was affectionately known, had been around the charts for three years.

With six UK hits to his name, including a number one with 'Only The Lonely' and a number two with 'Dream Baby', Orbison had a greater claim than most to top the bill over anyone, and it was perhaps his experience, as well as his innate good nature, that led him to give way to The Beatles, who were to close the shows, and to Gerry, who was to close the first half each night. Orbison's spot was to precede The Beatles onstage. Perhaps sensing which way the wind was blowing, he told *NME*'s Bruce Charlton on the eve of the tour that he had no previous experience of working in Britain and that he didn't mind being "slightly unobtrusive".

Though this wasn't a problem for Orbison, it gave the tour's promotion team a headache. The cover to the tour programme had to be redesigned with The Beatles in red lettering now appearing above Roy Orbison in yellow.

This was yet more good news for John, Paul, George and Ringo, but they were not entirely comfortable about following Orbison, not least because they clearly held him in some respect. Night after night he would bring the fans to their feet with a rousing finale, invariably leaving the stage after a series of encores. OK boys, follow that! All of The Beatles have gone on record about how daunting it was to follow the Texan star – but the screams always came to the rescue once The Beatles appeared. John recalled: "It was pretty hard to keep up with that man. He really put on a show – well they all did – but Orbison had that fantastic voice."

For The Beatles, Roy was yet another source of inspiration. Paul said: "I remember Roy would be at the back of the bus and he'd be writing something like 'Pretty Woman' and I remember him playing that to us and we'd think great song, and from that a little bit of competitiveness came in. We'd think we'd got to write one as good as that. We were just trying to improve all the time. We'd listen to something somebody else had done and try to beat it a bit."

This was the tour when The Beatles began to be bombarded with jelly babies. John and George had both confessed a liking for them with John playfully adding that George generally snaffled them ahead of him. Cue the arrival of boxloads of jelly babies from adoring fans – plus other sweets that were hurled at them night after night, causing them to duck and weave in order to dodge them. At least the British confection was softer than the American style jelly beans – as the four of them would painfully discover.

Their trusted friend and roadie Neil Aspinall, meanwhile, barely had time for a jelly baby. More and more was being asked of him as their fame grew, and along with his responsibilities for their equipment – making sure that it worked, helping them set it up and seeing nothing was stolen – came personal requests for this and that from The Beatles themselves, plus there was a growing need to protect them from the ever increasing number of fans desperate to get near them. There was also the aggravating problem of cinema sound systems that were inadequate for pop shows.

Another escalating problem was how to protect their privacy, not just from fans but from local dignitaries, cinema staff, reporters and general hangers-on who felt they had a right to enter their dressing room. Neil's weight plummeted from 11 stone to 8 stone that summer. "I just didn't eat for five weeks," he admitted.

The Beatles, meanwhile, weren't just dodging sweets. People knew they were smokers and packets of ciggies would be lobbed at them, too, and they weren't too proud to wrestle each other over them when they were down to their last one. Toys were also thrown – the most popular being teddy bears.

Then there was the issue of the disabled people in wheelchairs who were routinely brought into their dressing rooms to meet them. Theatre managers looked upon The Beatles as pleasant, easy-going young men who would be happy to exchange pleasantries with the disadvantaged, but an atmosphere of discomfort began to prevail at these meetings, so much so that John took the opportunity to mimic them onstage between songs in just about every performance.

Unlike the two previous Beatles UK tours, this one wasn't an Arthur Howes enterprise. Rival promoter Danny Betesh's fledgling Kennedy Street Enterprises of Manchester put together the package for 21 dates that this time around would include trips to Wales and Scotland. Danny had already formed a good relationship with Brian Epstein, having booked his Liverpool bands into key Manchester venues, and Epstein returned the favour in Liverpool for artists controlled by Betesh.

But Danny was new to the business and he felt that he needed the insurance of another promoter beside him for this tour, so he invited in Peter Walsh, who ran Starlite Artistes in Covent Garden, London, as an associate. Peter had been in the business a few years and his agency also had an office in Dublin where he had cut his teeth as an agent, manager and promoter. The jazz musician-turned-booking agent Tito Burns also had some involvement on this tour. "It's Peter's name that's often linked to this tour, but I did the day-to-day organising of it and I was at most of the performances," recalls Danny Betesh.

The tour had been in the planning for a while. In fact, when talks first started, Epstein had told Betesh that he wasn't sure The Beatles were ready to headline yet and suggested getting a big name American in. This wasn't a straightforward task. The original plan had been for the guitarist Duane Eddy to headline, then Ben E. King was suggested, as well as Frankie Valli & The Four Seasons, but in the end Orbison agreed to headline. The timing was perfect: as the tour got underway he was again in the Top 10 with his latest offering, 'In Dreams' and before long he had another single climbing the charts, ironically called 'Falling'.

So, depending on where you sat, an outlay of between 5s 6d (27p in today's money but £4.32 adjusted for inflation) and 10s 6d (52p/£8.24) bought you a seat for a show that featured no less than three major acts – and all in your local high street.

The Beatles still travelled with the others on the tour bus, but due to their rapidly expanding commitments elsewhere, they sometimes had to make their own travel arrangements between dates. Orbison, a fan of veteran cars and something of a movie buff, had a car at his disposal, but he preferred the camaraderie of the tour bus and generally travelled with the others. He got on well with The Beatles and often dined with them after shows. The bus, as so often happened on these tours, was sometimes targeted by excited fans, who even let the tyres down on at least one occasion – presumably so the fans could spend a bit more time with their heroes while the wheel was changed.

Aside from the perpetually heartbroken Roy Orbison, the tour featured other interesting characters, not least Louise Cordet, a pretty 18-year-old brown-eyed brunette, of French, Greek, American and Italian descent who'd had a hit the previous summer with her debut single 'I'm Just A Baby'. She was christened Louise Boisot and her background was about as far removed from working class rock'n'roll as you could imagine. The god-child of Prince Philip, the Duke of Edinburgh, she was the daughter of Free French pilot Marcel Boisot, educated at the French Lycee in Kensington and was attending a convent school in Switzerland at the beginning of 1963. She took her stage name from her actress mother Hélène Cordet and could already speak French, English and Italian and was learning Greek when the tour commenced. Louise had also taken a first step in her mother's profession, appearing in the pop film *Just For Fun* which had been released a few months before, in February 1963. Louise sang 'Which Way The Wind Blows', regarded as one of the highlights of the film.

David MacBeth, a hulking six-foot Geordie, had only one minor hit to his name, a song called 'Mr Blue' that peaked at 18 back in 1959. He dipped into TV and radio work, plus a touch of variety to pay the bills as he waited for a second hit record that never came. He sang his latest song, 'A Very Good Year For Girls', on this tour.

London-born singer Ian Crawford had emigrated to Australia in 1959 to further his career – and the move paid off with five Top 10 hits Down Under and 300 TV appearances. He then switched his attention to America, appearing in concerts in Hollywood, Las Vegas, San Francisco and New York, and he chalked up some TV appearances along the way. Signed to Kennedy Street Enterprises, the early summer of 1963 saw Crawford back in Britain and invited to join this tour to plug his latest record, 'Everlovin' Me'.

"We put a group together for him and called them Ian Crawford & The Boomerangs," recalls Danny Betesh. "They used to work on the local scene. Ian cut a couple of records with Decca and they were quite excited about him for a while, but it never really happened for him in this country. He married a girl singer and then decided to stop performing and concentrated on managing her."

Rounding off four solo singing acts on the undercard was Erkey Grant. Erkey hailed from Erith in Kent, and he and his regular group, The Tonettes, were to become well known to The Beatles. They comprised Eddie Wheeler on lead guitar, Brian Hatt on rhythm, Jim Hatt on bass and Danny Beckett on drums. Erkey was the singer, but he also played the keyboards on some songs. Danny and Eddie came from Gillingham and Brian and Jim from Dartford. Drummer Danny recalls that The Tonettes were originally going to be the backing group for the tour. "Terry Young used to get gigs for us as an agent and he said he'd do the first night for us, but his band ended up doing the whole tour."

Erkey, like Roy, wore dark glasses onstage, but his style was anything but laid-back.

"He was a real character," says Beckett. "There were stunts and comedy routines in his performance. He was a real showman. He was a steel erector and was used to working at great heights. The kids would be screaming with fear when he balanced on the edge of the stage or a piano, thinking he was going to fall. The Beatles thought the world of him and, among other things, John Lennon gave him two books of hand-written poems."

Erkey and the boys had released a strange comic song called 'I Can't Get Enough Of You' backed with 'I'm A Hog For You' on Pye in April 1963. They recorded it under the suitably comic name of Erkey Grant & The Eerwigs. Beckett believes that Tony Hatch had decided to call them The Eerwigs as a comic reference to Pye being one of the labels that had once rejected The Beatles.

The task of backing Erkey and the other solo singers (including Roy Orbison) on this tour once again fell to The Terry Young Six, with blond-haired Terry at least rewarded for all this hard work with a full page picture in the tour programme. Joining The Terry Young Six backing Roy onstage, was a young Bobby Goldsboro who had been called over from the United States. "I came over with Roy strictly to play guitar for him," recalls Bobby. "I was introduced as his MD. I thought it stood for Medical Doctor! I later found out it meant Music Director."

The very short-sighted John Lennon in particular benefited from Bobby Goldsboro's presence because Bobby introduced John to contact lenses, albeit an early and rather primitive variety. John's National Health-style glasses were a definite no-no for a performing Beatle, though he could hardly see a thing without them.

Bruce Baxter, Terry's guitarist, recalls that Goldsboro played only on the first few nights of the tour, a memory backed up by Erkey, who roomed with Bobby until he returned to the USA. On bass with the Terry Young Six was John Rostill, soon to replace Brian Locking as bass guitarist of The Shadows (which might explain why Shadows' rhythm guitarist Bruce Welch attended the opening night). It all made for a great line-up for pop fans up and down the country – and it made a pile of cash for Peter Walsh and the other promoters involved.

As everybody gathered at the Adelphi Cinema in Slough on Saturday, May 18 for the opening date it was obvious that a new dawn was settling on the world of pop. The Beatles were at number one with 'From Me To You' and even though the pulsating 'She Loves You' had yet to be recorded, let alone released, 'From Me To You' and all the excited reaction to it was a pointer to the future. The days of merely scattered screams and enthusiastic applause from girls who mainly stayed in their seats, were coming to an end. The first signs of full-on Beatlemania were in evidence on this opening night. The Big O was the big star – and what a star he was – but when The Beatles took the stage, girls who had sat patiently in their seats now rose to their feet and the din of the screaming was almost enough to drown out the band.

The Beatles knew how to work a live audience and so drafted in their old Cavern rocker 'Some Other Guy' to beef up the beat, along with a splattering of songs that were now recognisable to their growing followers. They now had three hit singles – 'Love Me Do', 'Please Please Me' and 'From Me To You' – that were mandatory for every show, plus 'Do You Want To Know A Secret' to please George's fans, and a couple of belters in 'I Saw Her Standing There' and 'Twist And Shout'.

Local newspaper the *Slough & Windsor Express* was switched on enough to understand the impact of the event. In years to come The Beatles, enthused its reporter, would look back on Slough with sweet memories. First there was the pleasure of playing to two full Saturday night houses of teenagers screaming their adoration for them and secondly they had the satisfaction of being presented with their first silver disc – to mark half a million sales of 'From Me To You' – onstage by the man whose song it had knocked from the top spot.

Of course, Gerry Marsden and The Beatles were friendly rivals and Gerry was delighted to present the disc to his mates while the audience erupted in approval. "From me to you for 'From Me To You'," quipped Gerry as he handed over the symbolic disc, and the newspaper dutifully published a picture of The Beatles proudly clutching their trophy. It was an historic moment for The Beatles, as Ringo emphasised later, telling the *Express & Star*: "When you're successful in show business you certainly look back on milestones like this show in Slough. I hope we'll be back again."

Tickets were a precious commodity. Cinema manager Nigel Lockyer confirmed that the show had smashed all Adelphi records with all seats sold for both houses within five days. "I could have sold them three times over," he said.

Chris Hutchins, in his report for *NME*, recorded that Roy Orbison had succeeded in the amazing task of inducing the audience to scream for more, even though The Beatles were on next. It was an astonishing performance, particularly as the Texan "without a single movement captured the audience, from the first notes of 'Only The Lonely'."

Roy played guitar and also a harmonica introduction to 'Candy Man'. 'Running Scared' went down so well that he immediately encored the chorus. 'What'd I Say', 'Crying' and 'Dream Baby' wowed the crowd and he followed that little lot with his latest – 'Falling'. Hutchins counted three encores for the big finish with 'In Dreams'.

Despite all the excitement generated by Orbison, the roof was raised for the show-closing Beatles. 'Some Other Guy' drove them into a rock'n'roll frenzy and Hutchins also mentioned 'Do You Want To Know A Secret', and of course they drove up the screams with 'Please Please Me' and 'From Me To You'.

Gerry & The Pacemakers had closed the first half in style and there were honourable mentions for solo singers Ian Crawford, Louise Cordet and the comedy singing style of Erkey Grant. This was the first time that Erkey had worked with The Beatles and he quickly learned about their Scouse wit. "This bloke came up to me and said are you Erkey Grant? I said that's my name. And he said to me 'Your group – The Eerwigs – are you taking the piss? I'm John Lennon out of The Beatles.' With that we shook hands." Erkey, known for his stage antics, knew that he was going to have to work hard to grab any attention in this company.

"I used to do this slow Ray Charles number 'I Can't Stop Loving You' and I got halfway through and started to strip off – the shirt, shoes and then made as though I was going to take my trousers off, then I heard this voice saying pull those bleeping curtains. And afterwards the tour manager said, 'Don't you ever do that again,' but I did. They knew I wouldn't take it too far – it was just to get a reaction, and it worked. They were screaming and shouting."

This was one tour that was to really rock. In the audience on that opening night was Bryce Martin, who went on to become a sub-editor on the *Slough & Windsor Express*. He recalls: "The star on the bill was Roy

Orbison, but those present were all gob-smacked to see that Roy – already a legend in his own right – had been demoted to supporting act.

"Our yearning to see and hear these truly fabulous four in the flesh made rational thought virtually impossible. But I remember we all sat rather respectfully in our seats through the warm-ups and through Roy. But, as one, we all wanted this to be over as quickly as possible. When the curtains eventually drew to reveal John, Paul, George and Ringo, everyone in the cinema went wild.

"I was transfixed by the sight and sound of these four individuals who had already changed me forever. My spine truly tingled and I felt like you did when you were with that girl you really fancied but never thought would like you. But in that here and now, these four were talking straight to me, like my own private audience.

"They went through their catalogue of hits – 'Love Me Do', 'Please, Please Me', 'Twist and Shout'. Nothing there hinted at the route these four were to take on their musical mystery tour, but we all knew on that night in May 1963 that they were something special – something we understood from people who understood us."

Pete Stone, yet to join the *Daily Mirror* as a photographer, was in the audience with his wife-to-be Jan who at 16 years of age witnessed the birth of a new revolution. "I used to love Elvis, but when The Beatles came along they just took over," says Jan. "Everything you see on the footage of Beatles concerts was there that night in Slough. It was just amazing. The sound was pretty awful because of the equipment they had then and all the screaming – but nobody cared.

"Roy Orbison was just excellent. He wasn't the type of performer you screamed at, but he was just fantastic. 'Only The Lonely' sticks in the memory all these years later."

That opening night in Slough was certainly memorable for Louise Cordet. "I was living in London and must have got to Slough early because I went into the town and was heading back to the cinema when a car went past tooting its horn, and there were these four mop-tops looking out and waving. I had already met them at my mother's club – The Saddle Room in Hamilton Place, just off Park Lane. They were so sweet. They were excited about the tour and said it would be great – that we would have so much fun.

"My mother was at that opening night. She turned up in her

Rolls-Royce and wanted to drive me off in it afterwards, but I went with friends in a battered old car with the doors virtually hanging off."

Louise took her actress mother backstage afterwards to meet Roy Orbison – with comical results. "Roy had fairly poor eyesight and when he was introduced to my mother he took my hand. With his thick dark glasses you couldn't see where he was looking either. It was so funny."

All of this fuss for The Beatles – and the girls screamed wildly at them in Slough – and yet Roy's impact on this night – and every other – shouldn't be underestimated. He once recalled: "On the opening night I had up to 20 encores and Paul and John grabbed me by the arms and said, 'Yankee go home!' They wouldn't let me take my last curtain call, but it was all in good fun."

The Beatles and Orbison were already a mutual admiration society, but there was some genuine discomfort on both sides. He couldn't draw the screams of excitement that they could from their young audience, but they were in awe of him as a performer and dreaded following him onstage.

The next morning the tour headed for Hanley in Stoke-on-Trent. The tour party had been told to be at the appointed rendezvous in London on time and there would be no big star treatment. The coach would pull out without any act that was late which meant they would then have to make their own way to the Potteries, a long trip on the road network of 1963. Paul had met Jane Asher just a month before, following a Beatles appearance at the Royal Albert Hall, and Louise Cordet recalls Jane turning up to see Paul onto the coach.

On the final night of the Shapiro tour back in March The Beatles had enough freedom to be able to enjoy a fish supper with *Sentinel* reporter Derek Adams before retiring to their humble digs in Hanley, but things had changed dramatically since then and the scenes at the Slough Adelphi on the Saturday night were repeated in Hanley. The screams emanated from the throats of 4,000 fans across two sell-out houses, breaking box office records for the Gaumont along the way.

Derek Adams was back and he caught up with The Beatles as they were relaxing during the break between houses. It was the group's fourth visit to the area "but this has been the best visit", said Beatle George. The conversation went on over the growing screams of dozens of kids who had gathered in the street below their dressing room window. Three enterprising girls, not content to merely wail from the streets, shinned their way up a workman's ladder and scrambled into the dressing room. They were promptly taken in hand by police, who, realising they were harmless, just as promptly released them. They were rewarded for their endeavours with autographs from The Beatles.

The *Sentinel*'s headline read '4,000 Pop Fans Have Big Night', but pop music wasn't the standard fare of regional newspapers in those days. Most readers were past the age of appreciating pop music and Adams still felt it necessary to describe The Beatles in his report as "a young vocal and instrumental group from Liverpool". He name-checked everyone appearing and noted that Orbison was making his first visit to the Potteries. The Big O, backed by The Terry Young Six, had the audience mesmerised, though the decibel levels of screaming were not at Beatle proportions. His current song 'In Dreams' and his new song 'Falling' were, of course, included and mentioned in Derek's report.

As Orbison rolled through his songs, the mystery was how he managed to hit those high notes with so little apparent effort – his mouth barely moving, but the vocal so dazzling. He stood virtually stock still, and yet moved people so much with his performance. Adams recorded that the fans loved Roy's set "but their enthusiasm reached frenzy pitch with the appearance of The Beatles".

Gerry & The Pacemakers were also riding the crest of a wave and they drove up the cheers and screams at the end of the first half, with 'How Do You Do It' in particular setting the Hanley Gaumont rocking, but it was The Beatles who closed both shows that night to a tumultuous welcome.

Danny Betesh: "You could hardly hear a thing when they were onstage. That's what it was like for most of this tour. Typically, the cinema's house PA would be used and then The Beatles' gear would turn up at 4pm or 5pm with Neil probably driving the van."

The touring party began their week the following morning, heading south-west for two houses at the Gaumont Cinema in Southampton.

Roy Orbison, quiet, unassuming, good natured, was held in reverence by his fellow musicians and his devoted fans. However, the American made quite another impression on the *Echo*'s reporter covering the shows. He dubbed The Big O "a sinister looking bespectacled American". And while conceding that Orbison had a good vocal range, he concluded that the singing star "wailed his glutinous material in an unattractively tear-stained manner".

But what really got his goat was the screaming – led by Beatles fans – that evidently spoiled his enjoyment of the show. The screams reached such a pitch when the group were onstage that the reporter – J.E.M. – wrote that he really couldn't make out if they were any good or not. Over-amplification and "feminine hysteria" had "left my critical faculties in a weakened state", he complained. Gerry & The Pacemakers cut through enough to make a more favourable impression and they were praised for their personality and drive. David Macbeth and Ian Crawford sang pleasantly, but poor old Erkey Grant apparently didn't live up to his programme billing as "a really sensational act" – at least not in that reporter's ears.

Terry Young was the one off sick, rendering the group as the now almost permanent Terry Young Five. However, the Five were alive to the task of accompanying the various singers and worked hard yet again to provide some quality backing. They also fared well in their own spot. Musicians like this were the unsung heroes of these tours – onstage for large parts of the evening and playing their hearts out to make the singing stars sound good.

The potential of Louise Cordet could be heard, although J.E.M. offered a rather back-handed compliment – "an attractive little Miss who will probably be a good singer one day" – that cannot have pleased her.

The *Melody Maker* carried only a brief report from Southampton, with its reporter pretty much coming to the same conclusion as J.E.M. Orbison's emotional performance didn't sit well with the reporter, and he pronounced the Southampton girls the loudest in the south, which put a dampener on The Beatles' performance in his eyes.

If these shows could sometimes test the patience of journalists of a certain age who were not necessarily taken by the charms of pop stars and the reaction they received, it was quite a different matter for the fans, both male and female. Grammar school pupil David St John was a fan of both The Beatles and Roy Orbison and he didn't consider it a hardship to queue all night on the pavement outside the Gaumont for his ticket. "In fact, it was an enjoyable experience," he recalls. "There was a great atmosphere between people, with fans singing songs. There was a lot of excitement. My mum came along and brought me a hot drink and some sandwiches and even took my place in the queue for a while to give me a break – quite a few parents did."

At 14 David had already taken his own first steps into the music world, but he was to make a bigger name for himself as a comedian, appearing on bills with Gerry & The Pacemakers himself in the 1980s. His memories of this night in 1963, though, are of The Beatles and The Big O.

"My seat was downstairs in the stalls, fairly near the front of the left, so just about facing Paul. There was just such a great atmosphere – such a buzz. They had those 30 watt amps and were doubtless singing through the cinema's house PA but you could still hear a reasonable sound, despite the screaming.

"Roy Orbison was just incredible. He didn't have the same problem with the screaming – he wasn't that kind of performer – but he was amazing. People were quiet while he was singing but they showed their appreciation when he finished each song. There was cheering and applause but they stayed in their seats – you could tell that people were there for The Beatles. I can't remember too much about Gerry that night, but he was great – a real cheeky chappie, and he'd have given a good show."

Dave Ward recalls the impact The Beatles had on their Southampton fans. "They opened with 'Some Other Guy'. Their presence was electric. I was in the second row from the front nearest to where John Lennon stood onstage. The girls were going frantic. Then George approached the microphone and raised his hands to quieten the audience. Then he made an announcement – 'We are very flattered by the screams. Thank you for that, but we would appreciate it if you could save them for in between the songs because we want you to hear our music.' This was followed by thunderous applause. And the fans did as George had requested and it was great. You could actually hear the songs. As I recall they didn't do an encore. They seldom did – if ever."

Dave was impressed by Gerry & The Pacemakers, and The Big O had a style all of his own. "He was not very visual. He just stood in one place and never moved throughout his act, but boy could he sing. He was fantastic."

Local musician Sid Carter was also in the audience. "Like anything that was 'of-the-day' we took The Beatles very much for granted," he says. "They were the same age as us. They came from working class back-grounds like us. They belonged to us and we belonged to them. I bought

'Love Me Do' in 1962 and there was no way I was going to miss their Southampton show.

"The biggest female response of the night was for the slightly chubby-faced bass player . . . with Gerry & The Pacemakers! It was so early in the careers of both groups that neither one was considered the top group. I felt that – instrumentally – Gerry and the boys were pretty superior to The Beatles. But the songs . . . I totally believe that they were, and still are, the best pop songs ever. But the evening wasn't about either band – it was about Roy Orbison. He was magnificent, spellbinding and, his limited guitar playing aside, utterly brilliant. I remember him getting about five curtain calls at the show I was at."

And so Monday passed into Tuesday, one of only two days during the three weeks when the performers had a day off . . . apart from The Beatles of course. They drove up to London from Southampton to record two shows for BBC radio at two separate venues. First they recorded six songs at the Beeb's Piccadilly Studios for Brian Matthew's *Saturday Club* that were to be broadcast four days later on the morning of May 25 when the tour was on its way to Sheffield. Rehearsals started at 2.30pm and the performance was recorded between 5.30pm and 6.30pm. As soon as this was over they dashed a couple of miles across London to the Playhouse Theatre on Northumberland Avenue to record six songs for the *Stepping Out* show. There was added pressure here as after a brief rehearsal they would be playing before a live audience from 10pm until 11.15pm. This show was broadcast on June 3. Recordings survive of two of the songs from that performance – 'Please Please Me' and 'I Saw Her Standing There' – and they provide a fascinating insight into the reaction the group was getting from live audiences at that time. Those two tight performances reveal an energetic young band on top of their game, with enthusiastic applause and a few screams from the audience *after* the songs had finished. Also appearing were their old mates from the Helen tour, The Red Price Combo.

There was an early start for everyone on the Wednesday as the package headed to Suffolk for two houses, the first commencing at 6.35pm and the second at 8.45pm, at the Gaumont Cinema in Ipswich. David Lowe, its manager, was an outgoing, genial man with a good eye for publicity, well known throughout the town, who got to know many of the stars down the years. Now 85, he has many happy memories, not least of this Beatles show and a second, on the Mary Wells tour, in 1964. A picture that survives of the Orbison tour shows The Beatles amidst a group of very happy children, with Ringo pretending to sign an autograph book with a drumstick. Some of Mr Lowe's nine children are in that photograph.

"When my kids went to school other children would say to them, 'That's your dad, isn't it, the manager of the Gaumont. Aren't you lucky,' and they were!" David Lowe has nothing but kind words about the stars who graced his stage, and that includes the stars of this night. He ushered The Beatles into his office shortly after they arrived so he could get to know them. The meeting went very well. "I have a soft spot for people from Liverpool," he told them. "During the war we went up to Liverpool to get on our ship – it was a down and out place at the time but the people came out and they gave us cups of tea and such a send-off. They may have been struggling but they came out for us and did us proud. I've never forgotten it and I told The Beatles so that night. They were very pleased to hear it and it all went very well."

Memories of this night were fairly typical. People listened to Roy – Gerry got an excited response, but you could hear him. But as for The Beatles . . . forget it. "The girls were just screaming too much. They would go mad and the screaming was exceptional for The Beatles," says Lowe, who also recalls arranging for Gerry and his Pacemakers to pop down to a local music shop where they did an impromptu version of 'How Do You Do It' for surprised punters. "Of course, word had got around. When we got to the Mulberry Tree a girl put her head out of the pub window and shouted at me. 'Which one are you?' Cheeky kid, I was much too old!"

Gerry and Roy, like The Beatles, left fond memories. "Gerry was first class – and still is. I can't think of anybody that wasn't likeable."

Pictured prominently in that photo with The Beatles are Ipswich schoolgirls Margaret Sewell (now Pope) and her friend Bridget Evans. The 11-year-olds had won one of the regular talent competitions held at the cinema where the prize was usually to meet the stars of the next show. Margaret and Bridget struck lucky – they got to meet The Beatles, and a famous picture, which appeared in the local papers and several books since, shows the girls staring adoringly at John Lennon.

"You can tell by the look on my face in that picture that I'm thinking, 'I can't really believe I'm here,'" says Margaret. "I was just 11 at the time and you don't appreciate what an important night it was at the time.

For some reason I only got two Beatle autographs – John and Ringo – but they were really friendly. I don't know why I didn't get all four! We went backstage after the show, too, to meet them again. It was quite something."

Not surprisingly for an 11-year-old, it was The Beatles and Gerry that Margaret was excited to see that night. "I seem to remember we were all sat in one of the box seat areas at the back. The Beatles were great and Gerry was very good, too. The Beatles were one of my groups – I was getting to the age when I'd started to take an interest in groups and music."

The original photo, in a frame, has pride of place on Margaret's wall today – but she finally sold those autographs in 2009.

Also in the audience was Colchester County High schoolgirl Maria Goodden who had booked tickets for her and two school pals – and she was surprised at how easy it had been to book those tickets. "I was a huge fan of The Beatles, but even I didn't know they were going to be playing so close to us that night. The box office had been open for a couple of weeks before I applied – and yet I was able to get us stalls tickets in the second row! It's surprising how quiet it was in a way. There was some screaming, but not much. You could clearly hear The Beatles singing that night in Ipswich."

Maria says she had been a Beatles fan since 'Love Me Do' and that she had an early number in the original Liverpool fan club run by Bettina Rose. She – and her friends – were there to see The Beatles and she was delighted to be able to hear them, too. "It was so different when I saw them shortly afterwards in Romford. By then there were so many crowds – and so much screaming – that you could hardly hear anything. Even the crowds outside were enormous. I remember getting pushed up against The Beatles' car and they just looked so pale and ill inside."

Ipswich on the Orbison night was another matter. "It was just so great to see them up there onstage really performing – looking at the audience and knowing they could hear them as well as see them. They were really trying and we could hear them."

Maria says it was the excitement of The Beatles' music that had made her a fan – but she was also a dedicated follower of fashion and the look was a part of what made them special for her and her friends. And it was the fashionable look that had already registered the young and cool Louise Cordet on her radar.

"She was very good and I knew her song 'I'm Just A Baby'. She was gorgeous and had that look that we all wanted – the long hair, short skirt and high boots. But The Beatles overrode everything. Roy Orbison was very good, but we were there to see them. Roy, with his dark glasses, looked pale and older in comparison – he barely moved onstage."

If that sounds a little harsh on Orbison, at least he was remembered. Maria was so besotted with The Beatles that she has no memories of Gerry from that show at all.

It turned out to be quite a night for Pat Hands (now Pat Jones), a 16-year-old local girl who worked at an Ipswich trouser factory – and she didn't even have a ticket. What she did have, along with her sister and a friend and a crowd of others, was the pluck to break through a stage door at the back, armed with her autograph book in search of the stars. Pat was harshly dealt with by a doorman who grabbed her new expensive coat and was manhandling her until a Beatle appeared to find out what all the commotion was about.

"Paul came out and told the doorman not to be so rough. He signed my autograph book. There were others there and suddenly there was a huddle of people clamouring for autographs. Then John appeared and signed my book and he handed it back to Paul who signed it again, adding the word 'Beatles'. Roy Orbison also came out and signed it – although he appeared a bit miffed that there was so much attention on The Beatles!"

All of this came in handy some years later when Pat needed some cash for a new washing machine. She had already given the Roy Orbison page to a friend who was a big fan, but she sold the two Beatle pages through a London dealer. She received a call from the buyer – to check the authenticity. That buyer was journalist and author Richard Younger from New York who paid her £600 – more than enough for a washing machine – and the two are still in contact to this day.

Ipswich man Terry Mayes is convinced that two Beatles – he doesn't know which – stayed at his mum's pub, The Masons Arms, in nearby Woodbridge Road that night. "My mum – Dolly Davies – was the landlady and quite a number of showbiz people popped in for a pint down the years. We weren't the nearest, but they could sneak out of the back of the cinema and reach us without having to cross the road," he says. "I was 25 and had married and moved out then – to one of the estates in Ipswich – but mum told me two of The Beatles stayed that night. In fact, she showed me the bill they paid, not that she knew much about them – she said it was some group called The Beagles!

"There may have been some fuss going on, but I saw them walk past the White Horse pub completely unmolested that night. But mum said girls appeared at the pub for autographs. They weren't old enough to be there so she wasn't going to let them in, but then The Beatles said if they don't come in we're not staying. So she let them in for their autographs and then hustled them out of the other door!"

Terry may not have made the show – but his sister Cheryl, who was 12 at the time, did. She was accompanied by the lodger in the other room at the pub and they sat together in the circle. Cheryl was quite a fan of Roy and Gerry, but remembers little of the show all these years later – apart from the screaming during The Beatles' set. It must have been straight home to bed, too, because she says that two Beatles did stay that night – but she didn't meet them. The Masons Arms went on to become The Orchard and then The Creams.

Such was the demand for tickets when the tour reached the Nottingham Odeon the next day that the sold out signs had gone up on the 2,500-seat cinema in Angel Row. The best hope if you weren't one of the lucky ones was to apply to the *Nottingham Evening Post* which had some tickets to give away in a lottery.

Meanwhile, although The Beatles had not yet made a breakthrough in the national press, they were already big news in the music papers. John Lennon was given space in *Disc* to report on life on this tour – and his ramblings were featured on the front page, along with his picture. He revealed that Gerry's bass player had a hairy moment at Nottingham. "Some Judy put her high heel in Les Chadwick's bass. He nearly went mad, but fortunately it wasn't damaged too much," wrote John.

The adulation may have been building up, but there was still plenty of fun to be had for The Beatles, and the rest. John revealed that The Beatles distinguished themselves this night by concealing themselves in the orchestra pit and making rude comments at compère Tony Marsh who was trying to maintain order. "We were trying to make Tony laugh, and he couldn't understand where the cracks were coming from. Then George poked his head up and we had to run for our lives!" They were still able to sign autographs for some lucky fans without being totally submerged, but there was an increased police presence to make sure that the stars – and the fans – were protected in case anything got out of hand.

It was an exciting night for local girl Gwen Speechley who had already seen The Beatles and was quite a fan. In fact, young Gwen had written to George Harrison – and received a reply. In his letter, George urged her to buy 'From Me To You' to help it to number one and said he was looking forward to meeting her when the tour reached Nottingham. Cheekily he added: "Don't forget to bring the sheriff." George sent the letter from his home address at 174 Mackets Lane, Woolton, and it also included a giant 'B' with antennae, an early Beatles logo. George also apparently sent Gwen a postcard and a lock of hair, but the cinema manager sadly thwarted her attempt to meet the Beatle on the night.

There was plenty of excitement inside the old Odeon, particularly when The Beatles were on. The screams rang out from the moment they took the stage and launched into 'I Saw Her Standing There'. Girls, over-come with excitement, were stretchered out and the audience decibel levels were rising. Police were needed out on the streets to hold the crowds back, but PC Peter Gibson had the job of guarding The Beatles' dressing room. He said they were talkative and friendly.

The Beatles headed to the police station in Shakespeare Street after the concerts. It was the perfect place to relax in peace. They were able to chat quietly among themselves in comfy chairs around a table with ciggies on the go and drinks in hand, before travelling the short distance to Mansfield where they stayed the night at the Swan Hotel.

The following day proved especially significant in the early career of The Beatles. Before their evening's show at the Granada Cinema in Walthamstow, the group had a date at the BBC's Aeolian Hall to record the first programme in their own weekly BBC Radio series. It was initially going to be called *Beatle Time*, but assistant producer Frances Line and her sister suggested *Pop Go The Beatles* as a laugh . . . and that was chosen as the final title. The Beatles were paid £42 a show with an initial run of four programmes, with an option of it being extended by a further 11 weeks if the gamble paid off. And gamble it was for the Beeb, as the group had only two big hits to their name and not everyone was in favour. Even the show's producer Terry Henebery wasn't a fan, as Jane Asher, sitting in the control room, discovered when she overheard some of his comments.

But the show was a hit and the group went on to make those 15 *Pop Go The Beatles* programmes. The rehearsals and final tapings on this opening day were completed between 2pm and 6pm and they included The Beatles recording the theme tune 'Pop Go The Beatles' – their version of the children's tune 'Pop Goes The Weasel'. The show was transmitted 11 days later, between 5pm and 5.29pm on Tuesday, June 4, as the group were preparing for their performances at Birmingham Town Hall on this tour. That 6pm finish didn't leave the boys much time to pack up their gear at the Aeolian Hall and travel the few miles up to Walthamstow in north London.

In fact, they had to take an emergency measure, as John revealed in his *Disc* column. "It (the radio session) was a load of fun, but we ran so late we nearly missed getting to the theatre. In the end we had to borrow Gerry Marsden's minibus."

John said that most audiences, despite the growing excitement, were behaving themselves, but not all . . . "They got a bit out of hand at Walthamstow when a few fans started leaping on the stage after our act. Even during 'God Save The Queen' they were still jumping about," wrote John. Those girls had to get past a firm line of stocky St John Ambulance Brigade men and not many did.

The show went on with the usual excitement. The *Walthamstow Guardian* reported that David Macbeth and Ian Crawford, backed by The Terry Young Six, were pleasant singers and Erkey Grant did his best to entertain. Louise Cordet made use of her language skills by singing 'I'm Just A Baby' in French as well as English. Tony Marsh, who hailed from nearby Chingford, may have been local, but the girls ignored his pleas for quiet and were just as vocal.

It wasn't just The Beatles. The girls were in full scream mode when Gerry & The Pacemakers were onstage, and the other singers were no doubt delighted to receive their share of screams on what was an excitable night, even by this tour's standards. As ever, only Roy Orbison was given a reverential welcome. The Walthamstow houses paid the great man the respect of listening before erupting into applause at the end of each song. 'In Dreams' – in the Top 10 that very day – went down particularly well.

Sandy Sharpe, in those days 19-year-old *Waltham Forest Guardian* reporter Sandy Brownstone, retains clear fond memories from this night. Young Sandy was in a privileged position. She had been on the paper for about a year and, being young and glamorous, she was an obvious candidate for covering the big pop shows when they called in at the old Granada in Hoe Street. Nicknamed Eyelash, and all lip gloss, mini skirts and high boots, she could get to places that stuffier, older reporters would have had trouble accessing. She was backstage with Roy Orbison and The Beatles between houses on Friday, May 24.

"I know it was between houses because I interviewed The Beatles when they had no trousers on," says Sandy, without a hint of embarrassment. "They had shirts on but were changing ready to go on for the second half. You don't tend to forget details like that. Roy was in there, too, and I've got a feeling that Billy Fury may have been in the dressing room that night, although I know he wasn't on the bill. Roy was very quiet and serious and withdrawn really."

And what of The Beatles? "I thought that Ringo was a bit thick, to be honest. George didn't make much of an impression, and John was quiet – serious and intelligent. It was Paul who was chatting away, and he was chatting me up, too. 'Do you want to come to a party?' . . . that sort of thing. In fact, Paul turned the tables on me by interviewing me. He wanted to know about people I'd interviewed and what I thought of them and about other things I'd done. I'm fairly sure that Billy Fury was sitting on a table, listening."

Sandy – now a proud grandmother of three – wrote a regular music column for the *Waltham Forest Guardian* and so was sufficiently clued-up. "Oh, I was a Beatles fan all right. I thought they were fantastic and was convinced they were going to be the next big thing – and I wasn't wrong."

The concert that night seemed to follow the familiar pattern. "Roy was just amazing – he was really good and the fans were quiet enough when he was on to be able to hear him. But there was a lot of screaming for The Beatles. People – well, the girls – were standing in their seats and dancing. The screams would irritate me now if I was trying to listen to someone, but back then I was of the age group – although I didn't scream myself – so it didn't seem to matter. Of course, I didn't feel the same way as the girls screaming, because I was often interviewing the people they were screaming at."

Also in the audience that night was George Sephton, one of the best known voices on Merseyside but not many know the face. For the past 40 years he has been the announcer at Liverpool Football Club. As a 17-year-old not long out of Liverpool Institute, he had a pretty good seat in the Walthamstow Granada. Although as a loyal Scouser he was a fan of The Beatles and Gerry, and had a healthy respect for Roy, it was none of these that got his blood racing. "I was a big fan of Louise Cordet," he says. "In fact, I was already a member of her fan club," George recalls. "But I didn't even know she was on the show when I booked my ticket. I was down in London visiting friends when I saw the show advertised in *NME* so I sent my postal order off to apply for a ticket, and it duly arrived through the post. I had a good seat just a few rows from the front. The screaming was so intense that when I got back to where I was staying it was the next day before I could hear anything. There was screaming for Roy, too, and the girl behind me must have been a big fan because when he was on she kept punching what she must have thought was the back of my seat but it was my shoulder and it was pretty sore by the end."

George recalls that the screams continued for Gerry but went off the wall for The Beatles. "It was just insane. I remember being disappointed at not being able to hear the music. Every now and again John would yell, 'Shurrup', but it didn't make much difference. It made my night when George leaned over and looked at me between a song and said, 'All right Bugs.' I think he knew the face because we had been at the same school."

George was at least able to hear his personal favourite Louise sing that night. "Everything was in reverse when Louise was on. All of a sudden the teenage girls went very quiet but I was sat there with my jaw on the floor. I was a big fan and had all her records. I just thought she was great and still do."

George is still the Anfield announcer and he still plays Beatles records to the faithful on match days. "They get twitchy if I don't," he says. "Particularly on the big European nights. I've taken to playing 'Hey Jude' at the end as well."

On the same day the tour played Walthamstow Gerry's second single 'I Like It' was released – and like the first, it would top the charts.

As the pop stars headed out of north London the next morning on their journey up to Sheffield for two houses at the City Hall, close on 100,000 football fans were heading in the opposite direction. Saturday was Cup Final day and the fans of Manchester United and Leicester City were converging on Wembley Stadium for the finale of football's showpiece competition.

But the screaming and shouting this day was not confined to London and the football. In fact, things threatened to get out of hand at the City Hall in perhaps the first, or certainly one of the first, examples of pretty much full-on Beatlemania. Worried City Hall officials rushed attendants to the stage door as hundreds of teenagers surged forwards. The centre staircase was lined by security staff throughout the show, but still the kids got through, running for the stage. Uniformed commissionaires had to rush onstage to prevent The Beatles being mobbed. Even a burly attendant, his chest proudly displaying service medals, expressed his fears that they just wouldn't be able to keep them back.

Compère Tony Marsh had more to do this night than just trot out the one-liners. "Just simmer down or the concert is off," he told the audience. In fact, he made several appeals for order, but to little or no effect. The Beatles' sets were largely lost in the wall of din from the screams. It wasn't just the ears being assaulted either. Missiles were being launched – autograph books, sweets, mascots and streamers from all parts of the hall. All of this would very soon become the norm.

The Beatles had to be guarded vigorously, and they barely stepped out of their dressing room. A reporter from the *Sheffield Telegraph* snatched a quick interview with Paul while the group snatched tea and biscuits between shows.

Paul spoke of their meteoric rise . . . and of some of the problems that go with it. "But if they stop screaming you know something's wrong and you are slipping. So in a way you accept it," he concluded.

Roy Orbison, who was accorded his customary polite welcome in Sheffield, also had time to give interviews that night, telling *NME* readers that The Beatles – and Gerry for that matter – had what it took to conquer the lucrative American market. Roy was explaining to *NME* writer Chris Hutchins why he believed The Beatles would top the American charts just as they were passing him in their stage suits ready for their performance. Paul hurled a large bag of jelly babies into Roy's lap. Paul could afford to be generous. "That's the ninth bag we've had given to us tonight and it's only 8.30pm," he said.

Chris and Roy had a fantastic view of that Beatles performance, watching from the wings as the Fabs marched onstage to be greeted by yet more jelly baby missiles. "It's a change to see new stars who are not just watered down versions of Elvis Presley," Roy told Hutchins. "This seems to be a sound they have made famous all on their own and I think it is the greatest. Though you know it as Merseyside music, I am sure this will be hailed as the new British sound in America."

The ovation for 'I Saw Her Standing There' went on *during* it, and 'Please Please Me' kept the beat going. The Beatles finished with 'From Me To You' to bring the house down.

The *Sheffield Star* wrote of the Beatles "blazing a riotous teenage trail" in what it called "unprecedented scenes". Such scenes would soon be repeated up and down the country – and then wider still. The screams, at various decibels, went on throughout the two-hour show.

High Storrs Grammar School girl Sue Mullins, who was to see The Beatles again at the end of the year and again at the Gaumont in 1965, was one of the many who were just there to see them. "My memory is of going with some girlfriends from school and getting there early, because really this was an experience. I had my copy of the *Please Please Me* LP by then. I can't be certain if I was screaming, but I probably was. I still have my ticket. We were in Row N of the stalls – so not that far back – but I can't remember hearing anything. Somehow, it didn't seem to matter. It was great – like being a part of something."

As for hearing The Beatles . . . some were luckier than others. The luckiest were those sat up on the stage – behind the performers, among them 19-year-old Derek Denton, who is now a cabbie. Denton and his wife-to-be Janet Beet were sat right up on the stage behind the stars with their friends David Wilson and Cynthia Laycock. It wasn't a bad place to be. "It was absolutely fantastic. We were sat behind them and they kept turning around and singing just to us. They appeared from a tunnel up some steps in the middle of the stage. We could hear them pretty well because all the girls were screaming out the front. The Beatles were in good voice, too, and we knew all the songs. It was great."

Derek was living at his parents' home at The Manor in 1963 and he had a job at a local cutlery factory. He was also a big Roy Orbison fan. "The fabulous Roy Orbison. He was great that night. About four years ago we finally got around to visiting Memphis and the studios where Roy and Elvis played. We had been meaning to do it for years."

Like many Sheffield fans, Derek bought his City Hall tickets for these big concerts at the record shop Wilson Peck. "My punters are generally shocked when I tell them about those days. You actually saw The Beatles live, they say. They are always amazed."

Local fan Mike Lawton, who was in the City Hall back in March for the Montez and Roe show, saw this one, too. There wasn't a chance he was going to miss it. He was already a Beatles fan, while Orbison was one of his all-time favourites.

"Such was the rise in popularity of The Beatles in a few short months that they had taken over the top of the bill spot from an established international star. I really loved the Roy Orbison section of the show, especially when he sang 'Running Scared'. I felt the hairs on my arms rise in response to the power and feeling he put into the song. Another reason for enjoying Roy's set was that members of the audience who had come purely to see The Beatles sat in silence while he was singing. That all changed when The Beatles came on.

"Advance publicity about their shows at other venues had mentioned the incessant screaming by young girls that I had experienced to a lesser degree when Tommy Roe had been on at the earlier concert. I hoped the Sheffield night would not be blighted by this but my hopes were in vain. From the moment The Beatles came onstage until well after they left the screaming was non stop and I heard very little of the performance, which was disappointing to say the least."

It was perhaps a happier night for Sheffield teenager Irene Snidall who accompanied a reporter on a complimentary pass backstage at the City Hall to meet The Beatles. All four signed her precious copy of the *Please Please Me* LP.

The next day – Sunday, May 26 – was always going to be a special date on the tour: an emotional return to Liverpool. The star of the city's favourite sons was now shining over much wider horizons and everybody knew that things would never be the same. The Beatles were from Liverpool but they didn't *belong* to Liverpool any more. New converts (the young girls) couldn't care less about that. They reacted in the same way as the new fans in every other town, city, or village for that matter. They didn't care where The Beatles came from. They just loved them. They bought the records, gobbled up tickets to see them wherever and whenever they could (pocket money allowing) and screamed their adoration at the mere mention of their names.

But there were others in Liverpool who had known The Beatles for far longer, fans who had shelled out a fraction of the price they were now paying to see the group, and who had watched them playing full-on, unfettered, rousing rock'n'roll, uninterrupted by screaming girls. Those Beatles wore jeans and leather jackets, swore and even ate onstage when they felt like it. The 1963 Beatles – limited to less than half an hour onstage, and all smart suits and freshly washed hair and showbiz bows at the end of each song – didn't have the same appeal to some of the old guard. And The Beatles knew it.

It had been more than six weeks since the group had appeared in Liverpool and there was an air of nervousness as they prepared for those two houses at the grand old Empire. How would Liverpool react? Would there be boos? Would there be empty seats? Would local fans reason they don't need us any more – so we don't need them? The answer, of course, was that Liverpool reacted on that late May day in 1963 just the same as everywhere else. If anything, the Liverpool reaction was wilder. Crowds lined the streets, with some holding banners proclaiming "Welcome Home Beatles". John later revealed that Ringo claimed he played better drums that night because he was so nervous that he couldn't think straight. But how much could The Beatles – let alone the audience – hear of Ringo's beat in the noise inside the Empire?

In amongst all the screams and adulation, the audience naturally included some who had seen the band in those early days. One was a young man called Ron Watson – now Sir Ron Watson, a distinguished Tory on Sefton Council. In the early 1960s Ron worked in the Royal Liver Buildings, not far from Mathew Street where the Cavern was located, and thought it was well worth the odd rollicking for being late back to work after lunchtime Beatle sessions there.

He estimates that he saw them up to 100 times from 1961 to early 1963 and firmly believes that the world never got to see the band at their best. "We didn't resent them achieving fame, it's just that if you had seen them at the Kingsway Club in Southport when they played two 40-minute sets to 200 people . . . and now people were being asked to pay five times that amount to hear nothing when they played for 30 minutes in a bigger venue.

"Those early gigs were something special. It was a great time to be 15, 16, 17. Sadly, nobody ever captured them as the phenomenal rock'n'roll band they were when they came back from Germany. By mid-1963 when they were becoming popular there was a certain element of disillusionment from people that had been following the band since those days. This wasn't The Beatles we knew."

Sir Ron admits that he was in the Liverpool Empire that day at least in part because Roy Orbison was on. "I'd always wanted to see Roy anyway, so I'm sure it would have been a factor. I reckon 25 per cent of the people in the Empire that night were people like me who had seen the group in what we considered to be their heyday. Maybe the reaction for some was more subdued because of that – and there were Roy fans there, too."

BBC Radio Merseyside presenter Spencer Leigh, who at the last count has also written 23 books – many on The Beatles and Liverpool music – was in the Empire audience that night. However, he too was primarily there to see Roy. "To be honest, I was a bit snobbish about The Beatles at that stage," he confessed. "I thought they were doing American music – but not as good. That view changed, of course, because I realised they did their songs with a charm of their own."

The screams for The Beatles were ringing out as Roy stepped out onto the stage to begin his set. Leigh: "Roy simply whispered, 'A candy coloured clown they call the sandman,' and that was it. They forgot about The Beatles for 30 minutes. Roy would use that whispering thing as a way of controlling the stage. It really helped that his fans didn't scream, of course. He wasn't the sort of person you screamed at. He looked as though they broke the mould before they made him."

Leigh was in the stalls about two-thirds of the way back at the end of a row. At the Empire you get a good view wherever you are, but he could hear reasonably well, too – even when The Beatles were on. "The Beatles were very good. I expected them to be. I thought they managed the stage very well. There was an awful lot of screaming, of course, but you could hear them."

Leigh maintains that Roy had a positive influence on The Beatles. "He would make a point of approaching all of the other acts to make sure they were happy and to thank them for being on the show. The Beatles picked up on that and they did the same."

Faron, of Faron's Flamingos, was there to witness the show and enjoyed meeting Roy Orbison backstage. "A lovely, lovely man," he said. "The fans were shouting we want The Beatles before he came on, but he didn't half shut them up. He was brilliant."

Also present that night was June Whelan (now June Ashley), another who had seen The Beatles many times before and who was looking forward to seeing Roy. June, who in those days worked at Johnson's Dry

Cleaners at Moreton on The Wirral, said: "It wasn't that I'd gone off The Beatles – it's just that it was *something* that Roy was coming here. The feeling was, well, we could see The Beatles any time. This night was a bit of a blur – but I really enjoyed it. I was a fan of Gerry's, too. I went out with his roadie for a while! I can't remember when it was, but I remember The Beatles being on *Scene At 6.30* and my friend Ann (Sheridan) was with me and I said after 'That's it, we've lost them. They're not ours any more.' And we were both there crying."

June says she saw The Beatles many times at the Cavern, and at other venues across the city. "They were playing at Hoylake YMCA one time and John Lennon begged us to go. He said nobody knew them there and they needed some friends!"

After all the cheering died down, The Beatles, despite their pre-show nerves, were able to look back on yet another triumph in their home city. "It was nice to be back, heading a bill at our own local theatre," John wrote in the second of his two tour articles for *Disc*.

The leaving of Liverpool is never an easy thing and The Beatles cut it fine, arriving at the Cardiff Capitol the next day 10 minutes after the first show had started. As it turned out, it was quite a clever move. Instead of having to elbow their way through a small army of screamers and autograph hunters, the boys were able to enter the theatre relatively peacefully, with the fans already in their seats and enjoying the show.

It was as yet not impossible to get within touching distance of the group. Among those who were around them this night were a couple of staffers from a local music store who were hoping to sell The Beatles some useful items, such as guitar strings and drumsticks. One of those lucky staffers was a young Dave Edmunds who recalled what happened in a 2001 BBC Radio Wales programme called *The Dragon's Breath*. "There was no security in those days," he says. "I stayed for the whole day. In the evening, I was just standing on the side of the stage watching The Beatles. We were too nervous to charge them, so we just gave them everything – all the sticks and strings. I gave Paul McCartney a set of bass strings."

Never mind out in the audience, even backstage was chaotic, as *South Wales Echo* reporter Philip Walker discovered. He witnessed typical Beatle humour among the carnage of their dressing room as they were waiting to go onstage to close the first house. The Beatles, still in the denim shirts and polo sweaters they arrived in, were accompanied by a bevy of girls.

Among them were two sat on a table writing furiously. "They're from Penarth, Austria," trilled George. "No, Australia," corrected Paul. "That's right, Australia," said George. Another girl walked in and Paul said to her: "Hello, my dear. I'm from the *South Wales Echo*. Would you care to give me a few details about yourself?"

If things were fun for The Beatles, they were positively shocking for Gerry. He bounded in, sweating from his stint onstage, to declare: "I got a shock from the mike. No one noticed it, but if you are dropping down dead you've got to make out it's part of your act!"

The Beatles began changing at their own leisurely pace with Paul still in playful mood. He warned Philip Walker of the *Echo*: "Don't talk to John. He's cultured. He makes all his money by suing papers that give us bad write-ups. We're all going to night school to get cultured like John!"

The Beatles, with the extra time allocated onstage as bill toppers, again added their old stage favourite 'Some Other Guy' – so beloved of the Merseybeat groups – to the six songs on their tour set list.

The Cardiff teenagers were, of course, in good voice. Even those in the fourth row of the stalls could hear only snatches of music above the din. One girl ran to the stage to throw her panties at Paul. Just one of the perks of being a Beatle in May 1963 . . .

Louise Cordet remembers that Roy Orbison had to deal with a potentially tricky situation after the shows that night. "He was going to take us to supper somewhere in his car – it was unusual because he usually just went off. But when he got to his car there were a couple of lads sitting in it who had refused to move. Roy was so polite and he had such a quiet manner but he talked them out of the car. I don't know to this day how he did it."

The tour headed for Worcester the next day with the local Gaumont housing the two shows. It was Worcester's first taste of the Merseybeat, and the fans screamed for The Beatles and Gerry just as long and just as hard as their Liverpool counterparts had. And no surprise that Roy made quite an impression.

For all the other acts, it was pretty much business as usual. That meant a long night onstage for the Terry Young Six who, as always, backed the solo singers, and did their own little spot, in both houses.

With the screamers not yet warmed up, at least Ian Crawford's singing could be heard – and it was pleasant enough, although lacking the excitement to get the girls going. Erkey Grant tried to do just that – but the *Evening News* reporter pronounced himself bored by his "vocal gymnastics".

David MacBeth was battling away and his version of Andy Williams' 'Can't Get Used To Losing You' was memorable. The few boys in the Gaumont that night would have appreciated little Louise Cordet and she received a cheer for her best number on the night – the classic song '500 Miles'.

But as ever, it was really about the chart stars. Gerry & The Pacemakers closed the first half and received a more than hearty welcome from the Worcester crowd. Gerry appeared all the more diminutive onstage thanks to his usual habit of wearing his guitar high – almost under his chin. Not so much walking through a storm as strumming through a storm of cheers as Gerry and the boys wowed them with 'How Do You Do It' and 'I Like It' among the highlights.

It took Roy a little while to spark the audience during his set, thanks, of course, to his rather laid-back style. But by the end, they were eating out of his hands. There he stood, feet firmly planted, reeling them off, one after the other, 'Dream Baby', 'Falling', 'In Dreams' and the rest.

This was why The Beatles were not entirely delighted to be following him. Every one of his songs was a classic, and every song was delivered with feeling. They shouldn't have worried, of course. Apart from anything else, they didn't need to sound as good as Roy. It was already a battle to hear them. Up went the screams, and up went their guitar amps, and it was difficult for the all-important vocals to get a look in. What the Worcester teens did get was that familiar driving beat – the shakes of the head – and the shrill oohs in all the right places. It was more than good enough.

The first house successfully negotiated, there were the now familiar scenes backstage. The Gaumont was big enough for the stars to have several dressing rooms and The Beatles were finding it difficult to get any peace, what with a crowd of girls gathered outside baying at full pitch while they worked their way through what autograph books they could. Gerry, by contrast, was lapping it up, parading his familiar grin to his fans at a window as they peered in, giggled and screamed. Meanwhile, Roy Orbison was as relaxed offstage as he was on. He made time to chat to *News* reporter Antony Willard about how much he was enjoying England, adding that he was about to sign a contract for a new tour. He praised the

Worcester fans for responding to Tony Marsh's appeal to hold off the screaming at least until he had finished each song. This was the treatment he was getting everywhere and he was genuinely pleased about it.

Willard also chatted to Louise Cordet and asked about her new record, 'Around And Around' which she sang that night. When the talking was done it was time for the show to start rolling again.

The Beatles battled to be heard, but enough of those recognisable hits got through to send the punters home happy. Another town conquered. As of 2009, the old Gaumont building still survives – but like so many cinema survivors from the period it is now a bingo house.

The next day the show moved on to York where The Beatles had made friends on their previous visits. One of them was *Evening Press* showbiz reporter Stacey Brewer who had been impressed with their efforts back in March on the Montez/Roe night, despite the absence of cold-victim John. Brewer ran a large story headlined 'Beatles' Sudden Fame', previewing this new show, complete with a sizeable picture of the smiling Fabs.

Rialto manager Don McCallion, so unimpressed with the truculent autograph hunters on the previous visit, was preparing for even more disruption this time. With 'From Me To You' still firmly entrenched at number one, and with Roy and Gerry to boot, the show had captured the imagination of the York teens. Mr McCallion was swamped by requests for tickets, but there was no chance. All had been snapped up weeks before.

Locals recall it as the night you could hear a pin drop when Roy Orbison effortlessly entranced them, opening with 'Only The Lonely' and running through a succession of hits and his current song, 'In Dreams'. Before Roy took the stage Tony Marsh could barely be heard above the din of 2,000 kids screaming over his efforts to announce him. And as for hearing The Beatles over the screams – well not too many people did.

Brewer, in his column, told readers of a night of "thunderous applause" not seen at the old theatre since Cliff Richard & The Shadows had appeared there. "The Beatles were a riot! They could have sung a Liverpool bus timetable and scored a hit," he wrote. Instead he recorded that they had sung 'Some Other Guy' and 'Do You Want To Know A Secret' (which I'm sure the boys would have been surprised to read was "a tribute to Billy J. Kramer") and the song that was currently at number one, 'From Me To You'.

Gerry & The Pacemakers didn't so much close the door on the first half

The third tour, May/June 1963. (*Courtesy Peter Nash*)

Living the dream: The Beatles, Gerry & The Pacemakers and Roy Orbison crowd into their dressing room at the Slough Adelphi on the opening night of the May/June 1963 tour that brought frenzied scenes to the British Isles. *(Harry Hammond/V&A Images)*

We love you Lou… The Beatles struck up a friendship with lovely Louise Cordet during the Orbison tour and she recalls that their antics sometimes drove road manager Neil Aspinall to distraction.

John and Ringo make sure that their friend Roy Orbison doesn't go hungry. (*Mirrorpix*)

Rival Liverpool quartet Gerry & The Pacemakers. *(Mirrorpix)*

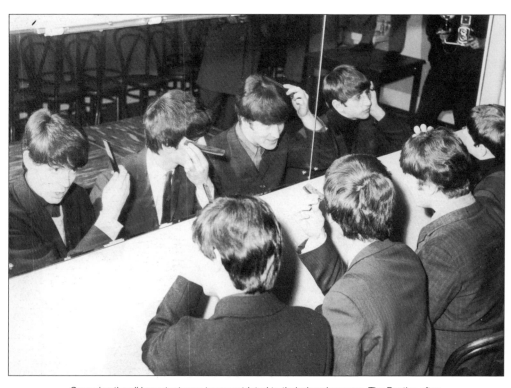

Grooming the all important mop tops: restricted to their dressing room, The Beatles often found themselves staring into mirrors like this when they ate. *(Express/Getty Images)*

Teenagers queuing in the rain at The Majestic Ballroom, Luton for tickets to see
The Beatles, April 17, 1963. *(Mirrorpix)*

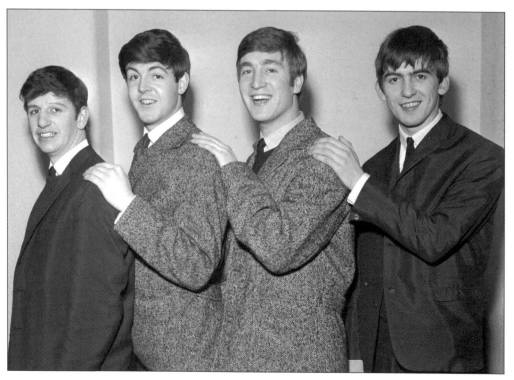

The toppermost of the poppermost… The Beatles wore confident smiles for this early publicity shot.
(Harry Hammond/V&A Images)

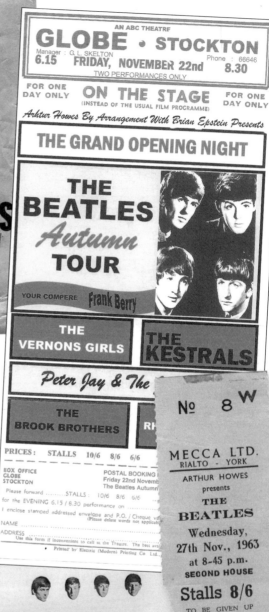

The fourth UK tour, November/December 1963. *(Courtesy Peter Nash)*

Ticket to smile… This lucky man and his girl have their tickets to see The Beatles.
The hundreds waiting in the rain hope to be similarly rewarded. (*Edward Miller/Keystone/Getty Images*)

"… the rest of you just rattle your jewellery": The Beatles with Marlene Dietrich and meeting the Queen Mother at the Royal Variety Performance, November 4, 1963. *(George Freston/Fox Photos/Getty Images)*

as slam it, wrote Stacey. 'How Do You Do It' and Gerry's new record 'I Like It' had sent the kids into ecstasy. 'You'll Never Walk Alone' the song that was to complete Gerry's hat-trick of number ones that year, brought the house down.

Stacey recorded that both houses that night over-ran due to the general chaos among the fans. McCallion would have enjoyed the success of the full-house shows, even if his small staff faced a big clear-up to get the cinema back in business the next day.

Supporting acts at least managed to make themselves heard. David Macbeth sang 'Oh! Lonesome Me', 'A Very Good Year For Girls' plus 'My Golden Chance' and Louise Cordet pitched in with 'I'm Just A Baby', 'Who's Sorry Now' and her latest offering 'Around And Around'. Ian Crawford enjoyed his moment in the spotlight, too, singing 'Some Kinda Fun' and 'Rhythm Of The Rain'. Erkey Grant turned out what was described as a novelty version of 'Jezebel' and The Terry Young Six did their usual sterling work backing them.

At the gig, along with half a dozen or so of his Nunthorpe Grammar School pals, was 15-year-old Alfie Shepherd, who went on to front his own band, Angel Pavement. "I remember us getting on our bicycles during school lunch to cycle down to the Rialto to buy our tickets . . . and getting a detention for being late back! If I'm being really honest, it was Roy Orbison I went to see," he admitted. "We were close enough to the stage to be able to see into the wings. Standing there for the whole of Roy Orbison's set were John Lennon and George Harrison. George, in partic-ular, seemed to be in total awe of The Big O as he went through his reper-toire – and you could hear a pin drop while he was singing. Roy had me mesmerised, too. It made the hair stand up on the back of my neck. Every-one sat silently and listened to Roy's songs throughout and then let rip when he finished. He just stood there with a guitar round his neck under a single spotlight and sang. Incredible!"

Alfie already knew of The Beatles, and he went away that night an even bigger fan.

"I went away knocked out by The Beatles. We were in the stalls – 15 or 16 rows from the front – so we had quite a good view. But when they came on, of course, everyone was standing on their seats and jumping up and down so we had to do the same. Of course, they were those cinema seats that folded so people were falling in between them, too. It was crazy.

It wasn't a riot. It was just adulation. People sort of got carried along with the excitement of it. I went away and thought it was great, but when I thought about it a couple of days later I realised I hadn't actually heard that much of it. You could hear a bit at the start of The Beatles' set, but it just grew until it became like a cacophony."

In the audience for the second house was Dave Brough, then a 22-year-old brickie with a York building firm, who now works part-time at York Central Library. "There are a couple of things that stick in the memory – one was John Lennon introducing Paul's 'Till There Was You' as from the film *The Muscle Man* (instead of *The Music Man*) and the other is of Paul sat on the edge of the stage afterwards and people queuing up the aisle for his autograph. I thought that was impressive that Paul did that – he was the only one."

Dave, who now lives in Fulford on the outskirts of York, said he was primarily there to see Roy Orbison and that he brought a bit of culture among all those hysterics. "There was such a wild reaction to The Beatles, I remember that," he said, "and Gerry gave a typical jolly performance."

Although both houses overran, there was still time to throw a party backstage afterwards in The Beatles' honour. They received their most unusual autograph requests yet when a couple of girls asked them to carve their names into their shoes.

Incidentally, reporter Stacey Brewer went on to have a distinguished career of more than 40 years in newspapers and radio, being awarded an MBE for services to provincial journalism in 1989. Among the tasks he enjoyed most were those of providing the good people of York with eye-witness accounts of those pop nights at the Rialto in the 1950s and 1960s for *The Evening Press*.

One man's life was to change considerably as a result of what happened at the Odeon Cinema in Manchester the next day. Derek Taylor had been a journalist since leaving school, first working for newspapers in his native Liverpool, but by May 1963 he was the northern area theatre critic for the *Daily Express*. However, as he explained in the *Anthology* series, he might never have gone along that night.

"I'd heard they were coming to the Manchester Odeon. We didn't, as theatre critics, cover these one-night pop shows because there was no continuity, so I bought a ticket myself. Gerry & The Pacemakers had been on and Roy preceded The Beatles."

As it turned out, Derek loved the show, and was knocked out by The Beatles, as the northern edition readers of the *Daily Express* were to discover the next day. So taken with The Beatles was Derek – and they with him – that he was given inside stories and he was soon writing a regular column for George (with considerable input from the Beatle). Soon he would join The Beatles' entourage, first as Eppy's personal assistant and later as the group's Press Officer.

Not everybody from Manchester knew everything about the Liverpool bands. The Beatles were dining in the otherwise empty restaurant at the Odeon before the shows when a local female reporter sidled up to ask them if they had a record in the charts. John told her their record was 'From Me To You' and she said that another Liverpool group called The Beatles was also in the charts. Apparently, John gave her one of his kinder replies. He revealed to *Disc* readers that the queues outside the Manchester Odeon stage door were the largest yet – at least partly due to Gerry and Paul sticking their heads out of the window above now and again to yell down at the girls. Derek Taylor wasn't alone in enjoying the Manchester shows that night.

Gerry's lively performance went down very well with the Odeon teens and both performances by The Beatles were greeted with rapturous screams. Roy, as ever, had them eating out of his hand as the Odeon girls took the opportunity to listen to the music as he sang his heart out. But when their Mersey faves were onstage it was back to the screaming.

The show went down well with the *Manchester Evening News* critic (initialled G.B.) who ventured that pop music was emerging from its "sickly phase". He called the show "the best pop bill in Manchester for months". He wrote: "The Beatles and Gerry & The Pacemakers are bringing a vigorous blast of sea air into the business, with robust beaty arrangements – and none of the deliberately sinuous body movements of recent years."

There were complimentary mentions for the rest of the bill, too, with name-checks for Ian Crawford, Lousie Cordet, Erkey Grant and The Terry Young Six. David Macbeth was described as "impressively professional" and compère Tony Marsh was damned with the faint praise of being "sensible".

The Beatles and the rest now headed south for the next few gigs. First up was a long trek from Manchester down to Southend for the two houses at the seaside town's Odeon Cinema on the evening of Friday, May 31. It was a gut-busting journey, but by this stage everyone on the tour knew that at the end of the long and winding road would be another two block-buster shows played to packed houses of baying fans. And so it proved.

All of the star acts wowed those two Odeon audiences, with The Beatles closing the show to deafening screams. Before that, the Big O, in his now trademark dark glasses, simply stood there and strummed through his classics 'Only The Lonely', 'Candy Man' and 'Dream Baby' and, as he had every other night, introduced the audience to his latest songs, 'In Dreams' and 'Falling'. There are only so many ways to say the same thing, but Southend was mesmerised.

It was now a familiar pattern that some of those who were just there for The Beatles came away also as fans of Roy Orbison. What a compliment to the man and his music. Roy won many new fans that night in Southend and they didn't have long to wait to see him again, as he was due to return to the Odeon stage in September.

The Beatles were getting used to following him onstage by now. They knew that the screams would drown out any flaws as soon as they emerged from the wings. Through the usual din they pounded out their bright and breezy set, so fresh to teen ears that had been used to tamer stuff in the run-up to 1963. 'Thank You Girl', 'Please Please Me' and 'From Me To You' provided the centrepiece to another tuneful, harmonic set. 'Thank You Girl' wasn't on their original set list for the tour, but their heightened status left them more time onstage if they wanted it. The song didn't last long on their play-list, so the Southend teens were lucky to hear it – if they did hear it among the screams.

Gerry wasn't being lost in all this. He and his Pacemakers showed their versatility and they got their screams, too. Gerry's infectious personality was winning him new fans wherever he went – and he made a big impact in Southend. "This group are obviously destined for the top bracket in show business," enthused the *Southend Standard*, which published a por-trait picture of The Beatles under the heading 'Take These Lads From Liverpool . . . And Show Really Packs A Punch'.

The Terry Young Six were continuing to be appreciated for their hard work as a backing band and for the cleverness of their own set. David Macbeth made an impact, too, but there was a feeling among some of the others appearing that the sooner it was all over the better. How many times can you appear onstage knowing that nobody's there to see you? Whether they were Gerry, Roy or Beatles fans, it made little difference. The best they could hope for was polite indifference – not the stuff of show business dreams.

If the screams drowned out The Beatles' singing at the Granada Cinema in Tooting the next evening it might have been for the better. It is highly questionable that their voices were in tip-top condition after eight hours spent recording two back-to-back *Pop Go The Beatles* radio shows at the BBC Paris Theatre in London before they dashed off to Tooting for the evening. They battled on without a break to record those radio shows, rehearsing and recording from 9.30am until 5.30pm before the two short stage appearances in the evening.

The irony is that fans who tuned into those radio shows (broadcast on June 11 and 18) heard songs that could no longer feature in the time-restricted concerts. Songs such as 'Too Much Monkey Business', 'A Shot Of Rhythm And Blues', 'Memphis Tennessee' and 'Youngblood' were already consigned to Beatle history as far as live shows were concerned, but the fact that they chose to include such songs in their radio sessions leaves us yet another priceless Beatles legacy. And The Beatles' efforts that night were appreciated by those Tooting fans, whether John, Paul and George's voices were strained or not.

All seats had been sold for both shows more than a week before. An advert which appeared in the *South London Press* the day before confirmed there was only "limited standing at the doors" for the 6pm and 9pm shows. The Tooting teens gave the entire package plenty of vocal support. Gerry & The Pacemakers closed the first half with their customary energy. They included several rockers from their Cavern days in their set, along with 'How Do You Do It' and 'I Like It'.

Roy Orbison more than held his own once again. He calmed the mood and yet enraptured everyone at the same time with those stunning songs. Tooting rose in tribute, mercifully sparing most of the screaming and shouting until each song was finished. Another big song, another big encore, he brought the crowd to its feet. Tony Marsh was then onstage to attempt a quick gag – lost in the din – before it was Beatles time again. They pounded out those early hits to non-stop cheering in both houses.

In the Tooting Granada that night was Max Clifford – in those days a young member of staff in EMI's press office. Max recalls: "As soon as The

Beatles came on, the girls just screamed and screamed and screamed. They really could have been playing anything and it wouldn't have mattered. They could have been miming. Nobody would have known. That's what it was like – even that early. Of course they were great and the girls reacted the way they did. Gerry did a good job, too, as I recall."

Max – and everyone else – was grateful to be able to hear Roy Orbison. "Roy was totally different. He was never a sex symbol – he was about his music and his singing. The Beatles were four great looking young kids and they were exciting, but Roy was a guy who appeared a lot older. He didn't move around or jump about. He was not the type you screamed at. He still went down a storm. He would just stand there, barely moving a muscle, and this amazing sound would come out."

As an EMI press guy Max was one of those allowed into the backstage area where he spoke to Roy. "He was a lovely man, Roy Orbison. He was a quiet man and he wasn't the least bit jealous about the reaction The Beatles received. I think he enjoyed it, but he was quite bemused by it all, and he certainly didn't appear to be bothered about it."

Some of the other acts endured occasional embarrassment due to the sheer popularity of the stars of the show. David Macbeth recalls: "I was winding up my performance at Tooting with a big Andy Williams song as my final number. I was walking along the front of the stage as I was singing and then heard this stentorian whisper from a girl who told her friend – 'I wish he'd get off and let Gerry on!'

"I felt I was out of my depth. The songwriter Don Black, who was in the audience, had some words of comfort for me backstage. You're wasting your time with this mob, he said. You should be out performing as Matt Monro does, to those kinds of audiences. Don was a charming man and he was right really, but I was just having such a great time and lots of laughs. Johnny Worth, who wrote Adam Faith's 'What Do You Want' among other great songs, was also in the audience that night."

Sometimes in life – even if you are flavour of the month – everything doesn't always go according to plan. And so it was at the Hippodrome in Brighton as The Beatles endured a disastrous opening to their set the next night. No sooner had the curtains parted for them to begin than after a few seconds everything went dead. Neil Aspinall got the theatre staff to close the curtains and they dashed onto the stage and checked everything. It seemed to be working again so the curtains were opened and The Beatles got ready to roar into action . . . only for the same thing to happen again. Neil later recalled: "It was ridiculous. We thought we were all going potty. This time John ran into the wings muttering something about the whole lot blowing up at any moment!"

Mercifully, the cause was soon discovered. It turned out that someone had accidentally placed a heavy bass drum on the mains supply point.

There were fewer of these kinds of incidents on the cinema and theatre circuit than there had been in the old Cavern days, but it was a major headache for Neil who at this stage had sole responsibility for setting up the equipment.

A group of friends who worked at a Portslade Village engraving firm were in the audience that night. Among them was 19-year-old Bonny Cother, who lived a few miles outside Brighton on the Mile Oak estate. Looking back in November 2009, Bonny said: "My mum worked in the box office at the Hippodrome so she was easily able to buy a ticket for me. We arranged to meet outside – about 5pm probably, because we were excited about the build-up – and the first amazing thing was the amount of people outside. There were already so many crowds, mostly teens or people in their early twenties. We were on the left-hand side, probably in the circle as I remember looking down, but we were all screaming. Despite that, you could still hear The Beatles singing, and they were awesome. The whole evening was fantastic."

Bonny remembers the security guys, as ever, lined up to prevent any over-excited teenager making the stage. What was it about The Beatles that made them react the way they did? "It was the first time I'd ever screamed at a pop star. Roy was very good, of course, and you could hear him sing, but he was more serious. But there was something about The Beatles. A lot of the stars were from America in those days but The Beatles were ours. And the music they played – it drew you away from your parents, and their control, and that meant such a lot to us."

The tour headed off from the seaside back to London the next day and two houses at the Granada Cinema in Woolwich. It seated 2,434 customers – but it seemed as if many of those customers were leaping out of those seats during the two houses.

The tension had been a long-time building. Fans had queued for hours for their tickets. School pupils risked suspension – or even the threat of being expelled – if they missed lessons to keep that precious place in the queue. Plenty thought the risk worth taking. Prefects could pull rank, of course, and bribe younger ones to queue for them in return for not reporting them. Any trick was worth pulling to get a ticket for the biggest pop show in town.

There was noise for Gerry, with fans out of their seats for their favourite songs. Gerry's impish grin was wide. How do you do what you do to me, he sang, and they screamed and waved in response. Roy was enjoying himself with so little effort and all the time the noise was rising.

And when The Beatles appeared – that's when the screams really started. It was difficult to hear anything else. The few (mainly boys) who wanted to hear the music reported that it was nigh on impossible. What they heard were hundreds of girls screaming and just an occasional beat in the background. At least they knew enough of 'Please Please Me' and 'From Me To You' to make out the words and sing-along, but only snatches of words or music got through.

The Beatles were becoming objects of desire, too. The main objects hurled at Woolwich were jelly babies . . . and they arrived by the shower-load. Among the excited girls up in the circle in the second house was 14-year-old June Sparrow, who attended Church Manor Way Secondary School and lived in nearby Abbey Wood. She was there with her friend Lorraine Young. "There was screaming near enough all the time The Beatles were on," says June (now June Coleman), "but you could still hear them. I had a day job at a sweet shop at the time and was already a Beatles fan. I shared a bedroom with my sister. She had her side covered with pictures of Elvis – she was a bit older than me – but I had The Beatles on my side.

"They were great that night, and so were Gerry and Roy. It was absolutely packed. Quite a crowd gathered outside, hoping to get a glimpse of the artists. We weren't at the front because we didn't think they'd leave through the front doors, so we gathered outside a side window where we could see the back exit. The only person we saw was Roy Orbison, who popped his head out of the window and waved and there was quite a cheer. There was such a buzz.

"After that we went round the front to meet my friend Cheryl Newman who was waiting outside with some friends because she couldn't get tickets. We went to the chip shop opposite before getting the bus back home and the girl in the shop went to put the chips down on my precious programme. I said, 'Mind my Beatles!' She thought I was mad. Not every-body knew about The Beatles yet!"

June, now of nearby Eltham, says: "I joined the fan club afterwards and still have four of their Christmas records and newsletters that they sent out to members."

Another of the besotted fans in the Woolwich Granada that night was Janis Hider, and such was the importance of the show in her young life that the details are as clear in her memory today as they were the morning after. She even remembers how she came to be there. "Maisie Hider, my mum, worked at the RACS (the Co-op) head office in Woolwich, and knowing that both me and my younger sister Jen were Beatles fans, during her dinner hour she popped along to the Granada opposite the Woolwich Ferry and bought us circle tickets to see the show. Easy! Up until then, we had only heard the groups on the radio or seen them on the nine-inch black and white television that's still in mum's loft! I had taken hours to get my make-up right, my hair backcombed as high as I could in a cottage loaf bouffant hairstyle, ironing my shantung bright orange blouse almost to extinction, my new brown pencil skirt worn as short as I dare, my white stiletto heels polished to a shine! Jen had gone through a similar few hours and then feeling all grown up, off we went to the show, driven by Dad [Albert Hider] in his green Standard 8 car, leaving us with instructions where to meet when it was all over so he could drive us home again."

The excitement built up for Janis and Jen from the moment the show got underway. "Along with everyone else in the auditorium, we were in a complete frenzy by the time The Beatles took to the stage. There had been lots of fun and singing along to the other artists, but when the Fab Four came on, the screams from all the fans really were deafening. With each one of us shouting their undying love for their own favourite Beatle, I swear we never heard a single note they sang. But it didn't matter, we were ecstatically happy. The Beatles were onstage looking good, and tears of happiness flowed freely, interjected by shrill screams from abso-lutely everyone."

Janis and Jen joined the throng at the back of the cinema after the show. Janis was 16 and about to leave Kidbrooke Comprehensive School for Girls – Jen was only 14. "We totally brought Woolwich to a standstill. It was while standing in the middle of the main road that the most magical moment happened. The Beatles opened the scruffy little black painted windows to wave to us crowded across the road below. And then it happened. John Lennon, my particular favourite, looked down, smiled and waved to me! I absolutely melted. Oh that smile! Etched on my heart forever!"

Janis, now Janis Burl, recognises what an ordeal the night was for her poor parents. "Mum and Dad had to drive to Woolwich from our home in Blackheath to pick us up after the show, but the whole area was at a complete standstill. Poor Dad was frantic as his little girls were caught up in what must have looked frightening to those not in the happy crowd. They ran through the streets to find us – but by the time Dad got to us, I must have looked like a panda that had been dragged over a hedge. No waterproof mascara in those days. Hairstyle still in place thanks to the lacquer, but clothes all screwed up and wet with perspiration. I swear my ears were ringing for days and my heart skipping beats due to that smile from John. Jen and me babbled on and on, telling a now relieved Mum and Dad what a wonderful night we had experienced. I still wonder how we all got to sleep that night."

Gaynor Holloway, aged 14 of Bexley Grammar School in Welling, was not only there that night, but she was one of those wonderful people who kept a diary! Her notes on the show were brief but they made clear that she and her pals enjoyed themselves. Gaynor, now Wingham and a respectable grandmother, was one of the screamers. Her diary records: "Monday, June 3, 1963. Whit Monday – cloudy. Went to see The Beatles, Gerry & The Pacemakers, Roy Orbison, and lots of stars. GREAT! Everyone was screaming. Had a Fab time. Went with Anne, Carol and Pauline."

Gaynor, who still lives nearby in Eltham, recalls: "Pauline was a friend and schoolmate and Anne was a family friend. I think Anne got the tickets – I didn't queue. All four of us went on the bus from Welling – the 89 bus and change for the 161 into Woolwich. We were upstairs in the Granada but I could see very well. There were lots of people jumping up and down and throwing things. Everybody went absolutely mad when The Beatles came on. Everyone was screaming – including us. I mainly went to see The Beatles, but Gerry & The Pacemakers as well because I liked the Liverpool groups. The whole thing was quite something for us. We were just ordinary 14-year-olds from the London suburbs."

Annette Pilbeam, the reluctant screamer at the Montez/Roe Lewisham date, was also there, with sister Christine. Annette recalls: "I was there to see The Beatles but I was blown away by Roy Orbison that night and became a real fan of his. I was excited to be there. I used to spend all my pocket money on concerts and records."

After four successive shows in the south the touring party headed northwards again with a trip up to Birmingham on the Tuesday. The Beatles played the city on five of their six national tours – but this was their only performance at Birmingham Town Hall. And among all the screaming chaos of a Beatles concert, what better vantage point could you have than right up on the stage?

That was the lot of 16-year-old apprentice electrician James Parsons who was in the wings looking after the lighting and sound in the control centre for the two shows. But it was a night that started with a rollicking. "We had a record player there because we would play records as people came in. We had a list which we were supposed to stick to, but we had an advance copy of The Beatles' forthcoming EP (*Twist And Shout*, released July 12) and I decided to play that instead and I got a telling off for that."

James recalls that the noise was there from the very moment The Terry Young Six started proceedings in the first house. The anticipation of what was to come meant that there was noisy excitement through the first half as Ian Crawford, Louise Cordet and David Macbeth performed their short sets. "You could have had Adolf Hitler on that bill and it would have been the same – such was people's excitement at what they were going to see," he says.

Tony Marsh sang his song and kept the show moving. "Nobody walked offstage. Everybody jogged off – it was as though there wasn't a second to waste. One would be off and the next would be on their way." The screams went up considerably as Gerry & The Pacemakers bounded onstage to close the first half. "When he came on, the place went into a frenzy. The reception they got and the way they played, they were up there with The Beatles in my eyes. They were that good. Gerry and the piano player really gelled. They made that place rock. Gerry was playing a Gretsch Country Gent – right up on his chest like he always did – and he had a voice that was comparable to John Lennon's – but you couldn't hear as well as you should have because the equipment just didn't have the power. Halfway through Gerry's act he broke a string and to this day I have this string, although very rusty, in an Epiphone string box."

Terry Young's band got the second half started and they stayed on to back Erkey Grant and then it was time for the penultimate act. "The one time the noise stopped was when Roy was onstage. He was held in absolute reverence. He came on to lots of applause, but when he started singing . . . you were blinded by Roy Orbison. There would be some noise when he started a song – people showing appreciation for their favourite song – and then it would go quiet. There was an electricity about him. He didn't have to shout. He would just speak into the mike and everyone would quieten down and listen to him. The guy was an awesome talent. At the end of each song – that's when the roar went up."

As Roy took his bows it was time for the show-closing Beatles and the screams were back with a vengeance. James continues: "The thing about Birmingham Town Hall is that it was beautifully designed for sound. You could drop a needle onstage and you could hear it right at the back of the auditorium. (Joseph) Hansom of Hansom Cabs fame was one of the designers. But when The Beatles came on the only way I can describe the sound is it was like a bomb going off. It just exploded for The Beatles. They were wearing their dark blue gabardine, collarless suits with Kildare shirts (known as such because they were sported by actor Richard Chamberlain in his TV role as *Dr Kildare*) and black Cuban heeled boots with seams down the sides. Stone Dri, a dry cleaning business in Corporation Street, Birmingham, made more money from selling them than they did from dry cleaning. I wore Cuban heels from 1962–1970.

"Their suits were buttoned up and John used his Gibson J-160E that night – the full acoustic with an electric pick-up. George was playing his Gretsch Tennessean – it was the one that later got smashed up on the motorway. Once The Beatles started so did the screaming and you just couldn't hear them. There were no fold-back monitors in those days so they wouldn't have been able to hear themselves. If you were watching from the audience, Paul was on the left and John was on the right, with George nearest to him. John and Paul introduced the songs – George and Ringo didn't say a word. John and George shared the same mike for harmonies."

There were a few seats set up on a podium directly behind the group, and The Beatles – never wanting to miss anyone out – turned and waved to the people in them, enjoying the carnival atmosphere.

James' duties also took him backstage with the stars. What did he make of them? "Roy Orbison was one of the most pleasant, calmed-down people I ever met. He was a very cordial, very pleasant man. He dyed his hair – and I asked him why he wore the dark glasses. He just said that he was not very photogenic and that was the reason."

So how did the Brit stars compare? "The Beatles were just The Lads. They were normal guys – they were no different from Gerry & The Pacemakers in that. In fact, all of those Liverpool groups had a certain air – very down-to-earth guys. They were just making their way through their chosen careers. People go on about John but it was Ringo who was the quickest with witty comebacks. When he found out I was the electrician he said, 'Make sure you get 250 volts coming down.' I said to him at one point, 'Don't tread on the cable because it will stop the power coming through.' He looked at me and I thought I'd better leave it there!"

There are no prizes for guessing that James discovered that George was the laid-back Beatle. "He was quiet – the politician in a way. He would pour the oil in the cogs. For example, you would hear John and Paul wanting to change things – drop a song and bring another in to break the monotony, but it would be George who would argue against it. You got the feeling that if anything was to pop it would be from John or Paul, but George would be there to pour the oil on troubled waters."

The toughest job of the night was endured by the staff who were literally holding the lighting. "There were four high beam spotlights – two on each side of the seats. They were very heavy and very hot. The guys had cloths or rags around their hands because they were so hot. They were paid £2 to operate the lights all through the show. Tough work."

The town hall had a big enough backstage area for The Beatles and Roy to have separate dressing rooms so they could put on their stage make-up in peace and prepare for the show. By this time, the sound check consisted of Neil yelling one-two-three a few times down the mike to check it was on. "There wasn't much point in doing anything else. Nobody was going to hear anything anyway," says James. "The Beatles had those little Vox 30-watt combo amps and a 50-watt bass amp – that was the maximum they used, and Birmingham Town Hall power system had a maximum of 100 watts. That's nothing today. Tables had to be moved and there was seating for 1,960. Everybody was seated – there was no standing. People got up and shouted during the performance, of course, but you couldn't go into the aisles."

Apart from all those crystal-clear memories, James has another valuable momento from that magical night. "I have the original amp that was used for The Beatles' PA system that night. It's in my garage!"

So that was the young apprentice's perspective. But what was it like for those out in the audience? Gerry Brooke, now a writer for the *Bristol Evening Post*, was there and he will certainly never forget it. "It was absolute bedlam," he recalls. "We were at the front of the balcony and we were in genuine fear for our lives. The girls were going mad, pushing and pushing us. It was all we could do to prevent ourselves toppling over the balcony. When The Beatles came on all I remember is the opening chords, because you just couldn't hear anything after that."

Even their arrival had been hairy. The fans chased the coach as it pulled up outside the Town Hall. They had spotted Paul. He was trapped in the coach for a while as John, George and Ringo scuttled into the theatre through a side door. Some fans worked out where The Beatles' dressing room was and they made a hole in the window. They were rewarded when George went over for a chat.

The Beatles never returned to the Town Hall, but it was one of the most historic venues they played, with the building predating most of the others by around 100 years. It was hailed as one of the finest music halls in the country when it opened in 1834. It was closed in 1997 but reopened, restored to its former glory, 10 years later after a £35 million renovation.

With just four places left to visit, the touring party headed north from Birmingham to Leeds the following day. Though the teenagers who adored The Beatles probably cared not one jot, the country was about to be plunged into a scandal that looked as if it might bring down Harold Macmillan's Tory government. Rumours of a relationship between the Minister For War, John Profumo, and party girl Christine Keeler had been circulating since 1962. Worse still, Keeler had at the same time been seeing the Russian naval attaché (and probable spy) Eugene Ivanov and this was the day when it all came to a head. Profumo, having misled the House of Commons and lied in his previous testimony, resigned from the government. Newspapers gave it enormous coverage, with banner headlines that would continue until another notorious event – the Great Train Robbery of August 8, 1963 – took over.

If The Beatles were to make front page news in the summer of 1963, they faced some tough competition. But espionage and political scandal was not on the minds of the teens queuing outside Leeds Odeon that night. They were not the least bit bothered about Profumo, Macmillan or how an alleged call-girl was threatening to bring down people in high places. They had far more important things on their minds. They were going to see The Beatles!

The crowds began gathering early around the cinema in The Headrow and there were 5,000 lucky ones who would have a ticket to scream. For the pattern was now fully set. The days of occasional screams when a Beatle shook a head or when several Beatles gathered around a mike to sing had now been consigned to the past. It seemed that just about everyone in the two sold-out houses this night just shrieked for all they were worth when The Beatles were onstage. The music was all but inaudible.

The evening started peacefully. David Macbeth and Ian Crawford were heard well enough and Erkey Grant felt confident enough to leap from the stage apron into the arms of girls in the front row without any fear. Looking back Erkey says: "I still remember that! As soon as I'd done it I thought oh no, I hope I'm going to be able to get back in one piece."

The charming Louise Cordet, so demure in a dark blue dress and white collar, was able to perform without the hindrance of any screaming. But the signs were not good when occasional screams punctuated Roy Orbison's set. Audiences normally sat in spellbound, reverential silence. Then The Beatles came on and the twice-nightly scream began.

It was all too much for reporter Ronald Wilkinson who simply wanted to hear the first house show that he was covering for the *Yorkshire Evening Post*. He described The Beatles as talented, but said he only had the evidence of their records to go on. "Their act was drowned out for the whole of its duration by one ear-splitting shriek which whistled with maniacal fury like some weird wind machine worked by a mad stage hand," he wrote.

Sadly, several appeals from the stage by Tony Marsh were ignored – probably unheard – and those in the audience who did want to hear stood no chance of quieting their neighbours either. "Any effort at appreciation of this show proves impossible," lamented Wilkinson. "The evening belongs to Bedlam." Added to the Bedlam was The Beatles repeating the stunt they played on Tony Marsh in Nottingham. This time singer David Macbeth was the 'victim'. "I still remember what they did to me at the Leeds Odeon. I was singing and I could hear all this coming from the orchestra pit. They were hiding there and trying to put me off – like they did at Nottingham to Tony. I couldn't help but laugh. I said over the mike 'Excuse me, is there a fire officer in the house? We've got some juveniles hiding in the orchestra pit.' The spotlight went on them and the screams started, of course."

Among the youngest in the audience was seven-year-old Russell Manning and his little sister Jane, who was six. The good news was they had seats in the second row – but the bad news was that when The Beatles came on dozens of fans charged to the front. "It was absolute mayhem. Just insane," recalls Russell. "People had just rushed forward and were jumping up and down and screaming – some fainted. We were now struggling to see anything and you couldn't hear much. It just went crazy. It was hysteria, really. The Beatles came on and the place exploded – that's what it felt like."

There was an early indication of what the night was to be like when Russell and his family arrived at the Odeon. "I remember arriving at The Headrow where the cinema was and there were what seemed like thousands of people milling about as you looked down the central reservation – probably without tickets a lot of them – and the atmosphere . . ."

At least the young lad was able to see and hear The Big O at close quarters – and that remains a cherished memory. "Even at that age I thought he was great," said Russell. "You could hear Roy that night and he was wonderful."

Russell has no memories of Gerry though. He is not alone in this – and yet both groups were enjoying great success. "I don't know the answer to that," says Russell, who now heads an estate agency in Leeds, "but The Beatles had a chemistry that was unique and their songs were so fresh – a rawness and edginess in songs like 'Twist And Shout' and maybe Gerry's seemed more mainstream pop in comparison."

There was a day off to enjoy on the Thursday as the touring party headed north to Scotland. Kennedy Street promoter Danny Betesh remembers them all gathering for a party. "It would have been the night before the Glasgow shows and it was held at the home of a well-known Scottish retailer. Everyone was there. Roy may not have stayed the whole night but I remember that The Beatles were there until the early hours. It was fun in those days. This was a time before the accountants and lawyers and everything getting heavy. Everyone had a good time and everybody got along. It was a happy tour," said Danny.

Louise Cordet has an odd memory of their coach arrival in Glasgow on the Friday. "I remember when we were on the coach in Glasgow John going up to the window and making mad faces out at people to see their reaction. He made some remark about them being short. 'This is a place full of midgets,' he said. There was a bit of sick humour, particularly from John."

The midget theme apparently wasn't John's invention. Paul made reference to it in a May 2010 interview with Scotland's *Daily Record*. "The country [Scotland] is a very special part of the isles we live in," he said. "It's had a kind of romantic thing for me since I first went there with The Beatles. Our tour manager told us: 'You've got to watch out. You'll see wee people there.' "We said, 'What do you mean, midgets?' But he said: 'No, people – only smaller.' Sure enough, the first two people we spotted were a couple of old folks – a wee Glaswegian man and woman."

The Beatles and Gerry & The Pacemakers had time to appear on *Round Up*, a teen programme for Scottish Television (STV), before making their way to the Odeon. It was a second appearance on the programme for The Beatles. They mimed to 'From Me To You' in the programme's Glasgow studios a few hours before their live appearance on the package tour. The Fabs had struck up a rapport with the show's teen presenters Paul Young and Morag Hood, but John didn't do himself any favours with older STV staff when he clowned about, trying to make Gerry laugh during a Pacemakers number.

While The Beatles and Gerry were having fun in the TV studios, fans were already surrounding the cinema in Renfield Street. Crowds started to gather six hours before the first show, and as early as 2pm cries of 'we love The Beatles, oh yes we do' were filling the air. The cinema seated around 3,000, and all 6,000 tickets for the two shows had gone within hours of being put on sale. Added to the 6,000 were hundreds – maybe thousands – of disappointed fans who couldn't get tickets, and police were preparing for trouble.

Chief constable James Robertson brought in reinforcements, and Chief Inspector John Kirdy was on the scene to help prevent the city centre being gridlocked. The number one task was to stop the fans getting into West Regent Street where there was a back door entrance to the cinema.

The first show got underway to building excitement as the teens waited for the stars to appear. The screams inside the cinema could be heard on the streets outside and by the time the big guns were onstage the body count from the fainters started to rise. And that wasn't the only problem. The Terry Young Six had looked on shocked when Chris Montez got pulled into the crowd on the previous Beatles tour – and this time it was Roy Orbison under threat. Girls stormed the stage during his set. Overrun bouncers started throwing them off the stage, but Roy didn't get away in time.

Terry Young guitarist Bruce Baxter recalls: "The girls had filled the orchestra pit at the front and then they surged up onto the stage. The bouncers were throwing them off but one girl got hold of Roy's glasses. He got them back and was unhurt, but he was shocked." Staff brought the stage curtains down.

Bruce said: "They weighed about three tons, but they dropped it and that was that. Again I had to unplug my guitar and just get off."

So it was a case of follow that for The Beatles. There would have to be a period of calm before they could even think about going on. Baxter: "It was a problem. Some nights Tony Marsh would be sat on the stage, his legs dangling over the edge just waiting for it all to stop so they could continue the show." Police then faced the problem of clearing the first house so the second could start, but tearful fans were desperate to stay.

The hysteria grew during the second show, with all sorts of objects hurled at the stage and several more attempted invasions. A drunk somehow managed to stagger past security onto the stage, perilously close to John Lennon, but the security guys bundled him away before he could do the startled Beatle any harm.

The Beatles were spirited away immediately after and headed for Renfrew Airport, but a huge number of fans refused to believe they had left, banging on the doors. The city's youth and the police may have been galvanised by the events of that night, but it passed some of the newspapers by. Only the *Glasgow Herald* covered the shows, under a headline '6,000 Pop Fans Go Wild'. The report referred to the stage being stormed during the performances of Orbison and The Beatles and concluded that it was "one of the most riotous receptions" since Cliff Richard & The Shadows had been there a few months before.

Needless to say, not much music was heard, but that didn't mean the usual pressures were lifted for the night. Ringo later recalled the down side of being the show-closers on a Roy Orbison tour. The Beatles were one of the few acts that could stand the heat of following Roy onstage at that time. "In Glasgow we were all backstage, listening to the tremendous applause he was getting. He was just standing there singing, not moving or anything. As it got near our turn, we would hide behind the curtain whispering to each other – guess who's next folks, it's your favourite rave. But once we got on the stage it was always OK."

Friday night in Glasgow quickly became Saturday afternoon in Newcastle as the tour descended for the two houses at the City Hall. This was home territory for David Macbeth who was given a rousing welcome. In fact, he recalls the welcome from the fans that day – and teasing a Beatle that it was all for him. "As we approached the City Hall you could see the fans out on the pavements where they had been queuing – many still with their sleeping bags. I turned to John Lennon and said I told you I was a big draw here! I packed the place, you know! We had quite a laugh."

In some ways Newcastle was similar to every other show on this tour – but in others it was almost an exaggeration of what happened elsewhere. The City Hall audience was simply spellbound by Orbison. There they sat, their collective breath blown away by this amazing performer who looked for all the world as though he wasn't performing at all. For, as ever, he didn't jump around. He just stood there and sang his heart out and how the Geordie nation paid tribute. It may have been a teenage audience there to scream at The Beatles, but they knew something special when they saw and heard it. As one, the audience rose to give the man a standing ovation – and a whole collection of encores. With a teenage audience this took some doing. Did it make life difficult for The Beatles? Of course not. The screams filled the place as soon as the Fab ones emerged from the sides.

David Macbeth could be relied upon to come up with something special this night, and he made himself very popular with the others when he managed to get them into the ultra hip La Dolce Vita nightclub in Newcastle after the shows. A quick whip-round later and the boys had a little kitty just in case the drinks weren't on the house.

David recalls: "La Dolce Vita club in Newcastle was the biggest club in the country at the time and after the show the boys asked me if I could get them in. I said of course because I knew the owners. I said we'll all have to put £2 in a kitty, though, and Roy – who was infamously careful with his money – said, 'You know I only drink Coca Cola.'"

David was already married then to Margaret, and the couple's daughter Tracey was just three. There was an added visitor that night. "Ian Crawford stayed with us that night. He was a smashing lad and all the girls went for him. He was an Australian with dark hair and very good looking – a kind of junior Dean Martin. He later became an agent. As for Roy he stayed at the Turks Head that night – it's no longer there. I remember his Transatlantic call to his wife that must have cost a fortune. The Beatles probably stayed there too that night."

Louise Cordet also remembers that night in La Dolce Vita. "It was memorable for me," she says. "I had my first alcoholic drink – gin and orange I think it was."

So now, after three incredible weeks, and all too soon for everybody involved, the tour was heading for its final destination. The foundations of the King George's Hall in Blackburn were laid in 1905, and due in part to the First World War, it was 1921 before it finally began its life as a grand concert hall for the people of the town. But its walls were rocked to their rafters the night The Beatles came to town.

The finale of the tour was a sure fire sign of things to come. Two full houses – a total of 4,500 people – trekked from all over Lancashire, and once there, the girls screamed for all they were worth – at least those who hadn't fainted did.

The Beatles had them jumping all over the hall and girls surged towards the stage at the end of the first house. But even their efforts were surpassed in the second house as the thin blue line of police was breached and some girls made it up onto the stage to realise their dream of touching a Beatle, while others were dumped unceremoniously back into the crowd.

One of those brave girls was 15-year-old Eileen Trippier (now Jackson), who lived in Oswaldtwistle and had just left Rhyddings Secondary. All these years later and Eileen can clearly remember the night she invaded the stage at a Beatles concert. "I was with my friend Betty Hope. My cousin Norma Gilmartin was in the balcony with her boyfriend John. Betty and I were downstairs near the front on the left side and there were some stairs up onto the stage. It was heavily protected by security but then at one point I noticed there was nobody there. I was amazed. I had to go for it. Louise Cordet was watching The Beatles from the wings and I pushed past her to make my dash onto the stage.

"John was my favourite, but the problem was he was on the other side of the stage. So I had to run right across to get near him, but John had moved to the edge on the stairs and when I got behind him I remembered this story that when someone had grabbed him at another gig he had kicked them. So I didn't grab him. All I wanted was a souvenir – perhaps his tie. They loosened their ties as the show went on to help with the singing, but I didn't get it. The security picked me up and carried me off. When Norma said, 'That girl onstage looked a little like you,' I felt compelled to confess it was me!"

The excitable behaviour wasn't limited to the girls. Darwen Grammar School girl Ros Kirkham (now Simpson) was upstairs in the balcony with friends when a boy risked his life by clambering onto the ledge of the balcony. "It was a waist-high ledge designed to stop people falling over but there he was on top of it. His mates were holding onto his legs so he wouldn't fall over. Quite frankly, I could have managed without that! It was a great night all the same, if a bit of a madhouse."

Ros described the concert as just that – "a madhouse" – in her diary the next day, and she also recorded how good the show was – especially The Beatles and Roy. "I had already seen The Beatles by then. They played at a Baptist youth club in Darwen where I live (Co-operative Hall, Friday, January 25, 1963). The buzz had gone round that there was this really good group from Liverpool. Paul was my favourite. I wrote in my diary after the Roy night that The Beatles and Roy were marvellous. There was some screaming but we could hear the music – probably because I wasn't screaming."

St Mary's pupil Steve Catterall, 13, was downstairs about halfway down in the middle section with his pal Stuart Butterworth and the boys were counting their bruises at the end. Steve recalls: "When The Beatles came on everyone stood up so we had to stand on the chairs to see anything. Then everyone else started doing the same so we tried to stand on the back of the chair to try to see. I fell off my chair – well, about 500 people did the same. The chairs weren't fixed. They had these canvas-backed chairs with tubeless steel and you were holding on to the shoulders of the person in front, trying to stay on.

"It was a great concert and you could hear the music, despite the screaming. I was a huge Beatles fan and was wearing ice blue jeans, Beatle boots and a Beatles jacket – black, with gold buttons and a round collar! But even as a Beatles fan, you couldn't take credit from Roy Orbison.

His voice was unbelievable. His hair was so black that when the spotlight hit him it appeared to be blue. He barely moved his mouth to sing, but he was phenomenal."

John Smith, a 17-year-old apprentice at the Blackburn Co-op, was in the balcony with three friends for the second house. He remembers the girls surging towards the stage as The Beatles finished. "They breached the security cordon and rushed the stage. Seeing this, John, Paul and George unclipped their guitars and ran for it, but poor old Ringo was stuck behind the drums and to see the abject look of fear on his face as he kicked drums and cymbals out of the way to get offstage was quite something. The other thing that sticks in the memory is the complete contrast in the reaction of the audience when Roy Orbison sang. You could hear a pin drop. It was quite amazing."

Smith recalls that a boy who had the temerity to shout "Up The Rolling Stones" was rewarded with a hasty clout from an umbrella wielded by a girl behind him!

The audience revelled in every song from Roy, but the screams reached fever pitch for The Beatles, who deemed it one of their best gigs. John Lennon, chatting to journalists from the *Blackburn Times* and the *Evening Telegraph* in the dressing room afterwards, was on cloud nine. "They were the best crowds we have had yet – the next being Glasgow. I could have played for another hour." Paul was impressed, too, adding: "That's right – we really got going this time."

As was often the case, it was 'Twist And Shout' that really got the party started. The sound smashed around the whole auditorium as teenagers swayed to the beat, while others twisted in the now crowded aisles and still others stood on their seats and screamed. The Beatles were on great form and loved playing to the wildest reaction yet. They smiled at each other as they dodged missiles from the audience – including, of course, those boxes of jelly babies that John and George had confessed they had a taste for.

Fans gathered at a side door afterwards – autograph books in hand – but there were no Beatles to be seen. According to the *Blackburn Times*, they rushed out of the front door and into their waiting car.

It had got to the point that anyone who even looked like a Beatle was putting himself in peril as *Evening Telegraph* photographer Milton Haworth was to discover.

Screaming girls – convinced the photographer was Ringo – descended on him at the end. "They tried to mob me but I managed to escape," he told readers the next day – and he vowed to get a haircut in case the Beatles came to town again! Speaking in May 2010, Milton, who now lives in Ulverston, recalls what happened, and says The Beatles didn't leave through the front as reported.

"I was leaving at the end through a side door when I happened to wave at someone I knew. The girls obviously thought I was Ringo and they descended on me. They went mad and were pulling my sleeves off. I managed to fight my way back in and security led me under the hall to the police yard where The Beatles' van was. They were inside with Neil Aspinall. Neil took me and The Beatles to a party at the Nelson Imperial Ballroom about 12 miles away. After a few drinks they dropped me back in Blackburn."

As a 17-year-old photographer covering the event, Milton had been in his element. "It was a great night. I took some pictures of The Beatles having a cup of tea before the shows and saw the first house from the back of the hall. I was in the wings for the second house and must have run off a stack of pictures. I think they were thrown away. I lived in New York for a while and I was offered thousands of dollars if I could find them! I got on well with George and had a good chat with Roy. He was a charming guy – an absolute gentleman. Gerry was a great guy, too, and still is."

Paul Earnshaw, who was in the balcony for the second show with his pal Gordon Walker, wasn't surprised about the photographer getting mobbed. "Milton lived near me in Little Harwood, Blackburn, and he really did look like Ringo," he recalls. "It wasn't just the hair – he had many of Ringo's features.

"As for the concert, it was just mad. Everyone was screaming and downstairs the girls got to the front. You could hear The Beatles despite the screams and, anyway, the screaming added to it. It was kind of fitting. We were in Blackburn but we were transported into this new wave sweeping Britain. We had seen The Beatles on TV and were now made to feel a part of it. The stage was absolutely littered with presents people had thrown on – some of them wrapped – all sorts of objects, teddy bears and the like."

Earnshaw, a 14-year-old St Peter's School pupil at the time, now lives in Oswaldtwistle. He concludes: "There will never be days like that again. You knew every record in the Top 20 and could sing every record in the Top 20."

Milton Haworth was also flavour of the month with June Wilby, who was at the show courtesy of a sixteenth birthday present from her mum and dad. June (now June Duncan) spotted Milton that night and he took her programme in for The Beatles to sign. "I cut the pictures out of the programme and stuck them up on my bedroom wall," she says. "Mum made me take them all down when I got married and most were thrown away – but I kept the signed photo and still have it today."

Chaotic it surely was, but the King George's Hall lived to tell the tale. It is still standing today, the same building that hosted the finale to this grand tour of all the talents in the summer of 1963.

Out of the third Beatles tour came some lifelong friendships. Gerry and the Beatles adored The Big O, and George Harrison became especially close to the Texas born singer. In early 1988 Harrison formed an ad-hoc group called The Travelling Wilburys which featured Orbison alongside Bob Dylan, Tom Petty and Jeff Lynne, and few doubt that Orbison's sad death in December of that year robbed the group of their greatest asset. Olivia Harrison, in a BBC tribute, recalled what George had said to her about this tour. "George told me they followed Roy. They would stand in the wings listening to this big ending and George said they'd be just trembling, thinking how on earth were they going to go out and follow this?"

It wasn't just The Beatles who were impressed by Orbison personally and professionally. Gerry Marsden, too, was fulsome in his praise, stating in the same documentary: "The way he sang was different from what we'd ever heard before. Elvis didn't do that – Roy did it and I think just the difference in the sound that that man made – that's why he was so popular.

"He loved England and he loved the British people. There was something about Britain, or the British people, that Roy liked. He would have to listen to accents and go and see places in Scotland and go and visit castles and walk the hills. We were in bed, and he was walking the hills! He just loved Britain, he really did, and we loved him. And that voice, my God, it used to annoy me, it was so good.

"He always reminded me of a preacher, he was so gentle. Very sweet. Loved his kids, loved his family and was just a lovely guy. We were all young and mad. Roy was very polite – a gentleman. We were just kids from Liverpool who knew nothing. We followed Roy Orbison, a massive star whose songs we'd sung for years and we're there with him and watching him. Oh – a dream."

Looking back in 2010, Bobby Goldsboro has equally fond memories. "I recall lots of laughter on the bus. Everyone made good-natured fun of my southern accent. I do a frog impression and I had everyone looking around for a frog for the first couple of days. When everyone realised they only heard it when I was around they knew it was me. After a while Paul McCartney could do the frog sound pretty well. I was with Roy Orbison in England touring with The Beatles and Gerry & The Pacemakers. I loved every minute of it."

Like The Beatles and Gerry, Bobby was utterly charmed by the Big O. "Roy was one of the nicest guys I ever met. We became like brothers. I don't think anyone knows what a great sense of humour he had. When we travelled together all we did was laugh. He always got along with everybody. Even after playing guitar and singing with him for nearly three years I still marvelled at the notes he hit night after night. And he loved his fans. To this day after a concert I stay and sign autographs until everyone has gone. I got that from Roy."

Bobby was simply amazed by The Beatles. "I had only heard a few of their songs when Roy and I arrived in England. I would stand in the wings every night and listen to them. I became a huge fan, like everyone else. They were all funny guys to be around. After travelling around on a bus together, you get to know someone. The Beatles had become the biggest thing in the world almost overnight, but they were just like everybody else on the bus. I ran into Ringo at a restaurant in Hollywood years later. A few years went by and I ran into him at the same restaurant. I said: 'We've got to stop meeting like this!' They were all great guys. In fact, when they were finishing their first American tour they were told to pick their favourite American singers and they'd try to get them to play the final concert at the Paramount Theatre in New York City. They picked all these great entertainers and then they picked me to be on the show. I got to see them all again and they hadn't changed a bit.

"When I sang onstage [on that tour] it's the only time I ever performed where I don't think one single person heard anything I sang. They were screaming so loud, I could have sung gibberish and they wouldn't have known. They were all there to see The Beatles."

Bobby also became a fan of Liverpool's other chart-toppers on the tour. "Gerry & The Pacemakers had a unique sound. I really liked to hear Gerry Marsden sing because his accent was different to everybody else. Again, the main thing I recall about the bus rides was the laughter. Back then, none of us had been on the road enough to let it get us down. I mean, who could gripe when you go onstage for a few minutes and thousands of girls are screaming, trying to get to you?

"It was a special time that I don't think we'll ever see again. There were no iPods, no computers, no digital cameras. No one was playing video games because they didn't exist. So, we all told stories, played songs, actually communicated! My only regret is that I didn't have a camera. Now that I'm doing oil paintings I'd love to paint something from that tour but I have no pictures. I've been fortunate since that tour to have my own music career and I've been blessed to have worked with some of the great names in show business. But, I can't recall a more fun time or a more memorable tour than the Beatles/Orbison tour."

Pacemaker Les Maguire, whose skilful piano playing was such a distinctive part of the group's sound, remembers the screaming of the kids and the boredom of the travelling. "You just got swept along with it all. There would be the kids and getting mobbed, but a big part of touring life was boredom. We would do up to 300 miles a day on the coach and you'd arrive at the theatre at about 4pm and then you were trapped inside until the show was over. Maybe someone would be sent out for a coke and a hot dog and if you were lucky you might be able to get to a nightclub at the end and have a couple of pints. Then it was back to the hotel and on the coach again the next day. It was a boring existence."

Les remembers The Beatles closing the show. "Roy would get a fantastic reception at the end of his spot and I thought they would have to put in quite a performance to follow that – but they usually did. My memories are sketchy now but it was fun. We had known The Beatles for years, of course, and we generally sat apart on the coach, but we all had a laugh. But the screaming of the kids . . . there were only 2,500, but it would really sting your ears."

Les describes Roy as "a real gentleman, a very cool character. He was a quiet person, but friendly".

Bruce Baxter is yet another fan of Roy Orbison. "He was absolutely super – a wonderful guy. He mixed in with everybody – there was nothing big time about him – and he looked after the band. He stood stock still onstage – there he was in his black sunglasses, black guitar and black clothes. He looked like a bloody fly!

"Of course the screaming was there on these tours. The fans couldn't really hear that much, but we could. Roy had a fantastic technique for controlling the crowd. He would open with 'Running Scared' and we would play very, very quietly. We would just carry on playing the intro chords until the noise died down. It would be five minutes some nights, but he would wait until it died down and then he would start singing."

Singer David Macbeth remembers that promoter Peter Walsh was nervous at the beginning of the tour. "Peter was my agent and he said to me one day do you fancy doing this tour? We've got Roy Orbison and I'm taking a chance on this new group, The Beatles, and Gerry & The Pacemakers.

"At the start of the tour we all travelled on the bus together, but that changed as it progressed. I had a car and I remember Paul picked up a car after Liverpool. The Beatles didn't always travel together. The Beatles were so naïve really. They would be playing cards and George Harrison went mad because he said he was owed two bob from the kitty. I was in hysterics. He wondered what I was laughing at and I said, 'Two bob? Do you know how much money you guys are worth?' They were very personable lads and always up for a laugh. They loved playing practical jokes."

It wasn't just the orchestra pit episode at Leeds. "During my act I would borrow John's guitar case and I'd put it down on the stage and announce to the audience that I had John's guitar case and shall we see what's inside? I'd usually open it and pull out a ukulele, but this night, I can't remember where it was, when I opened it a cat jumped out! Things like that would happen."

Macbeth remembers Tony Marsh being at the centre of the fun. "He had a tough job keeping the crowds amused as they waited for the stars to come on, but he was good at it. He always had great gags and he would bombard the audience. I remember asking him one night where he was staying, and he told me he was staying at this posh hotel. I said, 'That's going to cost you a few bob, mate.' 'No it won't,' he said, 'I'm kipping on the floor in John Lennon's room.' He said it was an old pro's trick. He'd just throw this quilt down on the floor and kip in that. It was typical of him."

David was to meet up with The Beatles again. "A few months later they were doing a one-nighter at the Floral Hall in Scarborough and I took my wife along to meet them. They were just the same, carrying on and

147

laughing. It hadn't gone to their heads. They were just the same practical jokers."

Like everyone else who met Orby, David admired him – but Roy was an unusual pop star. "I said to my wife I didn't think Roy was of this world. He must be a Martian or something. He wore the same suit on-and offstage for the whole tour and it never creased. It was amazing. I've never met anyone like him. I remember him working on his guitars – he'd be taking them apart with a knife. Very weird. I also remember him being on the phone to his wife in Nashville for ages. It must have cost a fortune."

David enjoyed being in the company of Gerry Marsden. "Gerry was full of fun – always a lot of laughs, and I bet he still is. We really didn't see much of Louise Cordet, though. I think she had chaperones. I remember Ian Crawford, the Australian singer on the tour, for the fact that you couldn't wake him up. It was like waking the dead. He missed the bus a couple of times because of it and had to make his own way there." David owned the hugely successful Greys nightclub in Newcastle for many years before selling out in 1996 following a heart attack.

Louise Cordet went on to appear in another pop film, *Just For You*, in 1964, performing the song 'It's So Hard To Be Good.' Gerry wrote 'Don't Let The Sun Catch You Crying' for her to record in 1964, but it made little impact. Gerry's own version just a few weeks later was a big hit.

Louise, with typical lack of ego, said in 2010: "I was the first to record it but my version wasn't very good. Gerry's was wonderful." Her 1964 version of the Bacharach and David song 'Don't Make Me Over' backed with 'Two Lovers', was well received but by 1965 her recording career was over. She was briefly a translator and publicist for Marianne Faithful. She married and is now Louise Yannacopoulos, living in Greece and with a home in London. She is a mother of three, one of which is the singer songwriter Alexi Murdoch.

Like the others, Louise enjoyed every day of this tour. "It was a very memorable period in my life and something that has stayed with me ever since. Now when I tell people that I toured with The Beatles I watch their jaws drop!" Louise remembers the japes that were always a part of touring life, and odd incidents stick in the memory. For example, John once letting her trim his precious Beatle cut. "Paul didn't want him to do that – the Beatle haircut was too important. But John was the most zany. I didn't just cut it, I ran my fingers through it and made his hair stand up so he appeared sort of crazed. Then he went up against the window looking out where he knew there would be a sea of faces.

"Neil Aspinall would sometimes get annoyed with the childish antics. We would have yoghurt fights backstage, things like that. I had a race with Paul to see who could drink a pint of milk straight down the quickest. We spent some of the time on the coach drawing squiggles. They would be passed on to the next person and the idea was to eventually create a picture. John once drew a portrait of me . . . but I didn't keep it! Can you believe that?"

A convent education was hardly ideal preparation for touring with a bunch of young rockers. Louise recalls: "John said I should go off and be a nun! I was 18 and unbelievably innocent. There was one particular person in a band who would mock me a little bit – speak in such a way that would shock me and there was an occasion when John Lennon and Gerry were sat in front of me on the coach on either side of the aisle and they both pounced on him. There was another time when there was chat about what one of them got up to with a girl and I said to Paul, 'Oh boys don't do that, do they?' He was quite coy about it. 'Well some might, I don't know', that kind of thing. The Beatles made a point of not talking about certain stuff in front of me. I did overhear them talking about girls they might pick up at the stage door, but they were always shielding me from seeing it or hearing about it."

"I did have a chaperone on this tour. It was the first time I'd been on a tour like this and my mother insisted upon it. The woman who was my chaperone had been an air stewardess but she was between jobs at the time and at a bit of a loose end so she ended up as my chaperone. She was quiet, too."

The Beatles were all smokers and Louise had also started smoking. "I was a secret smoker for a while but I had just admitted it to my mother. I was 18 by then. In those days, people were just so un-star like. The Beatles, Gerry and all of the others were like schoolboys really. We all messed around like kids. I was not at all star-struck. We said we would stay in touch – like you do – and we swapped addresses. I still have that envelope somewhere that they wrote their addresses on – and I think it was their Liverpool addresses.

"I didn't stay in showbiz very long so we didn't get to see each other very often. I would occasionally see Paul – he came to my brother's twenty-first birthday party – and very occasionally I'd see one of the others."

With the tour over, The Beatles returned to a life of one-nighters, pounding their way through a series of dances north, south, east and west – some of which had been booked many months before. Those performances included – on Saturday, August 3 – a farewell to the Cavern, their spiritual home, but now very much outgrown. While relaxing in their hotel after an appearance at the Majestic Ballroom in Newcastle on Wednesday, June 26, they began work on a song with a hook line "Yeah Yeah Yeah". A few days later, on Monday, July 1, they were at Abbey Road to record it.

'She Loves You', their fourth single, was released on Friday, August 23 and it sold more than half a million copies in a fortnight. During that very same week they performed a series of shows in a week's residency at Bournemouth during which, at the Palace Court Hotel where they were staying, photographer Robert Freeman shot the iconic, semi-shadow black and white photograph that was soon to adorn the cover of their second LP, *With The Beatles*. Earlier in the month they'd appointed a second roadie, Mal Evans, an old friend and former Cavern doorman, to work alongside Neil Aspinall.

TV and radio dates and studio sessions kept The Beatles busy in the weeks before their proudest moment yet, a bill-topping appearance on Val Parnell's *Sunday Night At The London Palladium*, broadcast nationally on ITV on October 13. If nothing else, this was recognition that the world of showbiz now acknowledged The Beatles as one of their own, but it was the pandemonium outside the Palladium that proved more significant in the long term.

In his book *John, Paul, George, Ringo & Me – The Real Beatles Story*, The Beatles' PR Tony Barrow pinpointed this day as the birth of Beatlemania. Fleet Street newsdesks on slow Sunday afternoons would send photographers and reporters to Argyll Street to get rehearsal pictures of that week's Palladium stars for their early editions. Beatle fans had seen trailers for days before the show and gathered accordingly, and the journalists were startled by the scenes that greeted them.

Barrow wrote: "When fans of The Beatles began to scream and shout in the street outside the theatre that afternoon, representatives of the full range of British dailies were on hand to hear and then see what was happening.

The newsworthiness of the scene was enhanced by the arrival of policemen from the nearby West End Central police station. The crowd suddenly shifted its focus from the theatre's front entrance in Argyll Street to the stage door in Great Marlborough Street. Were The Beatles arriving? Leaving? No, it was nothing more exciting than the arrival of roadies Neil and Mal carrying cardboard boxes of Cokes and hot dogs bought from a Carnaby Street café to feed their four masters. The crowd surged back round the corner into Argyll Street where energetic reinforcements of cops stopped them short of the Palladium steps and in doing so provided the ideal photo opportunity. The cameras flashed and the kids opened their mouths and yelled their heads off. The reporters collected quotes from a few fans and because this was the hardest news around that night the dead donkey was dropped yet again and Beatlemania was splashed across the front pages of Monday morning's editions. One paper called it 'Beatle Fever!' and the *Daily Mirror* coined the term 'Beatlemania'." Barrow added that the story also made Sunday's late evening news bulletin on ITV.

And so the snowball began to roll. On October 23 the group flew to Sweden for a series of concerts and TV appearances, arriving back a week later to unprecedented scenes at Heathrow Airport where they were greeted by hundreds of screaming fans. The mayhem made headlines in the popular press and was broadcast on national TV news, heightening the media frenzy about Beatlemania. By coincidence, US TV host Ed Sullivan happened to be passing through the airport at the time and witnessed the scene. It impressed him so much he would book the group for his show early the following year.

The very next day The Beatles set off on an enormous winter tour of the UK – their fourth this hectic year. With 'She Loves You' having already smashed its way to number one – and about to return there and top a million sales during the tour – they knew that the screaming crowds they had faced in the summer would be nothing compared with what was about to hit them on this tour. It was a roller coaster ride like no other before or since.

CHAPTER FOUR

The Fourth Tour
The Madness

November 1 – December 13, 1963
Featuring The Beatles, The Kestrels, Peter Jay & The Jaywalkers,
The Vernons Girls, The Brook Brothers, The Rhythm & Blues Quartet
Compère: Frank Berry

IF The Beatles thought their spring and summer UK tours were getting out of hand, they were a stroll in the park compared with the scenes on their third and final tour of 1963. Their tour opened in Cheltenham on Friday, November 1, and took in 34 dates in just under six weeks, including two shows in Ireland, all to a backdrop of increasingly wild scenes more associated with extreme civil disturbance than anything hitherto associated with the world of pop.

So what had changed? Firstly there was the unprecedented success of 'She Loves You' followed by the media coverage of the scenes outside the London Palladium. Then, four weeks into the tour, they released 'I Want To Hold Your Hand'. These two singles – the fundamental soundtrack to Beatlemania – catapulted the group into the hearts and minds of Britain's teenage population. From being merely the super cool princes of pop, over the summer of 1963 The Beatles ascended to god-like status, as far as their growing legion of fans was concerned.

'She Loves You' was the best-selling single of 1963 and remains the best-selling Beatles single in the UK, and until it was surpassed in 1977 by 'Mull Of Kintyre' – by Paul McCartney's group Wings – it was the best-selling UK single overall.

It entered the charts on August 31 and remained there for 31 weeks, 18 in the top three. It reached number one on September 14, dropped back to number three four weeks later then – on November 28, when the boys were heading off to Lincoln for two houses at the town's ABC Cinema – regained the top spot for a further two weeks until it was knocked off by 'I Want To Hold Your Hand' as the tour was nearing its end.

This staggering success realised Brian Epstein's famous boast that one day The Beatles would be "bigger than Elvis". But life is seldom that simple. However rosy things were, there was a price to be paid and by the end of 1963 that price was their freedom, their progress as a live act and all hope of enjoying anything approaching a normal existence for the remainder of their lives. All of this was the toll to be paid for the unimagined heights of celebrity that The Beatles lived through.

Brian Epstein's headquarters had by now moved from Liverpool to London, though the four Beatles had been bedding down in the capital since the spring of 1963, first at The Royal Court Hotel in Sloane Square and then at the Hotel President in Russell Square, Bloomsbury. But the sheer pressure of fans meant it was no longer practical for them to stay in hotels. By the start of this autumn tour, all four Beatles lived in a rented top floor flat at 57 Green Street in Mayfair.

The hundreds that had flocked to their earlier tour gigs had now become thousands, and The Beatles had outgrown the humble tour bus. By now it was decoy vehicles and elaborate escape routines, all planned with military precision. Getting them into and, even worse, out of venues was now a major concern, with hordes of frantic girls trying to grab them or even throw themselves in front of their car to stop them getting away. Neil Aspinall had secured an Austin Princess, and Bill Corbett, who worked for a car hire firm and was later employed by John to drive his Rolls-Royce, was hired as a driver. Even the Austin Princess was to feel the heat, breaking down several times during the course of the tour to add to the problems.

Neil, driven to a frazzle in recent months, certainly appreciated his full-time assistant Mal Evans. A part-time bouncer at the Cavern and full-time GPO engineer, 'Big Mal' had been known to the boys for some time and was welcomed into the group's inner circle during the autumn tour.

In truth, the 68 performances on those 34 tour dates over November and December 1963 could barely be described as concerts. The din of the screaming had now grown to the point that hardly anyone could hear the music – even those in the front rows – or The Beatles themselves up on the stage. No, these were not concerts. They were events. It didn't seem to matter to the fans that they couldn't hear the music. They could do that by playing the records in the comfort of their own homes. It was all about being there – just seeing them – and screaming – and maybe catching the attention of a Beatle for even the briefest of moments.

There was certainly no sanctuary in the dressing rooms that The Beatles often shared with the other performers – and the inevitable invited and uninvited guests. Cinema staff, journalists, local dignitaries, assorted hangers on – they all found their way into their dressing rooms before shows. The favourite Beatle tipple was scotch and coke and there was a little more scotch than coke going in.

Ideally, before gigs The Beatles would pass the time with a quiet game of cards, a bite to eat and a drink and then tune their guitars – but they were rarely, if at all, given time to enjoy such luxuries in peace on this tour. Beatle humour, however, was still much in evidence and it often saved the day as they faced the same inane questions in every town. Ringo, why do you wear so many rings on your fingers? Because I can't get them through my nose. John, are you wearing wigs? Well if we are they must be the only ones with real dandruff. Paul, how long do you think you'll last? . . . and so it went on.

This was the group's first national tour as bill toppers in their own right. No need for a Helen Shapiro or Americans like Chris Montez or Roy Orbison to sell tickets by now – or for Mersey rivals like Gerry & The Pacemakers to bring along their fans.

Accompanying The Beatles on this six-week descent into anarchy were The Kestrels, Peter Jay & The Jaywalkers, The Vernons Girls, The Brook Brothers (Ricky and Geoff) and The Rhythm & Blues Quartet. The latter were made up of Bob Francis on piano and the three members of The Brook Brothers' backing band, and they provided the backing for the brothers and The Vernons Girls. The compère was Frank Berry, a Canadian comic dubbed "Canada's Mad Man of Magic", who was also a bit of a dab hand at ventriloquism and the odd magic trick. For the greater part, he, and the others accompanying The Beatles on this tour, might not have bothered, as far as the fans were concerned. These artists, accomplished tour performers all, were standing between the fans and The Beatles and that wasn't a happy place to be. Their professionally honed performances were drowned out night after night with high pitched chants of We Want The Beatles! We Want The Beatles! Inevitable though it was, this was one of the less attractive aspects of Beatlemania.

The Beatles, now undisputed bill-toppers, had the luxury of being able to perform 10 songs per show. With the exception of Paul's show tune – 'Till There Was You' – the accent was on beat numbers. They usually kicked off with the song that was the opening track on their debut album, 'I Saw Her Standing There'. This would be followed by 'From Me To You', 'All My Loving', 'You Really Got A Hold On Me', 'Roll Over Beethoven' (sung by George), 'Boys' (sung by Ringo), 'Till There Was You' and 'She Loves You'. The shows would often finish with two Lennon rockers – 'Money' and 'Twist And Shout'. Later in the tour 10 became 11 as they added 'I Want To Hold Your Hand' to the sets. As we shall discover, they rather surprisingly threw in 'Anna' at Sheffield.

The hectic nature of their day-to-day lives is illustrated by the fact that after flying back from the week-long stint in Sweden on the morning of Thursday, October 31, the very next day they opened the six-week autumn tour with two houses at the Odeon Cinema in Cheltenham. On the way they enjoyed a relaxed lunch at a restaurant near Oxford, with heads turning as the now famous four settled down to mixed grills or steaks. Protective staff said the meals were on the house if they would sign their names. They happily signed . . . and paid.

The other artists travelled in the coach with tour manager Johnny Clapson. There was relief all round when the Beatlemobile glided through the lined streets of Cheltenham and the headliners were able to dart into the Odeon swiftly and without undue commotion. One tricky entrance negotiated – just 33 more to worry about and 34 departures. Clapson had been shepherding stars around Britain for 15 years, but he knew this would be his biggest challenge yet. To add to his woes, the Cheltenham gig coincided with a students' Rag Day and there was an audacious plan to 'kidnap' a Beatle and hold him to ransom as a stunt. This crazy idea was bought off with a £25 donation to student funds.

Some concert footage, with sound, survives from that night, showing The Beatles in their light, collarless suits going full pelt and sending the Cheltenham teens into raptures. Fragments from 'Boys', 'From Me To You' and 'Till There Was You' survive, along with slightly longer segments of 'Money' and 'Twist And Shout', plus footage of girls in the audience in various states of delirium. More importantly, the film shows The Beatles on the very first date of a daunting autumn tour enthusiastically giving their all onstage and looking very happy to be there. The music can clearly be heard over the screams, although the screamers and their neighbours in the stalls may not have heard that much.

The tension built up from the start as Cheltenham police, backed by others from nearby towns, guarded every gangway and exit while others made sure the girls didn't surge through the glass doors at the front of the house. The cries for The Beatles continued through the performances of the other acts and the girls were beside themselves by the time the Fab Four took the stage. Frank Berry attempted to introduce them, but was completely swamped. This was to be a nightly occurrence. What chance did Berry have? Even Lennon's appeals to "Shurrup" fell on deaf and ringing ears.

They opened with 'I Saw Her Standing There' and 'From Me To You' and were rewarded with a deafening response and a surge from the crowd that already had the police flustered. Appeals that they had tired of jelly babies were wasted breath. They rained down on the stage, along with programmes, coins and assorted debris. If The Beatles were put out by this new level of excitement, they weren't showing it, as George made clear in a dressing room interview with a reporter from *Disc* between the two houses.

"I thought this wasn't to be a show town, but the reception we got tonight has hardly ever been equalled," he said. The group were showcasing songs from their imminent second album, but George revealed that they were going to throw in some earlier hits in the second show – even though their efforts may have gone unnoticed. "I couldn't hear myself think out there tonight and we certainly couldn't hear each other singing or playing," George added.

The boys faced the media and changed out of their stage suits during the break. They puffed on cigarettes and chomped on hot dogs. Five portions a day of fruit and veg was a diet unknown to anyone, let alone pop stars on tour in 1963. Neil Aspinall was already asking Berry to appeal for calm – at least until the end of each song. He knew he was fighting a losing battle. Even back in the summer the girls were ignoring such pleas. The screams in the second house were reportedly even louder than the first.

Meanwhile, outside the Odeon on the streets of sleepy Cheltenham, were scores of stricken teenagers. Some had fainted, others had minor

in early by filming the crowds with his own cine-camera. He was reportedly delighted at the mass of waving fans, commenting afterwards: "We felt like royalty."

It wasn't much fun for the police and ambulance men, though. They worked flat out to keep the city centre open to traffic and there were dozens of fainters to deal with, too. Sadly, some of the innocence was disappearing. Touts were out again, with one boasting that he bought sixty 5 shilling tickets that he was selling on "like hot cakes" for £5 each. Worse, there was a bomb hoax just five minutes from the end of the second house – too late for the police to be able to clear the building, but three fire engines stood by.

There was still some innocent fun, though. Two 14-year-old schoolgirls had baked a cake for the group and they were rewarded with a kiss from each Beatle after being taken through to meet them.

Music blasted out of The Beatles' dressing room, with Little Richard and The Contours among the records played. A Chinese waiter appeared from a local restaurant and The Beatles all chose English dishes.

As for the concerts, predictably, there was more screaming than music. It is a compliment to Peter Jay & The Jaywalkers that they performed well enough to stop the girls screaming for The Beatles during an act that was polished, professional and funny in all the right places. However, The Vernons Girls, The Brook Brothers and The Kestrels struggled to be heard, as did poor old Frank Berry trying to make announcements. There was no bitterness towards The Beatles, but Maureen Kennedy of The Vernons Girls broke ranks by going on record to say how tough it was for the other acts while the crowds were screaming for The Beatles during their sets. "I think the boys are fabulous and deserve all of this," she told Ray Coleman, "but it's a bit rough on all the other acts."

The two sell-out 2,500 houses went wild when The Beatles came on. Apart from the din, The Beatles had to cope with sweets, dolls, streamers, programmes and even several handbags launched at them from the audience. They kept their own announcements to a minimum during their half-hour spots.

The *Yorkshire Post* described the scene: "Usherettes were lost in a seething mass of waving arms and shaking legs. It was as if the whole audience had been sprayed with an infectious screaming virus." The Beatles concluded with 'Twist And Shout', sparking a mass surge for the stage. A few minutes of one of their performances were recorded for use in a court case involving the Performing Rights Society. The tape apparently no longer exists. If it did, there probably wouldn't be much music on it.

Fan Lesley Cooke recalls her mum queuing all day to get a ticket for her, but Lesley confesses that she didn't hear anything over the screaming. Another fan, John Beckett, was a secondary school boy living in Wakefield back then but a pal had got them tickets and they travelled in on the bus. "It was only when I got into Leeds that the full force of their popularity hit me. The whole area was choked with hundreds of people, mainly young girls who were screaming and chanting for them to make an appearance at the windows just above the entrance. Ordinary people passing by were of course grumbling, and moaning as ever people do. Newspaper sellers were probably sold out.

"My pal and I fought our way through to the queue for entry, grasping our tickets. I was in shock, and trying to act cool as a defence mechanism. Everyone walked excitedly into the auditorium, and behaved themselves really well when the support acts were on. We were seated about halfway back, downstairs in the stalls on the left, so we had a pretty good view. When The Beatles finally came on, most of the audience downstairs began screaming, abandoned all reserve, and charged down to the front – jelly babies being hurled at the stage – and general pandemonium ensued.

"The Beatles were clad in their stock silver grey suits. I remember seeing them in colour, especially hair colour, because the TV and press were black and white of course. Because we were acting cool we refused to charge to the front, as this was seen to be a bit girly! We remained in our seats."

Peter Jay recalls that The Beatles escaped the fans afterwards by heading out of Leeds to stay in a hotel in Bradford.

Having suffered the car breakdown on the way to Leeds, The Beatles took no chances heading out of Yorkshire the next morning (Monday, November 4). They flew down to London for the Royal Command Performance before the Queen Mother and Princess Margaret at the Prince of Wales Theatre in a show that was screened the following Sunday (November 10). They arrived in Coventry Street with Epstein in a car with the now customary autograph hunters besieging them, but at least they were in good time for rehearsals.

The Beatles performed four songs that night – 'From Me To You', 'She Loves You', 'Till There Was You' and finally 'Twist And Shout' which

John famously introduced by inviting the people in the cheaper seats to clap their hands and the rest to just rattle their jewellery.

This was the one night, of course, when the music wasn't drowned out by screaming. The refined audience was far too well mannered to scream while The Beatles were singing, so there was plenty at stake as they performed before royalty on a show in which the audience could hear every note and which was later going to be seen by millions of television viewers. Paul gulped nervously as he introduced 'Till There Was You' but the group put in an impeccable performance on their most important date yet. They were able to hear themselves singing and playing – an unusual event at the time – and they were rewarded at the end of each song with prolonged applause.

It was a triumph for them, raising their profile yet further, and the Queen Mother was said to have been impressed when she met them after the show. She asked them where they were playing the next night. Slough came the reply. 'Oh, that's near us,' she said – Windsor Castle being a mere couple of miles down the road.

In the Royal Command audience was Peter Jay who confessed that although he was getting to see a lot of The Beatles on tour, he couldn't normally hear them because of the screaming. So he quietly forked out for his ticket and settled back in his seat with the lords and ladies to enjoy the unique experience of hearing them in concert. Few daylight hours were wasted for The Beatles. They were up early the next day to be filmed as they were driven around London in a hired car discussing Beatlemania for a BBC current affairs programme.

If The Beatles enjoyed their brief sortie into a privileged world at the Prince of Wales Theatre that Monday they crashed head-on back into their own crazy world on Bonfire Night in Slough. Rumours that youths with firecrackers were plotting to do their worst hardly eased tensions around the Adelphi Cinema in the countdown to the shows. Police reinforcements were drafted in from High Wycombe to contain the hysterical fans and deal with anyone out to cause trouble. Operation Beatle involved 40 specials working alongside 40 regular officers, with ambulance men, cinema staff and St John Ambulance Brigade volunteers also doing their bit. Even the garage next door had staff on duty to allay fears over the 18,000 gallons of petrol stored underground while youths with fireworks and firecrackers were about.

The earliest arrivals that day were 15-year-olds Pat Turner and her friend Brenda Koning who camped out on the cold pavement from 9.15am with a flask of tea as their only comfort. Joining them later were a group of girls from Warren Field School and Slough High School marching under their own Beatle banner lovingly made by Madeline Harridge. They sang their own Beatle song to the tune of 'Onward Christian Soldiers' as they advanced on the Adelphi, and were pictured in high spirits in the next day's *Slough Observer*. There were around 150 girls lined up along Bath Road when The Beatles arrived in their Austin Princess at 4.25pm, dashing through the front doors as police held the girls back. Waiting for them were three giant boxes of autograph books to be signed.

The soundcheck included an impromptu jam session featuring Ringo and George and several Jaywalkers in front of around 30 policemen who would later be overworked protecting the stars from their excitable fans. Not everyone loved The Beatles. A sign bearing the words Ban The Beatles was spotted in a car outside.

The tension built up inside the cinema as the other acts tried their best to make the girls forget about The Beatles for a while. But still the screams came. In the circumstances, you wouldn't think that the Canadian compère needed to work the crowd, but that's just what he did. When the moment came he shouted out: "Let's hear! Who do you want?" The shrieked reply rivalled a jet engine for decibels. "You're not loud enough," baited Berry. Another almighty screech. "Come on now. I can't hear you!"

After half a dozen such teasers the curtains finally opened and there, as large as life in their black corduroy jackets, were the four pop princes who had dazzled the Queen Mum and Princess Margaret the night before. They pounded out 10 songs in 25 minutes of pure anarchy, 'From Me To You', 'I Saw Her Standing There', 'She Loves You', 'Twist And Shout' and the rest, all lost to the wall of screams. The average age of the girls in the first show was estimated at 14 or 15. For the later show, the girls were slightly older and slightly quieter. The accent is on the slightly. The body count stood at 11 fainters treated by ambulance men. Local papers were there to report on the pandemonium, which they did with lengthy articles and pictures the next day.

The *Slough Observer* recorded that two girls legged it from the back of the stalls during the 'Twist And Shout' finale in a bid to make the stage –

only to be dragged back by attendants. The *Slough & Windsor Express & Star* reported on excited, but well behaved, fans. Police were also impressed with The Beatles. Chief Supt Harman, in charge of operations, said of the group: "You could not wish to deal with a more co-operative group of lads." The Beatles made a clean getaway – straight offstage and out through a side door to their waiting car. Two police Jags, their sirens wailing, kept 400 fans at bay. One girl, overcome, had to be rescued by police as she attempted to throw herself into the path of the racing cars. Beatlemania was building up speed.

The following night *Chronicle & Echo* reporter Barry Newcombe was there to witness 4,000 girls descend on the ABC Cinema in Northampton for the two November 6 shows. "Every flick of slim tailored hips," he wrote, "every clap of hand and tap of winklepicker was echoed with wave upon wave of screaming so deafening that only the electronic beat stood any chance of being heard."

Newcombe's eloquence aside, this was a Beatles concert much like any other. Away from the screaming, he managed to get himself a nice exclusive – a one-on-one interview with Lennon backstage that found the Beatle in a relaxed mood. "The only time you can get away from the noise is when you're in bed," John told him. "But the noise doesn't get you down, and although everyone expects us to crack up under the strain, we're getting along nicely. We thought we had reached the top a long while ago. Then came the Royal Command Performance and soon we shall be making a film. You just can't tell when it will all end. Once, when we were out in the car, it was only girls that used to point and say 'There are The Beatles'. Now we notice that older people are noticing us. I hope we can become entertainers for the family. We love what we are doing and get a tremendous kick out of making people happy, and that's something we'd like to do for a long, long time."

The two shows got underway with the usual nightly scenes of chaos as The Beatles tried to make themselves heard. When the shows were over the usual game began. A decoy coach was sent charging out of the Lower Mounts exit with girls in hot pursuit. Finally the coach was mobbed, but The Beatles had already made their dash for freedom with a police escort across the car park behind the cinema and through what was a factory in St Michael's Road. The *Chronicle & Echo* reported that there were crowds milling around outside the ABC for another hour, but there was little trouble. A couple of youths caught trying to clamber over a wall at the back and some earache from the screamers was about as tough as it got for the police on this night. This was one of the easier ones.

Looking back now, some of those who were there remember the screaming. Spencer Secondary Modern schoolgirl Linda Ward (now Linda Gardner) recalls the excitement around Northampton that night: "I remember 'Twist And Shout', the final number, and the panic it created. Everybody just went wild. When we ran out of the cinema after the show our ears were still ringing. In fact, they were throbbing for at least an hour. We ran around the back and were convinced that we'd seen two of The Beatles at one of the windows but then we read that they had already left by then. I went with three other girls to the second show. One of the girls went to school near the ABC and she queued for the tickets. We couldn't hang around for too long afterwards because we had to dash for the last bus home. I lived in Northampton, but a couple of miles away on the other side of town. The whole town was buzzing that night. It seemed everyone was talking about The Beatles' show and asking about it. Even older people on the bus were talking about it and one said to us that we were very lucky to have gone."

Some fans went to great lengths to make sure they were there. It's not every 16-year-old girl that would have the confidence to organise a coach trip for her and her pals to enjoy something special but that's exactly what Janet Edroff did, so keen was she not to miss out. Janet, a Welwyn Garden City High School girl at the time, didn't have the pennies to get to the show from her home in Hertford, a full 60 miles from Northampton, so – thanks to her mum stumping up the deposit in advance – Janet hired a coach from Reg's Coaches of Hertford which she regularly used to get to school, and Beatle mission improbable became a reality. Looking back 46 years later, Janet, who now lives in Stevenage, says: "I can remember the terrific noise and being there to see them. I worked out that by putting my fingers half into my ears I could cut out the worst of the screams and still hear them singing – although I was probably screaming myself!" It was a life-size poster of John that adorned Janet's bedroom ceiling back then, and she is proud today that it was John who was her favourite. "I could tell even then that there was something about John," she says. "He was different from the others. I don't know how, but I could tell that he was very important. The coach picked us up and dropped us off at the school and our parents took us home from there. It certainly improved my popularity at school for a while!"

Also in the audience that night were pals Elizabeth York and Lyn Marlow who had seen the Montez tour performance at the ABC back in March. They had been there to see Roe in March – but both were now besotted with The Beatles.

Elizabeth says: "They were brilliant – and the songs they sang. They were just different – the fringes, the Beatle suits. We walked about two and a half miles from Kingsthorpe to Northampton to queue all night for the tickets. My younger sister Sandra came with us and she didn't even like The Beatles. It was a long queue, too. It went from Abingdon Square where the cinema was round the corner and up The Mount and into St Michael's Road. But it was all very nice. I remember a policeman walking by to make sure everyone was all right. I'm not sure people today would be happy to have their teenage daughters out all night like that on the pavement.

"The show itself was absolute mayhem. The screams. You could barely hear The Beatles. It started from when the compère called their names out. We stood on the seats, screaming. You couldn't help it. It was a form of hysteria really. It was just seeing them. The excitement of young girls seeing their idols. Paul was my favourite – then George. This was purely for the looks, I hasten to add. Now I think John Lennon was fantastic. As you get older, the lyrics and the songs are more important."

What was pure unadulterated bliss for the teenage girls was viewed with suspicion by their parents. "At the time the older generation didn't approve of pop stars. My dad did – he loved The Beatles – but he was very much in the minority. The older generation generally regarded them as long-haired gits. It hadn't been long since the war and they now saw younger people with money in their pockets and getting more freedom and independence."

Elizabeth's friend Lyn adds: "We knew we had to go down and queue all night to get tickets for this one. Elizabeth and I were both working at Barratt's shoe factory and we wanted to get down early so we could enjoy all the excitement of the build-up, so we went straight from work. We had dressed up for work that day. We went to the second house so the first show would still have been on when we arrived. We had good seats, too. We were on the left hand side – row J – in the stalls, so Paul was the one facing us and he was our favourite. There was so much screaming and everyone was throwing things on the stage. The papers were full of it afterwards – the locals and the nationals."

The Beatles were now preparing to fly over to Ireland for a Thursday night in Dublin and a Friday in Belfast before heading back to London on the Saturday for two dates at East Ham. And if they thought their English fans were maniacal, they hadn't seen anything yet. The Irish fans were in a class of their own for Beatle riots. Just imagine the scenes in England – and then triple them.

Even before The Beatles arrived on their flight from London there were those ready to desert Dublin as if some natural disaster was about to befall the city. They had memories of the city hosting pop concerts before and of the mayhem that could result. They also knew that with The Beatles, that mayhem would be off the scale. The Dublin date had taken up what had initially been a day off, but it made good sense to do an overnight there, and Peter Walsh had persuaded Arthur Howes to let him take it on.

The Beatles would be well looked after. Walsh had organised for his colleague, the multi-faceted Paul Russell, who ran his Starlite Artistes office in Dublin, to look after the Beatle team. Russell was a well-known personality – an entrepreneur and a drummer and vocalist with a show band. He also presented a television show. Best of all, he knew The Beatles, having spent three weeks around them on the Roy Orbison package in May/June.

There were some boys wearing Beatle haircuts along with the girl screamers to greet Aer Lingus flight E1 155 which landed at Dublin Airport in the early afternoon of a cold and damp November Thursday. The whole tour package was on this flight, with The Beatles in First Class, and when it touched down airport staff and stewardesses left their posts to ogle the group. A press conference was held in the VIP lounge, and among those present was George Harrison's mum Louise, proud of her son, The Beatles and her family's Irish roots. Russell met the group and they were soon ready to depart for the upmarket Gresham Hotel in O'Connell Street where police were already holding back lines of girls. No battered van or car that would break down this time. Russell was proudly chauffeuring them in his Chrysler Saratoga car, while the rest of the package would make their own way on a tour bus.

The impact the group had already had on the way young people behaved, dressed, wore their hair and the music they listened to cannot be exaggerated, but the impact of The Beatles in Ireland was bigger even than Beatle-barmy England. The chaos can hardly be overstated from the moment The Beatles stepped foot in Dublin until the moment they left. Brian Epstein never liked being away from "his boys", but while they were in Dublin he was in New York negotiating a deal for them to appear on Ed Sullivan's TV show. Arthur Howes was in Dublin and with him was playright Alun Owen, getting his first taste of what a day in the life of The Beatles was really like as he began researching his script for the Beatles' first movie, *A Hard Day's Night*.

The Gardai were holding back a group of girls when The Beatles arrived at the Adelphi Cinema in Middle Abbey Street around 4pm, after being smuggled in through the Prince's Street entrance.

Colm Keane in his book *The Beatles' Irish Concerts* reveals that Bob Geldof, then 12 years of age, was at the Adelphi press conference, in the company of his 16-year-old sister Lynn who had managed (as did a few others) to blag her way in. Keane's book also reveals how media savvy The Beatles were as they checked with photographers whether they wanted a portrait or landscape type shot before they took their pictures, and then posed accordingly.

As the first show began there was a fevered atmosphere. A full house of 2,304 (plus more in the aisles) got ready for a giant screamfest. Not many of those 2,304 stayed in their seats or stayed silent. The Dublin shows took the same format as those in England, with Frank Berry fighting a losing battle to be heard or even noticed as he introduced the acts. First up were The Rhythm & Blues Quartet before Berry was bouncing back onstage to introduce The Vernons Girls – a trio of Liverpool girls – Maureen Kennedy, Jean Owen and Frances Lea – who were the latest incarnation of what had originally been a 16-strong choir set up by the city's Vernons Pools company.

Amazingly, in all the furore, a heavily disguised Ringo and John managed to sneak out of the Adelphi and into a nearby pub with Kestrels Geoff Williams and Roger Greenaway to sample the delights of Guinness in its homeland. They made it back in time for their spots after the interval of the first house.

People were worshipping The Beatles, but The Vernons Girls, who had been in the business that bit longer and were of similar ages to the boys, treated them more like little brothers and Maureen in particular wasn't averse to telling a Beatle where to go if he were annoying them. Frances, the blonde one, took centre stage, with the dark haired Maureen and Jean on either side. The girls sang 'Passing Strangers' and 'Funny All Over' before launching into their latest single, 'Tomorrow Is Another Day'. All the time the tension mounted as 'Beatle time' got nearer.

The Brook Brothers were on next. Real brothers from Winchester and styled on the Everly Brothers, the Brylcreemed Ricky and Geoff had been on the showbiz circuit for five years and had catchy Top 20 hits such as 'Warpaint' and 'Aint Gonna Wash For A Week' to their credit. They battled away well, opening with 'You Gotta Learn Your Rhythm And Blues' followed by 'Warpaint' and 'Seven Daffodils'.

The colourful seven-piece Peter Jay & The Jaywalkers closed the first half. Drummer Peter knew every trick in the book – and invented a few more – to hold an audience and put on a show. They crashed straight into 'Do You Love Me?' and earned loud applause. They had the benefit of featuring well-known music by equally well-known stars in their act and it paid dividends as they played tunes made popular by The Temperance Seven, Acker Bilk, Russ Conway and The Shadows. They also played their own neat little trick on the audience. The lights went out and Jay announced, "Ladies and gentlemen, the moment you've all been waiting for . . . The Beatles!" The curtains opened and the audience took in those familiar four mop-tops taking a big bow. The screams hit the roof for some seconds before the teens gradually realised it was Jaywalkers in Beatle wigs taking the bow. They closed out with their own hit record, 'Can Can 62'.

The biggest Beatle riots were seen in Dublin, but it is to the credit of those audiences that the other artists on the bill were given a fair hearing. The Kestrels, ever professional, went down very well – their humour, mimicry, first class singing and stage presence endearing them to the Dublin teens after Berry introduced them at the start of the second half. Their version of Lennon and McCartney's 'There's A Place' got a loud cheer, as did 'Green Green'. It was soon time for Berry to wind things up for The Beatles. Not that things needed much winding up.

He led the crowds in chanting "We Want The Beatles" until the curtains parted and there on the stage they were, letting rip with 'I Saw Her Standing There'. Great song followed great song – 'From Me To You' and then 'All My Loving' (a song as yet little known to most fans as their second LP, on which it featured, was still some days from release). Ringo was given his customary song – 'Boys' – and then the spotlight was on Paul for 'Till There Was You'. They stepped it up with the big one – 'She Loves You' – but it was virtually obliterated by the screams. The stewards had managed to keep some semblance of order but when the group finally launched into 'Twist And Shout' it was greeted by the big charge. It seemed like hundreds rushed the stage from the stalls. Anyone who stood in their way – including burly attendants – was simply crushed by the mob. Among the many objects lobbed at the stage was a torch someone had snatched from an usher. Others stood on their seats, screaming, clapping and stamping their feet. Pandemonium ruled.

Peter Jay recalls: "We were off first and there were just thousands of people screaming at you. We weren't trying to look like The Beatles but it was the style – the quiffs had gone and the hair was forward. I went to America just after that tour – just for a holiday – I can remember walking down the street in Miami and people were shouting at me from the other side of the street. You could have landed from another planet – and this is just because you had long hair. I had a leather coat on and I know it was hot. I went into one store and there was almost a riot. Because you had long hair, a leather coat on and an English accent, you had to be one of The Beatles, and they would start coming at you and you would have to leave. It seems unbelievable now."

The 2,304-plus fans left the first show, but didn't want to go home. Outside, waiting to get in for the second house, were another 2,304, plus around 2,000 ticket-less fans desperate to hear what they could from outside and perhaps even get a glimpse of a Beatle later. They would not be budged. It was a recipe for disaster. Up to 7,000 people were now milling around outside and the Gardai were beginning to fear the worst. The back doors of the cinema were opened so that some people could exit via Princes Street, thereby relieving pressure at the front of the house, but the sheer volume of people surrounding the cinema was getting out of hand.

Many headed towards Middle Abbey Street once they got out and the Gardai were soon forced into taking steps to seal off the road. This was a pop concert, but the scene was rapidly descending into a street riot. People were getting hurt – fans and officers. Youths began to launch themselves at the Gardai. Barriers were knocked down, fights broke out and a teenager was stabbed. Traffic was gridlocked, windows smashed and squad cars raced to the scene . . . and all this while St John Ambulance volunteers attempted to treat around 20 young fans who had fainted. The normal trick of sneaking The Beatles out in an evening newspaper van worked and they travelled the short distance back to the Gresham Hotel while thousands remained outside the cinema, convinced they were inside.

Looking back, Peter Jay says: "It was crackers. They were turning cars over and setting fire to them. In our minds, at that stage, this was pretty cool. If you were going to have a riot, yeah, have a proper riot. I didn't even see it. We just heard about it. This was all a bit of fun when you're 18 or 19, because Dublin had a reputation for being quite a wild city. I can't remember anything about the plane trip. All I remember is just getting off there and getting all this reaction."

The Beatles did a quick interview and George headed off to meet family in nearby Drumcondra. The Beatles rose the next morning to unwelcome headlines in the Irish newspapers that reflected on the scenes of devastation the night before, and of those injured in them. The inside pages carried little about any music they made. The reporters hadn't heard much of it.

The Beatles remained in their bedrooms digesting the bad news until departing The Gresham Hotel shortly before noon in a car with darkened windows. But people knew who was in that car. They were cheered as they passed through towns and villages on their way to Belfast and what they hoped would be a calmer reception.

Predictably, there was a sizeable crowd outside the old Ritz Cinema in Fisherwick Place when they arrived in Belfast shortly before 4pm. The 2,200 seat venue had sold out for both shows – and could have done so several times over. The Beatles met their Irish fan club secretary and posed for pictures at their press call and then headed for the sanctuary of their dressing room.

As always, once The Beatles – and the other performers – were inside the theatre there was no getting out, short of a disguise and a very large risk of injury. Colm Keane in *The Beatles' Irish Concerts* quotes photographer Stanley Matchett as saying the press conference was held in the auditorium itself, The Beatles sitting on seats in the empty theatre to answer questions from a few local journalists. Conditions were reportedly stark, too. The Beatles were cold, hungry and tired, huddling around a one-bar fire backstage when they met one journalist before retreating to their room.

The first house commenced at 6.30pm and the other acts went through their well worked routines – The Kestrels earning a cheer for 'There's A Place'. When it was time for The Beatles, they trotted onto the stage to a wall of screaming and a mass of lobbed objects. St John Ambulance volunteers were again kept busy reviving the fainters. It's hard to exaggerate the effect they had on that crowd by just simply setting foot on the stage. Mass hysteria is perhaps the best description.

Fan Teddy Copeland, who was upstairs in the front row of the balcony, and projectionist Danny Devlin, who was high up at the back working the spots, were amazingly able to hear the music despite the din.

The group played their usual 10-song set list, with their regular patter and introductions and their now famous bows at the end of each song. From 'I Saw Her Standing There' at the start to the rip-it-up 'Twist And Shout' at the end the screaming never stopped. The first house was considered relatively orderly, compared with the second. Several girls made a dash for the stage, while others jumped up and down on their seats and shrieked their heads off. Missiles – from all directions – had to be dodged. It was getting to the point where all appeals were useless.

The police insisted on their own tactic for extricating The Beatles after the concert and the usual disguised van trick was abandoned. Instead, the theatre was cleared and The Beatles were led out through the front into their waiting car so people could see them leave and not hang around the streets.

Even as The Beatles walked through the foyer fans were passing out at the mere sight of them. It is no exaggeration to suggest that even in a country as devoutly religious as Ireland, those who worshipped them reacted as though they were witnessing the Second Coming, working themselves up into a kind of spiritual fervour. This exit was an odd tactic that was not to be repeated, and it was an uncomfortable parting for the Fabs. Some were close enough to maul them and they did so as The Beatles were bundled unceremoniously into their car.

People swarmed around the Beatlemobile so it was forced to inch its way along on what would normally be only a five-minute journey to the Grand Central Hotel in Royal Avenue where The Beatles were to spend the night. They headed straight for their rooms, where food was waiting for them, and there they stayed. In England, a few stragglers might be hanging around outside the hotel, hoping for a glimpse of a Beatle. On this night in Belfast there was up to 2,000.

Around 100 were still there the next morning as The Beatles set off rather late for Aldergrove Airport and a flight back to London and two houses at the Granada Cinema in East Ham. The Beatles' whirlwind tour of Ireland had left scenes of devastation in its wake. The other performers had been caught up in that whirlwind, too, but they largely enjoyed the experience, if Peter Jay is anything to go by. "Our trip to Ireland was planned like a military operation," he says. "Not even the members of the package knew the departure time. Dublin was fantastic. The fans there really do go mad. Girls who fainted in the crowds outside the theatre were carried into their seats by attendants. Outside, there was the biggest riot yet. Cars were overturned and the police had to make several arrests. Inside, it was incredible for noise and appreciation. Belfast was the same – like a Wembley football crowd. All streaming towards the theatre. We all had to live on fish and chips sent in because anybody in the show would have been mobbed if they strayed into a restaurant."

Jay recalled that customs allowed The Beatles straight through with no checks. Brook Brother Rick was not so fortunate. Customs opened his suitcase and sent all his personal gear along the conveyor belt – toothbrush, pyjamas, comb, underwear, the lot – for all to see.

There was no time to recover from the tumultuous Irish adventure. No sooner had the boys landed in London than they were off for the two shows that Saturday night at the Granada Cinema. It was only a week into the tour but The Beatles were showing signs of strain. They looked and felt drained from the travelling and the sense of being constantly under siege, in fear for themselves and for the safety of their fans as night after night extraordinary, bewildering scenes were being acted out. The authorities were at full stretch as teenagers took leave of their senses, behaving outlandishly wherever The Beatles went. If they were already exhausted, there was one very welcome bit of news. Their fifth single, 'I Want To Hold Your Hand', which was not due to be released for nearly three weeks, had pre-orders that were set to top the million mark. This set a new record in UK chart history.

Every silver lining had a cloud, though. "That's great, but how are we going to top that?" asked John when George Martin visited them in their dressing room before the East Ham shows to give them the great news.

Meanwhile, momentum was building up fast again outside. The thousands who turned out in Ireland were almost matched in London that afternoon, with an estimated 6,000 fans waiting outside the Barking Road cinema.

The Beatles arrived at 3.50pm and scuttled inside. They were able to have a soundcheck and an unfortunate volunteer was sent out for cheese sandwiches. He was duly mobbed, with The Beatles watching on from the safety of a dressing room window. Peter Jay watched from another window, amazed that The Beatles' sandwich carrier had to be given a police escort. There was dessert, courtesy of four local office girls who had baked a cake. Strangely, the same volunteer had an easier ride later, slipping in through the front doors largely unnoticed to bring in a hot supper for the group.

The Beatles were very photogenic and a couple of noted photographers were inside the cinema to capture the magic of a Beatles concert that night. The celebrated *Observer* photographer Jane Bown took some classic pictures of the group relaxing backstage. They could have been taken on any night, if truth be told, because one cinema was very much like any other in 1960s Britain. Jane's photos, though, had a charm of their own, capturing the boys in relaxed mood before the shows.

"Ringo was playing patience, Paul was reading, John strumming and George was sitting by an immersion heater," Jane recalled. "It went on for a very long time. I could have taken a lot more, but I didn't. They didn't seem to mind me. I think they rather enjoyed it because someone said perhaps it's time I went and one of them – it may have been Ringo – said, 'Oh no, we like her here'. So that was nice." Jane also took photos of some cherub-faced fans queuing outside, Beatle photos, pens and auto-graph books in hand. An up-and-coming young society photographer called David Bailey wasn't going to miss out on an opportunity like this on his East Ham doorstep either.

The concerts? A giant screamfest of course, with the group, in their light blue collarless suits, battling to be heard, their Vox amps a tiny presence on the giant stage with huge gathered curtains, after the rest of the package had battled equally hard for some attention. The Beatles put in an energetic performance, despite their Irish blitz, and despite the fact that few could hear them.

Some locals remembered the night in a 1994 *Memory Lane* TV segment. They talked of the long queues for tickets beforehand – and again to get in on the night – and the excitement in the area in the run-up to the show. The jelly babies rained down on those in the front row of the stalls, and as for hearing The Beatles that night – it depended on where you were sitting.

Amy Cook, who has since died, did hear them, because she was one of the lucky ones near the front. In the programme, she told viewers: "I can't remember who was on with them because all I cared about was seeing The Beatles. When Paul sang 'Till There Was You' I just melted. People just screamed and screamed and jumped up and down and I know it sounds crazy, but I could hear the songs."

Others reported that the noise wasn't just coming from the girls – the boys were on their feet hollering, too, with all efforts by the stewards to keep them in their seats doomed to failure. Peter Jay: "It was nice to be back in Cockneyland, but the crowds outside the theatre were just as big [as Ireland]." The excitement was showing no sign of abating. The cinema building is one of those that survives . . . as a bingo hall.

Next day The Beatles set off for the Midlands for two Sunday shows at the Birmingham Hippodrome. It was evidently a quieter night, largely because fans stayed at home to watch their appearance on the Royal Variety Show on television. The *Birmingham Mail* reported that there were far bigger crowds outside the stage doors for other pop shows than there were this night for The Beatles. The newspaper said there was a maximum of 400 outside the stage door and even those waiting to get in were relatively orderly.

The lucky few with tickets for the Hippodrome saw The Beatles in the flesh but missed a rare opportunity to see them on the telly. All four Beatle songs were included in a show which began shortly before 7.30pm and finished at 10.30pm, and from the fans' point of view it was a pity that video recorders weren't around in 1963. But from the point of view of The Beatles, the TV appearance offered a welcome relief from the chaos. They arrived in a police van to be smuggled in but for once didn't need it. They even had time to pose for smiley pictures in police helmets before the show – an unthinkable prospect on normal tour nights. A po-faced police spokesman said: "No official order was given for The Beatles to wear the helmets. The fact that they did so was purely a spontaneous gesture on their part as they stepped out of the van near the stage door. Uniformed police had been with them in the van."

With so many excitable youngsters safely at home watching The Beatles on television, it meant security staff inside the venue had a much easier time. Maureen Beresford was one of those who didn't make it. At 13, she was considered too young to be there, but her brothers John, 19, who was in the Territorial Army, and Tom, 23, who had just left the Army, were among a group of tough young lads hired to beef up security around the stage.

Although Beatle-besotted Maureen was disappointed to miss the show, her brother John put a smile on her face. Maureen (now Maureen O'Neill) says: "John brought home the programme for me. It was signed 'To Maureen with love from The Beatles' in Paul's handwriting, and John, George and Ringo had added their names. Peter Jay and The Brook Brothers also signed. John also gave me Ringo's cigarette packet and two toy fluffy dogs that had been thrown on the stage."

Maureen was the envy of her pals at Lozells Girls School in Birmingham. "We were all Beatles fans. One girl was called Georgina Harrison. As you might imagine, everybody used to ask her, are you George's sister?"

Despite the smaller waiting crowds, it was the normal secret squirrel routine. The Fabs had arrived in Birmingham a little late due to an unexpected hitch. Their Austin Princess, rapidly knocking up the miles on this tour, broke down again on the M1 on the way up from London and had to be towed off. They had a meal while it was repaired and then arrived at the rendezvous – the police headquarters in Steelhouse Lane – rather late. Even so, there was time for them to drink tea and sign autographs while they prepared for the next leg of the journey – to Digbeth police station a few streets from the Hippodrome. A van was prepared to take them into the lions' den. However, this was one night when the storm never materialised.

Even at the change-over between the two houses when 2,000 teens were ushered out and 2,000 more were ushered in, there were no reported incidents. Of course, some things don't change. The Beatles battled the constant screams during their two sets, with both audiences unlikely to have heard much above the din they were themselves making. The Beatles, and the whole entourage, were doubtless grateful, however, for a relatively calm night. The Beatles in their van, chased by only a small group of teenage girls, were heading out of Birmingham even as the National Anthem was being played at the end. The only damage reported that night were some tributes to the group, penned in lipstick on the rough-cast.

Hippodrome manager Wilf May was unquestionably the most relieved man in Birmingham. "Every credit must be given to the Birmingham police for the way they organised the evening," he says. "Everything went smoothly. The audiences, in their own way, were good, too. They came in quietly, had a long scream and shout, and then went home."

Of course, this is The Beatles we are talking about, so something out of the ordinary had to occur. One of five youths who had climbed onto the top of a nearby building managed to put his foot through the roof but survived unscathed and, just to soothe any fears that The Beatles were losing their magic powers, several girls inside the theatre had to be treated for hysteria. Thank goodness for that!

On a more serious note, the price to be paid for fame on such a ridiculous level was illustrated by John's absence earlier in the day from the christening of his son Julian at a church in Hoylake. Though efforts were made to conceal the existence of Julian and John's wife Cynthia, fans soon found out and – in truth – it didn't seem to harm The Beatles' popularity one jot.

The next stop on the tour, after a rare day off, was Portsmouth for two shows at the Guildhall on Tuesday, November 12. The *Portsmouth Evening News* had been building up the event for days with 'The Beatles Are Coming' tasters publicising the show, and had even produced a lavish four-page supplement inside the newspaper on the day. All police leave had been cancelled and security beefed up in anticipation of another bout of Beatlemania – but then rumours began to spread that The Beatles would not be appearing.

The *News* carried a Stop Press confirming that the group had arrived in Portsmouth – Ringo on a flight down from Liverpool and the other three by car from London – in spite of reports from London that Paul had been struck down with gastric flu. The paper quickly gathered enough details to run an article headlined 'The Beatles Go On – Despite Flu'. The report stated that all four were suffering with flu, but quoted John as saying: "The show must go on."

The boys had been concealed in a Corporation van which made its way safely to the Guildhall entrance without drawing much attention from a crowd of about 50 fans. They soon realised what was happening but police held them back as the group were ushered in. No sooner had the City Extra edition ran the story saying the show was on than a message got through saying that Paul was too unwell to appear. Another Stop Press was published in a later edition confirming the bad news.

Sharp-eyed viewers who tuned into Southern Television's *Day By Day* programme that evening would have noticed Paul visibly wilting during an interview with reporter Jeremy James in their dressing room. John did most of the talking as they fielded the usual round of questions. Are you boys beginning to find it tough going round the country at such tremendous speed, asked James, as if sensing their discomfort. A straight bat from The Beatles. Well what about being mobbed? "The police get mobbed, we don't," replied John. The group then explained how they were smuggled into the venue by van before the inevitable question, "What will you do when it's all over?'" "Sail away on a yacht." piped up George. The reporter commented on Ringo's scarf and he replied with commendable humour: "It's my old school scarf – Borstal High!" As the interview continued John noticed Paul wilting and Paul raised his eyebrows and gave a quiet whistle. At that moment it was clear they would not be playing that day. The Portsmouth headlines the next day wrote themselves. 'Crowds Weep Over Beatles', declared the *News*, with another edition reassuring: 'The Beatles Are Not "Cracking Up"'.

Even as the Fab Four lay in the bedroom of their hideaway, the Royal Beach Hotel in Southsea, reading about the show that never was, they vowed to return. It was John who sent down a message to reporters saying they were aware that fans had camped out for days for tickets, and a spokesman confirmed that Paul had gone straight to bed with a temperature of 102. A police inspector guarding The Beatles was ready to call for reinforcements should enough girls discover where they were staying. Back at the Guildhall, the 2,000 with tickets had gathered in disbelief as a *News* bill pasted on the venue confirmed 'The Beatles Show Off'. Nobody was moving until, in desperation, Guildhall entertainments manager David Evans grabbed a stage loudspeaker to broadcast the news. "You can vent your enthusiasm somewhere else – not on the Guildhall steps," he added.

Tearful girls craned their necks to look through the windows, only to see Portsmouth's city councillors gathering for a meeting. Three girls who had queued for two days were sobbing in despair, another threw herself on the ground, weeping. Others remained, defiantly singing 'She Loves You' for some time outside before eventually moving on to nearby coffee bars, many of them still tearfully clutching precious copies of that four-page *News* supplement. The Wednesday Late Extra edition ran a more optimistic story headlined 'Beatles Returning To Portsmouth' with a pledge from the group that they would be back. "The promoter is already fixing a date," said George.

After a night's rest The Beatles emerged, ready to face a new day. Hotel employee Lilly Morin had the much envied job of serving them a breakfast of boiled eggs, toast and tea and instantly pronounced them a hit. "I think they are lovely," she said. "They are good boys. They were very considerate to me and I would like to wish them luck!"

Paul looked in much better shape, cheerily greeting the waiting press as they left the Royal Beach Hotel through a back entrance at 10.45am the next day. George confirmed that all of the group had been unwell, but Paul was worst hit. Promoter Arthur Howes, meanwhile, had his business hat on. The show goes on at Plymouth tonight, he told the press, and a doctor was on hand if needed. The Beatles and Neil Aspinall, in their Austin Princess, met a Westward Television team headed by producer John Bartlett in the car park of the Lyneham Inn just off the A38 at Plympton. The Beatles, as if to underline that they had recovered, emerged from the car to clown for the cameras.

They donned their coats, and Paul playfully collapsed into the arms of John and George, with Ringo fanning him furiously. George held up the *Daily Mirror* which had run a front page story about Paul's illness, along with a picture. It was classic knockabout Beatle comedy to show they were back in business. They politely declined an offer of a Pickfords van and headed for the TV studios with their guests in the Austin Princess.

Stuart Hutchinson briefly interviewed them for Westward's teen show *Move Over, Dad*, on which Paul dismissed exaggerated reports of his illness while John, still wearing an overcoat, coughed and thumped his chest. There was a secondary benefit to the TV appearance: a tunnel ran from Westward Television to the Athenaeum Theatre just yards from the ABC Cinema in George Street where they were to play.

Among those at the 4pm press call that day was 19-year-old Mike Cox, a photographer for the *Western Evening Herald* and the *Western Morning News*. Cox had a tough night, dashing back to the office a couple of hundred yards away to leave the press call pictures to be processed before rushing back to the ABC to photograph the massive queues of girls and then – with the best view in the house – snapping The Beatles from the edge of the stage as they ripped their way through their first set. Then it was another dash back to the office with live pictures, then back to do it all over again for the second show.

Cox, a Beatles fan, was running on adrenalin that night, but he said the Fab Four were taking everything in their stride. "They were so relaxed, so laid-back it wasn't true. We just sat on chairs drinking tea and chatted to them like we were chatting to our mates. There was no security in those days. That's how it seemed. Once they got inside the cinema away from the screaming fans, they could just relax and be themselves."

Cox wasn't embarrassed to ask for autographs – and The Beatles obliged. "The funny thing is I was talking to George the most, but I ended up with my programme signed by the other three . . . and John had signed twice for some reason. Onstage, they were great. There was nobody like them. Everyone was on a high and really enjoyed it. They were light years ahead of everyone else."

Silent black and white footage remains of The Beatles onstage that night, thankfully bouncing with health in their dark, velvet-collared stage suits, bashing out their hits to the usual barrage of screams from more than 2,000 fans at each house. The footage was taken for the BBC by Colin Rowe who was at the show with his wife Peggy and their eight-year-old daughter Gina. "I filmed the performance and the crowd and there were some fantastic scenes – all the screaming and throwing of knickers at the stage," he says. "I just kept shooting and shooting and shooting. When you are filming you are so single-minded that the event passes over you, and I was 30 at the time, with a young family. I was not at the age to be impressed by all that. But Peggy remembers the noise all right and that when she was driving the few miles home to Hartley afterwards her ears suddenly popped and she could hear again!"

Gina's abiding memory is of the screaming and of joining her dad when he filmed before the show. "I remember hiding behind dad's leg when he was with them. I was eight at the time and very shy. I could hear talking, but I was hiding away. I joined my mum and her friend Jean for the show. It would have been the first house as I was so young – and I remember our ears popping on that journey home and my mum's relief when they did. We were a long way from the stage so I couldn't see much of them either."

Among those who rubbed shoulders with The Beatles that night was Stephan Chase and he witnessed some classic Beatle banter. "I happened to be in Westward TV visiting the editor Lefcos Greco," he says. "I knew some of the personnel, having worked on the odd programme myself. I waited with several other people on a stairwell overlooking the dark passage and as the Fab Four emerged one by one we followed them upstairs to a larger landing near the rear exit. It was very exciting. They all looked so Beatley, dark fringed and skinny in their Beatle suits. We hung out together inside the unlit exit for about 15 minutes.

"I remember one little bit of dialogue when in the general confusion of the exit Paul's voice called out 'Hey George, where's Ringo?' From somewhere behind, Ringo's lugubrious voice answered, 'I'm over here you bloody fool!' My then girlfriend was egging me on to ask for autographs but, thinking myself rather cool, I didn't want to be so obvious. After a bit more nagging, however, I consented, saying something irritable like, 'Oh, all right then, I might as well.'

"The coat in front of me turned around sharply at my remark and I found myself nose to nose with Mr Lennon who said, in that laconic yet threatening Liverpudlian way of his: 'Yes, you might as well, mightn't you!' He grabbed the grubby little bit of paper proffered, signed for me and passed it on around all four of them to various sarky comments. I stuffed it in my pocket. Paul underlined his autograph with the word 'Beatles' in case of any confusion!"

Stephan asked Ringo what he thought of Marlene Dietrich, whom the group had met at the Royal Command performance. "Old," replied Ringo, rather uncharitably.

Chief Constable John Fawke Skittery described the Plymouth teenagers as "highly excited, but perfectly well behaved". And they were – so long as you deem jumping on the seats, hurling objects and screaming at the top of your voice as good behaviour. The tunnel made the perfect escape route at the end, but not everything went exactly as planned. Hundreds of fans, armed with their Beatle photos and autograph books, waited at the back. The Beatles dashed out of the cinema into the theatre and on to the tunnel leading to the TV studios to the Austin Princess in the car park.

However, there were so many fans milling about that, inevitably, some had found the car. Police advised The Beatles to sit quietly on the stairs and there they remained with the door slightly ajar for 10 minutes until the police arrived in the Austin Princess to rescue them. They spent that night at the Imperial Hotel in Torquay ready for the next day's short trek westward to the ABC cinema in Exeter.

As ever, word had got around as to where they were staying and about 100 girls were loitering outside the hotel by mid-afternoon, hoping for a glimpse of them. Once inside The Beatles didn't leave their rooms, but they were in good spirits the next day, joking with fans and signing autographs as they left.

At Exeter, as everywhere else, tickets for The Beatles were a precious commodity. They were reportedly changing hands for up to £5 (approximately £78 today with inflation) in the hours leading up to the show, with ABC manager Bob Parker explaining to reporters that the cinema could have sold their 1,800 seats for each show a dozen times over. "Cancellations because of illness? Certainly not. They would crawl on their hands and knees to see The Beatles, however ill they were," he concluded.

Such was the excitement that several of the London Inn Square cinema's side windows were broken by fans desperate to get in, while others contented themselves with singing, shouting and screaming in the streets outside. The Beatles had managed to sneak in through a side door while members of other groups on the bill were signing autographs at the front. Once inside, as ever, their biggest problem was boredom after they'd finished the soundcheck.

This was solved by their personal Mr Fix It Neil Aspinall who brought a large parcel into their dressing room. Inside was a Scalextric set – a model car racing track – with four racing cars for four Beatles. When playtime was over, they held their pre-show press conference, with John remarking about how life on the road had changed. "It's a bit dodgy if you all go out together, but if you go out alone it's all right," he said.

Exactly how well The Beatles played this night was almost impossible to tell, unless perhaps you were in the front two or three rows. Each night seemed to be more chaotic than the last as the excitement built everywhere on this tour. Berry tried his best. "And here they are . . . John, Paul," but George and Ringo were lost to the din. A hail of jelly babies rained on the stage, with George appearing particularly flustered. With 25 police trying to keep order, backed by Red Cross volunteers, delirious fans in their seats were waving scarves and programmes. They made so much racket that The Beatles could have been singing anything.

It was an unusual exit, even by Beatle standards. An ambulance and two police cars – with policemen huddling around – created a great deal of attention at one side door, while few fans took any notice of a van parked at the other side with a young girl called Ann Maddison at the wheel. The Beatles sneaked through a side door into Ann's van to be driven away, with only a handful of fans getting near enough to touch them. Ann's father was a friend of cinema manager Bob Parker and she was doubtless delighted to come to the group's rescue. They didn't have far to travel that night, staying in the upmarket Rougemont Hotel in Queen Street, though some fans were in hot pursuit. It was 2am before they finally turned in after a turkey and ham supper with (not very rock'n'roll) Horlicks to wash down the sandwiches.

The Beatles were up at 9.30am to breakfast on fruit juice, Corn Flakes, toast and marmalade and tea . . . before going back to bed at 10am for a couple of hours of extra kip. By 12.30pm they were heading out of The Rougemont towards Bristol for Friday afternoon and evening shows at Colston Hall. They didn't spare the horses on this particular journey, with the Austin Princess reaching up to 70mph. There was no question of them breaking the law. Exeter police escorted them to the city boundary – dubbed Checkpoint Ringo – where a Devon police car took over to see them to Checkpoint McCartney on the Somerset/Devon boundary, at which point another car led them up the A38 to Bedminster Down where Bristol police took over. They stopped briefly in a Bedminster side street to phone Colston Hall to let them know they were a few minutes away, then, guided in by a *Bristol Evening Post* van, they cut through the busy traffic and into Colston Street across the yard into the hall. They were safely inside before the gates closed in front of a pack of screaming girls.

Operation Get The Beatles Into Colston Hall Safely was deemed a success and the heat was off for at least a few hours until Operation Get Them Out Again. There were literally hundreds of girls around Colston Hall for up to eight hours. Many had skipped work, risking sack. The hall's famous red doors were now adorned with messages of love for various Beatles. Tickets were being hawked at inflated prices, along with Beatle photos, and local sweet shops sold out of jelly babies.

BEATLEMANIA !

It's happening everywhere.. even in sedate Cheltenham

*Out of this world!
These are the symptoms of Beatlemania.*

The with-it bug bites so hard ..

EVERYONE, everywhere is catching it. IT is called Beatlemania.

Earlier this week it swept Sweden.

Last night it hit sedate Cheltenham—traditional home of retired brigadiers, colonels . . . and the Ladies' College.

And if you haven't got it yet, these fantastic pictures show just what Beatlemania can do.

Cheltenham loved it.

The four pop-singing Beatles took the place of classics for two concerts—the start of a five-week British tour.

Screamed

And 1,890 Beatlemaniacs squealed and screamed right through the opening number.

Beatles' leader John Lennon, 23, bawled for quiet. It but brought more squeals.

As Lennon and his fellow-Beatles, Paul McCartney, Ringo Starr and George Harrison, struggled manfully on, girls rushed to the stage.

Two fans fell into the orchestra pit. The second-house reception was even more ecstatic.

Hundreds stood on their seats, waving coats and umbrellas.

Programmes were thrown on to the stage—with telephone numbers written on them in lipstick. . . .

OUT OF THIS WORLD! The strong arm of the law holds back a fan with a bad attack of Beatlemania.
Pictures by Mirror Cameramen Bill Elmann and Maurice Tibbles.

By the middle of the November/December 1963 tour The Beatles were headline news wherever they went. *(Mirrorpix)*

Beatlemania, Sunderland, November 30, 1963. (*Ian Wright*)

The Beatles on stage at the Globe Theatre, Stockton-on-Tees, November 22, 1963.
(*Ian Wright*)

A breach of the peace. Frenzied Beatles fans and a harassed policeman watch the
band perform at Manchester ABC, November 20, 1963. (*Press Association*)

Shake it up baby now… the girls react in the usual manner to John, Paul, George and Ringo. The blonde in the leather jacket may look familiar – she seems to pop up at every Beatles gig! *(Press Association)*

Final preparations… A member of staff polishes handrails as The Beatles soundcheck at the ABC Cinema in Manchester, November 1963.
(Mark & Colleen Hayward/Getty Images)

December 2, 1963: The Beatles in cabaret at the ballroom of the Grosvenor House Hotel in London's Park Lane for a charity show. *(Popperfoto/Getty Images)*

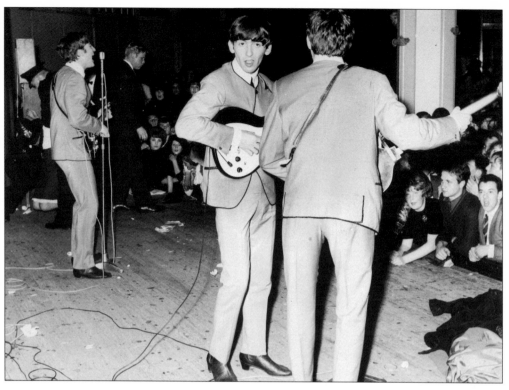

George turns away, perhaps to dodge flying jelly-babies, at Sheffield City Hall, November 2, 1963. *(Bettmann/CORBIS)*

The Beatles backstage at Sheffield, November, 1963. *(Bettmann/CORBIS)*

December 15, 1963: The Birmingham *Evening Mail* competition winners meet The Beatles;
left to right – Cheryl Fellows, Paul, theatre manager Edward Turner, Carol Ann Young, George,
Patricia Thacker, John, Mary Hatwell, Ringo and Yvette Jones. *(Mirrorpix)*

John and George sign autographs for PC T. Payne at the
Hippodrome Theatre Birmingham, November 10, 1963. *(Mirrorpix)*

The Beatles backstage with local promoters, Stockton-on-Tees, November 22, 1963. (*Ian Wright*)

Poker faces… A game of cards was one way for Beatles to amuse themselves as they waited their turn on stage during the autumn/winter tour of 1963. (*Express/Getty Images*)

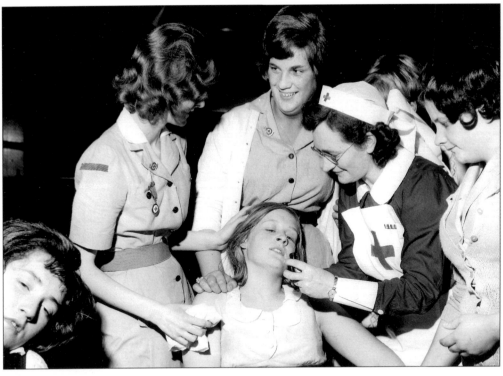

Nurses tend to one of hundreds of fans who fainted during The Beatles UK appearances, this one from the Globe Theatre, Stockton-on-Tees, November 22, 1963. *(Ian Wright)*

An usher carries away another fan who fainted during the Stockton-on-Tees show on November 22. *(Ian Wright)*

Fans and paparazzi surround The Beatles' limousine during their November/December 1963 UK Tour. *(Popperfoto/Getty Images)*

The *Evening Post* spoke to 15-year-old Sue Godfrey of Avonmouth, who captured the mood with: "We'll see The Beatles, even if we have to break in." But it was another girl who tried to climb a 15ft wall at the back to get in.

Bristol was the hometown of The Kestrels and they took the opportunity to talk to their local newspaper about the pressures of going on just before The Beatles. Roger Greenaway told the *Post*: "It's quite a struggle. By the time we go on the fans are getting worked up to fever pitch for The Beatles. They scream and shout for them and frankly, they just don't want to know us. They think we are keeping them from their idols." He made it clear that it hadn't affected their relationship with their illustrious touring mates. "We enjoy The Beatles. They're a great crowd to appear with," he said, "but this screaming isn't our cup of tea."

The *Post* published a series of photos that perfectly captured The Beatles' visit. There was a picture of the group relaxing in the hours before the storm, and the customary shot of St John volunteers leading out stricken girls, plus a picture of The Beatles performing, with a line of security men protecting the stage. Not every newspaper was allowed to take pictures of The Beatles onstage on these tours. Kestrel Geoff Williams recalled that cinemas tended to have different rules from concert halls. "Charles Lockier did the Colston Hall shows in Bristol and he wouldn't let any photographers backstage to take photos. We went over to the green room and met the press and borrowed a camera and there is a picture of all of us together. Similarly, Arthur Kimbrel had the De Montfort Hall in Leicester and I'm pretty sure that he wouldn't let photographers take stage pictures. The cinemas were a different kettle of fish."

Reporter Roger Bennett, sporting his very own Beatle haircut, tried to hear what he could over the screams, and saw one girl evade the lines of security to leap onto the back of an astonished Lennon. Around 30 girls fainted. After the shows the fans left the hall to join many more waiting outside to catch a glimpse of them leaving. Police estimate that up to 5,000 people were in the streets around Colston Hall chanting and screaming for The Beatles.

A police van took The Beatles to the outskirts of Bristol to their Austin Princess, which took them to the Francis Hotel in Bath where they stayed that night. Around 500 fans had somehow discovered the group was staying at the hotel, and they proved a major headache for police trying to get The Beatles inside. Girls tried to squeeze through the revolving doors, and other guests staying at the hotel were trapped inside for three hours. Things were beginning to get out of hand. The cloak and dagger operations may have been amusing at first, but when it was night after night the novelty wore off quickly, particularly when there was a real chance of people being seriously hurt if things went wrong. It's not difficult to see why The Beatles were beginning to feel they were under siege.

Next day the tour was headed for the seaside with two Saturday shows at the Winter Gardens in Bournemouth.

To be in prime position for a ticket at a Beatles show, you had to be dedicated. For this tour such dedication meant camping out on the pavement on a chilly or wet autumn evening about a month before the big day. On the front page of the *Bournemouth Evening Echo* on Saturday, October 26 was a photo of three teenage girls huddled in a blanket camping outside the Winter Gardens. They had been there for more than two days to secure their tickets for The Beatles' visit, which was to take place three weeks later. The girls held up copies of music papers to cover their faces, claiming their parents and bosses didn't know they were there.

Queues that had started forming at 8.30am on the Thursday had grown to 60 overnight and then grew and grew, stretching from the steps of the Winter Gardens down the paths to the edge of Cranborne Road and then up another path and around to the back of the theatre, until they numbered around 600. It was considered worth it for prime tickets to see the Fab Four. To write in was not enough, even when you were paying an enormous sum. The theatre returned a cheque for £134 10s for 316 tickets to the Junior Leaders Regiment at Bovington Camp!

It was no longer just a matter of hurling jelly babies to tickle a Beatle's tastebuds. Cake baking was becoming a regular thing. Teenage sisters Tania and Marion Turner made an iced cake, complete with Beatles and chocolate guitars, to present to the band. They weren't alone. Winter Gardens' manager Samuel Bell reported that dozens of assorted toys, sweets, cakes and other gifts were sent in. Screaming girls were gathering from 11am and by show time the theatre was under siege with 120 police trying to keep order.

The Beatles were brought to the front of the theatre in a windowless police van at 4.30pm. There was to be no decoy vehicle on this day. Police sprang from behind the curtained entrance doors at the front and linked arms to form a corridor for the smiling Beatles to run the gauntlet of the screaming hordes.

They met the press and were quickly led to meet the Mayor and Mayoress and inspect the hundreds of goodies sent in for them by the fans. One letter – 55 pages in total – contained more than 10,000 "pleases" for autographs, at a cost to the writers of three pens, three writing pads . . . and two sprained wrists.

The Beatles were soon relaxing in the privacy of their dressing room, the Scalextric Neil had bought in Exeter once again the centre of attention. A picture of them with it graced the front page of the *Bournemouth Evening Echo*. Journalist Dave Haith was accorded the privilege of joining them for a race. "I was working for a press agency and had been sent along to cover the show. I was taken to their dressing room and they were having great fun with it. I thought it would be a good thing to have some fun with them so I asked if I could join in. One of them handed me a controller and there I was, racing The Beatles . . . until I crashed on a corner! They were a fun bunch of lads. They had a quip for every sentence. It amazed me that they didn't show any sign of nerves at all about the fact they were going to go out and play for all those people.

"I suppose it helped that nobody could really hear anything because of all the screaming. They were a sensation. You didn't quite know why it was happening. Sam Bell told me some of the seats were absolutely soaking afterwards."

Haith had enjoyed special privileges in the dressing room, but he was left standing for the concert. "Sam used to dish out free tickets to reporters and often their wives or pals, too. I remember in this case it was different, though, because there was such a clamour for seats that the press were asked to forgo their tickets. 'Just arrive,' he said, 'and we'll let you in – but you'll have to stand at the back.' And stand we did, along with a lot of other worthy folk who also had presumably pleaded with Sam to bend the fire regulations. At least it gave us a full view of the packed audience."

The theatre's 1,755 paying customers for the first house gave a good reception to all the performers, with the screams, however, not drowning out their efforts. Peter Jay & The Jaywalkers' mimicking of The Searchers, The Shadows, Freddie & The Dreamers, and particularly The Beatles, went down very well, and The Vernons Girls and The Brook Brothers got a good reception. The Kestrels, in that tough spot before the Fabs, put in their usual polished performance, backed by the hard-working Rhythm & Blues Quartet. It was one of those rare nights when most of the music could be heard, and when people heard The Kestrels they realised how good those songbirds were. They went off to an enormous cheer – but they knew in their hearts that it wasn't for them. The screaming was relentless by the time Frank Berry attempted to introduce the main men. The Beatles' two 20-minute spots that night were almost inaudible, accompanied by hysterical scenes. There to capture the excitement were television cameras from the NBC and CBS television giants of America.

Because the TV cameras were there, some remarkable footage remains of The Beatles in action that night. It includes film of them being "delivered" in the van while the police have to work hard to hold back the girls. Cinema staff close the front doors quickly behind them. There are clips of them singing 'From Me To You', 'She Loves You', 'All My Loving' and 'Roll Over Beethoven' and, unusually, they were filmed doing 'You Really Got A Hold On Me'.

The cameras capture all the excitement and the screams; girls jumping out of their seats, waving frantically, and several in the front row dancing in time with 'She Loves You'. In amongst the chaos a police sergeant and the odd bemused bobby in uniform can be seen trying to make sense of it all.

Between houses The Beatles watched *Thank Your Lucky Stars* and *Juke Box Jury*, courtesy of a portable TV loaned to them for the night, and the motor racing game was brought out again. There was even time for press and TV interviews. This was the night that the Second World War fighter pilot and all-round hero Terry Spencer, latterly a photographer with *Life* magazine, began to cover the story of The Beatles. He did so at the behest of his 13-year-old daughter Cara, and he was to spend quite some time around them, taking around 5,000 photographs, as they toured the country.

The second show carried on in pretty much the same fashion, with the police concentrating on protecting the stage. Only one girl tried to crack the tough blue line. This didn't mean The Beatles were safe, though. George was hit in the eye by one of the many objects hurled. The seaside theatre had played host to quite a few entertainers down the years, but it had seen nothing on this scale. One over-wrought girl was taken to hospital while another injured herself running into the police van taking The

Beatles away. Just another mad day in the touring life of The Beatles.

The Beatles spent the night at the Branksome Towers Hotel between Bournemouth and Poole, leaving shortly before noon on the Sunday for the Midlands and two houses at the Coventry Theatre. The plan was for them to arrive at Coventry Police Station at 3.30pm, but they stopped for lunch along the way and were half an hour late. Their Austin Princess headed out from Little Park Street down the High Street into Broadgate and then round into The Burges and Hales Street, before finally arriving at the back of the theatre. Around 200 girls had gathered on a rainy afternoon to welcome their idols, but the barriers quickly came down to allow The Beatles in safely.

Supt E. Townsend was pleased with his team's efforts. The Beatles arrived in good enough time to get the Scalextric out again to amuse themselves in the hours before showtime. The press – still concerned over Paul's health, though he was now back fighting fit – were on hand and John commented caustically: "Now everyone is waiting for us to crack up under the strain. I'll tell you this. When we are breaking down we'll make a public announcement so everyone can come and take pictures." Of more concern to them was the growing danger of being injured by the many objects hurled at the stage, with George mentioning being struck in the eye the previous night. The more thoughtful girls settled for handing their Beatle gifts to policewomen at the stage door while the boys performed but most simply lobbed items from their seats. It was Ringo's turn to cop it at Coventry – he was struck on the head by a shoe.

Vernons Girl Jean Owen was celebrating her twentieth birthday. The local newspaper reported that The Beatles made her day by presenting her with a Ludwig drum kit as a present, but in a radio interview with BBC Radio Merseyside's Spencer Leigh in August 2010, Jean, now known as Samantha Jones, revealed the truth. "We were having a jam session before the shows and then I was talking with John Lennon and he was looking out at all the press guys. He said, 'Look at that lot, they'll believe anything you tell them. I'll show you,' he said. So he went out and told them they had bought me a complete Ludwig drum kit as a birthday present. Sure enough, it was printed."

Among those backstage eager to meet The Beatles was actress Julie Christie, who was pictured chatting to Paul. John posed with stage door keeper Nan Egginton and her cuppa for another photo.

The theatre held just over 2,000 and all seats had been sold for both houses within four hours of them going on sale just over a month before. Around 250 teenagers waiting in line for tickets had been left disappointed. In the hours leading up to the show, the rain continued to fall on Coventry and onto the poor, ticketless fans gathering outside. Those with tickets for the most exciting show in town couldn't have cared less about the weather. The Rhythm & Blues Quartet got the party started and compère Berry, as ever desperate to ratchet up the excitement, announced: "And now, from Liverpool, we have . . . [cue screams from the audience as an image of The Beatles was projected onto the curtains] . . . The Vernons Girls!"

The Brook Brothers, Ricky and Geoff, battled through their set amid growing chants for The Beatles. Peter Jay & The Jaywalkers had the benefit of a group of their own fans in the audience to cheer them on as they closed the first half. The Kestrels did their best to make themselves heard after the break and then Berry was back to introduce the headliners. Cue hysteria. Some girls put themselves in mortal danger, running to the edge of the circle to lean over and wave at the group in a frantic bid for attention. The Beatles tried their best, but nobody, surely, could hear anything in this racket. The screams went into overdrive for 'She Loves You', by now the national anthem for teenagers, and then the boys loaded up for the big finale with 'Money' and that show-closer of all show-closers – 'Twist And Shout'.

The second house was reportedly a little calmer, and the Coventry fans were deemed to have been better behaved than some. But we are always dealing in relatives.

Dear Mrs Egginton was on hand again to help the group's hasty exit at the end of the night. As usual, they were in their car and racing off before the fans knew what was happening. Many were milling around for some time afterwards, convinced The Beatles were still inside. The Beatle car sped back to the police station and from there they headed off to a hotel two and a half miles away at Brooklands Farm. Sadly, the Coventry Theatre is one of many no longer with us – it was demolished in 2002.

The next day, Monday, was a day off from the tour, but that didn't mean a day in bed for The Beatles. They were due to meet up with EMI chairman Sir Joseph Lockwood at EMI House in Manchester Square, London, where they would be presented with a number of silver discs for their record breaking achievements in 1963. They received silver discs for sales of their LPs *Please Please Me* and *With The Beatles* – remarkable considering that *With The Beatles* had not yet been released. There were further discs for several EPs and for 'She Loves You', the latter presented to them by Gerald Marks, editor of *Disc*. The Beatles then attended a cocktail party followed by a formal lunch in the boardroom with EMI bigwigs and their guests.

While the Fabs were in London, Mal Evans was driving their guitars and amps in the group's Bedford van to Wolverhampton, ready for the next day's two houses at the Gaumont Cinema. Unfortunatley, he crashed at Bridgtown about nine miles from Wolverhampton and ended up in Staffordshire General Infirmary with head injuries. Mal was kept in for several days but was nevertheless said to be "fairly comfortable" by a hospital spokesman. Inside the van, nine Beatle guitars and various amps had survived the battering, although some of the guitars needed minor repairs at a local music shop. Mal had been heading towards Longford Island when he crashed into a lamp post.

Wolverhampton signalled a worrying new trend when two ticketless teenagers pretended to attempt to take their own lives by swallowing a large quantity of tablets. The 16-year-olds, one from Surrey and the other a local girl, had left their homes and hitch-hiked to the previous two shows at Bournemouth and Coventry. Arriving at Wolverhampton without tickets, they were turned away from the Gaumont and ended up in a café where one of them claimed to have taken a handful of tablets with a glass of water. She left a suicide note which read: "Tell The Beatles we are sorry to do this, but we have taken 50 aspirins because we were so desperate to see you. Please, if we live, come and see us in hospital. Please know now that we really adore you. We want to die, with or without you."

Police inquiries revealed that the girl had actually swallowed peppermints but she and her friend were able to see the show, courtesy of tickets bought for £2 each from a tout. John Lennon was sickened by the story. "This sort of thing is dangerous," he said. "Some people may think it is flattering for young girls to try to commit suicide just because they want to see us, but if every teenager did it when she could not get in, some of them might die."

The Beatles had dashed into the Gaumont from their car in the afternoon and they were visited by Sean O'Mahony, the publisher of *The*

Beatles Book monthly fanzine, which he also edited under the name Johnny Dean. He was there for an exclusive picture session with The Beatles onstage before the shows, in their stage suits and playing as if to an audience. He also witnessed a 15-minute jam session featuring John, plus Peter Jay and one of The Jaywalkers and one of The Rhythm & Blues Quartet.

The Beatles Book also published a picture taken that night of Paul doodling on the piano with Tony Burrows of The Kestrels. The accompanying article recorded how the boys had time for a quick wash between the two "houses" and how Neil, apart from all his other duties, would see that The Beatle diet of steak and chips, washed down with cola or tea, was maintained.

The Vernons Girls took their turn for a soundcheck, singing the song 'Misty' while press photographers looked on. Ringo walked on, with a rolled umbrella, to greet Peter Jay in a posh accent with: "Hello Charles, going to the club tonight?" A bout of earache that day prompted Ringo to ask for a doctor. John, in a brown corduroy cap and glasses, arrived a little later than the others and they settled down to steak and chips, brought in from a local café. They would hardly have gone hungry. Local fans, having heard of the difficulties of getting food in for the stars, had sent in sandwiches by the score.

It was a special day for Valerie Lloyd of Shrewsbury who had two front row tickets and the opportunity to meet The Beatles before the show, courtesy of winning a national music paper competition. Valerie took her brother and they were driven down by their parents. They were joined at the cinema by several other winners and they went in three at a time due to the limited space in the group's dressing room. The Beatles were invariably charming in these situations and the youngsters were entertained by some Beatle looning, and George handed round some humbugs. Valerie gave the boys a drawing she had done of them. Paul told her it was the best he had seen, and George chipped in: "You've won another humbug!"

There was time for more photos and to field the usual questions from the press. But they loved to make time for banter, too. A Beatle reply to one question went: "Yes, we are doing a film set in Korea. It has to be there because we are Koreans. There, John has his leg amputated."

They made much bigger headlines in the Wolverhampton *Express & Star* than they had back in March on the Montez and Roe show – even though the newspaper's reporters couldn't hear much of their set above the screaming. Teenagers rushed the stage during the performance, bottles and jelly babies were thrown and hundreds of girls were weeping uncontrollably at the end. Two girls fought with stewards, who held them back, and only the extra security on hand prevented a riot.

Grammar school boy Keith Farley, who had been in the Gaumont for the Montez/Roe night in March, was there again, this time up in the circle – to see, but not hear them. "You couldn't hear a thing," he says. "It felt like an event in one way – because The Beatles were there – but in another it was something of a non event because you just couldn't hear any music."

The hysteria continued outside with thousands of screaming youngsters gathering under the dressing room window. The kids were kept off the road by crash barriers and the police. There was danger, too. One policeman risked his life by climbing onto a glass roof to coax some girls down. He fell through, cutting his boots to ribbons, but mercifully, he was not seriously hurt.

The Beatle getaway was set in place. A police car pulled up in front of The Beatles' car outside and while teens chased both, the boys jumped into a van that hared off in another direction. Meanwhile, about two dozen youngsters had gathered outside the local hospital where Mal was still recovering after the crash, expecting the group to visit their friend. However, it was deemed too much of a security risk and the teenagers were left disappointed.

The Beatles had enjoyed (although that might not be the right word for George, who loathed flying) the luxury of a flight into Manchester the next day, touching down at Ringway Airport in good time for the trip to the ABC Cinema at Ardwick, Manchester, for the two Wednesday night houses. Travel by air didn't change one thing – there were hordes of girls waiting at the airport. Dozens swarmed around a female reporter in the entourage who was spotted holding onto a Beatle arm for a few seconds. The girls were desperate to touch the glove that had touched a Beatle.

The full drama of a Beatle gig in an English city was captured on film that night thanks to a deal that Epstein had struck with *Pathe News*, which filmed scenes in and around the cinema, including The Beatles backstage and onstage performing two songs during the first house. In return for their co-operation The Beatles received a share of the profits, and the eight-minute film was shown at selected cinemas for a week from

December 22. The footage has been seen many times down the years, and survives – in colour – as a glorious example of a Beatles performance in late 1963.

Many fans will by now have watched John, Paul, George and Ringo playing 'She Loves You' and 'Twist And Shout' to a backdrop of incredible screaming. Close-ups of girls in the audience appearing to lose control of themselves told their own story. The backstage footage shows the cinema manager inspecting his female staff as they prepare to open the doors – a common procedure at the time. The Pathe film also shows The Beatles larking around in their dressing room and being photographed by the press as they pose with a toy panda sent by a fan. Around 5,000 people queued for up to two nights for tickets. The thousands waiting on the night, crammed up against the doors ready for them to be opened, also appear in the film, with some excitedly displaying their tickets.

With the concert in full flow the film briefly shows a young constable with his fingers in his ears as the screamers attempt a fair impression of a jet taking off. The film provides evidence that plenty of music was coming out of those tiny amplifiers and speakers, as The Beatles' voices and instruments can be heard clearly, but the screaming probably prevented much of it reaching the audience. One man in the audience stuck out like a sore thumb in the baying, cavorting crowd that night – and not just because he was a man. The *Manchester Evening News* had brought along Professor John Cohen, head of the Psychology Department at Manchester University, for his verdict on the behaviour of the girls. Sat in the front row of the stalls, Prof Cohen, fingers in ears, observed the seething mass all around and promptly shouted his verdict to the reporter sat right next to him. Referring to the screaming, he ventured: "It's just healthy exuberance. Remember, this is the only world they have that's completely theirs." The screams reached a yet higher level. Prof Cohen, fingers still firmly in ears, told the reporter: "This is not really hysteria. Hysteria is pathological. It is a disease. This is an emotional release. It is an expression of complete undiluted enthusiasm." So why do the girls scream? "You might as well ask a flock of geese why they fly and flap their wings," replied the professor.

Pathe wasn't the only company filming that night. Granada filmed similar backstage scenes together with an interview that was broadcast on Monday, January 6, 1964, on *Scene At 6.30*. The Beatles also spoke to a radio station.

Even in those days, it paid to nail your property down, particularly if you were a pop star on the road. Stolen from the tour coach this night was a guitar belonging to George, a six-string bass belonging to Jaywalker Geoff Moss, two suits and a guitar belonging to one of The Kestrels. There was a happy ending for George at least. His guitar was later discovered hanging on some nearby railings. However, as we shall discover, the incident was still playing on his mind several weeks later.

Manchester had fallen to Merseyside for the night and now The Beatles and the rest of the package were heading up to Carlisle for two Thursday shows at the town's ABC cinema.

There was nothing as precious to a teenager as a ticket for this tour and the excitement in Carlisle in the run-up to the event matched that at other places. ABC Cinema manager Norman Scott-Buccleuch, interviewed on television when the tickets went on sale, said: "They all say the live show is dead. I don't think so. After all, these kids are enthusiastic. They've been queuing for 36 hours."

Girls and boys queued side by side for their tickets, with some of the girls wearing cowboy hats with the word Beatles on them. They were queuing around the block for tickets and those queues grew to such an extent that the police decided something had to be done. Norman's son Calum, 24, who was to work as a stagehand on the night, recalls the excitement of the teens queuing for tickets a month before the concerts. "The queues had started on the Wednesday and the ticket office wasn't due to open until the Saturday," he said. "In the end the police insisted that something had to be done. They didn't want these kids spending another night out on the streets, I suppose, and so we opened the box office at 11pm on the Friday and sold tickets through the night. It was all quite orderly, as I recall, but it was the first time I had seen police dogs. All 1,880 tickets for each house were sold by the morning, which didn't go down well with people who were arriving from West Cumbria on the Saturday expecting to get their tickets, but there was nothing we could do. The police had insisted."

When the day of the show arrived, The Beatles were smuggled in the back of the cinema and there was an atmosphere that Calum had never seen before. "There was a buzz, a real buzz," he said. "We went in just before 6pm – and it was a struggle to get in, believe me. There was an air about it that you didn't get with the other shows. I've never seen anything like it before, or since, and I don't think anyone who was there will ever forget it."

Calum was working the curtains from the right-hand side of the stage that night and helping with the equipment. He should have been ideally placed to hear The Beatles. "You just couldn't hear anything for the screaming," he said. "It was so different from when they were here before on the Helen Shapiro package when you could hear them above the screams. This time the noise was like you get when you put a sea-shell up to your ear – a sort of hissing, but much louder. It was like a wall of sound. It was amazing – for both houses – I've never heard anything like it.

"When they came onstage everybody just stood up and for a moment I was frightened that they were all going to storm the stage." Calum recalls Frank Berry stirring things up, rather than calming them down. "He had them singing 'We Want The Beatles. We Want The Beatles'. It just got louder and louder. He was whipping up the hysteria."

The stage and the dressing room were protected by 30 security guards, while outside police dog handlers kept the crowds under some semblance of control.

Mike Mitchelson, who went on to become the Tory leader of Carlisle City Council, was a 15-year-old pupil at White House Grammar School when The Beatles came to town. "My over-riding memory is just of the hysteria and the screaming," he says. "Everyone was whipped up into a frenzy before they came on and when they came on it was total hysteria. You really couldn't hear any music, that's my memory. I was also in the audience for the Helen show earlier in the year – I went to quite a lot of pop shows. There was some screams at the Helen show, but you could hear them over it. But not this time."

The Beatles, who memorably strolled up to the Crown & Mitre Hotel with Helen and Kenny Lynch the previous February, made their getaway from the ABC this time in a Royal Mail van driven by Carlisle police sergeant John Walker. But it was a something of a ruse for they stayed overnight again at the Crown & Mitre before heading east to Stockton-on-Tees the next day, a day that would go down in history for an event that occurred just over four and a half thousand miles away.

Friday, November 22, 1963, had been anticipated with great excitement by Beatles fans, and not only those in the north-east of England. *With The Beatles*, the group's eagerly awaited second LP, was due in the shops that day, and the anticipated crowds were gathering outside Stockton's Globe Cinema for the first house at 6pm. It was of no concern to them that on the other side of the world the youngest ever president of the United States, John F. Kennedy, was about to embark on a motorcade in an open-top car to greet cheering, flag-waving supporters in the streets of Dallas, Texas.

By the time those hoarse-voiced excited children left the Globe at around 8pm the awful news had been confirmed. President Kennedy, very much the symbol of youthful optimism for a new generation, was dead. The fateful bullets struck him shortly after 12.30pm in Dallas (6.30pm in England) and he was pronounced dead at Parkland Hospital half an hour later.

A series of newsflashes kept television viewers up to date with the latest information. ITV's *Take Your Pick* was interrupted with updates of his condition, and the president's death was confirmed at 7.30pm (UK time), followed by a two-minute silence. The parents waiting to meet their children outside the cinema at 8pm were white faced with shock. Many were in tears. The excitement of their children turned immediately to sadness and journeys home were silent and tearful.

The performers were having to come to terms with the news, too, as Geoff Williams of The Kestrels recalls. "We heard the news that JFK had been shot before we went onstage. That would have been around 7pm. It wasn't until afterwards that we found out he was dead. I don't think there was a TV at the cinema – it would have been just word of mouth. Our coach driver Johnny Sparks may have been the one keeping us up to date because he was always popping in and out and talking to people.

"We went back to the hotel [the Eden Arms Hotel at Rushyford] after the shows and watched it all on the TV. People couldn't believe it. We were all stunned. We all sat there before the TV – stunned to silence. Nobody said anything. Nobody was into politics in those days, but Kennedy was a popular guy. Everyone loved him as a president. We just couldn't believe that it could happen."

Peter Jay recalls: "Word went round maybe the show's cancelled. President Kennedy's been shot. Everybody was like 'I can't believe it. Oh my God.' And there was mayhem going on outside anyway. At this stage when you've been on that roll for a few days and weeks you don't know whether you are coming or going. You have no idea of where you are or what you're doing. There was a big discussion going on. We were all in the theatre and was the show going to go ahead, or not?"

It was Alan Day, who worked at the Globe, who broke the news to The Beatles. "They were flabbergasted. They just couldn't believe it," he says. Tough though it was, the show had to go on for The Beatles and all the other performers. There was a second house (from 8.30pm) to be entertained, however strained the circumstances.

Geoff Williams explains: "We had a job to do. People were there . . . and we had to carry on. And we did. I honestly don't think the audience reaction to that second house was any different to any other night of the tour. It might seem strange but this was an audience of young people who loved The Beatles, and they had come along for a good time. They were too young to have understood the implications of what happened. They didn't understand about politics. We had to carry on. It was no good going out half-hearted – we still had a job to do.

"It was only afterwards that you had time to reflect on what happened. We were all staying in the same hotel that night – The Beatles included – and that was very unusual. We all gathered around the television and watched it together and we were all stunned into silence. Kennedy was such a young man and he was very much liked, as was his wife. It was unbelievable that the President of the United States could get shot, with all that security around him. It was so poignant when John Lennon got shot because of course we were with them when it happened to JFK."

The Beatles were abruptly halted onstage that night, but not as a mark of respect to Kennedy. Midway through their final number in the second house, a girl three rows from the front somehow managed to escape the grip of burly stewards to make a mad dash for the stage. Confirming that it really was business as usual for some fans at least, she flung herself across the 10ft-wide orchestra pit and scrambled onto the stage where she made a beeline for George and held him in an embrace for a few moments before turning her attention to John, who was belting out 'Twist And Shout'. She grinned up at him and was about to pounce when the breathless stewards finally caught up with her and bundled her off through the stage door. As they did so the curtains were suddenly dropped – with John in mid-song – and the show was halted there and then. The Fabs were immediately whisked away in a police car.

The story made page seven of Saturday's *Daily Express*, complete with a picture of the girl about to make a lunge at John, with a steward about to move in. Theatre staff were embarrassed by the girl who beat their security. Her friend, quizzed later by journalists, piped up innocently that she had told her she was determined to kiss a Beatle.

Despite The Beatles' swift exit, and the gravity of what had happened in Dallas, hundreds of chanting girls remained outside until they were finally cleared by mounted police. There was no 24-hour news service in 1963 and many of the youngsters – inside and outside the Globe – would have been blissfully unaware of the tragedy that was unfolding in America.

Vernons Girl Jean Owen, now Samantha Jones, recalls: "We were just about to go onstage when John Lennon said, 'Have you heard, John Kennedy's been shot?' Maureen said, 'Oh John, don't be so sick'. It was only after we came off that we found out it was true. In those circumstances, you know anyway that you still have to carry on. Your first thought is – God, the audience will be crap tonight. It's not selfishness. You still have your job to do. I can't recall the audience being any different that night. I'm sure I would recall if they had been."

One of those screaming fans was 16-year-old Melody Grainger (now Bahou), who lived in Middlesbrough, but is now in Ontario, Canada. "I had just finished school and was working at C&A's department store," she says. "My church youth club had arranged a trip to Stockton to see The Beatles. There was a whole busload of us. I remember being picked up at the end of my street and hearing someone say, 'Tell Melody.' 'Tell Melody what?' I said. 'President Kennedy's been shot!' was the reply. There was no other information. I was shocked and yet there was no further discussion that I can remember."

Melody recalls what happened when The Beatles came on. "I couldn't see much. We had seats in the 'gods'. I couldn't hear much either for all the screaming! Mind you, if you plugged your ears real hard you could hear them singing. What else can I say? It was The Beatles, live in person! I was screaming, too, Lord knows why, and tears were streaming down my face. I liked John, the sexy one – didn't care much for Paul, the baby face. Then it was all over, we piled on the bus and headed home. We hashed over the songs they sang, what they had said and how great they were all the way home to Middlesbrough. It was past 11 when I got home. Next day it was confirmed John Kennedy had been shot dead in Dallas. I had been screaming and crying tears while Jackie Kennedy had been doing the same, only in bitter anguish . . . and my lovely John, murdered in America 17 years later."

As newspapers dropped on doormats the next morning there was only one story. People all over the world were digesting the shocking news about JFK. The Beatles, meanwhile, as shell-shocked as everyone else, were preparing to travel the short distance from Durham to Newcastle for their two shows at the City Hall that night.

Although many newspaper column inches were taken up with the grim news from Texas, the papers, as always, had space for Beatle news. The *Daily Mirror* carried an appeal from Brian Epstein for fans to stop throwing things at the boys while they were performing, for fear of injuring them. "It all started with jelly babies," he was quoted. "Then the fans started to throw things, including teddy bears and boxes of sweets. We don't mind the jelly babies so much, but when they're in boxes it's a different matter."

Epstein pointed out that John, Paul and George had little chance to see anything hurtling towards them because of the spotlights. Ringo had a better chance further back on his drums. Elsewhere in the *Mirror* that day was a story – headlined 'They're In The Beatle Class' – about 14 boys "who want to be Beatles when they grow up". Just to prove that it wasn't all straight-laced classical music lessons back then, the children were pictured enjoying their first guitar lesson at Weston Park Secondary School in Southampton. Unlike most teachers up and down the land, forward-thinking headmaster Leslie Fish caught the mood by saying: "If ever you get into The Beatles' financial class, I hope you'll remember your poor old head!"

The Beatles were guaranteed a warm welcome on Tyneside. More than 4,000 fans had queued around the block from 3am to get tickets for the show. Visits by The Beatles were always memorable, but for local newspaper reporters they were sometimes memorable for the wrong reasons. Newcastle *The Journal* reporter Rodney Pybus confessed that although he liked The Beatles, watching them in concert was an experience he hoped would never be repeated. He wrote: "This quartet of modern minstrels appeared on the stage about 40 minutes before the end of the show. From that moment until they finally leapt out of the spotlight there was a non-stop, near unendurable Niagara of audience participation. Between me and The Beatles there was a solid wall of sound and bodies that prevented me from hearing much more than intermittent snatches of Ringo

Starr's drumming and Paul McCartney's bass guitar for the first 20 minutes."

He observed that the stewards were fighting a losing battle to keep the excitable Beatle fans in their seats, and he had a novel way of explaining to the uninitiated just what it was like being caught up in the whirlwind of Beatlemania.

"I have not attended the mass torture and execution of 5,000 assorted farmyard animals, but I imagine the noise they would make would be very similar to that which forced my fingertips deep into my ears. In any case, I could hear more of the music that way," he wrote.

He found it a good deal easier to hear all the other performers that night. The screaming really didn't start until The Beatles came on. "A word of well-earned praise for the supporting groups," wrote Pybus. "They were very, very good indeed and in fact produced the evening's musical entertainment."

The Beatles, having effected their escape from the City Hall, headed for the comfort and security of the picturesque Eden Arms Hotel where they were staying that weekend. All four signed headed hotel notepaper for a staff member, but they were to run into yet more trouble with their Austin Princess, which failed to start the next morning. The AA were called but failed to find a cure and the hotel was soon targeted by the fans, as always not slow to track them down.

The Beatles hired a new getaway vehicle from Minories Garage in Newcastle and were on their way to Hull within the hour, but the poor AA man, trapped in the car park by screaming Beatlemaniacs, was having to battle his way to freedom. The hotel manager was reportedly not amused. "This Beatlemania makes me sick," he muttered.

When tickets went on sale in Hull, teenagers broke through crash barriers and had to be forced back, some fainted and were gently passed over the barriers by police, and a police horse arrived to help keep the seething mass under control.

By 4am there were already around 1,000 kids in the queue. Fortunately, Hull had Jack Nicholson to take command of the situation. Not *that* Jack Nicholson, but Supt Jack Nicholson who took the loudhailer just before the booking office opened at 8am to tell the teenagers: "There will be no sale until you settle down."

The queues were boosted by teenagers from Middlesbrough, Wigan,

Grimsby and Goole and by 11.20am all 4,720 tickets for both houses had been sold, and around 100 very disappointed teenagers left without tickets.

Not everyone was dreading the big day. One shop did brisk business with its Beatles brooches, a gentleman's outfitters was looking forward to selling plenty of Beatle-style suits and boots, and record shops and hair-dressers were also preparing to make hay. On the night there were 40 police on duty inside the cinema and double that number on the streets.

A 2009 article in the Hull City Police Old Comrades Association news-letter reveals that The Beatles were late for their rendezvous with Hull police at the station in Gordon Street due to their earlier car trouble. Rookie cadet Mick Beckett, 16, was a Beatles fan and he was delighted to learn that he would be joining colleague (and fellow Beatles fan) PC Andy Lowthorpe, 19, on duty inside the ABC Cinema. The Beatles were gathered together in the charge room with Sgt Ted Holt to discuss arrangements for their journey to the cinema. Sgt Holt was old school and he was unimpressed by long-haired Scousers, and even less by the language coming from John Lennon's mouth. "If you don't stop swearing in my charge room, the only place you're going is them cells," the Beatle was warned.

Happily, no Beatles were locked up and they emerged from the station into the police yard where they climbed into the vehicle, affectionately known as Big Henry, ready for their ride to the venue.

Already inside the van was PC Lowthorpe. Looking back in 2010 he recalled: "All of a sudden the doors opened up and The Beatles jumped in. You can imagine how I felt. I was 19 and into pop music and for me to meet The Beatles was something I'd never forget. The driver was told to take a round-about route to the cinema."

The van pulled up at the side entrance and The Beatles had no trouble getting in as the screaming girls were all at the front behind barriers. With The Beatles safely inside the ABC, Lowthorpe joined colleagues on crowd control on the streets outside, but he was delighted that he was to be on duty inside the cinema during the shows. The Beatles, meanwhile, met the press, dealing with the usual run of questions as a group, and then breaking off to meet reporters individually. John was questioned by the *Hull Daily Mail*'s reporter. How was fame affecting them? "It changes other people around us," he said. "We get very little peace and quiet but we find it no more tiring than we find anything else."

The Beatles, of course, got a riotous reception. Twelve fans fainted during the first performance, 11 during their second. Others leapt from their seats to be restrained by police and stewards. Among them were four rugby league internationals, John Taylor, Brian Tyson and Jim Drake of Hull Kingston Rovers who became comrades in arms for the night with former Hull forward Mick Scott.

PC Lowthorpe was upstairs in the balcony, where he had his work cut out. "You really couldn't hear much music where I was," he says. "All you could hear was the screaming and shouting. You could feel the balcony vibrating – you could feel it under your feet. The girls were fainting and being carried out and I thought they have paid all this money and probably queued for hours and ended up seeing very little of the concert."

The *Mail* reporter heard enough to record details of The Beatles' "twangy sound, big beat and non-stop energy" as they pounded out the hits for Hull. The Beatles cast regular glances at each other in their attempts to co-ordinate, at the very least, the start and finish of the songs.

Mounted police cleared a way through thousands of excited teenagers to allow buses in and out of Ferensway station between the two houses. Crowds of ticketless youngsters gathered outside chanting 'We Want The Beatles' while fans inside were enjoying the second house. The newspaper was impressed with the whole Beatles operation. "The Beatles showed all the showmanship expected of them but perhaps their snappiest routine was not during their act at all. As soon as the final curtain fell they left their instruments and made a dash through the side stage door into a waiting police van."

The Beatles were heading back to the police station before the fans realised they had left. Hundreds gathered at the back, waiting for them to appear. There were more chants of 'We Want John'. Buses were still struggling to get in and out of the station due to the number of kids sitting in the road. The police were struggling to clear them. Despite the furore, the police and cinema manager John Fisher later praised the teenagers for their comparatively restrained behaviour.

As for PC Lowthorpe, he has more than just memories of that night to cherish. "While I was in the car with them, The Beatles signed two sets of autographs for me. I kept one set but ended up giving the other autographs away. There was a lad who was hurt falling over a barrier in the crush. I felt sorry for him so I said pick an autograph. So I tore it off for him and then I tore away the other three and gave them to girls in the crowd."

Mondays generally represented a day off from the tour and The Beatles spent the afternoon of November 25 in Manchester at the Granada TV studios, miming to 'I Want To Hold Your Hand' and 'This Boy' and being interviewed for *Late Scene Extra* and *Scene At 6.30*. The interview section with programme host Gay Byrne included a memorable 10-minute ad-lib session with Liverpudlian comic Ken Dodd in which they indulged in some classic cheeky banter. Dodd claimed to be involved in a film script for the boys in which Ringo was cast as Charles II "and he goes along to Nell Gwynn and pinches her jaffas". There were several moments of riotous laughter, not least when Ken says he'd consider forming a group and invites suggestions for an earthy name for him. "Sod" piped up George, to great laughter.

The following night, Cambridge, that proud and cultural seat of learning, fell just as much under the spell of The Beatles as all of the other UK towns and cities. The queues for tickets had been no shorter there. In fact, it stretched all the way around the old Regal Cinema in St Andrew's Street. Taking no chances, The Beatles were met by the police at an agreed destination a mile away several hours before the show, arriving at the cinema in the back of a police van.

Each town employed its own unique methods and equipment for dealing with a Beatles show. The Cambridge police force had the use of a 12-man Vespa motor scooter team – their great advantage being that they were cheap to manage and could travel slowly enough to equal a foot patrol, or quickly enough to give escaping burglars a run for their money. This night they were drafted in to try to make sure that the 4,000 kids getting in and out of the Regal over the two houses were kept in control and nobody came to any harm. The Vespa squad included former Cambridge goalkeeper Roy Coxon, and backing them up were Red Cross volunteers to revive the fainters, plus the same burly collection of Shelford Football Club members who had controlled the crowd so well on the Montez/Roe tour night.

Of course, they had a few more problems to address this time. In the event The Beatles made it inside safely, ready to face a posse of reporters and photographers whose numbers had grown since their Palladium triumph. In fact, each Beatle was surrounded.

They were also interviewed in their dressing room by the now late reporter Jean Goodman for the local BBC TV news magazine programme *East At Six Ten*. Her interview included what was now becoming a nightly question – "How long do you think you'll last?" "About five years," replied John. "Will the group stay together?" "Don't know," he fired back.

Despite the increasing hardship of touring life, The Beatles were generally good-natured in dealing with questions that irritated them. "What's your favourite colour?" "What kind of girls do you like?" "How did you get those haircuts?" "Why the name Beatles? "How long are you going to last?" The same questions, over and over, from venue to venue.

The talking done with, it was show time – fun for the fans but a challenge to those in authority – especially when The Beatles were onstage. The bar where they had earlier met the press was now an emergency first-aid area with a dozen nurses at the back ready to deal with girls who fainted.

Shelford Football club secretary Jim Dean, who also worked at the cinema, recalled: "You could feel the vibration coming from the floor. There was a lot of excitement, and it was all for The Beatles. It was an atmosphere you could never dream of unless you were there."

Dean and the footballers, who had already been drafted in to help the ABC in Northampton, were old hands at this job and they were up to the task again. "It was good fun. We enjoyed ourselves," he says. "Only two or three got onto the stage and they were all comfortably dealt with by the stage hands."

Fellow football club member Tony Smith recalls more problems than the previous visit. "The thing I remember most was the noise. We were down the side aisle and in front of the stage stopping any runners trying to get onto it, and trying to dodge jelly babies being thrown at the stage. We were taking the fainting girls outside and removing the girls from under the seats. They were also hiding in the toilets between shows – anywhere they could hide so they could see The Beatles again."

That dealt with the security, but of course nobody could do anything about the screaming. Noel Knights was just 16 and he had queued all night to get his ticket. He was able to make out enough of the music to proclaim that it was worth it. "Their performance was memorable," he says.

Also in the audience was local girl Rosemary Preston who has subsequently spoken of how she loved seeing The Beatles, but heard little. She did, however, manage to make it onto the pages of a national newspaper. "The next morning my mother came to my room with a copy of the *Daily Express* in her hand with a photograph of me and a couple of my friends at the concert screaming. The caption was: 'City of learning and culture bends to the sound'."

There was little respite for The Beatles. Even the short break between the two houses was taken up talking with Peter Yolland who was to produce their forthcoming Christmas show, which would run for 16 nights at London's Finsbury Park Astoria from Christmas Eve. The interview was recorded during the break to give them at least some chance of being heard above the screams.

Then came the second house of full-on screaming. Once the concerts were over it was the usual problem – getting the boys out in one piece. The decoy car routine, so vital to the group at that time, was put into effect with military precision that night in Cambridge. A standard Black Maria police van of the period went screeching along Downing Place with headlights full on towards where the screaming girls had gathered. The Beatles, of course, were not in it. They were securely inside another van, driven by Police Sergeant Arthur Quinney, that quietly made its own way through a back gate into the university's Downing Street site and then along Tennis Court Road, Lensfield Road, Gonville Place and Parkside before sneaking through another back door that led through to the plush University Arms Hotel where The Beatles were to spend the evening.

There was no rest for The Beatles, even at their hotel. First they had an interview with American journalist Michael Braun who was compiling a book *(Love Me Do – The Beatles' Progress)* about their early rise to fame. With their planned conquest of America around the corner, they were happy to oblige.

They even made time to put smiles on the faces of two young fans. Jean Chainey, who had been in the audience when they played the Regal back in March, went one better this time. Although she hadn't seen The Beatles play this night, she spent up to an hour with them at the hotel before they were finally able to retire for some kip. Jean, now living in the United States, explains: "I occasionally worked at the University Arms as an evening telephonist/information clerk. The food and beverage manager had told me that The Beatles were staying there the night of their show and would I like to meet them. To be honest, I thought he was just trying to impress me. Nevertheless, I and a friend whom I decided to share the experience with turned up dressed alike – we wore red tartan calf-length skirts, black roll necks and high boots and we waited in the lounge playing cards . . . and we waited and waited.

"Then, suddenly, we were alerted to their arrival and we rushed to the hallway and saw the four Beatles, with a small entourage, run in through a side entrance down the corridor and into the lift. They were wearing black macs with the collars turned up, in an apparent attempt to conceal their identities. We went back into the lounge and resumed our wait.

"After a while the food and beverage manager came in with Brian Epstein and Brian asked us if we were ready. Brian escorted my friend and me down the corridor into the lift, down another corridor and into the room where they all were. The lights had been turned down because they, and we, were about to watch some slides from their Hamburg days. Four upright chairs had been placed in a row for us to view the slide show.

"I cannot say enough about how kind Paul, George, Ringo and John were. They were absolute gentlemen, especially Paul, and they paid us a lot of attention. They seemed genuinely interested in us. I remember Paul was operating the slide carousel and narrating, George sat in an upright chair (next to me), John was lying on top of the bed with a bottle of drink, possibly scotch, and Ringo was flitting around the room making jovial comments and generally clowning around."

There was a sleep-in the next morning for The Beatles, who were finally driven away at noon in their black Austin Princess with staff lining up at the drive to wave them off while assorted fans and neighbours looked on.

The extensive preparations now needed to host a Beatles visit were illustrated by the authorities in York as the Fab Four headed in for their two houses at the Rialto, now known as the Mecca-Casino, in Fishergate the next day. The group had provoked much excitement on their three previous visits, but everybody knew that this time it would be off the scale. All police leave was cancelled and traffic diversions arranged. Around 40 special constables were drafted in to support the 60 or so regulars in the bid to maintain order. Chief constable Cyril Carter, noting the growing Beatle chaos in other towns, was laying down the law: "We expect the young people of York to set a good example to those lesser cities," he stated, somewhat optimistically.

The St John Ambulance brigade, meanwhile, had recruited extra volunteers to deal with the inevitable fainting fits. Not everybody was looking forward to the event. A reader who dubbed him or herself 'The Observer' had sent the press this unduly pompous letter which was published on November 6: "Many young people these days complain that adults tend to condemn them. But when one sees the disgusting behaviour now occurring up and down the country under the name of 'Beatlemania' it is impossible not to draw certain conclusions."

Evening Press columnist John Blunt wasn't impressed either. "Ask any teenager in York and they could name the four Beatles," he wrote. "Now ask those same teenagers for names of a few other well-known personalities. The Secretary General of the United Nations, for example, or even our own Prime Minister. The answers, in many cases, will not slip so easily off the tongue. Such is fame. Such is our sense of values in this modern world."

Blunt evidently had no issue with The Beatles themselves, who he described as hard working and likeable, but he did have a problem with "the howling, screaming, bustling, shoving, fighting mobs which collect whenever they make an appearance."

Most members of the press, however, were lining themselves up with the kids. Entertainment reporter Stacey Brewer's story headlined 'Only Four More Days To The Beatles' stirred up the mood. Brewer was well aware there would be little chance of a repeat of niceties observed on previous visits to York by The Beatles. "Last time they were in York, Paul McCartney and George Harrison were able to sit with me in the empty theatre after the show and talk into the small hours about showbusiness, their hopes and plans. There'll be no opportunity for relaxing like that this time," he lamented.

All the signs were there that Beatlemania was coming to town. A local shop that placed a Beatle-embroidered pillow in the window was rewarded with a permanent stream of girls with their noses pressed up against the glass. An entrepreneurial confectionist invented a new brand of sweet – the Jelly Beatle. The police ploy was to seal off the streets around the cinema. A police car had been waiting at the city boundary at 3.30pm ready to escort The Beatles' Austin Princess limousine to the venue, but The Beatles caught everyone on the hop by arriving early and calling in at the York Motel in Tadcaster Road first for a meal, to the surprise and delight of other diners. George telephoned the police and they sent a car, also containing theatre manager Derek Lacey, to meet them.

Lacey had been wrestling with the dilemma of how to get them in and out safely. Ingeniously, he appealed to the fans themselves for ideas. Suggestions included disguising them as telephone engineers or landing a helicopter on the roof. What they settled for in the end was good old fashioned crash barriers with the baying girls held back for up to five hours on that chilly autumn afternoon. It worked reasonably well. One girl was hurt as she was nearly run over by a car – but that was the only casualty, if you discounted the eardrums of anyone within screaming distance.

Most fans had expected the group to arrive at the back, but they ran out of their still moving car through the front doors to catch them on the hop, with the girls held back by the barriers and the thin blue line. The doors were opened only 15 minutes before the first performance. Beatle goodies were on sale in the lobby – Beatle aprons and belts at 9s 6d – the red and blue striped aprons complete with a beetle – yes, a beetle – playing a guitar and the words 'From Me To You'.

The Beatles were already under virtual siege from 30 photographers, flash-guns firing off everywhere as they posed for pictures. Two York girls from Queen Anne Grammar School in York were then able to scoop the press with their own exclusive interview for their school newspaper. Unlike many of the professional reporters The Beatles encountered, Christine Glensor (17), of Millfield Lane, and Bronwen Pickering (also 17), of Lord Mayor's Walk, had some intelligent questions to ask, too. Bronwen to Ringo: "We know you like jelly babies, but what do you think about politics?" Ringo knew enough to neatly sidestep that one. George was asked about Sweden, and then how he thought they would do in America. Cue the cute grin and the sensible answer: "We'll have to wait and see." During the interview The Beatles were also busy reading fan letters and signing autograph books.

The cinema management had received hundreds of requests for autographs, and even a dress which the owner wanted The Beatles to sign so she could raffle it for charity. Paul was briefly handed a baby by a couple who had travelled from Hull for the show. "It's just like a christening," he joked.

The insightful questioning over, it was the turn of the seasoned journalists and the usual run of banal questions. The tiring journey up from

Cambridge had left John feeling under the weather. "He'll be all right after a kip," predicted Paul, and so he was after getting his head down in the dressing room for three hours.

The shows got underway to a backdrop of screams. Local historian Van Wilson recalled: "There were 1,800 fans inside the auditorium and another 400 outside jammed between crush barriers shouting 'We Want Paul, George, John and Ringo' throughout the concert."

The shows weren't without the odd hiccup. Peter Jay revealed in his music paper tour column that first all the theatre's lights fused, and then the curtains wouldn't work. Four men – two on each side of the stage – were eventually tasked with holding back the curtains. All the performers – the Fabs included – endured some bitter-tasting tea due to some bright spark filling the sugar basins with salt. The show, however, left no sour taste in the mouth.

Stacey Brewer recorded that the York teens, however excited they were about The Beatles, treated the other performers well – with no cat-calls or impatient stomping – and he credited Frank Berry for creating the right mood. With the luxury of actually being able to hear them, Brewer registered his approval of The Kestrels, Peter Jay & The Jaywalkers, The Brook Brothers, The Vernons Girls and The Rhythm & Blues Quartet.

Berry had got his introductions down to a fine art. "Do you want to see John? [screams], George? [screams], Paul? [screams], Ringo? [pandemonium]." The girls waved, held up pictures, and screamed and they kept it up as The Beatles ran through their 10 songs. But the York teens generally did not indulge in some of the excesses that had gone on elsewhere. One girl tried to clamber onto the stage during the second house, but she was gently restrained by the security men. A senior police officer was moved to note: "There were no disturbances, just good natured enthusiasm."

Brewer liked the blend of hit songs, mentioning 'From Me To You' and 'She Loves You' with numbers from the new album *With The Beatles*. He also name-checked 'Till There Was You' and 'You Really Got A Hold On Me' and described a rip-roaring version of 'All My Loving'. He also noted that Ringo's 'Boys' went down well. He wrote: "But the real frenzy came with the final number – a whoop-it-up styling of 'Twist And Shout'."

The Beatles, as ever, were quick off the mark with their exit. As soon as the curtain closed they dashed from the stage to their waiting Austin

Princess before the National Anthem was played. In that more respectful age, the girls stopped their screaming as it struck up and resumed only after it had ended. It was long enough for a clean getaway. The Beatles were well on the way to their hotel, via a detour route along Cemetery Road, before the first fans had even left the theatre.

Following the Beatle car was a Jaguar driven by Arthur Howes, sporting his very un-Beatle-like cropped hair and a snakeskin coat. With him were two girls from the teen magazine *Boyfriend* – a reporter and a photographer. Arthur confessed that he'd rather be back in London than heading for a hotel lounge, but he owed The Beatles more of his time than simply signing their cheques.

Back in the hotel after dinner a tired George retired early, but John wandered down the corridor in a T-shirt and trousers to the room shared by Paul and Ringo. Paul was holding court about a film called *The Trial* which he had recently seen. The conversation soon turned to their forthcoming trip to America, and whether they would fare any better than Cliff Richard who was relegated to fourteenth on a bill starring Frankie Avalon. Conquering Britain was one thing, but America? They weren't feeling confident. Double scotches and cokes were ordered and the talk turned to fame, fans, Liverpool and how friends, and even some family members, now looked at them differently. The Beatles could afford a late night. Tomorrow's journey was comparatively short – a quick drive down the A1 to the ABC Cinema in Lincoln.

It was like that scene from *A Hard Day's Night*. Show time was approaching and Ringo, dressed in an over-sized overcoat and heavy disguise, was nowhere to be seen. This was no jolly jape, however. Ringo had been hit with a nasty bout of earache after the press conference inside the ABC and a doctor was called. It took her 20 minutes to convince the security she was genuine and then she was rudely interrupted by Neil Aspinall who burst in, demanding to know who she was and why she was peering into the drummer's ear. The brave decision was taken to cart Ringo through the waiting fans off to hospital for treatment – hence the heavy disguise.

Again, like the harassed Victor Spinetti in *A Hard Day's Night*, the cinema's area manager sat biting his nails in the hospital as Ringo was examined. "He has to be onstage in 15 minutes," he wailed. At last Ringo emerged, his ears having been syringed. Only Ringo would offer a cigarette to the hospital's ear, nose and throat specialist as he did so. It was politely declined.

A *Daily Express* reporter asked about Ringo's health. "He's here to see a friend," came the reply. Who said the art of spin started with Alistair Campbell?

The matter of Ringo's ear was briefly mentioned by Peter Jay in his weekly music paper column.

Beatle humour carried on regardless. Ringo returned to the theatre in good time and on his dressing table found a tube of Yardley's Shampoo For Men to which a fellow nameless Beatle has added the words "and Ringo".

It wasn't just Ringo who was in the wars before the show. Fan Richard Cooper (16), from Scunthorpe, vaulted a fence near the cinema thinking he was going to land on a towpath – but he miscalculated and ended up in the river Witham. He was rescued by two friends and taken to the police station to dry out . . . and then home by his parents.

This was one of those nights when everyone on the bill got screamed at. The din started as soon as the curtain went up, and it never let up. The Rhythm & Blues Quartet got an enthusiastic reception when they opened, an almost certain indication that everyone was in for a noisy night. They brought on the lovely Vernons Girls who set the scene with 'Be My Baby' and 'I Went Funny All Over'. The Brook Brothers followed with 'Warpaint', 'Forbidden Fruit' and 'Whistle In The Wind'. The crowd created plenty of noise and the audience were invited by Berry to take part in a 'Yeah Yeah Yeah' competition just to make sure they hadn't forgotten who who was closing the show.

Peter Jay & The Jaywalkers knew how to put on a show. They rocked it up with their own version of 'Kansas City' followed by 'Parade Of The Tin Soldiers'. Then came their own show-stopper, 'Can Can 62', complete with spectacular drum solo. They were big on presentation – especially their leader. Sparks flew from the cymbals, and the drums featured their own light show with the beat. It was a ripping end to the first half.

The Rhythm & Blues Quartet opened the second half, remaining to provide backing for The Kestrels, with 'Green Green' and 'Michael Row The Boat Ashore' standing out for the reporter covering the show for the *Lincolnshire Echo*. The Kestrels were highly regarded but as ever they had to fight to be heard over screams not intended for them. It was very nearly

Beatle time and Berry had a desperate battle to make himself heard as he attempted to introduce them.

Cinema manager Mr Clifford and his staff patrolled the aisles and police took their positions as the girls stood on their seats, waving and screaming as The Beatles bounded onto the stage. 'From Me To You', 'All My Loving' and 'She Loves You' just about cut through the screams as the Fabs pounded away for almost half an hour. 'Till There Was You' was the lone ballad and as usual they finished on full power with Lennon belting out 'Money' and 'Twist And Shout'.

Excitement there was a-plenty but Lincoln teenagers set a good example in the run-up to the event, according to Mrs M. Leachman, chairman (women could still be chairmen in those days) of the local Electrical Association for Women. "We have all heard of the disgraceful behaviour of young people in other places and the noise they have made queuing during the night," she told colleagues at the branch's annual dinner. But the York teens had risen above that and Mrs Leachman congratulated the city police on how they handled the event.

It wasn't exclusively teenagers who followed The Beatles. Following their car away from the ABC at the end of this night were a couple of Lincoln housewives – June Clarke and Anne Blair. It was a good job they did. The Beatlemobile hurtled along West Parade but then turned into a cul-de-sac. Mrs Clarke pointed them in the right direction . . . in return for Beatle autographs. They were now headed for their hotel in Doncaster – a good halfway point for the next day's shows in Huddersfield.

However, the night's dramas weren't over yet. American journalist Michael Braun, still travelling with them, reported that the driver was lurching all over the road in his haste to deliver The Beatles to their hotel. "Hey, this is not the continent. We drive on the left in England," said Lennon. Then the car ran out of petrol. Neil had to flag down a passing lorry at 1.30am.

The Beatles' second album had been released the previous Friday and 'I Want To Hold Your Hand', their fifth single, was officially issued in the UK on November 29, with advance orders suggesting it would break all records. As it went on sale they were heading from Doncaster to Huddersfield for two shows at the town's ABC Cinema. Huddersfield was primed. When tickets went on sale a few weeks before, the fans, as everywhere else, lost sleep to join the queue.

Peter Whittle, a member of the Round Table in those days, remembers colleagues going down to provide soup for the children – for that's what most of them were – who were in the long queue. "It was an unbelievable atmosphere. I don't think Huddersfield has ever seen anything like it," he says today.

Local lad Bob Joynson was one of those in that long queue. "I slept in a car park at the booking office that night with a mate. When the doors opened there was this big rush. I never got there, but my mate was smaller and he managed to nip through the crowd and got two tickets."

Peter Garry (17) had beef and onion sandwiches and a bottle of Guinness to keep him going. "In the morning hundreds of bleary eyed teenagers rushed towards the front door to get the best seats. To our dismay a bus load of people pulled up, the police created a cordon and they strolled in and grabbed the best seats. Eventually, I walked away with my prize of six tickets at about six bob each." Another in the queue was Stephen Carter, who went on to spend 30 years as a policeman and was then appointed librarian at the *Examiner*. Stephen was a 20-year-old clerk at the time with R. S. Dyson and Co., wholesale grocers in Macaulay Street in Huddersfield town centre. He lived in digs at Dalton and got to know another lodger called Ray Jones, who was a footballer for Huddersfield Town.

It was Ray who suggested going to see the show – they were to take two girlfriends along with them – but it was Stephen who drew the short straw and had to queue overnight for the tickets.

Stephen explains: "The tickets were to go on sale on Saturday, November 2, but Ray was due to play for Town's Reserves that day so I was somehow volunteered to queue. The queue started on the Friday and I got a spot in it about halfway up Fox Street. It started raining, but there were two young women just in front who were a bit better prepared than me. They had a groundsheet and a large umbrella balanced against the low wall that ran up the side of the small ABC car park. They realised I was on my own and invited me in under the umbrella. I think they also had a half bottle of rum. Happy days.

"I remember that the police had to link arms outside to keep people back because the crowds were surging and the glass doors were bending a bit."

It was a difficult night for young police officer Margaret Rose, who was on duty and remembers that bending glass door. "I got trapped by the crowd outside the glass door and was being squashed so hard I thought I was going to pass out. There was glass all around me and it could have gone. I was on my own but I was facing the foyer glass door in the end and luckily someone inside could see how distressed I was and opened the door to let me in. It saved me. I was in danger of passing out. It was only later when I realised how vulnerable I'd been."

When the big day arrived the police were well prepared, having spent some time perfecting their Operation Beatles strategy. The cinema seated just over 2,000 and though every seat was sold for both houses, there would be plenty of ticketless fans lingering in the streets outside. The plan was to close the neighbouring Fox Street and the car park behind the ABC, while keeping the traffic flowing in Market Street. Fans would queue single file with barriers tied in place by string.

Cinema windows were blacked out so fans couldn't see where The Beatles were. It all looked a bit over the top when only three fans turned up in the morning with their Beatle photos. They weren't going to stay all day, they said. By mid-afternoon five policeman stood outside an otherwise deserted cinema. It was the quiet before the storm, of course, but it was good news for the Fabs who arrived at 4pm to be greeted only by an enthusiastic bunch of press photographers and the odd passer-by. They had been given a relay service into town. Having met up with police six miles away, they were escorted by a white police car into Huddersfield. Their timing was perfect. Within an hour there was a large crowd gathering around the cinema. The policeman driving The Beatles was PC George Banks and it was he who would be waiting to drive them away after the shows.

The Beatles met the press and were pictured on the front page of the next day's *Huddersfield Weekly Examiner* tucking into cocktail sausages at their own reception. Joining the hard-bitten journalists were two pupils of St Gregory's Roman Catholic Grammar School, Ian O'Brien and Michael Hartley, both 15, who were there to report for their wonderfully titled magazine, *Crank*.

It was all going swimmingly until half an hour before The Beatles were due onstage. With the show underway, and many teens already in their seats and hundreds, maybe thousands on the narrow streets outside, the fire brigade received a call claiming there had been an explosion at the cinema. Three fire engines, sirens blaring, raced through the streets and pulled up outside the ABC.

Cinema manager Roy Hartle had checked every inch of the building before the doors were opened, so he was able to reassure firemen that it was a hoax. The panic was over. Steve Earnshaw, a fireman at the time, remembers the incident. "I was on days and was about to finish at 6pm. After we discovered it was a hoax we headed back to the fire station and then returned to the ABC to help with the security. Some of us were outside and some inside. I was backstage in the wings. I got The Beatles' autographs on a programme but they got lost somewhere when we moved home."

Stephen Carter, Ray Jones and their dates had got their tickets and were at the first house that night. Carter later became aware of the hoax call but confirms that those in the first house enjoyed an uninterrupted show, unaware of the drama that had briefly unfolded. They were near the back of the stalls – perfectly placed to hear the screamers at full pelt. "When the show started everyone was just waiting for The Beatles to come on," he says. "When they finally did there was just this tremendous screaming and it continued through the entire performance. You couldn't really make out what they were singing – apart from the odd moment when the screamers near you paused for breath. Then you'd think, 'Oh they're singing that one now!' I remember that we left the cinema and went into a bar called The Shoehorn in New Street and my ears were still ringing.

"It was great to be there, though. I liked The Beatles, but I wasn't an avid fan. It was a once in a lifetime moment to see them in Huddersfield."

Marjorie Bryar (née Brooke) was also delighted to see the Fab Four that night, particularly as she got in for free. "I was a nurse at Huddersfield Royal Infirmary and we received some complimentary tickets – probably from the cinema. But the deal was we had to sell ice creams during the interval. A group of us went along. I can remember two of them – Margaret Dempsey and Maureen Osbourne. We felt so fortunate. The police were holding back the crowds on the way in but we managed to stick together to get to the front and we showed our passes at the glass and they let us straight in. There must have been plenty of people without tickets because people were begging us for ours."

Once inside, the nurses – ice cream girls for the night – were taken to the balcony to receive instructions. "We didn't have seats. We stood in the aisles with the ice cream trays around our necks, but it was worth it to see

The Beatles. It was great, being in the circle, because you could look down and see everything. People were fainting and screaming and falling about. I've never seen anything like it. And we also got to see The Beatles. We just couldn't believe it at the time."

And did the ice cream girls join in the screaming? "I was 18, going on 19 at the time and I was not given to screaming!" says Marjorie. "But there was great excitement. The screaming went on through the show but it was horrendous by the time they came on. People were so jealous afterwards, to think that we had seen them and didn't even have to pay. It was an absolutely fantastic experience. When I walk down that street I can feel the atmosphere even now. It was quite scary in its way."

Peter Garry, who had queued for his six tickets, was dressed for the occasion. "I put on my Italian suit with my winklepicker black boots with silver coloured beetle brooches fastened to each boot. I boarded the bus and headed for the ABC. I was in the stalls two-thirds of the way back behind two giggly girls who fidgeted all night. The other acts were watched in silence, apart from Peter Jay & The Jaywalkers who did a bow, the lights dimmed and a Beatles song started up. Of course the screaming started until the lights went back on and it was Peter Jay etc with mop-top wigs. The screams soon turned to mock booing. The Beatles eventually arrived onstage to an ear splitting scream and opened up with 'I Saw Her Standing There'."

When the first house was over The Beatles retired to their dressing room with the usual round of people to meet and greet. Among them was a shy young man from the Huddersfield Tape Recording Society, on a mission to undertake separate interviews with each Beatle for the society's monthly *Music Box* programme, broadcast to several local hospitals. The interviewer who politely asked each Beatle to read out record requests was Gordon Kaye, the actor the nation took to its heart when he played the part of the loveable René in the hit television comedy *'Allo 'Allo*.

John Lennon, meanwhile, was in the awkward position of receiving a gift he was unable to accept. A black kitten with a pink bow was left in a shopping bag on a stalls seat with a note for John. The cat was safely back in the care of its young owner by the end of the night.

The pattern of polite applause for the other acts continued in the second house as another sell-out crowd waited for the Fabs. Local lad Brian Senior and his pal got in – despite falling victim to a trick. "We were offered two tickets by a mutual acquaintance. It was the day after my six-teenth birthday. We arrived early to join the queue which, as you can imagine, was manic. When the doors opened, everyone was pushing and shoving trying to get in as quickly as possible. When we handed our tickets to the usherette she told us that we had got only one ticket – the original and the counterfoil. We had been duped! Because of the crowd all around us, she told us to go ahead into the cinema as there was no way we were going to get back out through the melee! We had to share our seat, but as soon as the show began everyone was up on their feet anyway.

"I was a hairdressing apprentice at Deighton at the time. One of our regular customers was a police constable who lived in the area. When he called in the following week he told me that he had been on duty in The Beatles' dressing rooms and had he known that I was a fan he would have got me their autographs!"

Sheridan Smith (now Earnshaw) was a 13-year-old schoolgirl in the second row of the stalls with a pal that night. They were not screamers and were trying to hear the music, but they were disappointed to be whisked off by parents at the end when they wanted to head for the stage door.

The *Daily Examiner* referred to Peter Jay & The Jaywalkers, The Vernons Girls and The Rhythm & Blues Quartet in its report on the shows, but described them as "hors d'oeuvres" with only a little screaming during their acts. The newspaper suggested that the effect The Beatles had on such young girls was frightening. Paul was asked about the screaming and he compared the behaviour of the girls to that of the boys when they are at a football match, "It's just that it's screams rather than cheers."

The Beatles were spirited away within 90 seconds of the curtain closing at 10.30pm. As the last strains of the National Anthem blared out, they dashed out of an emergency door into PC Banks' waiting police van at the Fox Street car park and off they drove at breakneck speed, straight through a red light. PC Banks, now 81, describes The Beatles as "a smashing group – four great guys".

His van was normally used as a prison van. "We used to take prisoners to Leeds Prison in it," he says. "We also used it to occasionally take dead bodies to the mortuary." PC Banks served for 27 years on the local force and still lives in Huddersfield. "The Beatles seemed happy after the show, commenting about how good it was and how good the Huddersfield people were. I had my noteboard – foolscap size – and I handed it to them and said, 'Right let's have your autographs then.' Two of them signed it and I still have it. We got away OK. A lot of the fans were at the front where there was a decoy car."

In fact, Beatle instruments and belongings were being placed inside the police car at the main entrance. All were reunited at the Peel Street Fire Station where they changed and left in their own car to meet up with the rest of the touring party. It is estimated that there were about 80 police on duty, with specials drafted in, and all that preparation had once again paid off.

Policewoman Margaret Rose, who had been rescued when the tickets went on sale at the beginning of the month, was on duty inside the cinema. Margaret, who was also part of the police First Aid competition team, recalls: "All I could see and hear were screaming kids who didn't know how to behave themselves. I was standing downstairs at the back and watching out for anybody who might be in difficulty. I was a sort of dampener really. People were passing out and getting hysterical. I would say 'Control yourself, you silly so-and-so.'"

Don Levitt, who played in a group called The Embers, remembers what The Beatles left behind that day. "We used to play at the ABC in Huddersfield every Saturday morning for the young kids – the ABC Minors. We used the same dressing room as The Beatles the day after their concert, and they left loads of fan mail in sacks which we sat and read!"

Beatle humour – their default mechanism when things were uncomfortable – could have a cynical edge and it got them into a bit of bother at the Empire Theatre in Sunderland the next day. Among those in their dressing room before the shows was a local priest, and his conversation with them, robust but good natured, was reported in an unpleasant story that appeared in a national tabloid and embarrassed everyone involved.

For once it wasn't John, but Paul, who posed the awkward question, asking of the priest: "Why are there so many big churches in countries where people are starving?" Ringo then offered scotch and cokes all round, including one for the priest. "Are you allowed to drink?" quipped George. John, never one to let an uncomfortable moment pass without making it worse, joined in with a remark about Aleister Crowley and black masses.

The subject of the wealth of the Catholic church was discussed and the priest said he was on a humble rate, to which Paul replied that The Beatles were on "the going show business rates". Paul offered to play a show at the church for nothing and the priest – demonstrating his lack of awareness in worldly matters – was said to have slipped a 10 shilling note into Paul's pocket.

At that moment Neil Aspinall walked in to hurry them onstage and the priest said he wished he had time to convince them of the benefits of faith, but he wouldn't talk to them as he would to his parishoners. John and Paul – in unison – asked "Why not?" as they dashed past him for the stage.

The story found its way into a Sunday tabloid where The Beatles stood accused of being disrespectful to the priest. But Peter Melvin, then a 19-year-old member of St Benet's Parish Youth Club in Roker Avenue, of which the priest was the chaplain, maintains the group had not behaved badly. Peter was among a group of excited youth club members to whom the priest had spoken the next day about his meeting with The Beatles.

At the end of 2009 he recalled: "What was said to the priest was no different from the daily banter I got from my workmates during the week. He gave the impression that there was mutual respect and they parted on good terms. Sadly, the 14- and 15-year-olds in the club went to school the next day and told their friends. It was passed around the playground like Chinese whispers. The story got distorted and things got added on. Some of the girls at school told their teacher. She said something to the effect of . . . 'If they are that bad don't buy their records.'"

The exaggerated story was leaked to the newspaper. Peter Melvin: "The priest told us The Beatles were very hospitable and witty. He enjoyed their company. No one pushed him. The reporters on the other hand behaved disgracefully. They hammered on the doors and windows of the priest's house and shouted through the letterbox, terrifying the housekeeper. These were guys who had falsely accused The Beatles of being disrespectful to a priest. I learned the meaning of hypocrisy that day."

There was a more welcome headline the day after the shows in the *Sunderland Echo*. The newspaper's entertainment writer, Barry St John Neville, confessed that he had hardly heard a thing over the screaming, but he knew he had witnessed something special. Under the headline 'Overwhelming, Overwhelmed Yeah! Yeah! Yeah!' Barry said he had shared a joke with the Fabs before settling down in his seat for the show and he attempted to put his finger on just what it was that made them so special.

"During the years I have been interested in theatre, I have seen some of the world's leading stars, and watched the way in which different audiences have reacted to them. But Saturday was something quite different," he wrote. "Every young member of the audience felt that he or she was fully entitled to take part in their performance, and did so with great gusto. It was only when The Beatles announced anything that the noise subsided and one could hear anything from the stage at all.

"When a Beatle asked them to stamp their feet and let themselves go . . . they obliged, and I feared for my safety, feeling the dress circle move with all the stamping. The boys are certainly the epitome of teenage adulation. Perhaps it is the way they have of looking at each girl in the audience and saying I Love You? Perhaps it is their voices or body movements?"

Like so many before and after him, Barry was frustrated at not being able to hear The Beatles. "The moment we had all been waiting for was ruined by the screaming of thoughtless individuals. On the other hand, the parents of those thoughtless individuals shout at Roker Park on Saturday afternoons. But that, I will concede, is different."

The Beatles didn't stay in a local hotel that night. They travelled more than 120 miles down to the then Normanton Inn (now renamed the Clumber Park Hotel) in Worksop to shorten the journey to Leicester the next day. While there they signed a menu for a waitress. That menu fetched more than £3,000 at a rock'n'roll auction in London in 2006. It was bought by the owners of the Clumber Park Hotel and now hangs proudly in the hotel where it was signed.

Leicester police were taking no chances. Around 200 guarded the grounds of the De Montfort Hall the next day. Patrolling in shifts, another 30 joined stewards inside who would be protecting the stage. Police and stewards could be seen with protective cotton wool in their ears.

The decoy routine worked too well, with The Beatles' arrival offering no hint of the excitement to come. There was even a hint of disappointment from Ringo, who said: "Where is everyone?" and from Paul, who commented: "That's the most uneventful arrival we've had anywhere." The excitement was building at the University Road side entrance to the De Montfort Hall where anxious looking police and stewards had gathered to mingle with the crowds that had been growing all afternoon. But as all the attention was on that entrance, the Beatlemobile – guided by a police jeep and motorcyclists – calmly made its way through the main gates in Regent Road with only about 50 teenagers in tow.

The arrival was quiet, but the show was typically chaotic, with police on virtual riot patrol and shocked stewards and St John Ambulance crew under siege. The police had to fight off the fans, too, as all respect for law and order was briefly washed away by a tidal wave of Beatlemania. The front seats had been removed to create a no-man's-land between the audience and the performers. Girls stood on their seats screaming and quite a few fainted. The Beatles, despite protestations that they were sick of them, were still being bombarded with jelly babies. But in their growing excitement, the girls didn't stop at that. Full boxes of chocolates, which can give you a nasty bump when hurled from 200 yards by a frenzied fan, were also being flung. Autograph books were chucked, along with a doll, a giant panda, a shoe – even an umbrella landed onstage. Talk about raining in on them. John playfully waved a fist at the audience in retaliation. The result – even louder screams.

Steward Ray Millward, 59, wasn't enjoying it. He copped for the shoe and umbrella and he was kicked and punched by a delirious girl for good measure. He told the *Leicester Mercury*: "I have never seen anything like this. We used to get a lot of hysteria with Cliff Richard, but this beats everything. I had a shoe and umbrella thrown at me. One girl fought like a wildcat. I had to force her arm behind her back to get her to sit down. She was scratching, kicking and screaming the whole time."

Another girl flung herself at the line of police and stewards as The Beatles left the stage at the end of the first show. One might expect that Councillor Robert Scott, chairman of Leicester's Youth Committee, who was in the audience that night, would have been horrified by the scenes . . . but he wasn't. "I think they have been marvellous," he said. "They were quite well behaved in general. They were just enjoying themselves. If they don't do anything worse than this they won't go far wrong."

Fan Barbara Corderoy was the hands-down winner of the most amusing comment award when she told the *Leicester Mercury*: "I didn't hear anything . . . I didn't see anything . . . but it was fab!"

The evening ended on a bizarre note when a boy leapt off a balcony straight onto the stage and threw his arms around the neck of a startled Beatle at the finale of the second house. Not every fan was at the De Montfort Hall to scream at or grab hold of a Beatle. The odd one wanted to hear the music. Wyggeston Grammar School boy Richard Buxton, who had been at the earlier Montez show, had to work harder to enjoy them this time. "We were again in the stalls underneath the circle balcony overhang and as soon as they came on everyone stood on their seats and started screaming. So I had to stand on my seat, too, otherwise I wouldn't have heard or seen anything. I worked out that by standing on my chair and cupping my ears I managed to hear a bit more. I remember the vocal quartet The Kestrels came on before The Beatles and people actually booed them. They didn't deserve that, but it was just that everybody wanted to see The Beatles. The screaming was frustrating, but then we knew that was going to happen. We just wanted to see The Beatles."

The Beatles' departure at the end of the evening was every bit as smooth as their entrance had been. They were off and away before the fans knew a thing. Photographs published in the *Leicester Mercury* the next day capture perfectly the emotion and chaos of a Beatles gig: joy and desolation at the same time on the faces of the teenagers and the stage and hall afterwards looking like it had just withstood a riot.

The following week had been earmarked by The Beatles as a holiday, with the tour not resuming until their hometown shows the following Saturday. However, there was still business to be taken care of, with two events on the Monday – one of which they enjoyed very much, and the second, perhaps a little less so. First they drove to ATV's Elstree studios in Borehamwood to film a hilarious sketch – and three live songs – with their (and everyone else's) favourite comedians, Morecambe and Wise.

Eric and Ernie were on great form with Eric memorably greeting Ringo with the words "Hello Bongo". Some witty banter followed – particularly between John and Eric. The Beatles performed both sides of their new single 'I Want To Hold Your Hand' and 'This Boy' before the live audience, and threw in 'All My Loving' for good measure. They even donned striped blazers and boaters to join Ernie in a comic version of 'Moonlight Bay' as the credits came up, with Eric interrupting by singing 'Twist And Shout' and, comically, 'I Like It', Gerry's hit. The Beatles were slick in these situations. Quick witted and lively, they enjoyed the banter and came across well. A little bit of John loved the idea of being a comic.

The fun out of the way, they headed into London for an evening charity event in the ballroom of the Grosvenor House Hotel in Park Lane. Their mini concert was part of a cabaret style show for an audience in evening dress – an unusual, and probably slightly uncomfortable, event for the group who nevertheless performed with their usual professionalism.

Tuesday ended up being a working day, too, with a return to the Portsmouth Guildhall to make up for the cancelled show following Paul's bout of gastric flu on November 12. But three weeks can appear a very long time in the fickle world of pop. The *Portsmouth Evening News*, having published a four page special to welcome the group last time round, was now, rather surprisingly, questioning whether their popularity was fading. Despite 'She Loves You' that very week achieving the unheard of feat of returning to number one and 'I Want To Hold Your Hand' having already achieved record sales, the newspaper was openly questioning whether Beatlemania was on the wane.

Under the heading 'Cool Portsmouth Awaits Return Of The Beatles', it referred to a girl who had only last month cried herself to sleep, but who this time "is not even taking a packet of jelly babies to hurl at dear George tomorrow".

David Evans, The Guildhall's director of entertainments, also thought he detected a slight cooling of ardour, but he wasn't taking any chances. "There does seem to be a drop in the interest there was last month. We do not think there will be the same furore. But we cannot risk it. We are following the precautions we took last time. There are 4,000 coming. Tomorrow we will judge how they feel about The Beatles."

Evans – and the local police – were wise. The Beatles, as ever, received a tumultuous welcome. They were late in arriving – their car broke down yet again on the way – but they were determined to overcome their Portsmouth hoodoo. George said: "We were supposed to be on holiday this week but after the disappointment of last month's show, we felt we had to come back."

Local College of Art students Vicki Mitchell and Bernice Goodall, both 16, had the unbridled joy of spending time with John, Paul, George and Ringo before the shows, having won a competition to design clothes for them. Paul smuggled the girls and a *News* reporter in through security as police held the crowds back. Paul and John looked through the girls' designs for possible new capes and suits and the group told the delighted girls they liked their ideas and they would be passed on to their tailors.

The excitement built up through the support acts, and entertainments director Evans soon realised how wrong he was in suspecting fans were losing interest. "If you try to get on the stage you will be burnt by the footlights or electrocuted," he warned the baying mob. "I have a lot of policemen and strong-arm men who will take you out if you do not behave – and you will not come back."

From the moment the curtains parted on The Beatles in the first house, the cries went up and that's how it stayed for their full set. Two girls were treated for hysteria and an exasperated Paul tried in vain to plea for quiet. The boys were naturally keen to plug their new single, so 'I Want To Hold Your Hand' was added to the set list, with girls bobbing in their seats, screaming and shouting their approval. As with everywhere else, little could be heard above the din, but several half-crowns were found on the stage after they belted out 'Money'. Pleas by Frank Berry not to throw jelly babies were all too predictably ignored.

The great and the good always seemed to find their way into Beatles shows. Stood at the back, witnessing everything, were the Lord Mayor and Lady Mayoress, making goodness knows what of the chaos all around them. The second house was slightly calmer but there was to be an uncomfortable exit for The Beatles at the end of the show.

After their final number they dashed out of a side door while 'She Loves You' was played through the cinema's speakers. Many fans remained inside ready for a possible encore, but up to 1,000 – many of whom had attended the first show – were waiting outside and The Beatles' car was already surrounded. For once, the ruse hadn't worked. Police jostled with a screaming mob trying to get to the car, which could only inch its way to freedom. The girls were screaming, pleading for them not to leave. Then the car stopped completely as a girl slipped through the cordon and jumped in front of the wheels. The crowd seemed to grow while the car was halted and it was some seconds before she could be rescued and bundled away to be treated for shock. Police struggled to clear a route and they had to run alongside the car as it picked up speed to prevent other girls from doing the same. It seems that suggestions of Beatlemania being on the wane were unambiguously premature.

The group enjoyed an unprecedented three days' leave during the remainder of the week, managing to pop in and out of their Liverpool homes virtually unnoticed, but they paid for it when they returned to work on Saturday, with a home-town schedule that was as hectic as anything they'd ever faced, even by their own workaholic standards.

In the early afternoon they recorded a BBC *Juke Box Jury* special at the Empire Theatre, followed by an abbreviated Beatles-only concert in front of 2,500 members of their Northern Area Fan Club, also at the Empire and also filmed by the BBC, then they sprinted over the road to the Odeon Cinema for two evenings shows as part of the package tour.

Amazingly, there were no fans to meet them when they arrived in a BBC van at the Empire Theatre in Lord Nelson Street that morning to rehearse for the two TV shows. 'The Only Squeals Came From BBC Van's Brakes' screamed a headline in the *Liverpool Echo*, with 19-year-old Maxine Aspden, a Wigan shop assistant, named as the lone fan to face a wall of 30 police officers. Even Maxine gave up the ghost, leaving before they arrived. "I suppose the rest of the girls must be too busy doing their Christmas shopping to bother about The Beatles," she commented wistfully.

The Fabs made up the entire panel of *Juke Box Jury*, which was normally recorded in London. They then performed 12 songs for the fan club. Both events were screened that evening, securing 23 million viewers for the BBC. They even managed to squeeze in an interview for a BBC radio pop show to be aired on Christmas Day, before their mad dash to the Odeon. Pudsey Street, between the two venues, was closed to clear their route.

All four Beatles crowded round a TV set at the Odeon shortly before 6pm to watch themselves on *Juke Box Jury*. It was soon time for them to take the stage to close the first house on the tour package and any lingering doubts that their home city still loved them were rapidly blown away. They got a great reception from more than 2,600 people who screamed their every movement. They ran offstage at the end of the first house to watch themselves on the television again – this time in the fan club concert – entitled *It's The Beatles* from 8.10pm–8.40pm, and didn't much like what they saw or heard.

They – and TV staff – had insufficient time to prepare and they were horrified at what they considered a fairly shambolic show going out to so many millions of viewers. In the chaos, the cameras had occasionally focused on the wrong Beatle, the sound levels were poor and, worst of all, there was the odd bit of flat singing due to the poor sound balance. The BBC received complaints from viewers that the show did not do justice to the group and a mental note was made to do things differently next time. Fortunately, there was no time to concentrate on the negatives – there was a second full-house at the Odeon to entertain.

Ray O'Brien, the author of several books on The Beatles, was a member of their Northern Area Fan Club at the time and had been sent a ticket for the afternoon Empire concert and *Juke Box Jury* show. His abiding memory is of the sheer volume of fans that were there for this homecoming. "The atmosphere was just amazing. I remember George waving out of an upstairs dressing room window and the screams from the waving girls down in Pudsey Street, which was completely packed.

"I was just so very proud that a group from Liverpool was causing such excitement through the whole country. And when I saw them trapped in that upstairs room, I thought back to not much more than a year before when I'd seen Paul walking down Mathew Street in his black leather jacket with a guitar slung over his shoulder, and he would have had to come in on the bus from Allerton, and people were just saying 'Hiya Paul, all right Wack', that kind of thing."

Like Sir Ron Watson who saw The Beatles on the earlier Orbison tour, Ray had seen the group many times in their leather jacketed days and he wasn't a fan of the suits and the mop-top image. "What Sir Ron said goes for me, too," he says. "It wasn't a resentment thing, it's just that I had seen The Beatles probably 50 or 60 times in those days – mostly at the Cavern – and I preferred them then.

"Watching the *Juke Box Jury* show and Empire concert I detected a slight change within the group, with John now appearing more as the leader. Back in the Cavern days it was Paul who always had so much to say, but now John seemed to have taken over. I noticed that."

All the acts rocked the Odeon during the second house, with The Beatles getting a truly deafening response in their home city. With the three concerts this day, The Beatles achieved yet another piece of history – being screamed at by the biggest numbers yet during the course of a single day. The Liverpool Odeon was closed in September 2008, and a 14-screen Odeon multiplex was opened the very next day in the Liverpool ONE shopping centre.

The Beatles were spared the ordeal of a long road journey down to London for the next leg of the tour. They flew out of Liverpool Airport on the Sunday morning.

Thousands had slept out on the streets to queue in the pouring rain the previous month for 6,000 tickets for the two sell-out shows at the Odeon in Lewisham on Sunday, December 8. In that respect Lewisham was the same as everywhere else, but on the day The Beatles arrived the cavalry was needed in the form of seven mounted police, 18 regulars and 12 specials whose job it was to keep the fans at bay. A couple of girls injured in the melee were treated by policewomen. The queues had been forming for hours on a bitterly cold winter's day and police moved in when a window shattered in a side exit due to the sheer pressure of numbers of waiting people.

The Lewisham adventure began in the usual manner with The Beatles' Austin Princess arriving without much fuss in the yard of Ladywell Police Station where it was met by a photographer from the *Lewisham Borough News* and police staff, autograph books at the ready. Police then escorted them to the Odeon where a bingo session had just finished. Several stowaways were found hiding after the bingo and they were swiftly ejected. Outside, hordes of fans were waiting, and the mounted police were swiftly brought into action to get The Beatles in safely.

Brian Epstein joined the group for the pre-show interviews and he gave an insight into how they were coping with the tough touring schedule. He denied a story that a maisonette was being bought for the group so they could write songs in seclusion. He said the group rarely stayed together, even when they were in London. "They generally split up after a show. John may have his wife with him and some of the others usually take a relative along," he explained.

The Beatles were in good form, chewing popcorn, cracking jokes and engaging in witty banter with the press. Paul, ever aware of a photo opportunity, showed his versatility when he got behind the drums to prove that he could lay down a good beat, along with his other skills.

The Lewisham public, much to their credit, gave all the other performers a fair hearing, but they didn't hold back when The Beatles' moment came. The crowds of nearly 3,000 for each show were larger than most – and that meant even more lungs being used to full, eardrum-shattering effect.

Local reporter Paula Gracey, who had met the group on their previous visit in March, was with them the whole time again, but confessed that they were so tight that outsiders felt they weren't with The Beatles, even when they were around them.

Little music could be heard that night and St John volunteers had their work cut out with fainters inside and outside the cinema. Not all of it was directly to do with swooning over The Beatles. Girls had queued for hours – some without food or water on a bitterly cold day – and they emerged from the shows in a vulnerable state, many dazed and hysterical. One girl got on the wrong bus and ended up stranded miles from home, but kindly bus company staff laid on a special run to get her back safely.

Not everyone had come to scream. The *Kentish Mercury* carried a photograph of a group of girls from Eltham carrying placards appealing for other fans not to scream over the music. Some hope!

Lewisham could probably claim the most unusual fainter award when it was reported that a man aged around 40 had to be revived. This truly was mania. Police Supt W. K. Hansome patted himself on the back after their clean getaway at the end. A few minor injuries, a few fainters and the odd shattered window was a relatively light price to pay for the pleasure of hosting a Beatles concert.

Nevertheless, it was too high a price for local Tory MP Henry Price, who made the headlines a few days later after addressing a Conservative ladies' luncheon. He bemoaned the hypnotic effect the Fab Four had on teenagers and suggested that the challenge was to find something better for teenagers to get excited about. Perhaps fortunately for him, most Beatles fans were too young to vote.

The usual Monday off went by the board at the start of the final week of the tour as the package was to play two houses at the Odeon Cinema in Southend. The Beatles had to be on their best behaviour, too, for they had an early morning visitor to their Mayfair flat – a reporter from the teen magazine *Fabulous* who would be spending the next week with them to give readers a flavour of life on the road. He arrived at flat L on the top floor at 57 Green Street to find most Beatles, never the best of early risers, in a state of disarray. Ringo, apparently more asleep than awake, buzzed him in. George, with rumpled hair, had not long been conscious and John was still deep in the land of nod . . . until Ringo started blaring out records from The Miracles, The Shirelles and The Ronettes on their communal record player. Paul, by contrast, was not only up, but he was already out visiting a friend.

The reporter – bylined Paul Fry – found himself carrying out most of the breakfast duties – making tea and serving cornflakes, eggs and toast. His introduction into the Beatle world was instantaneous. Their phone number had been rumbled by the fans and Paul, who had just returned, turned on his best Beatle charm and wit to deal with a rogue call. Then the group's PR man Tony Barrow arrived and Fry discovered there was more to a Beatle touring day than just turning up for the gig. They first had to negotiate a couple of photo sessions, then a couple of interviews, a visit to their fan club headquarters, and finally a trip to Abbey Road for a meeting with George Martin. Lunch was for wimps – even in 1963. The Beatles made do with a quick snack in the Abbey Road canteen – interrupted by waitresses wanting autographs – before the Austin Princess showed up mid-afternoon to ferry them to Southend. The boys were quiet in the car. George was still bemused by the incident in Manchester more than two weeks before when his guitar was taken, only to be found nearby, and the boys discussed, with some amusement, the dumb questions they faced on a daily basis from reporters.

They arrived at the Southend Odeon to find the police holding back the crowds and Paul Fry got his first taste of panic – a dash for a stage door through hundreds of grasping hands. Once inside he then discovered how The Beatles kept sane amid all the madness. While their gear – which had been on the coach with the other artists – was being set up onstage he made his way to the dressing room where the Scalextric track had already been set up. John summed it up: "Once we're inside we can't get out. We'd go barmy just looking at each other, so we've become competitive with this gear."

By this time Neil and Mal were too recognisable, so one of the cinema staff was sent out for sausage rolls and egg sandwiches. The dark brown suits for the Southend shows were neatly pressed and hanging up, but there was plenty more to do. Autograph books by the bundle were shipped in to be signed, along with photos. There were bundles of letters to read and presents to open.

The excitement had started long before cinema doors opened on the day. Tickets for the Southend shows had gone on sale nearly a month before – on the morning of Sunday, November 17 – and such was the desperation for tickets that fans began queuing on the night of Thursday, November 14. Heading the queue were two girls from a convent high school who were keeping places for some of their friends. All police leave was cancelled and they set up a mobile headquarters in a nearby car park with radio contact to headquarters. An ambulance was on stand-by to monitor the welfare of girls sleeping out on the pavement for several nights in the ever encroaching winter.

And for those who might assume that 1960s teenagers didn't lead their parents a merry dance, newspapers reported that girls drafted their parents in to take their place in the queue when they had to go to school. The police bill to keep an eye on this little lot was £400 – a sizeable amount in 1963.

Among those St Bernard's Convent School girls at the head of the queue was Bernadine Kennedy, who had just turned 17. She queued from the Thursday with a school pal and two boys, one of whom, Ian, became her husband. Looking back at the end of 2009, Bernadine said: "I can't think that I'd queue on a pavement for a few days to see anyone now, but it was all so exciting – this was The Beatles! It is the queuing that I remember now – the atmosphere and the excitement of it – and the cold."

When night fell, only the nearby bowling alley was open for the odd fan to obtain supplies of coffee while their mates held their place in the queue. By the Saturday police were turning newcomers away, telling them they had no chance of getting tickets. Everything comes at a price, and in Bernadine's case it was getting into trouble with both the school and her parents. The long stint in the queue inevitably meant some bunking off – but this was one school that was not beneath playing a trick of its own. "They had someone with a camera and they were walking up and down filming the queue so they knew who was playing truant. Then the local newspaper took a photo that appeared on the front page and there was I, right in it!"

Perseverance paid off for Bernadine and her friends, though, as they secured tickets in the second row of the stalls, just feet from the stage, and right in the middle, too. Did it help them hear the music? Not really. "We had a fantastic view and it was a good sound, what you heard of it. The Beatles were exactly as you would have expected. We'd seen them on TV and now we were watching them playing right in front of us. But it was just so noisy, with the screaming, and I was screaming, too," said Bernadine, now an author of romantic novels. "It was a form of mass hysteria I suppose."

Bernadine recalls young men waving from the dressing room windows afterwards and the screams going up. It was widely presumed to be The Beatles – perhaps her favourite, Paul – but she later discovered, of course, that Paul and the others had long since fled the scene.

Their Austin Princess was given a full police motorcycle escort to the cinema that afternoon, and the huge crowds surged forward to reach it outside the stage door. There were no Beatles inside. They were safely camped in a police van that had been gently patrolling all day, thereby attracting little suspicion from the fans. The Beatles, as was their routine, had switched vehicles some miles away.

Southend's Chief Constable, W. A. McConnach MBE, had planned the operation with such skill and cunning that he was accorded the rare privilege of having The Beatles pose for his own exclusive picture session while the press were kept waiting, much to the amusement of the watching Vernons Girls. The police chief, who also had to deal with a bomb scare, had pulled off two master strokes – closure of Luker Road, thereby isolating a stage door, and driving The Beatles through Middleton Garage to sneak them into the cinema.

John entered the Odeon first, in a suede cap and dark glasses, Paul and George followed in matching black polo neck sweaters and leather jackets. Ringo was last in. The appreciative Beatles were then given a warm welcome with cups of tea from local teenagers Linda Daniels and Susan Pledge.

They also had their meals brought to them in their dressing room, a far cry from their May 31 visit on the Orbison tour, when they had been able to have a stroll in town. "It's always like this," said John. "We have visited many towns on our tour, but all we have seen is the backstage of the theatre and dressing rooms and the inside of a police car or van."

Local and national press were there to cover the event and The Beatles spent half an hour posing for pictures and chatting to them. They lined up with their backs against the stage, then huddled together on the stage and stood with two senior cinema staff for yet another photo. *The Southend-on-Sea & County Pictorial* had produced a special Beatles edition and the boys were pictured with that, too.

Disc carried a report which included remarks from John and Paul bemoaning the lack of square meals on tour. John commented: "We bless the co-operation of all theatre staffs for at least receiving us with hot meals. Trying to get out after a show to eat is impossible. A year ago, before all this happened, we could enter and leave any theatre, stay in a hotel, have a night out and go shopping without being mobbed. Things we really enjoyed have now become pipe dreams."

George was cheered up by the thought of their upcoming tour of Australia and New Zealand. "I'd just like to spend a few weeks in the sun," he said. Apart from the regular press interviews, they were also interviewed in their dressing room by a BBC TV news team – an increasingly regular occurrence.

Odeon manager Arthur Levenson, fully aware of the riotous scenes at Beatle nights, had hired Securicor heavies to beef up the men protecting the stage. The *Southend Standard*'s reporter at least managed to hear enough of the supporting acts to enlighten readers of their efforts. The Rhythm & Blues Quartet were "good, in their own, bouncy way". There were a surprising number of males in the audience to appreciate those other Liverpool headliners, The Vernons Girls. The Brook Brothers performed 'Warpaint' and their latest record, 'Whistle To The Wind', in their slick set but the crowd was getting a bit impatient by the time the energetic Peter Jay and his mates were onstage. The tension mounted through The Kestrels' act as everyone waited for the main act.

The Beatles were getting used to breaking records by now – but yet another was achieved this night. A police noise meter recorded the screaming at 110 decibels – equal to a "sustained artillery barrage", according to the *Southend Standard*. To put that into perspective – a prolonged burst from a pneumatic drill reached just 100. A police noise expert warned dryly: "Prolonged exposure to noise of this intensity could result in an injury to the ear drums."

As usual, they kicked off with 'I Saw Her Standing There' and then 'All My Loving'. 'You Really Got A Hold On Me' from *With The Beatles* kept the heat on.

Ringo tried to make himself heard singing 'Boys' while keeping the correct beat – an almost impossible task in these conditions – and it was mercifully quieter when Paul took the spotlight for his let's-take-a-step-back number, 'Till There Was You'. John and Paul then totally unnecessarily appealed for even more noise for the show closers – 'Money' and 'Twist And Shout'. Southend fans had come to party and the girls, needless to say, were beside themselves. One 16-year-old blonde rushed for the stage and tried to climb the orchestra pit, pleading "I must touch them." She threw a toy pooch on the stage and John threw back a Beatle brooch for her. She was carried out by security but was seen later trying to break a police cordon at the stage door. Her exasperated mum told the newspaper: "She's always been a bit headstrong and a tomboy." She went back to work at a Southend café on the Tuesday proudly wearing her Beatle brooch.

Chief Constable McConnach was pleased with the Fabs' trouble-free escape through the same exit, still in their stage make-up and suits, and into the van even as the first strains of the National Anthem were being played. All police leave had been cancelled, of course, and the cost to the taxpayer had been hotly debated in the newspapers in the run-up to the shows. Ringo countered: "We pay income tax and of course we are ratepayers, so we know all about additional rate costs. These things are necessary, believe me. Some of these girls need protecting from themselves."

On a lighter note, the *Standard* reported that Beatle-besotted Sally Ross (11), of nearby Westcliff, was the envy of her pals at Crowstone Preparatory School because she met them before the show and they gave her their autographs and posed for pictures with her. This act of kindness was set up by Levenson after Sally spent two nights making models of The Beatles from chocolate boxes, cigarette tops and dolly pegs. Photographs from this night, taken by press photographer Derek Cross, were featured in an exhibition at the Atelier Gallery at Leigh-on-Sea in November 2009.

From Southend the party headed back to Mayfair and Paul Fry was to discover why Beatles find it hard to get up in the morning. He reported to readers of *Fabulous* that it was 3am before they finally turned in – with Ringo emerging in his bright red pyjamas to finally turn off the record player – and this with the prospect of a 162-mile journey to Doncaster the next day. Oh well, at least they could kip in the car.

On the way they stopped for a light lunch at a hotel but there was no escape from the prying eyes. George was the most discomfited by this type of behaviour. "Sometimes they look like they think we're from another world," he told Fry, but they all willingly signed autographs between bites of lunch, and smiled as they did so.

But despite the screams and excitement, the riotous behaviour that was becoming the norm was conspicuous by its absence in Doncaster. The Gaumont had drafted in extra staff from nearby cinemas and reports spoke of orderly queues and teenagers moving in and out of the old cinema peacefully for both houses. Police Supt R. Coggan was relieved, commenting of the youngsters: "They are a credit to Doncaster. They behaved themselves when they queued for tickets [a month before], and again on Tuesday evening."

Gaumont manager Colin Meggison also reported that fans had been on their best behaviour when several days of queuing began for those precious tickets. He had been up all night supervising the queues that had been building up. First in line was 13-year-old Highfield Secondary Modern School pupil Brian Elmy, of York Road, Doncaster, with 16-year-old shop assistant Sandra Smith in second place. Several mums queued on behalf of their daughters. By dawn it was raining and the queue stretched down into East Laith Gate. Wet and cold, the youngsters were admitted into the box office, 20 at a time.

The kindly theatre manager laid on hot dogs for the fans shortly after midnight and, minutes later, another 500 were brought out. By morning there were none left. It seemed as though every teenager within 10 miles of Doncaster wanted a ticket. The cinema manager praised the youngsters for their calmness, but added wryly: "All we have to do now is get The Beatles in and out of the place on the night!"

When the big night came the problem was solved by the usual careful planning. The group turned up at the Gaumont in a newspaper delivery van, thus successfully dodging the expected welcoming committee. They had arrived in Doncaster in their car an hour later than planned. They were due to meet police outside Doncaster Rovers' football ground at 3.40pm for a briefing, having travelled up from London after the Southend shows.

"We overslept," explained Ringo. "We always seem to these days." It's likely that Ringo didn't mention to the police or the press that they hadn't gone to bed until 3am. They switched over to the *Yorkshire Evening Post* van, using piles of newspapers for seats. It wasn't the most comfortable mode of transport but that wasn't a problem. Paul told the *Post*: "I'm in a great mood for tonight. I've never felt better for months."

As the van pulled up in front of the cinema, the Fabs leapt out, ran to an alley by the side entrance, and into the Gaumont. Safely settled in their dressing room, but struggling to be heard over the screams outside, they were interviewed by Australian journalist Dibbs Mather for a radio broadcast that was to go out later on the BBC Transcription Service. The interview lasted nearly 10 minutes. George talked about losing their privacy, but didn't appear to mind too much. It was part of the territory now. He reckoned they would have at least another couple of years at the top and was asked what might happen to him then. George said maybe he might have a little business to run.

John, though, was in straight-bat mode. He told Mather he [John] hadn't "got a nice personality" and denied being the Goon-style humorist of the group. Asked if he fancied branching out into comedy, John retorted: "I don't stand a chance of being a comedian. I'm not funny enough." But he did give a preview reading of one of his poems that was to make its way into his book *In His Own Write*. Paul tried to explain how they came across the name Beatles. All the while girls could be heard outside chanting 'We Want Paul' or 'We Want John'.

Time was also made for an interview with the *Yorkshire Post*, with John denying there was such a thing as The Mersey Sound, and Ringo saying that the screaming of the fans didn't unsettle him – but he confessed to still having "a bit of stage fright sometimes".

Of course the calmness of the earlier queuing hours disappeared rapidly as show time neared. Pictures in the *Post* the next day capture the excitement of the screamers, the high spirits outside the Gaumont and the arrival of The Beatles in that van.

The fewer screams that night was probably because of the number of mums in the audience. One commented: "I'm not a Beatles fan, but I'm with a small daughter. I trust her to behave quietly. It's the others I don't trust!" As ever, the atmosphere for the 105-minute shows built up from the moment The Rhythm & Blues Quartet got the first 2,000-strong house underway.

Martyn Vickers, who had seen the Montez show the previous March, was back inside the Gaumont to see – if not hear – this show, and ended up with his cherished programme signed by John, Paul, George and Ringo as Martyn's policeman father Cyril helped bundle them out. "My Dad wasn't a big fan, to be honest," he says. "I remember him going down to meet them at Doncaster Rovers football ground that day. He thought they were a bunch of long-haired idiots, but he did get them to sign the programme for me. He drew the line at The Rolling Stones, though, when they were here. The gig itself was absolute mayhem. It was an electric atmosphere, but you really couldn't hear anything. The girls were going absolutely mad."

As he had the previous March, meticulous Martyn noted the set list not just of The Beatles, but of all the performers inside Doncaster's Gaumont. The Rhythm & Blues Quartet played 'Sticks And Stones' to get the show underway and stayed on to provide the backing as Frank Berry introduced The Vernon Girls who sang four numbers, 'Be My Baby', 'Passing Strangers', 'Funny All Over' and 'Tomorrow Is Another Day'. Then it was time, with the atmosphere still building, for The Rhythm & Blues Quartet to play for their regular front men, The Brook Brothers, who sang 'Whistle To The Wind', 'Seven Daffodils', 'Clap And Shout', 'Warpaint' and 'The Apple'. Berry reappeared to bring on Peter Jay & The Jaywalkers to close the first half. They belted their way through 'Can Can 62', 'Kansas City', 'Parade Of Tin Soldiers' and 'Do You Love Me' plus their impressions spot – including, of course, their take on The Beatles.

The Rhythm & Blues Quartet opened the second half and provided some masterful backing for The Kestrels, who were given five songs to battle through as the fans became increasingly frenzied. Nevertheless, the Bristol boys gave it their best shot through 'Walk Right In', 'There's A Place', 'Only You', 'Dance With Me' and 'Green Green'. Then it was back to Berry to try to make himself heard to introduce the next act.

And through a hail of jelly babies, autograph books and a frenzied wail of screams, John, Paul, George and Ringo emerged from the wings for their 11 numbers. With 'I Want To Hold Your Hand' now thrown in to accompany 'She Loves You', 'From Me To You', 'Twist And Shout', 'All My Loving' and the rest, it was a blockbuster. But how much could be heard through the din of the screams?

Anne Worslade, wife of photographer Charlie who took photos of the February show, was in the audience. She recalls: "I was just about still at school at the time and I was lucky to get a ticket. They were very hard to come by. But a friend got them and we were downstairs quite near the stage. It didn't help though. It was just one noise. There was so much screaming. We were expected to scream really! I don't remember much about the songs that night – just the screaming.

"We went round the back afterwards to see if we could see a light on – they might come out or even just wave out of a window. But we wouldn't have been able to stay long. We had to get the bus home!"

Mick Longworth, whose father ran the Regent Hotel, recalls: "The kids were sleeping out for days for tickets for this show. The noise was deafening, of course. The music was loud, too. In fact, you could have heard the music clearer outside because of the big air vents at the back. There were crowds of girls outside the cinema who couldn't get tickets and they were screaming over the music, too."

All too soon for the fans, it was time for 'Twist And Shout' to bring the second house to a finale. Supt Coggan leapt back into action as the

National Anthem was being played, helping bundle the boys into Inspector J. Oldfield's car to take them to their own transport out of town.

Peter Jay chatted to fans at the back afterwards and Supt Coggan was able to reflect: "I was extremely satisfied with the way everything went. I could hardly believe it went so well."

The Beatles settled for a comfortable hotel this night, but even at that late hour there were phone calls. Brian was on the phone wondering how things had gone and there were a couple of press calls plus fans who had worked out where they were. It was well past midnight again before any Beatle was sleeping.

The Futurist Theatre in the seaside town of Scarborough was used to hosting packed houses, originally as a cinema when it opened back in 1921, and also as a theatre from 1957, but never had it witnessed scenes like it did the next day. Police and specials were at full stretch to hold back the surging crowds of fans who had come to worship at the altar of the kings of pop. Two crowds of just under 2,400 fans screamed themselves hoarse during the two performances that night, and they stamped, jumped and climbed on their seats for good measure.

It wasn't such a lucky day for one teenage girl, Barbara Dobson (now Barbara Price). The police inspector who met The Beatles that day at Yeadon Airport north of Leeds, and who had the task of getting them to the theatre in one piece, was prepared to make a detour. He was a friend of the Dobson family and he asked The Beatles if they would mind calling in at young Barbara's home in Stepney Road, Scarborough, to say hello. They readily agreed and stopped off at Stepney Road. Alas, when they knocked on the door nobody answered and so they continued to the theatre. It later transpired that Barbara and her family had been down at the bottom of the garden and had not heard a thing!

Peter Nickson, who died aged 77 in November 2007, was the policeman charged with looking after The Beatles inside the venue. He reportedly described George as the best Beatle and John as a mickey-taker.

In the crazy world of the Beatle fan, any souvenir was worth having. Judith Gullen (17) was as pleased as punch when Ringo presented her with two half-smoked cigarettes backstage and she wasn't parting with them for all the world. Souvenirs were one thing, but the hysteria of fans was quite another. The increasing fear of being hit by missiles from well-meaning fans was mentioned by The Beatles in a series of weekly individual interviews that were published in the popular weekly magazine *TODAY* in the run-up to Christmas. Ringo and George both urged the fans to hold back, in interviews that also provide an insight into what they thought about touring at this time.

There was typical George humour laced into his plea, as he urged: "Please don't throw things – or, if you must, throw them on John's side of the stage. His head's tougher – and a bigger target as well, come to think of it. But seriously, please stop bombarding us. But if you have to throw something – just throw kisses!" Missiles apart, George said The Beatles were still enjoying life on the road. "Touring, of course, is tough on you physically. Sometimes you really feel dead beat and you just don't feel like going out to face an audience. But once you get on the stage, the tiredness vanishes and everything is great. How could anybody be unmoved with a couple of thousand fans clamouring and screaming? Sometimes it's a job to hear ourselves play – and I'm sure lots of people in the audience never hear more than a few notes. John tells them to 'Shurrup!' every so often, for the sake of the quiet ones in the theatre – but we don't really mind the screaming. The kids have paid their money, and they are entitled to do what they want."

Surprisingly, George is quoted as not missing the loss of his privacy, but less surprisingly he was missing being behind the wheel and expressed a love of fast cars. "Nowadays, we are driven everywhere. I'd love to own a racing car – not necessarily to race it myself – but just to be in on the racing scene," he said. George was also dreaming of owning a big house somewhere hot, but as for musical ambitions . . . "Well, of course, I'd like to hear John sing in tune!"

After two concerts at the Futurist in Foreshore Road on Scarborough's South Bay, The Beatles escaped via Blands Cliff, with police tempers fraying as they struggled to hold back the crowds. The Beatles were driven south to nearby Filey where they stayed at the elegant white-painted Hylands Hotel on The Crescent. The Hylands has since been converted into a retirement home.

After almost six gruelling weeks, the penultimate show was just over 100 miles away, at the Odeon Cinema in Nottingham. As ever, preparation was in hand. All police leave had been cancelled and Supt Ossie Sutton, in charge of the top secret Operation Beatles, was feeling confident. However, a fleet of ambulances stood by, just in case. "Security arrangements have been made and we shall have a sufficient number of officers on duty, with an adequate strength in reserve," he told the city's *Evening Post* beforehand.

He believed the fans would be well behaved and would have a good time in Nottingham. "We are anticipating the biggest crowds ever drawn by an entertainment event in Nottingham. I expect our youngsters will be like our football fans – good humoured and well behaved."

But had he allowed for tearful hordes without tickets in Old Market Square and the area outside the cinema in Angel Row?

As far as The Beatles were concerned, the familiar routine was followed. They met up with police at the city police headquarters and with perfect timing arrived at the cinema shortly before 4pm. But were the fans wising up at last? Moments later the crowds that had been gathering outside mobbed a police van that had pulled up outside a side entrance.

Mercifully, the timing was perfect and The Beatles had a clear run – and they did break into a run – into the cinema via another entrance with only a handful of followers in tow. As they tucked into a meal inside the cinema, crowds continued to swell outside, with all sorts of Beatle merchandise on sale at all sorts of prices. This night, as all others, was to have its share of screaming, of fainting and tearful hysteria. There was also the increasingly familiar game of dodge the missile onstage as all sorts of objects were hurled at The Beatles.

Along with the usual jelly babies and cards, a gift-wrapped box hurtled past Paul McCartney's head. "That was a close one," he said into the microphone before carrying on with an announcement. Several appeals were made for calm, yet still the missiles rained down and the screams along with them.

The biggest problem facing the police now was getting 2,500 people out after the first show and 2,500 more in for the second. As The Beatles played, the fans jumped up and down, waving and screaming their undying love.

At the end it was an elaborate, top secret, double-decoy routine that began with them being smuggled out while a Beatles record was being played behind the curtains. They were bundled into a black police van which whisked them away from St James's Street to the police headquarters in North Church Street where their own vehicle was waiting to take them down to Southampton, via London.

A separate police van had picked up their luggage from a side entrance while their guitars and amps were taken out, amazingly, through the front of the house. The thousands inside were reportedly unaware that their heroes were already heading away from the Odeon faster than one of Robin Hood's arrows. Outside, the cinema police held back the crowds. There were several fainting victims and one poor man was kicked in the head as he fell over one of the fainters.

The Beatles' car left the station with two policemen in a police car following to ensure their safe passage. One was 27-year-old PC Terry Lambley, who now lives in nearby Wilford, and recalls: "They headed over Trent Bridge past Forest's ground and the Trent Bridge cricket ground and headed down the A606 towards Melton Mowbray. When they got to the Melton Road Post Office in West Bridgford the car stopped and I saw John Lennon dash out and post a letter in the post box. It's still there.

"As soon as they got into the countryside we turned tail. That was our job done. It had been quite a night. It was supposed to have been my day off but with all leave cancelled I was drafted in and ended up carrying the radio – it weighed about 5 tons and had an aerial that was about 12 feet. I had to stand outside the cinema with it so the inspector, who was next to me, could have contact with the police who had walkie-talkies guarding The Beatles in their dressing room. With all that power it could only just about transmit between the street outside and the dressing room, but it was the height of technology back then!"

All the effort was worthwhile, though. Supt Sutton, the policeman charged with dispensing Operation Beatles, declared, with some relief: "It went very smoothly."

The final show would be down on the south coast at Southampton with two houses at the town's Gaumont cinema. The Brook Brothers, who had their big break on Southern Television's *Home Grown* show, hailed from nearby Winchester, and in honour of being the local lads were elevated to second on the bill. The *Southampton Evening Echo* gave them a mention in a three-page supplement which also included a particularly well-written and engaging article on The Beatles by a talented young writer called Jim Arlott, then 19 and the son of the late and much-lamented cricket commentator John Arlott.

Jim Arlott somehow managed to squeeze in with the boys when they made their traditional flying getaway during the National Anthem that night – but things didn't quite work out as he'd hoped. Jim's younger brother Timothy, in his book *John Arlott: A Memoir,* recalled: "The Beatles were in the ascendant, and when they played at Southampton Jim managed to get into the back of the transport van that took them from the concert. He tried to conduct an interview with John Lennon, but his abiding memory was of Lennon saying repeatedly to the chief roadie: 'Where's the fucking bread, man?'"

Tragically, Jim was to die in a road accident in his sports car in the early hours of New Year's Day, 1965.

The Gaumont (now The Mayflower Theatre) had been hosting the stars since the early days of rock'n'roll. Bill Haley, Buddy Holly, Chuck Berry, Eddie Cochran and Gene Vincent were just some of the big names who appeared at the famous old cinema in Commercial Road, and The Beatles had already been added to that list back in May when they played there on the Roy Orbison tour. But this was different.

Southampton was on red alert for the invasion. A total of 4,460 fans (the girls outnumbering the boys by an estimated three to one) had snapped up every ticket for both houses and worried police and cinema security staff knew that many more would be descending without tickets. There were around 100 police on duty. Gaumont manager Ken Watts was at the centre of a military style operation to get the Liverpoplians in and out without harm to them or their fans. The Beatles swapped their Austin Princess for a Ford Consul on the outskirts of town. It parked up at the front around 4pm for them to dash through the main doors while a decoy coach distracted fans at the back.

The getaway plan was top secret, too. "Even my mother wasn't told," said Watts. However, even the tightest security could be breached by Beatles fans. Teenagers Penny Allen and Judy Stewart had been hiding in the theatre for 24 hours before they were finally discovered in a dressing room and turfed out just an hour before the show. Penny, who lived in Winchester, said: "It's heartbreaking. So near and yet so far."

The cinema's third projectionist, 18-year-old Les Acres, wasn't on duty that night as he had recently broken his ankle, but he had gone into the cinema to sort out his sick pay. He didn't stay for the show as he wasn't a Beatles fan, but he was there long enough to hear about an incident between George Harrison and Archie the doorman, who was in his eighties. "I don't know what was said between the two but it was a verbal exchange and it ended up causing quite a commotion," he says. "My wife's uncle, Ken Shave, who had been hired to work the ropes that night, had to be held back by quite a few people. Ken was a huge man but a very nice chap. He was a signalman on the railway but the cinema would pull in casual labour for the pop shows, and he was just the sweetest guy. The group had minders but they had decided they weren't going to get involved and The Beatles were shuffled off to their dressing room."

The shows were typical. The girls shrieked, screaming like banshees and bobbing in their chairs. The supporting acts could be heard, but not the main men. The cinema's second projectionist, Ken Butler, worked the spotlights that night but remembers only the screaming. "You really couldn't hear them sing because of it," he said.

Those last few words summed up the whole tour, of course. Every day just seemed to be crazier than the one before. Added to all the other commotion in Southampton was the traditional last night tricks that performers would sometimes play on each other. Vernon's Girl Jean Owen's big moment was her lead on 'Tomorrow's Another Day' with Frances Lea and Maureen Kennedy harmonising on the other mikes, but a Beatle was out for a bit of gentle sabotage.

Jean, now Samantha, recalls: "My mike stand started moving, but I just tried to carry on. Fran and Mo started giggling and I said 'Come on girls'. Eventually I turned round and there was one of them, possibly Paul, at the piano with a coat over his head with something hooked around the stand, pulling it. I was laughing too then. We were just like big kids really."

Samantha says The Beatles were largely unaffected by the way everybody was behaving towards them. People who met them were still talking about them being "down-to-earth" and "normal" and they were determined to keep their feet on the ground and not get carried away with how people were reacting. In fact, *Fabulous* told readers of discussions they'd had about what they would do if it all went sour. John and Paul still wanted to be songwriters, George would still have guitars around him and Ringo thought that opening a string of women's hairdressing salons would provide him with a good living.

On the last big tour of 1963 it was the simple things that saved them – the Scalextric in the dressing room, the record player wherever they went, a constant ciggie on the go, and the banter between each other.

The year that had begun with them virtually unknown outside the north-west now ended with John, Paul, George and Ringo recognised in every corner of the British Isles. It would be almost another a year before they would set off on their fifth tour of the United Kingdom but as 1963 drew to a close, more adventures were being lined up. Early in 1964 would come concert dates in Paris, followed by their first visit to the USA – perfectly timed as they were number one in the American charts at the time – and shooting their first film. Next up was a huge tour involving visits to Denmark, Holland, Hong Kong, Australia and New Zealand on which the crowds in the streets sometimes topped six figures. There was the usual run of seaside shows, recording sessions for new singles, EPs and two more LPs, plus radio and TV work . . . and then a giant 25-date tour of America.

You might think that The Beatles would be ready for a rest when 1964 neared its end. Instead, they faced another big British tour, including dates in Scotland, Wales and Ireland. In the world of The Beatle there was barely time to draw breath.

CHAPTER FIVE

The Fifth Tour
Mary Had A Little Band

October 9 – November 10, 1964
Featuring The Beatles, Mary Wells, Sounds Incorporated,
Tommy Quickly, The Remo Four, Michael Haslam and The Rustiks
Compère: Bob Bain

PLAYING the enormous stadiums of America had presented huge problems for The Beatles in the summer of 1964, the biggest of which was security. It is no exaggeration to say that due to the enormity of the crowds there were moments when they felt their lives were in danger. There were genuine fears for the safety of the fans, too, as the hysteria regularly surpassed the level where the police felt they could safely contain the situation.

It was an incredible achievement for The Beatles to conquer the USA in the way they did, but there was good reason to return to Britain when all the shouting was over. For all the importance of being the first British artists to conquer the giant American market, The Beatles knew they couldn't neglect their fans back home. The notoriously fickle world of pop moves quickly and new contenders for the throne, most notably The Rolling Stones, were waiting in the wings.

In hindsight it appears there was never any real threat to The Beatles' status as the country's most popular group but back then there were times when it didn't seem that way. They were constantly being asked how long were they going to last, or were they starting to slip? Alongside worthy contenders like the Stones were upstarts like the London-based Dave Clark Five whose 'Glad All Over' knocked 'I Want To Hold Your Hand' off the top in January 1964, prompting fanciful newspaper stories about how the 'Tottenham Sound' would soon replace Merseybeat.

It would have been unthinkable for a Beatles' single not to reach number one, but reports indicate they weren't that confident about the song that was to end up as their eighth single, which they began recording on October 6 at Abbey Road – just three days before the start of their fifth UK tour. The Beatles, understandably, didn't enjoy having guests – invited or uninvited – in their dressing room before shows when they just wanted to relax and prepare for their evening's work. But it was inevitable that there would be occasions when that rule was bent. And Beatle conversations overheard early on this tour reveal their doubts about whether 'I Feel Fine' would be good enough to land them another number one. Indeed, they were observed tightening up the song's tricky little riff in their dressing room at the Gaumont Cinema in Bradford on the opening night of the tour.

The boys would still have clear memories of the chaos that followed them all around Britain on that final tour of 1963 and though they made the right noises about being delighted to see the fans, they were dreading facing another month of chaotic touring, as well as having to fit in Abbey Road recording sessions on rare rest days. But they were persuaded that the tour was necessary to keep them where they wanted to be.

A new chauffeur – Alf Bicknell – had been hired to drive them around in their famous Austin Princess. The boys took to Alf, and they respected his loyalty and professionalism. He was to join Neil and Mal in the trusted inner circle of friends and protectors.

Reports across the country suggest that although shows were still selling out, the atmosphere was slightly calmer at Beatles concerts, compared with 12 months before. Were The Beatles slipping was the question beginning to be whispered, by journalists at least. Or perhaps the fans had done a little growing up, too?

The excitement was still there, but fans were losing a little less sleep queuing for tickets and the riotous behaviour was, well, a little less riotous. That's not to say that the 1964 scenes were not chaotic and the screaming intense. They were. And for The Beatles there was still the general discomfort of travelling on the road in cold, damp foggy Britain as autumn turned to winter. World stars they may have been, but touring the UK in 1964 wasn't a life of luxury. Pre-show meals were snatched in pokey cinema dressing rooms. Their favoured steak with chips and peas was often eaten as they perched at small tables dressing rooms, facing themselves in a mirror.

On the plus side, there was always some enjoyment at playing live onstage, despite the frustrations of largely not being heard, and they were being paid £850 a night (which after inflation is about £13,000 today). The tour was a joint promotion by Arthur Howes and Brian Epstein. Tony Barrow, in his book *John, Paul George Ringo & Me – The Real Beatles Story*, explains why. "By then, Brian had realised exactly how much box-office cash from concerts was being allowed to leak away to outside impresarios who put on The Beatles' stage shows and he plugged the hole by co-presenting the new tour with our usual promoter Arthur Howes."

The tour was the usual format of two houses a night, starting at 6.15pm and 8.40pm. It meant 54 shows at 27 venues in just 33 days. And what did the fans get for shelling out ticket prices ranging from a top price of 10s 6d, down to 5s 6d in the cheap seats? Well they got The Beatles for about half an hour onstage, an improvement on earlier tours. The Fabs had 10 songs as their basic set list this time – songs from their summer blockbuster film and LP *A Hard Day's Night*, interspersed with two or three classic Beatle rockers.

The Beatles were delighted to have Mary Wells as their special guest on the tour. Her song 'My Guy' had been a smash hit on both sides of the Atlantic that summer and the Fabs were big fans of Motown artists, and Mary in particular. They were also happy that Mary, who was still only 21, was another genuine star on the bill, to take at least some of the spotlight off them and perhaps take on some of the press calls. Of course, it didn't quite work out that way.

Mary Esther Wells had suffered heartache in her young life. Born in Detroit, her father died when she was four and she contracted spinal men-ingitis which had serious implications for her health. By the age of 12 she was helping her mother eke out a living as a cleaner. Out of all the misery, Mary found a joy in music. She composed her first song, 'Bye Bye Baby' (not the Bay City Rollers song), when she was 15 and ended up recording it herself and it launched her in America. By the end of 1964 she had followed it up with 'I Don't Want To Take A Chance', another massive States-side hit with 'Two Lovers' and had several successful albums to her name. But it was 'My Guy' that launched her to superstardom and The Beatles were among her devotees.

However, Mary had become engulfed in conflicts with her recording company and it was announced that she was leaving Motown as the tour was getting underway. 'My Guy' was to be her one and only hit in the UK, although she continued to have a degree of chart success in America.

Mary took the saying 'An Englishman's home is his castle' literally, as Arthur Howes' staffer Malcolm Cook recalls. "I didn't work on The Beatles' tours, but I do know that Mary didn't understand all of our values. As she travelled the countryside on the tour she wondered why we hadn't demolished all the old ruined castles and abbeys and replaced them with nice modern buildings," he said.

Costs were being kept to a minimum to maximise profit and Mary was the only artist on the bill not from Epstein's North End Music Stores (NEMS) Enterprises, which by then was based in Argyll Street near the London Palladium.

Sounds Incorporated were old pals of The Beatles from their Hamburg days. They had a first-half spot plus the job of backing Mary on the tour, and *Disc* published a photo of her rehearsing with them in London shortly after she jetted in from America. Hailing from Kent, Sounds Incorporated were primarily an instrumental band comprising John Gilliam (aka John St John) on guitar, Richard Thomas (aka Wes Hunter) on bass, Tony Newman on drums and a brass section of Barrie Cameron, Alan Holmes and David Glyde (better known as Griff West).

Epstein considered that one bonus in signing them was that they could provide backing for his solo artists. They had already accompanied the Fabs on their world tour in the summer of 1964, proving a popular support for The Beatles Down Under. The last of six Beatles shows over three nights in Melbourne was filmed and screened in a television special entitled *The Beatles Sing For Shell*. The footage reveals that the fans gave Sounds Incorporated a great reception during their set. Would they fare as well in the UK? It had been a breakthrough year for them with first 'The Spartans' and then 'Spanish Harlem' bringing them chart entries.

Tommy Quickly (real name Thomas Quigley), a Liverpudlian, was the baby of the tour. He shared a July 7 birthday with Ringo – but at 19 was five years younger than the Beatle. Brian had first set eyes upon him at the Queens Hall in Widnes in September 1962 and Tommy was pretty quickly entertaining at the Cavern. There had been high hopes for Quickly, who Brian paired with The Remo Four, but his career was

PROGRAMME

BOB BAIN

1 THE RUSTIKS

2 MICHAEL HASLAM

3 BOB BAIN

4 SOUNDS INCORPORATED

5 **MARY WELLS**

INTERVAL

6 THE REMO FOUR

7 BOB BAIN

8 TOMMY QUICKLY
not appearing at Birmingham on 11th October

9 BOB BAIN

10 **THE BEATLES**

the BEATLES
SPECIAL GUEST STAR direct from AMERICA
MARY WELLS
TOMMY QUICKLY   SOUNDS INCORPORATED
MICHAEL   THE   THE
HASLAM   REMO FOUR RUSTIKS   BOB BAIN

The fifth tour, October/November 1964. *(Courtesy Peter Nash)*

Tommy Quickly, who was down the bill for The Beatles' fifth UK tour in the autumn of 1964, was also managed by Brian Epstein. (*David Magnus/Rex Features*)

Lights, camera, action… Sounds Incorporated, made up from accomplished session players, were on The Beatles' 1964 tour and they toured with them again in 1965, culminating in the famous Shea Stadium concert before a crowd of 55,000. (*Dezo Hoffmann/Rex Features*)

The Remo Four from Liverpool backed Tommy Quickly and had their own spot on the 1964 tour.

(*Siegfried Loch - K & K/Redferns*)

Tamla Motown star Mary Wells.

(*Michael Ochs Archives/Getty Images*)

My Guys… The Beatles with Mary Wells, their special guest on the 1964 UK tour. *(Hulton Archive/Getty Images)*

Police and St John Ambulance men keep a wary eye on the audience while The Beatles perform on stage at the De Montford Hall, Leicester, October 11, 1964. *(Mirrorpix)*

John and Ringo dodge fans by escaping from the Birmingham Odeon through an underground passage, October 11, 1964. *(Mirrorpix)*

The sixth and final tour, December 1965. *(Courtesy Peter Nash)*
Paul and John in perfect harmony for 'Baby's In Black' at Hammersmith Odeon,
London, December 10, 1965. *(Bob Whitaker/Getty Images)*

The Paramounts – Gary Brooker, Diz Derrick, Barrie Wilson and Robin Trower – from Southend made quite an impact with their single 'Poison Ivy' in 1963 and were on the December 1965 Beatles tour. They were later to form the nucleus of Procol Harum. (*GAB Archive/Redferns*)

The Moody Blues – Clint Warwick, Graeme Edge, Ray Thomas, Mike Pinder and Denny Laine – were admired by The Beatles and attracted plenty of screams from their own fans during the 1965 tour. (*Dezo Hoffmann/Rex Features*)

Singer Beryl Marsden from Liverpool joined her friends
The Beatles on the 1965 tour.

Liverpool band The Koobas – Roy Morris, Keith Ellis,
Tony O'Reilly and Stu Leathwood – were on the
1965 tour and were known for their lairy trousers as
well as their own distinctive brand of rock'n'roll.

(Michael Webb/Keystone/Getty Images

Paul and John backstage at a news press conference at the Glasgow Odeon on December 3, 1965. *(Mirrorpix*

Ringo and John on the run from theatre to car at the end of another concert. (*Mirrorpix*)

Crowds throng the streets as Beatlemania takes hold. *(Mirrorpix)*

Beatlemania – a temporary and nowadays unimaginable madness that gripped the teenage population, especially the female half. *(Friedhelm von Estorff/K & K Ulf Kruger OHG/Redferns)*

struggling to take off. He had the unwanted distinction of flopping with a Lennon and McCartney song when 'Tip Of My Tongue', released in August 1963, failed to make the charts. He did at least trouble the charts briefly during this 1964 tour with 'Wild Side Of Life', which at least made the top 40 (it peaked at 33) and stayed in the charts for eight weeks.

The Remo Four also hailed from Liverpool. They were among the pioneers of Merseybeat and had been regulars at the Cavern. Bass guitarist Don Andrew was the leader, Colin Manley was on lead guitar and vocals, Phil Rogers was on rhythm guitar, and on drums was Roy Dyke (later to become one-third of Ashton, Gardner & Dyke). They were signed up to NEMS in 1963 and secured a recording contract with Piccadilly.

West country boys The Rustiks comprised Keith Taylor (rhythm guitar), Bill Covington (drums), Rob Tucker (lead guitar) and Dave Gummer (bass). They were from Paignton just outside Torquay and were the surprise package of the tour. They caught the eye of Brian Epstein when he was on a panel judging a TV talent contest, which they won. Brian, to the surprise of some of his team, signed them up and immediately put them on this tour. They had made their TV bow on *Ready Steady Go* in the first week of September with their debut Decca single 'What A Memory Can Do'.

Michael Haslam, from Bolton, was working in a leather tannery until Brian walked into a club in 1964 and heard him sing. Michael (24), regarded primarily as a ballad singer, had cut his teeth in the tough clubs and pubs of the north-west and Epstein clearly enjoyed what he heard. He signed Haslam to NEMS and issued his debut single, 'Gotta Get A Hold Of Myself', on Parlophone and lined him up to appear in The Beatles' Christmas Show which was to begin its run at the Hammersmith Odeon once the tour was over. The future looked bright – but it would depend on whether Brian was willing to devote enough attention to Haslam's career and come up with good enough material for him to sing.

The compère for the tour was Bob Bain, a well-known name on the comedy club circuit in those days. The tour programme spoke of his warm personality and rapid-fire wit and that he was up for a gag off-stage as well as on. Like those who had walked this walk before him, he would need that sense of humour.

A tour coach ferried everyone around – apart from The Beatles. The tour manager – John Clapson – would be on it, tasked with keeping the show on the road and everyone happy.

First up each night would be The Rustiks, followed by Michael Haslam. Then it was time for a gag from Bob Bain and then he would bring on Sounds Incorporated. Mary Wells would close the first half. The Remo Four would open the second and then Bain would introduce Tommy Quickly, with The Remo Four staying on to provide his backing. Then Bain would be on to try to introduce The Beatles.

The action got started with two houses at the Gaumont Cinema in Bradford on Friday, October 9. The Beatles' last UK tour had omitted Bradford, but they made up for this by staging the first of two previews of their Christmas Show at the Gaumont six days after that tour ended, with the second in Liverpool the following night. The Christmas extravaganza incorporated a gruelling 17 shows, with two a night, at London's Finsbury Park Astoria.

Friday was a great night to start a tour with the weekend beginning and fans in good spirits, though it hardly made much difference to the touring party. Heavy traffic meant the Fabs arrived at the Gaumont later than planned and they made their way in through the crowds, John in his dark glasses, but they got down to some important work that evening. Anyone around the Bradford cinema on that opening evening may have heard a nice bonus . . . four Beatles playing a song they would soon be recording. 'I Feel Fine' was to hit the shops six weeks later, and they worked on it in what privacy they could, with all doors and entrances firmly locked!

Covering the show for *NME* was Gordon Sampson, and he was quickly able to dispel any rumours that The Beatles were losing their touch. Just to underline the point, his review was headed 'Beatles Still Tops' and he wrote of fantastic scenes, of banner-waving fans trying to break through police barriers and all sorts of objects being lobbed towards the stage, including a giant teddy for John, who was celebrating his twenty-fourth birthday.

The Beatles, in their smart, black suits, opened with a short burst of 'Twist And Shout' and then launched straight into 'Money'. Paul then somehow managed to make himself heard over the screams as he gave his traditional audience welcome of: "Ta. Thank you very much and good evening. How are you, all right?" before launching into 'Can't Buy Me Love', the first of five songs from *A Hard Day's Night*. He slowed the pace with 'Things We Said Today' and then George fans had a treat as he took the spotlight for 'I'm Happy Just To Dance With You'. Then John belted out 'I Should Have Known Better'. He accompanied himself on harmonica as well as guitar, and George was on his 12-string Rickenbacker. Then John was joined by Paul for their duet 'If I Fell'.

Ringo, as ever, was given his number. He didn't have a song on *A Hard Day's Night* so it was back to 1963 as he launched into 'I Wanna Be Your Man' with gusto, supported by the others on the chorus. According to *Disc*, Ringo's song earned the biggest screams. The paper also complimented John on his harmonica work. John introduced 'A Hard Day's Night' to send the screams even higher and then Paul hit them with 'Long Tall Sally' for a full-tilt finale. The curtains came down while an instrumental version of 'Twist And Shout' was played over the speakers. These 10 songs were the group's basic set list for the tour. The opening night, as you might expect, was to set a pattern for the rest.

Sampson had covered the Helen show at the Gaumont for the *NME* in February, 1963. Looking back, he considered the difference between the two: "The screaming of course. And the fact that you couldn't get a seat this night. I was covering the show for the *NME* and the best the manager could do for me was standing up under an alcove to the side, near the front. It was where you were put if all the seats had gone. It was one of the best views in the house, but it was difficult to make out many of the words. It was a complete madhouse, but it was just exuberance. It wasn't like the early rock'n'roll tours when they were ripping the seats up. This was just kids getting excited. The atmosphere was electric. It was unprecedented really."

Russell Manning, who at seven had seen The Beatles in Leeds on the Orbison tour, was in the front row of the circle this night with five or six relatives and he enjoyed the experience much more this time around. "We had such a great view and you could see everything on the stage. I remember the whole thing being not quite as manic or as intimidating this time. We went to see my aunt in Pudsey first and seeing The Beatles on television in her house in an early evening news programme before leaving for the concert. It was exciting to watch them on television and know I was going off to see them."

Even an artist as talented as Mary Wells struggled with an audience that had really only come to see The Beatles. She closed the first half, wearing a pink dress for the first house and a black for the second, but the reception was the same . . . lukewarm. 'My Guy' went down well, but 'What's So

Easy For Two Is So Hard For One', 'Time After Time' and 'Two Lovers' went over quite a few teeny heads.

Sounds Incorporated, who had backed Mary, tried hard in their own slot, with 'Spanish Harlem' followed by 'Maria' from *West Side Story*.

Tommy Quickly had the slot before The Beatles and he fared a bit better. He looked quite a sight decked out in a bowler hat, with an umbrella in one hand and a toy dog in the other for 'Walkin' The Dog'. The knockabout theme continued with 'Humpty Dumpty' and he got his biggest cheer for his single, and the nearest he ever came to a hit, 'Wild Side Of Life'.

He was backed by The Remo Four, but it had proved tough going for them, The Rustiks and Michael Haslam. They performed well enough but fans weren't there to see them, and reporters weren't there to write about them. The two houses done, it was time for the quick getaway. Fans waiting outside Bradford's swankiest hotels after the show hoping for a glimpse of The Beatles were to be sadly disappointed. The Fabs had kept one step ahead by finding somewhere nice to stay . . . in Halifax.

It was wrongly presumed that The Beatles stayed at The Raggalds Inn in Queensbury this night (the confusion may have come about because the police set up a road block just before Raggalds), but they carried on along the same road to where they were booked – an imposing Jacobean mansion called the Cavalier Country Club, which was actually a private dining club and not a hotel. This meant that owners Freddie and Rita Pearson relinquished their comfortable beds for the night so that Beatles George and Paul could get their heads down, while their daughters Gail (14) and Kim (8) gave up their shared bedroom for John and Ringo. Brian Epstein was also present, but he was obliged to bed down on a put-me-up bed in the room where they dined.

The stay was so top secret that Freddie and Rita didn't even tell their daughters. Gail, all grown up in 2010, says: "I can't believe that they would conspire to keep the news from us and there was never a chance they would let me go to the concert either. In the end my father relented and told me about a week before, but I was sworn to secrecy. In fact, I told one friend but luckily she could be trusted – she went on to be head girl at school. I had made a wise choice. My mother had been terrified that our home and gardens would be trampled so they weren't particularly looking forward to it and certainly didn't want the news to get out."

Gail was in bed by the time The Beatles arrived that night but she made it her business to find out every juicy detail. "I wasn't allowed anywhere near them. I didn't see them at all that night. But the (club) members were amazed of course when The Beatles strolled into the bar. They stayed up late and John was very funny, putting on a Yorkshire accent. It was said that they had visited a wool mill in the past few days. They went upstairs to have their dinner in a private room. It was brought up to them by our chef, Pepe Palomar."

Pepe originated from northern Spain, near Barcelona, but there ends the comparison with Manuel from *Fawlty Towers*. The Beatles' meals that night were by no means typical of the general diet in 1964. Pepe said: "I remember what they ate, of course I do. They had prawn cocktail, melon, turtle soup, fillet steak, monkey gland steak (a flattened fillet steak), and cold duckling," he recalls. "And I remember specifically what Paul McCartney ate because he wanted to eat it his in room. We sent in smoked trout and steak Diane on a tray."

After dinner it was back down to the bar, and surprisingly it was birthday boy Lennon who was first to retire. "John had toothache, apparently, and so went to bed before the others," says Gail.

Having missed out that night Gail was hoping The Beatles would at least have their breakfast in the dining room the next morning. She was inconsolable when they didn't appear but instead ordered a meal in their rooms for 10.30am. "I was crying my eyes out and my mum finally said this is ridiculous and she went up to Paul and George's room, knocked on the door, and when they answered said that I'd been waiting all that time to see them and thrust me into the room. Of course I was struck dumb but they were very nice and chatted to me. Paul said what a wonderful place we had. He had been reading this book we had about Ibiza and said that it looked great and he fancied going there. He even offered me a ciggie, but I refused, of course.

"Then my sister, who was very shy, was brought in and John and Ringo came in. Dad took two pictures of us with them. They had to be taken by the window because his camera didn't have a flash. Mine never came out, but Kim's did. As for my parents, they thought The Beatles were terrific. They were probably a bit wary of how pop stars could be, but The Beatles were so well behaved."

Some more precious photos were taken outside before The Beatles headed out of Yorkshire to Leicester and their two Saturday night shows at the De Montfort Hall. The Beatles' hotel bill was settled a few days later – with a cheque for £42 13s 6d, courtesy of The Beatles Ltd.

"My father asked the bank manager if we could have a copy of it – you could do that back then – and he was duly given a photocopy," said Gail. "It's not worth as much as the Bayeux Tapestry, but it means a lot to us." The Cavalier Country Club still stands proudly, although it has long since been called Holdsworth House and is now a popular hotel, very proud of its link with The Beatles and a few other high profile guests down the years. Gail (now Gail Moss) and sister Kim are joint owners.

Gail says: "The room where The Beatles dined that night is just as it was back then, right down to the beautiful Edwardian chairs they sat in."

The Beatles were driven down to Leicester, stopping off for some lunch at a hotel just outside Nottingham. Ringo, who had passed his driving test the previous day, spent part of the afternoon looking for a new (and preferably fast) car. In the event he settled for a Facel Vega, reportedly reaching a top speed of 140mph during his trial drive on the M1. Perhaps it was fortunate the police were elsewhere that afternoon, probably on duty at the De Montfort Hall. The 100 officers outside were controlling crowds that gathered around the entrance from 3pm. Happily for John, Paul, George and Ringo most of the fans were unaware of it when they sneaked inside. Ambulance men linked arms with police to form a human chain to protect the stage when they finally took to it.

Photos appeared the next day of some of those hard-pressed ambulance men carrying girls out of the arena in varying stages of hysteria. The Beatles played on, despite mass fainting and screaming.

Leicester Mercury reporter Denis Downes – fingers in ears up in the balcony – took his 12-year-old daughter to the show and he captured the early show chaos in his amusing column. "A shower of jelly babies rained round the unfortunate men on the stage, ricocheting off the impassive line of policemen, stewards and ambulance men looking stolidly outwards from the front of the hall. John (or was it George?) ducked nimbly as a half pound block of chocolate, suitably wrapped, hurtled past his left ear."

Denis' daughter gave her own verdict on some of the supporting acts. Sounds Incorporated came out very well. "Fab! Second only to The Beatles – 'Spanish Harlem' especially," she said. Mary Wells was apparently let down by some faulty equipment. The daughter's note read:

"Backed by Sounds Incorporated. I could only hear them, with an occasional squeak from her. Faulty mike!"

There was good news for Rustiks' drummer Bill Covington. "Pretty good for a comparatively newly heard-of group. Smashing drummer." The Remo Four verdict was: "Same as anyone else you might mention. Not great; not bad." The Beatles were perfection, of course, although she did confess that she couldn't hear John, Paul and George speaking!"

Richard Buxton, who had already seen The Beatles twice, saw them for the final time this night. He was probably there for the second house, because he did get to hear Mary sing. "I was there with my sister and we were probably upstairs in the balcony because I remember looking down to see Mary Wells. She was terrific. I also remember that Tommy Quickly was on before The Beatles and he was applauded. People liked him and thought he did well. Maybe some of the applause was because of who was to follow. If we had been where we usually were – in the stalls underneath the overhang of the circle – it would have been claustrophobic with all the screaming."

The Beatles' getaway was chaotic, despite the best laid plans. They dashed offstage and were bundled into a black saloon at the back while the National Anthem was still playing. Unfortunately, the teens weren't respectfully standing and saluting Her Majesty. A mob of 60 to 70 girls rumbled the ruse and swarmed around the Beatlemobile in University Road, hammering on the windows and roof.

The saloon careered into another car in the panic before the police finally managed to free them. The Beatles were reportedly driven down to London to spend the night before heading back up to the Midlands the next day.

Ingenious – that's what The Beatles team had to be by now to stay one step ahead of the fans, and the way they managed it in Birmingham on the Sunday demonstrated a touch of genius. Instead of turning up at the Odeon in New Street, they were passengers in a police van that travelled the wrong way up a one-way street and dropped them off at the Exchange pub in Stephenson Place. They then walked down a long passage, through the cellar, out the back and clamoured over a wall! It might sound undignified, but it was a way of bypassing a screaming crowd of 2,000 fans who were braving heavy rain. The police heroics weren't appreciated by one unsuspecting motorcyclist who was quite unprepared for a van speeding round the corner in the wrong direction before screeching to a halt at the Exchange cellar doors.

The girls had been packed outside the cinema all afternoon, their cries reaching fever pitch every time they saw a vehicle that just might contain pop's most celebrated stars. Around 60 police had the difficult task of keeping them in some semblance of order and an inspector threatened to have them all cleared away when one section started to surge. Then the rain got heavier and the crowd thinned as some girls tried to find cover. At least 300 were still wailing outside as the first of the two houses got underway, drowning out the nearby Salvation Army band.

The *Birmingham Mail* reported that many adults joined the fans blocking New Street and screaming at cars that pulled up by the cinema. Inside, there was something of an eerie quiet before the storm that would erupt when the shows got underway.

The newspaper's reviewer (F.N.) wrote: "The show itself started very quietly. It seemed for a while that this was going to be a Beatles concert in which one could actually hear what was going on. There was a strong supporting bill (although Tommy Quickly was absent that day) and none of the hysteria and mounting tension that had ruined other shows as fans grew impatient for the star turn. Indeed, the atmosphere was singularly restrained. Could this really be a Beatles show?" The reviewer's ears were in for a rude awakening.

"The answer came when the famous foursome appeared onstage. Suddenly there was a mass explosive scream. Teenagers were on their feet and tried to rush towards the stage. An army of attendants, with uniformed police standing by, went into action. The supervision was excellent. The flashpoint passed. The moment anyone leapt out of a seat he (yes, he!) was politely but firmly told to sit down again.

"But the screaming continued at a remarkable pitch. Then, just half an hour afterwards, the curtain came down and the National Anthem was played. Some did not stand. It was not a disrespectful gesture. They were simply exhausted."

Marty St. James, the Professor of Fine Art at the University of Hertfordshire, and a highly rated video and performance artist, was a bemused boy of 11 when Beatlemania erupted all around him. His sister Sheila (18), an Odeon usherette, took him to concerts there, but she insisted he stay in his stalls seat before, during and after this Beatles show.

Looking back in 2010, Marty recalls: "It was really strange as a boy of 11 to see all these older women – in reality they were probably 14 and 15-year-olds – becoming hysterical, screaming, shouting and fainting. The compère was winding it up and by the time the curtains opened and The Beatles came on the first few rows were on the floor. There must have been some who didn't see anything.

"You could hear the beginning of the songs – you could make out the opening words and chords, but then it would get lost as soon as Paul made a coy look or The Beatles sang some oohs or shook their heads and then it was deafening and The Beatles couldn't hear what was happening and we couldn't hear what was happening.

"It must have been terrible for the other groups because nobody was interested in them. Everyone was just waiting for The Beatles. I recall that they appeared larger than life onstage. The Odeon stage was quite big but The Beatles looked big. The presentation was quite theatrical – when the curtains opened it was like looking into a giant television."

Marty, who had travelled in on the bus from the family home in Kings Heath, south Birmingham, was rescued by his sister afterwards from the empty but battle scarred arena. "It must have taken its toll because I was tired at school the next day and my teacher asked me why. He gave me a telling off when I told him."

Maybe it was something to do with the acoustics, but John Harte of Sheldon in Birmingham, who was upstairs with his mate Bobby Hall in the very back row during the second house, recalls hearing the concert very clearly. "Don't ask me how because we were right at the back, but for some strange reason we could hear them singing over all that screaming and it was a fantastic concert. You could hear everything," he said.

John, who was 18 at the time and working in a warehouse, adds: "There were police in uniforms placed all along the wall upstairs, but the girls downstairs were trying to get up on the stage. I couldn't believe that we could hear every word. When the curtain came down at the end everyone was waiting for them to come back out and take their ovation, but when the curtains opened there were just their guitars on the stage."

The Beatles had of course been whisked away instantly after the show, back to Digbeth Police Station, and the boys in blue were being cagey about how they did it. A coach was driven off from a side entrance with only a driver appearing to be on it. Four suits were draped from coat-hangers over the back seats, with luggage sitting on others, and fans drew their own conclusions. "I bet they're lying on the floor – the cowards," rapped one. Teenagers broke through the police cordon and pounded on the side of the coach, but it somehow managed to pull clear of the throng with no casualties.

After a day off on the Monday the show was back on the road on the Tuesday, and while The Beatles were heading to Wigan for their two houses at the town's ABC cinema, Epstein had business of his own in London. George Martin joined him for readings from Brian's auto-biography *A Cellarful Of Noise* which had been ghost-written by Derek Taylor, later a key aide in The Beatles' organisation.

In the world outside The Beatles, Britain was preparing for a General Election. Although The Beatles told reporters they had little interest in politics and would not be voting, Brian sent Labour leader Harold Wilson (or Harassed Wilsod as John would dub him) a telegram wishing him well.

The Beatles suffered a breakdown in their car on the way to Wigan (memories of the autumn 1963 tour) but arrived in time to enjoy a bowl of soup each – and to pose for pictures with those same soup bowls. They dashed in through a side stage door and after their 25-minute sets in each half they made a lightening getaway into a waiting police car in an operation that had apparently been planned over weeks, rather than hours. It helped that cinema manager Neville Ward had considerable experience of staging pop shows. He had been the ABC manager for 17 years and this was his fifth pop night.

Ward went that extra mile to see that the world's hottest pop group had at least some home comforts while chaos was reigning all around them that night. He made sure the boys had a television in their makeshift dressing room, and plenty to eat. Today one might expect that would be a standard offering, but this was the black and white world of 1964.

Everyone knew what to expect at a Beatles concert by now and there were 40 St John Ambulance personnel at hand – smelling salts at the ready. Chief projectionist John Ellwood and his six staff were helped by six volunteers from the Wigan Amateur Operatic Society acting as stage hands and trying to keep order. And what a job they had on their hands.

The Wigan crowd gave a more generous welcome than others to the undercard acts. The Rustiks, Michael Haslam, Sounds Incorporated and

Tommy Quickly all received generous applause, as did special guest Mary Wells. Nothing, though, could disguise the truth. The teens were mentally fast-forwarding the clock hands. The newspaper reported that "a deafening scream, hurled towards the stage from 2,000 throats, pierced both air and eardrums" and there was no let-up during The Beatles' 25-minute performance. Despite the incredible excitement and noise only one girl was said to have been hauled back from the stage.

In the audience was Jackie Kirk (née Foster) who recalls how she felt.

"Then came the moment we were all there for, the Fab Four, live onstage. I could hardly breathe, my throat was dry. I thought I would pass out. It was really that bad. The noise of screaming girls drowned out their singing. I've never seen as many jelly babies in my life, either. They could have opened a shop. I had two programmes for years – God knows where they've gone!"

As the spotlight switched to the ABC in Manchester the next day one of George's guitars was in need of repair. Fortunately they knew of just the right man to turn to. Brian Higham, of Barratts music store in Manchester, was an old friend. While The Beatles spent the day at Granada television studios in Manchester being interviewed and miming to 'I Should Have Known Better' for the *Scene At 6.30* show, Neil was despatched to the store – complete with the Gretsch – to see if Brian could work his magic on it in time for the two houses at the ABC Cinema (now the Apollo) in Stockport Road, Ardwick.

Higham recalls: "Neil explained that the third tuner was bent where it had taken a knock and others were loose. I told him that I'd have to ring round and see if I could find some. I told him I was gigging in Manchester that night and I'd drop it in in time for the shows."

He drove to Denton to pick up a new set and still has the old ones to this day. After closing the shop he headed to the Piccadilly Club where his own band, The Harbour Lights, were to play that night. Who should be in there but another friendly face. "I bumped into Norman Rossington (who had played The Beatles' fictitious manager in *A Hard Day's Night*) and we had a quick drink and then shared a taxi to the ABC to drop off George's guitar."

ABC executives ushered the pair backstage and Higham presented George with his fully restored Gretsch. They stayed for the whole of the first show before Brian dashed off to the Piccadilly for his own gig.

"I remember chatting to them that night. Brian Epstein was there, too. Paul was asking about the latest bass strings and I made a note in the little blue book that I always carried in my pocket. I knew the NEMS number well enough but Paul added another number and I got him to sign it, too. They all did. I did wonder where Ringo was, though, as he was missing. They said he was upstairs in the dressing room watching TV with Sounds Incorporated, who I also knew."

Brian headed up to the dressing room where he was to see another well-known face. "It was Jennifer Moss who was playing Lucille Hewitt in *Coronation Street* at the time. And the thing that has stuck in my mind ever since is that Corrie was on the television in The Beatles' dressing room when Jenny was brought in and she was introduced to them. John, who had actually been watching the programme, just said to her, 'Hello. How's your knickers?' That was all he said to her and then he just went back to watching her on the telly."

Among the press guys The Beatles spoke to that night was Alan Walsh of *Disc*. He found them in upbeat form as they discussed the release of their imminent single and plans for the Christmas shows that were to commence on Christmas Eve. Typically, they were tucking into steak and chips in their dressing room and had cigarettes on the go. Paul, referring to the single, said the release date of November 27 had been pencilled in, but they had not yet selected the song. "We recorded five or six tracks before this tour started, but we all seem to be keen on different ones," he said. George, his feet up on an armchair, spoke of the Christmas show and diplomatically said The Beatles were happy to be entertaining their fans at home after a busy year of dates abroad.

Reference was made to a second film, with Paul predicting it would be in colour "and will have more of a story". George dealt with the perennial question of how they were handling their fame and said it wasn't too much of an issue for them. "After all," he added, "everyone looks like us now anyway!"

Walsh also interviewed Tommy Quickly who was hoping that exposure of his latest song – 'Wild Side Of Life' – on this tour would finally bring him a hit. Speaking as he applied stage make-up for the first house, Quickly said of the song: "I like it and I'm hoping this will be the one which finally clicks for me. My A&R man, Tony Hatch, found the number and did the arrangement."

The interview revealed that Tommy was trying to write a song and was taking driving lessons and that while The Beatles would be hosting their Christmas shows in London, Tommy would be joining Gerry & The Pacemakers for a week at the Liverpool Odeon, followed by a week each at Leeds and Glasgow.

The interviews done with, it was show time and Manchester gave the Merseyside pop stars and their American star guest a tumultuous welcome. It was the same format – The Rustiks opening the show and staying onstage to back Michael Haslam and then it was time for Sounds Incorporated's solo spot, with the 'William Tell Overture' prominent, as ever. They stayed on to provide the backing for Mary Wells to close the first half, with added accompaniment from her own guitarist. The Remo Four kicked off after the interval and stayed onstage to back Tommy Quickly, who went down well with the Manchester crowd. The proverbial roof was raised for The Beatles during their 28-minute set, as it had been the year before.

Brian Higham watched the show from the wings before dashing off for his Harbour Lights gig. He saw the irony in George taking such care to have his cherished guitar repaired. "They were great, but why they bothered tuning up I don't know. You couldn't hear a thing for all the screaming," he said.

The Beatles' first visit to Stockton-on-Tees had occurred on the day President Kennedy was assassinated in November 1963. This second and last visit to the north-east town also had a political edge – it coincided with the General Election, which narrowly returned the Labour Party, led by Harold Wilson, to government after 13 years of Conservative rule.

So The Beatles faced some topical political questions in their Stockton hotel room before the shows at the Globe Cinema on Thursday, October 15, when interviewed for Tyne Tees for the news-magazine programme *North-East Newsview* to be screened the following evening. They were suitably diplomatic about their political views, but did provide some typically witty Beatleisms. The exchanges would have happily fitted into the script of *A Hard Day's Night* . . .

"What do you think is going to happen to you if they nationalise you?" asked the reporter.

"Well we'll have to move out won't we?" offered George. "We'll have to go and live in Germany or some place like that."

"Southern Ireland," said Lennon and McCartney in unison. Paul was asked if he had aspirations to one day become Prime Minister, but he dismissed the job as "a hard day's grind".

He offered the non-smoking interviewer a cigarette, and Ringo chipped in: "They're going up, you know."

"We'll have to give up then," said George and Paul. "Aye! None of these luxuries," ventured Ringo. "Don't tax them, Harold," said John, with Ringo adding: "It's bad enough as it is."

Returning to politics, referring to the party leaders, the reporter said: "During the last few weeks, the Grimond group (Liberal), the Hume group (Conservative) and the Wilson group have been edging you off the papers. Have you been envious of all these groups?" Paul replied: "No. We sell more records than they do!" George came out with: "The situation looks pretty Grimond, doesn't it!"

Along with the politics came the usual How Long Will You Last question. This time it was in reference to an apparent misquote from the irascible Prince Philip, accompanying the Queen on a tour of Canada. The Beatles are on the wane, he was reported as saying – later 'corrected' to "The Beatles are away".

"What about this business of being on the wane. Is that all over?" asked the TV interviewer.

Paul replied: "Well, we get it about every two months. Somebody says, 'You're finished. You're on the wane.' You know, they say Dave Clark's in, Brian Poole's in."

George chipped in: "But we're still having a laugh, aren't we."

The reporter continued with: "You don't look too bad for four lads likely to be on their way to the dole queue, do you?"

"No. Well, we passed one the other day, didn't we, Paul?" said John.

"Yes, we passed a dole queue," said Paul. Again, it was George with the punch line . . . "We're still on the dole as well. Don't tell Harold."

The Beatles were an hour behind schedule and by the time they got to the cinema the streets were teeming, boosted by children who were off school that day. A press conference was hastily arranged in the office of Globe manager George Skelton. The Beatles were still in playful mood, with Ringo hiding in a cupboard until he was unearthed by an *Evening Gazette* reporter.

This initially proved to be a sad day for local girl Geraldine Davison.

Geraldine, who was in a wheelchair, had been bought a ticket for her twentieth birthday by a family friend. However, it wasn't considered safe for her to be admitted so she had to miss the show and the friend bought her a Beatle record instead. Geraldine wrote to Ringo, explaining her predicament and wishing him luck for the show. He sent her a signed photo and delighted Geraldine said it more than made up for missing out. There was even better to follow. Kindly cinema manager George Skelton presented Geraldine with a programme signed by all four Beatles.

The 2,500 packed into the Globe for the first house screamed their little heads off and showered The Beatles with jelly babies. They beat their way through 'Money', 'If I Fell' and 'A Hard Day's Night' and the rest to a backdrop of constant noise. Ringo again got a huge response for 'I Wanna Be Your Man'.

Stockton Express reporter Paul Screeton, in his report headlined 'Beatles "Whistle-Stop" A Screaming Success', noted that the group enjoyed themselves more than The Rolling Stones who had looked bored when they played the Globe the previous month. The score in fainters was 4–0 to The Beatles too – the four ambulance men and six nurses on duty in that first house were able to deal with a relatively modest total. John was waving comically at the crowd and George, Paul and Ringo were all smiles and enthusiasm.

Paul Screeton was also impressed with Mary, in her slinky, silver lamé dress, but he feared her material was too sophisticated for such a young audience. Even so, Mary, who was backed by her own guitarist and musical director Melvin Turrell as well as Sounds Incorporated, was given a good reception for her renderings of 'One Who Really Loves You', 'My Guy', 'Two Lovers' and 'Time After Time'.

Screeton caught up with Mary, who was listening to a song on her portable record player with her secretary, Maye Hampton, and Tommy Quickly, in the dressing room during the interval. Mary praised The Beatles and predicted that her latest record 'What's Easy For Two' was going to be a hit.

Tommy drew his fair share of screams – and laughter – from the Globe audience. His bowler hat and umbrella for 'Humpty Dumpty' was taking audiences by surprise. Tommy revealed that the 'Wild Side Of Life' would be a hit because his mum had bought five copies and he was saving up for one himself.

'Maria' and 'Spanish Harlem' were two of the tunes that earned Sounds Incorporated yet another round of applause.

Not everyone in the audience was a screaming teen. Captured in a *Gazette* photo was 68-year-old Winifred Kirby, of Thornaby, who had taken her granddaughter Susan (16) to the show. During The Beatles' performance, Winifred, fingers in ears, looked as though she'd rather be anywhere else in the world at that moment.

The touring party was headed for Hull next, with Friday afternoon and evening shows at the city's ABC Cinema. Hull was ahead of its time with its one-way road system, but The Beatles, hoping to slip unseen into the theatre, found the back door locked. With fans already gathering at the front they turned tail and headed for the police station. Plan B was put into action and they were placed in a police van that got them into the cinema with the minimum of fuss.

In fact, they were relaxed enough to gather round the cinema's piano with Paul belting out some old-fashioned classics like 'Roll Out The Barrel' with John, George and Ringo, beer glasses in hand, pitching in with some vocal support. Cilla's 'You're My World' proved too high, even for Beatle voices, according to the *Hull Mail*.

George and Paul told the newspaper that the group had been too busy to vote in yesterday's General Election. George revealed that the boys would be working with Dick Lester again on their second film with filming due to start on February 22. Ringo, meanwhile, was happy to talk about his new car. Paul had an Aston Martin and George an E-type Jag, leaving John as the only Beatle without wheels. Lennon had the usual routine questions to deal with. Crowds had begun to gather shortly before the first show and inside the cinema there was plenty of excitement.

Showtime saw The Beatles in sparkling form for both houses. They cracked gags, smiling and laughing, and seemed to enjoy the excited reception they received. The audience, as ever, played its part in making it a memorable night.

Rugby players and other burly helpers had been drafted in to support police in protecting the stage. However, even they, and the barrier around the orchestra pit, couldn't prevent the girls getting through, and at least two managed to launch themselves at the stage. First aid volunteers were kept busy reviving the fainters. Love letters, cards, jelly babies and presents rained in from every angle, but this was one night when The Beatles took it all in their stride.

They exited in the usual manner, taken back to the Gordon Street police station, and they had time to visit the chippie over the road in Redbourne Street before they left Hull.

There was a weekend off from the tour before it headed up to Scotland for three dates from the Monday. There was, however, travelling and work for the busy Beatles. They drove down to London on the Saturday and spent a marathon nine hours at the Abbey Road studios on the Sunday. Astonishingly, they completed six songs from scratch (five for *Beatles For Sale* plus 'I Feel Fine'), re-recorded another and finished yet another in those nine hours.

The Beatles were spared the ordeal of a lengthy road trip up to Scotland and instead flew up to Edinburgh, arriving at the city's Turnhouse Airport at noon. For once word hadn't got out and only a handful of girls were there to greet them, but things went horribly wrong at the ABC Cinema in Lothian Road, where both The Beatles and Epstein were submerged in the huge crowds outside and buffeted up against the glass at the front door.

Bill Barclay, who later went on to achieve fame as a comedian and actor, was a local 19-year-old who had been hired as security. He was in the foyer when he heard the screams of the girls and looked up to see John Lennon's face pinned against the glass of the locked doors. They managed to somehow smuggle The Beatles in but then realised Epstein was still outside in the mob. They had to open the doors again to let him through.

Thankfully, it was calmer inside the ABC than it was on the desperate streets outside. The Beatles were each given a security guard and Barclay's job was to look after George. There was the usual cut and thrust with the press, with John fielding a question about why there were so few fans to greet them at the airport, and why they were not doing the Royal Command Performance.

There was also the usual clowning for the cameras. Ringo was pictured in the *Daily Record* doing a passable imitation of a mother playing the piano to entertain a small boy and doing a spot of fortune telling as he read Paul's palm while George and John looked on. But it was the quiet before the storm. Those busy streets outside were getting still busier. The fans that had queued deep along Morrison Street for their precious tickets were determined to give The Beatles a warm Edinburgh welcome they would never forget. One of those fortunate enough to see – if not hear – The Beatles that night was 16-year-old Royal High School pupil Chris Warbrick who was excited beyond belief when the envelope containing his two tickets dropped on his doormat. He was to take his girlfriend Pauline Barry to the show. Chris, who now lives in Dumbarton, said: "My school bus passed the ABC and I remember being on the top deck on the way home about 4pm and seeing the crowds of people already gathered outside. It was fantastic. I was thinking I'm going to be there tonight. I went to the 8.30pm show so I had plenty of time to prepare before calling round for Pauline.

"We got the bus and it went along Fountain Bridge and there were crowds and crowds of people in Lothian Road outside the cinema. It was pandemonium. There were so many screaming and tearful people and I remember holding on tight to my ticket in case someone tried to wrest it from me. The Beatles were the biggest thing on the planet. It was so exciting to be there."

Chris recalls that the other artists got through their performances with only an odd scream of interruption. It meant that he was able to hear Mary Wells fairly clearly. "She was so good. 'My Guy' was a terrific song and it sounded so good, but I didn't recognise the other songs she sang. Tamla Motown was only just starting here and Mary – apart from 'My Guy' – was not that well known to a lot of people. They were just there for The Beatles. Mary closed the first half – at least it was better than coming on just before them. It was a problem for everyone else really. Sounds Incorporated were very good musicians, but I was a three guitars and drums person. I was only 16 and not too sophisticated and maybe they were a wee bit out of their time."

Someone who definitely appeared out of his time was the show's compère Bob Bain. "He was a Brylcreemed comedian. A small fellow, quite tubby and totally non fashionable. A really strange choice of person to compère a pop show." Bob had a tough job controlling the teenagers. "People just wanted him off really – let's have The Beatles. But of course that's about the last we heard – him introducing them, and then the noise went up. I couldn't really hear anything and we had a loudspeaker at the end of our row! It was just constant screaming, but it didn't really matter. It was just a matter of being there – to be part of the occasion."

It was a trouble free evening, discounting the overworked Red Cross volunteers who were kept busy dealing with over-excited fans. The *Daily Record* reported on dozens of fainters being carried out of the cinema and three girls being carried from the queue for the second show after passing out.

A large crowd gathered outside the cinema between houses singing songs of devotion to the Fab Four as tearful girls left the first show. The Beatles battled to be heard from the moment they took the stage. The screams from the girls were clearly audible in the streets outside the ABC. With The Beatles due to play Dundee the next night, a reporter from the Dundee *Courier & Advertiser* was there to witness all the excitement and pronounced that "Dundee fans are certainly guaranteed a treat".

Chris reflected on how newspapers dealt with teenage entertainment in those days. "The *Edinburgh Evening News* pop reports were covered by a guy called John Gibson, who was always quite 'straightforward' about such shows. In those days there was no hype in such newspaper reports. My impression was that he was older than us teenagers, and perhaps wasn't quite on the same wavelength as us."

Nevertheless, Gibson was in tune with his younger readers that day. In his review of the two shows, he recorded: "Beatlemania on the wane? Don't you believe it. They are maybe being pushed a bit by some dishevelled people called The Rolling Stones, but as far as Edinburgh goes they are still the greatest, and still Fab. There wasn't the slightest hint of a slip from the absolute pinnacle in pop entertainment."

After the show The Beatles headed off for some well deserved rest at the classy Four Seasons Hotel at St Fillans on the banks of Loch Earn. Despite the lateness of the hour, special arrangements were made for them to enjoy a gone-midnight steak dinner. They slept in the next morning. John and Paul, who shared a chalet, rose first to enjoy a bracing coastal walk, returning for lunch in the hotel dining room. George and Ringo had breakfast in bed. A few hours to themselves was a rare luxury, and four police detectives were hired by the hotel to make sure that nobody invaded their space.

All four Beatles, accompanied by Neil, went boating on Loch Earn at 1pm. It made a nice picture spread for the *Daily Record,* with the Fabs, wrapped in coats and scarves to keep out the Perthshire chill, getting away from it all before reality intervened. All too soon it was time for a road trip to Dundee and two Tuesday houses at the Caird Hall. It was back to the usual routine, with their car met by police three miles outside Dundee, who escorted them in.

It had been just over a year since The Beatles had last played the Caird Hall and such was their impact on that fair city that there was considerable excitement at the prospect of their return. The authorities were determined that nobody would be allowed to spoil the fun. The police, together with the Malcolm Nixon Agency, who were handling the bookings, had taken on at least 50 stewards inside the hall, "and they'll be men who can use themselves in an emergency", warned city factor Charles Macdonald. "There will be no young boys, girls or anyone who might run away from trouble. The more I can get – 75 or more if possible – the better."

And just to ram home the message, it was pointed out to readers of the Dundee *Courier & Advertiser* that The Beatles would also have their usual squad of "heavies" with them. The Agency stressed that The Beatles would not be staying within 35 miles of the city – which was true as the Four Seasons Hotel was just over 50 miles away.

When The Beatles had touched down at Turnhouse the day before John had issued a message for the Dundee fans as only John could. "Hi Jocks! Delighted to be back in awricht-the-noo's-ville. Looking forward to meeting you all in the Caird Hall tonight. Thanks for all your Hielan' support. Och aye the noo, from Jock MacLennon."

Before the shows the boys were interviewed in their dressing room by June Shields for Grampian Television, and plenty of irreverent humour was again on display. They made some weak jokes about Dundee cake and were then asked if they have any heroes in showbusiness. John said George, George said nobody, Paul said everybody – especially American coloured groups – and Ringo agreed with that. John was asked if he had a message for fans in Aberdeen because the group were not playing there. He obliged by going into some Lennon gibberish in a mock Scottish accent.

The TV crew was impressed enough to remain and shoot a few minutes of silent footage of the concert mayhem that was to follow – including snatches of the other performers. The Beatles had another visitor as they waited to go onstage. Margaret, Countess of Strathmore, was dropped off in her chauffeur-driven Rolls-Royce and ushered backstage to meet pop's royalty. What was said remains unrecorded but the Countess didn't enjoy her evening and subsequently wrote to the *Courier & Advertiser* describing fans as appalling and bad mannered for screaming so hard that she couldn't hear the music.

Meanwhile, Charles Macdonald had been as good as his word. Shoulder to shoulder in front of the stage stood 40 powerful men, among them local and national wrestling champions. At various points across the hall were another 35 – all too ready to reseat excitable teens – but such was the devotion of Beatles fans that the dire warnings already issued, plus appeals for calm before both houses, counted for nothing once those curtains parted. Cries of We Love You Beatles suddenly convulsed into one gigantic scream. The *Courier & Advertiser* recorded that the noise was far louder than the previous visit and there were casualties from all over the hall, with 50 carried out in 5 minutes, all of them girls sobbing ecstatically or in a state of collapse led from the hall by the tough security guys.

From the distinctive opening notes of 'Twist And Shout' through to Paul's 'Long Tall Sally' finale it was one giant scream in Dundee. The six-man Sounds Incorporated were once again hailed as the pick of the rest. Not being screamed at didn't necessarily mean you weren't appreciated. Their fine arrangements of 'Maria' and the 'William Tell Overture' were listened to in almost total silence by the bemused teens. But there was an explosion of applause at the end of each number, "the kind you get at opera houses" noted the *Courier & Advertiser*.

Mary Wells' classy act wasn't to everybody's taste. Fans wanted material they knew and girls who had come to scream at The Beatles weren't Mary's audience. There was to be no clean getaway from the Caird Hall. Bob Bain was onstage imploring the audience to call for an encore by The Beatles – but too many fans had wised up to the routine by now. The Beatles dashed out to find a crowd of up to 1,000 people and police with dogs trying to control them. They were mobbed all the way to their car and desperate fans flung themselves on it as they were driven away. Screaming girls fell on the road as the car disappeared down Castle Street.

Leaving the screams behind, The Beatles enjoyed a second night in the tranquil setting of the Four Seasons, but police were called to disperse several car loads of teenagers who had followed the group back from Dundee. The hotel again pushed the boat out for their star guests, hosting a party for them. Paul retired first and John followed. Ringo and George decided to take a boat out and spent some time exploring the pier. Such rest and relaxation was a rare luxury for them on tour. Little was seen of The Beatles at the hotel the next day and the handful of fans who gathered hoping for autographs were disappointed. The group were quietly driven off to Glasgow.

Scenes in and around the Odeon Cinema in Glasgow before, during and after the Wednesday shows provided more firm evidence, if it were really needed, that Beatlemania was still kicking and screaming. The shows had sold out within hours and ticket-less fans, waving placards of protest and screaming and chanting, took out their frustration on the streets surrounding the venue.

In scenes reminiscent of Dublin the previous year, there were reports of cars and shops being attacked, and police were fearing a full-on riot. It reached a head when 3,000 fans leaving the first house merged with the huge numbers of disappointed fans outside. Shop windows were smashed in Renfield Street and a car in West George Street was overturned. Mounted police sent youths running for cover and there were nine arrests for disorder and seven charged with causing a breach of the peace.

Fans were herded into West George Street and fireman had to hose down the road after petrol gushed out of the overturned car. The *Glasgow Herald* reported the sorry tale the next day. "At one stage West George Street had the appearance of a field hospital, with dozens of girls propped up on the pavement being attended by nurses. More serious cases were taken to Glasgow Royal Infirmary," it reported.

The Fabs had arrived at the cinema a good hour before the show – enough time to deal with the battery of reporters, photographers and TV crews hoping for that bit of gossip that would make the headlines. The Beatles played ball, revealing that they would start shooting their second film in February and that John was to publish a second volume of his poems, stories and drawings.

Sadly, though, as in Dublin in 1963, the next day's headlines were all about the near riot The Beatles' appearance had caused. The *Glasgow Herald* wrote of it being "A Hard Day's Night for police" while the *Daily Record* led with the story, under a banner headline 'Bedlam For Beatles'. Beatles fans could give football supporters a run for their money. Police were drafted in from Scotland's World Cup qualifier with Finland at Hampden Park four miles away as things got out of hand between the two houses. The window of a shoe shop in Argyle Street was smashed and a car was overturned in Sauchiehall Street and a second car was ransacked in West George Street. A man was arrested for throwing an object at a police horse as they tried to restore order.

There was a happier atmosphere inside the venue, but the music was predictably lost to the screamers. Maximum crowds of 3,000 screamed through each Beatles set. Two people not screaming were Celtic foot-baller Bobby Lennox and his wife Cathy. They enjoyed second row seats, courtesy of Bobby's team-mate Jimmy Johnstone who had to give them up after being called into the squad for Scotland's match. Bobby and Cathy dodged the jelly babies and heard what music they could above the screams. Lennox told *The Beatles In Scotland* author Ken McNab: "It was like nothing I had heard before. Just Bedlam. When you play football, you're so focused on the game you hardly notice the crowd. But I had never heard a noise like this in my life."

The Beatles leapt into their getaway car at the end for a dash through the crowds and back to the sanity of their hotel. Scotland had been rich in its contrasts – the silent beauty of its countryside and the wild mania of its big cities. There was no time to rest. It was back over the border into England and a trip to Yorkshire for two big city houses the next day.

They came out in their thousands for the return to Leeds of The Beatles. Almost 5,000 fans packed into the two Odeon houses, while many hundreds – possibly thousands – more gathered outside. Screaming fans left their seats in a mad dash for the stage during both houses, cramming around the front of the orchestra pit when The Beatles came on. Security and St John Ambulance volunteers were in danger of losing control and being over-run. Cinema manager John Clark told the *Yorkshire Post* that he had never known an audience so determined to get on the stage.

Six girls broke through the cordon to climb over the organ onto the stage during the first show. One girl was inches from Paul before being dragged away and taken out by a guard. Typically, she simply went round the front of the house and persuaded a policeman to let her back in. The Beatles were top earners, but they should have been paid danger money on top. All sorts of things were still being lobbed at them, despite repeated appeals in the press and from the stage. The Leeds fans were certainly not holding back. Among the objects showered on The Beatles was a cigarette lighter which landed straight on Paul's head.

He held the offending lighter up for reporters to see when he spoke to them the next day at Kilburn. "See this," he said. "It hit me on the head at our concert in Leeds last night. That's how excited the audience was getting! They were throwing all sorts of things at us in their enthusiasm. I've got so many bumps on my head from being hit by flying objects that I feel more like a prizefighter!"

Ambulance workers beefed up the stage security for the second show, in front of a marginally older audience that included four adults who refused to leave their seats after the first house in protest at being unable to hear or see anything for people jumping in front of them and screaming. They were allowed to stand in a circle aisle for the second show. Why would they think that would be any better? They could barely have heard any more second time around.

The Beatles talked about the album cover of their forthcoming *Beatles For Sale* at the Odeon. John signed a photo for a fan and on the back he sketched four possible designs for the cover. The photo surfaced at a Bonhams auction in 2008.

The next day's shows in London took place in grand surroundings at the largest and most palatial cinema in England. The Gaumont State in Kilburn High Road seated 4,000 and boasted huge chandeliers and ornate carvings along with the customary deep-pile carpets.

The Beatles met the press, and being a London venue, reporters and photographers from the big dailies rubbed shoulders with the regionals looking for an exclusive interview or photo. The boys were photographed seated on the steps leading up to the stage, John and Paul in dark suits and ties, Ringo in a striped suit and George in a roll-neck sweater, dark jacket and striped trousers.

The press, as ever, were firing their questions. Paul was asked what he thought about Tamla Motown artists achieving great chart success in the UK. "They're great, and will continue to go down well here," he said. "They're all exciting entertainers, as those Supremes showed during their trip."

Paul thought he noted a difference between fans in the UK and America. "The odd thing is, though, that these coloured singers aren't really appreciated by the white people in the States – they come over to Britain and are knocked out by the reception they get. It seems it's only their own kind that likes them back home."

Tight security meant that Mary Wells' planned visit to the *Ready Steady*

Go! studios was cancelled. Once the artists were safely inside the cinema at 4pm it wasn't deemed sensible to let them out again, so Mary missed out. Disappointed Mary was nevertheless free to speak with *Disc's* Penny Valentine, to the backdrop of a Jackie Wilson song on Mary's portable record player – quite a luxury. It wasn't the only luxury for Mary, who was accompanied on the tour by her friend and secretary Maye Hampton.

Mary revealed they both had a passion for British cream cakes. "Maye and I buy a box every day to take on the coach . . . and I'm trying hard to lose weight," said Mary. "It's been real funny on the coach. The boys are always laughing at us with our boxes and the other day one of Sounds Incorporated came up and thumped the top of my box so the cakes were all squashed. We all had a good laugh and then I opened the lid, got a handful of cream and pushed it into his face. Then he got a handful and pushed it into mine!"

Mary and The Beatles were not travelling together, but she had been around them enough to be worried for them, telling Valentine: "You have no idea how surrounded they are. There's always someone wanting them. Their lives are certainly not their own. Sometimes Paul or George will come into my dressing room and play a couple of records and then leave again."

The Beatles, and all the others, were surrounded again this night. But the crowds outside were gathering later than during the whirlwind autumn 1963 tour – and the behaviour of fans – in London at least – appeared to be not quite as desperate.

Willesden & Brent Chronicle reporter Christopher Eorwine, who covered the first house, noted with some relief that fans were no longer rushing the stage in such numbers, and neither were they ripping their own clothes in ecstasy. Not all of The Beatle photos being hawked outside the Gaumont State were snapped up either, although that may have been down to the prices the touts were asking.

The crown was not about to be ripped from those mop-topped heads just yet. Eorwine ventured that there wasn't a group that could hold a candle to The Beatles and the reception they received at Kilburn con-firmed the matter. "The solid wall of noise, screams, whistles and shouts from a theatre packed with deliriously happy fans left no doubts that The Beatles are on top for a long time to come," he wrote. The first house, though excited, was remarkably well behaved. The warm-up acts were accorded a polite reception – something akin to the applause that accompanies a decent pass in a football match. Mary Wells, closing the first half, and Tommy Quickly, just before the main event, made the biggest impact on the crowd as tension mounted during the countdown to Beatlemania.

That countdown was lengthened by Bob Bain who took great delight in whipping up teenagers already in a state of deep frenzy. He "cavorted around like a juvenile cheer leader" as thousands of teenagers collectively willed him to oblivion. The curtains closed as he at last dashed off and they parted again for the arrival, to screams and delirium, of The Beatles.

The girls were immediately on their feet, handkerchiefs, scarves, anything that came to hand being waved madly in the hope that it might, it just might, be spotted by a Beatle. The Fabs responded with an enthusiastic performance. 'Can't Buy Me Love' – only five minutes in – brought the first fainting case. A girl from the front stalls was rushed into the aisle by her boyfriend and into the arms of a St John's Ambulance nurse who took her out through the exit. She was back 10 minutes later as good as new. Girls were alternately laughing and crying, one was pounding her head on her arms crossed on the seat in front of her.

The Beatles crashed though a set still dominated by songs from *A Hard Day's Night*, rousing the girls to fever pitch. Encouraged by the security detail, most mustered the self-discipline to remain in their seats as Beatle heads bobbed in unison and the beat pounded on. They finished with 'Long Tall Sally' and dashed off for the sanctuary of their dressing room. The curtains were greeted with wails and as the National Anthem died away a struggle began in the front stalls. One girl had refused to budge. Outside, the queue was already forming for the next performance half an hour later. It was a bigger crowd – a longer queue – and the men hawking the Beatle photos were back.

The author, journalist, record producer and founder of soul music.com David Nathan was then a 16-year-old schoolboy living with his family above their chip shop right next door to the Gaumont State. His father Mark's friendly relationship with the cinema manager paid dividends as tickets were made available for the second house for David and his sister Sylvia (12) who dressed appropriately in Beatles tights and a Beatles scarf.

David's father was even involved in an elaborate end of night getaway plan for The Beatles whose plan-B escape route would take them out of the back, then up and down ladders set up on both sides of the wall so they could hide in the store – where the chip shop kept its huge vats of oil – until the crowds had cleared. Happily for The Beatles, but sadly for David and Sylvia, plan-B wasn't needed. But at least the Nathan family had the kudos of feeding The Beatles that night as someone was sent out to their shop for a fish and chip supper.

David credits The Beatles, along with Dionne Warwick, for awakening his interest in the music of the great black artists. Looking back, he says: "I was a Beatles fan, so this was a huge treat for me. But it was a mental night. Even just trying to get through the crowds was just mad. The second house was so loud. I was there to see Mary, too, but you just couldn't hear much over it all and we had pretty good seats, too. I was a little upset because I was already immersed in the music of Motown. The only two songs I remember Mary doing that night were 'You Beat Me To The Punch' and 'My Guy'.

"I definitely remember The Beatles singing 'Can't Buy Me Love' and 'A Hard Day's Night'. Funnily enough, I'd won a copy of the *Hard Day's Night* LP not long before in a school raffle. I remember begging Mum to let me stay up that night just in case The Beatles ended up staying in the storeroom, but she said 'I don't care if it's the Queen of England – it's your bedtime!'"

For the touring party, Friday night in Kilburn was to be followed by Saturday at Walthamstow. At least there wasn't a long road trip this time and they could all hit their favourite London clubs. Pop stars on tour were grateful for such blessings.

The tickets for the shows at the Granada Cinema in Walthamstow had gone on sale months before. Even though the box office wasn't due to open until the Sunday, queues had begun forming shortly after the schools turned out on Friday, June 26. Police sent the early birds home, fearing they would get in the way of Saturday shoppers. Fans returned the next day but had to hang around Hoe Street until the cinema closed at 11pm on Saturday before queuing could officially start. Thirty police were on duty to make sure the girls were safe and there was no queue jumping. The box office opened at 7am on Sunday and by the time it closed at 9pm around two-thirds of the 6,000 seats (taking in both houses) had been sold. By the end of the week, both performances were sold out. Granada manager Ralph Papworth was relieved that it had all passed off peacefully.

The girls (and quite a few boys) had months to look forward to the big day, which finally arrived on Saturday, October 24. The crowds began gathering outside the cinema, but they missed out on the arrival of The Beatles. The boys had travelled from the West End in their own car after a press conference to officially announce that 'I Feel Fine' backed by 'She's A Woman' was to be released on November 27 as the group's eighth single.

The Beatles had jumped out of their car and into a Granada TV van outside Walthamstow Police Station. They were driven along a service road behind the Hoe Street/High Street shops and quietly into the back of the cinema. They were able to enjoy a meal inside their dressing room while the crowds continued to grow outside.

The first house would usually contain the younger fans but they kept the authorities at full stretch inside and outside the cinema. Around 50 extra police were called in, including a mounted policeman who helped control the crowds outside. Police and ambulance volunteers inside were also hard pressed.

The *Walthamstow Guardian* carried a picture, taken from the Circle, showing girls surging around the stage as The Beatles were playing. Within seconds of the curtains opening the shriek had gone up and all sorts of gifts headed towards the stage. They were personalised with labels such as 'To Ringo With Love' or 'To John My Favourite'.

The Beatles opened with 'Twist And Shout' and reporter Rex Pardoe noted that it had an immediate effect. "Like a well-drilled chorus line the downstairs concert-goers rose to their feet row by row – from the front. Before 'Twist And Shout' was over every seat on the ground floor had been tipped up."

There was a little more restraint up in the circle, but four or five girls put themselves in grave danger as they raced to the balcony rails at the front, causing fears that they might fall. The screams rang out, the girls jumped up and waved their scarves, but enough music was heard for Pardoe to namecheck some songs and pass judgement on the performance. "The Beatles' two half-hour sessions, one at each house, were gems of pure professionalism. Relying on their chart-topping hits 'Can't Buy Me Love', 'Twist And Shout', 'A Hard Day's Night' and 'Long Tall Sally'*, The Beatles drove their fans into fits of frenzy," he wrote.

---

* Of these songs only 'Can't Buy Me Love' and 'A Hard Day's Night' were chart-topping hits of course.

Then, at 8.30pm, with barely time to draw breath, it was time to do it all over again. The mayhem carried on. Two dozen fans were treated for hysteria, some carried out by bewildered security and St John volunteers. The downstairs foyer was likened to a "casualty clearing station" afterwards and hundreds gathered outside to see The Beatles depart. As in Kilburn the night before, they were thwarted. The boys were out the back and away while the National Anthem was blaring out.

McEntee Technical School pupil Janice Drew was lucky enough to be in the front row for that second house. Now Janice Crott and living in Kansas, she remembers the magic of being there to see The Beatles. "My school friend Maggie had lined up all night and was one of the first, if not the first in line for tickets. I am not sure if her parents knew where she was that night but Maggie bought a few tickets for us and some friends. Maggie and I made banners to hang around our necks. Hers declared her love for Ringo and mine was for Paul. We each made extremely tall top hats with pictures of The Beatles to wear. We also made a banner of sheets that stretched across the front of the seats. It declared our dedication to and love for The Beatles. The banner was pulled out of our hands by other crazy girls not long after the show started!"

Janice and Maggie really were in the front row of full-on Beatlemania. "When The Beatles came onstage the theatre was alive with screaming, which did not die down at all. I was rather annoyed because I could barely hear The Beatles, even in the front row, although I hasten to add I must have been screaming as well! We stood on our seats and were in awe. At one point I looked at the girls I was with and there was only Maggie in the seat next to me. The others had been carried out by St John's Ambulance Brigade people because they had fainted. Then Maggie threw her cardboard, moveable puppet she had made of George onto the stage. George picked it up and put it on his amplifier and so I turned to Maggie to say something, but she had collapsed in a heap in her chair. They had to carry her out! So I was the only one left and I decided I didn't want to miss the show and was there until the end.

"When The Beatles finished Maggie came rushing back down the aisle, but The Beatles had gone. We rushed outside to see if we could watch them leaving, but they were not in sight. So we tried to storm the backstage, but were sent back out. We hung around for quite a long time waiting for the departure of The Beatles, but never saw them. The newspaper the next day stated that they had left the theatre over a wall right after the show."

Walthamstow pop fans didn't have to wait long for the next show. A month-long tour starring Gerry & The Pacemakers, Gene Pitney and The Kinks was to start out at the Granada a few days later on Saturday, November 7. The Beatles and co., meanwhile, were heading for the seaside.

Converted into a variety theatre in 1902, the Brighton Hippodrome had hosted many great performers down the years, including the legendary Brighton comic Max Miller, and the return of The Beatles on this Sunday was guaranteed to be a lively affair. They were sneaked inside with the usual efficiency, through a garage in West Street that led out into Middle Street where The Hippodrome was situated. There were fewer visitors to their dressing room when they were outside London, but one welcome friend here was Sean O'Mahony (aka Johnny Dean of their monthly fan mag *The Beatles Book*), who chose tonight for the monthly picture and interview session with the group.

Sean revealed that they had another visitor that afternoon, *Melody Maker*'s Chris Hayes who lived in nearby Saltdean and wrote the paper's Any Questions column, to which readers would write to inquire about what equipment was favoured by the stars. Sean asked The Beatles about 'I Feel Fine' and was surprised to find them nervous about how it would do. Paul picked up a guitar and played it to him and O'Mahony predicted that it would be a big hit, but they were still expressing doubts.

Hippodrome staff, meanwhile, had been undertaking a 90-minute search for stowaways. The venue had hosted a Beatles show just a couple of months before and was well aware of what fans might get up to. Neil Aspinall came in to tell The Beatles it was time to change and Sean took photos of them in their dressing room before heading to the wings to prepare for some stage shots. He was to note how difficult it was for the other artists on the bill – each knowing that everyone was there to see The Beatles. Even so, the musical ability, and audience-friendly style of Sounds Incorporated won them new fans in Brighton. Tommy Quickly made quite an impact, too, but he had that awful spot before The Beatles. Bob Bain's attempt to introduce them wasn't heard beyond John.

The Beatles wore their black mohair suits and tore it up from the start with 'Twist And Shout'. 'Can't Buy Me Love' was followed by Paul's 'Things We Said Today' before George's solo spot with 'I'm Happy Just

To Dance With You'. John donned his harmonica holder for 'I Should Have Known Better' and then John and Paul shared the vocals on 'If I Fell'. Ringo then took the spotlight with 'I Wanna Be Your Man' and then it was 'A Hard Day's Night' before Paul's rip-roaring show-closer, 'Long Tall Sally'.

O'Mahony was aware of the songs they belted out that night, but not many of the screamers would have heard anything over their own voices. The usual array of objects was hurled as soon as the curtains had parted – jelly babies, dolls, programmes, declarations of love – they all headed into the spotlights. The Brighton *Argus* referred to "wild-eyed hysterical girls" rushing down the aisles and hurling themselves at the stage. The police formed a human barrier in front of the orchestra pit.

Supt A. M. Probyn was in charge of the 40 police on duty. Naturally, all police leave had been cancelled. "We are not so much here to protect the group as to protect the girls from themselves," he said. "If we let them, they would just throw themselves in front of The Beatles' car."

A band of 20 St John Ambulancemen, under Supt Edward Sanderson, treated 18 hysterical girls in the nearby Middle Street Primary School.

O'Mahony wisely gave The Beatles a few minutes to cool down before joining them in the dressing room between the shows. They had some time to spare before they were due onstage again at 9.45pm. What they wanted was to relax and watch some telly – what they got, as ever, were more visitors.

Being the seaside, one of them was a fortune teller! The mystic, Eva Petulengro, wearing her black hair in a beehive and dressed in a coat with fur cuffs, read George's palm. He was keeping mum about her predictions, but she hadn't said anything worrying judging by his demeanour afterwards. When the mystic vanished they settled down to watch TV . . . only for Neil to bring in film star Richard Harris and his wife. The Beatles could be pretty blunt when they didn't want company, and though they didn't say anything rude to him, their body language made it clear they didn't want visitors.

George sank into the sofa and pretended to be asleep while John wrapped himself in a green plastic mac and dropped to the floor. Paul and Ringo grunted one-word answers, explained that George and John were tired, and signed autographs for Harris' children and with that he and his wife were gone.

John and George then perked up to watch television and eat their meal of steak, peas and chips, pretty much the stock diet for The Beatles on tour. Pictures in *The Beatles Book* indicate their dining conditions were cramped to say the very least. They were perched, shoulder to shoulder, on the dressing table, facing themselves in the mirror. Promoter Arthur Howes turned up while they were eating and wanted to talk about further tours – probably another one-way conversation.

Sean O'Mahony was also the publisher of *Beat Instrumental* magazine and he'd brought some copies along for The Beatles to read, along with pictures from an earlier session. Soon Neil popped his head around the door to say it was time to get ready for show number two.

The press were also hanging around backstage for more questions and photos as the Fabs made their way to the stage. After a frenetic second show, for which they wore their grey suits, they exited through the stage door side entrance with Mary Wells and were swept away in a post office van. At the final curtain hysterical girls were collapsing and the mass screaming continued through the National Anthem.

The *Argus* wasn't the only newspaper to cover the show. The *Brighton & Hove Gazette* carried a story a few days later headlined 'Who Says The Beatles Are Slipping?' which included a photo of The Beatles arriving in their car and another of excited, banner-waving fans behind barriers awaiting their arrival.

The *Gazette* wrote of the chaotic scenes around the cinema as evidence that the group were not about to surrender their crown to any pretenders just yet: "The 'knockers' say The Beatles are on the way out: The Rolling Stones are taking over. But if they had come to Brighton on Sunday and seen the overwhelming enthusiasm of hysterical, faithful Beatle fans, they would have left shaking their heads in amazement," wrote the *Gazette*'s reporter. Sadly, this was to be the last show at the Hippodrome which closed soon afterwards and later became a bingo hall.

The next two days were rest days for the tour, but The Beatles headed from Brighton to London for recording sessions at Abbey Road. They attended a mono mixing session on the Monday morning and Ringo recorded his vocal for *Beatles For Sale* track 'Honey Don't' in the afternoon. In the evening the group recorded their 1964 fan club Christmas flexi disc. Paul and Ringo, accompanied by their girlfriends Jane Asher and Maureen Cox, then headed off to the group's favourite London nightclub, the Ad Lib Club in Leicester Place, above the Prince Charles Theatre just off Leicester Square. There was more mixing work at Abbey Road the following day.

On Wednesday they headed west to Exeter for two houses at the ABC Cinema but the journey was anything but straightforward for The Beatles. A combination of not leaving themselves enough time for the journey, stopping off for something to eat and getting lost meant that they arrived at the cinema only five minutes before the show started. It had been arranged for them to switch to a decoy van at Honiton before heading to the cinema, but it all went wrong. The driver got the blame for turning down the wrong road but at least they had the consolation of finding a good chippie. Of course, rehearsals hardly mattered as the fans never got to hear anything anyway, and the screamers were out in force at Exeter.

Police and cinema staff had an additional worry tonight. There were growing fears for the safety of 13-year-old Elizabeth Freedman from Massachusetts, who had been missing from her home for several weeks. Elizabeth was thought to have been heading for Britain to try to see some of The Beatles' concerts and police and cinema staff were given a description and asked to keep a lookout for her. They faced a difficult task. Elizabeth was slim, 5ft 7in tall with long blonde hair and spectacles. She wasn't spotted at Exeter.

The Beatles were at the centre of a screamfest from the moment the curtains parted. Thank goodness the fans had the records to play when they got home because little could have been heard wherever you were in the ABC for either house. One young fan gave a quote which could have come from any of them: "I cried all the way through. Someone put their arm around me and I didn't know who it was. We couldn't really hear the music because of all the screaming."

The group made their secret escape at the end but there were hundreds of people milling around outside the cinema afterwards, hoping for one last sighting of them. The traffic was nearly at a standstill outside, with buses full of still weeping girls heading away from the cinema and back to sanity.

The Beatles were already on their way out of Exeter, bound for their hotel in Torquay, where they recorded a taped interview with journalist Jean Shepherd that was to appear in the March 1965 edition of *Playboy* magazine. Shepherd had spent some hours around The Beatles since they played the Edinburgh dates and he produced an absorbing look at the group and how their extraordinary experiences had (or hadn't) affected them. He wrote of "sweaty T-shirts, trays of French fries, steak, pots of tea, and the inevitable TV set". He tasted just a few days of life on the road with The Beatles, but it was enough to give him a window into their unusual world. "It became impossible to tell one town from another, since to us they were just a succession of dressing rooms and hotel suites. The screams were the same. The music was the same," he wrote.

Their duties all done, The Beatles were not yet ready for bed. They reportedly took driver Alf Bicknell out for a night on the town to celebrate his 36th birthday.

The next day The Beatles' late arrival at Exeter prompted some questions from the press when they met them before the two houses at Plymouth's ABC Cinema. Ringo admitted: "We were very late – five minutes before we went on in fact," he said. Asked why, he replied: "Oh, all sorts of things happened. It took us longer than we expected – we stopped to eat and we got lost and everything, all in all, made us late."

Another reporter appeared and put his microphone under George's nose and asked the annoying question: "How much longer are you going to last, that's what we want to know?"

"Last what?" said George.

"Last year?" said Ringo.

"No," persevered the reporter, "last the pace?"

"I dunno. Till we get fed up," said George.

"What will you do then – become an MP?" asked the reporter.

"No, a railway driver – engine driver, or a fire engine driver. Something like that," said George.

Trying to escape from banality for a moment, George commented that he enjoyed filming and they were due to start work on their next film in February. But another reporter collared Ringo. "Did you vote?"

Ringo: "No. Did you?"

Reporter: "No."

"Well there you go then. That's two of us so don't go picking on me if you didn't vote either."

Turning to John, Ringo continued: "Hear that Johnny? He comes up here . . ."

A reporter asked Lennon if he voted. "No. Didn't have time," he replied curtly. Ringo explained that they were touring, which a reporter misheard as Tories, but John cut in: "British Nationalist I'd vote!"

This exchange gives a flavour of meetings between The Beatles and the media at the end of 1964. This is how it would go on night after night on this tour. Their tactful, if sometimes impatient response to inane and often ill-mannered questions was testament to their willingness to play the game in order to protect their wholesome image. Given a free rein, George, and John in particular, would no doubt have taken great personal delight in telling many of the reporters where they could stick their questions.

Reporters were also latching on to the fact that although most Beatle concerts were selling out – and quickly – at a few venues empty seats were beginning to appear and the crowds waiting to greet them appeared smaller than the year before. Recently discovered television interview footage of Paul at Plymouth before this concert sees him dealing with these doubts. "All the business that there may be small crowds and things, it doesn't worry anybody except newspaper men who maybe use it as a good angle," he said. "They say, 'Ha ha . . . The Beatles must be finished because there are no crowds there', but you know that sort of thing doesn't matter. Records matter, whether a place is sold out or not matters and we are doing OK on those things, thank you."

The Beatles were more comfortable talking with representatives of the music press, most of whom they knew and respected and who would talk to them about their music, and what music they enjoyed listening to. Music papers always wanted their own exclusives and all four Beatles chatted at Plymouth to the *Melody Maker*'s jazz-loving Ray Coleman about 'I Feel Fine'. John was relieved that the recording of the single and *Beatles For Sale* was over with and that he was pleased with the results.

Of 'I Feel Fine', he ventured: "I suppose it has a bit of a country-and-western feel about it, but then so have a lot of our songs. The middle eight is the most tuneful part, to me, because it's a typical Beatles bit."

The *Western Evening Herald*'s concert report remarked that if The Beatles were to start slipping, there was no sign of it happening just yet. Under the headline 'They Still Scream For Beatles' the *Herald* reporter made it clear the fans were at least as noisy as their last visit (in November 1963) and to underline the point a photo accompanying the article captured ecstatic girls in the audience. Amps and speakers turned to maximum volume "fought a long battle with noisy hysteria that was quite equal to the frenzied screams which greeted the Liverpool group in 1963".

Around 30 stewards policed the kids inside the cinema, while a similar number of uniformed policemen were on duty outside. The stewards formed a line in front of the stage, but things didn't get too out of hand. The body count at the end was around a dozen hysteria victims . . . and one broken seat. A decent result at the end of a Beatle night.

The Rustiks were on home territory and it was a happy night for them. They received a fair amount of screams – as did all of the performers. Even Bob Bain got a spirited response from the screamers and, of course, they went into overdrive during The Beatles' two barnstorming sets.

The Plymouth girls were generous towards all the acts and even Her Majesty was treated with respect. The screaming continued when the curtains closed as The Beatles were dashing off, but stopped immediately the National Anthem started. There was another brief bout of screaming afterwards before the teens quietly queued for the exits. The Beatles had already made their getaway through the back door into their waiting car, almost unseen.

Paul, though doubtless frustrated at the levels of screaming, was putting on his usual diplomatic face. "They create atmosphere, which is important," he said. "And we don't mind the fact they can't hear what we sing. They hear us on the records."

The Beatles were back in Bournemouth the following night, this time at the Gaumont Cinema, and their impending demise – imagined, of course – surfaced again in the *Bournemouth Echo* review of this show. The boys were familiar with the south coast holiday resort, having played a one-week season in August 1963, plus their tour date the following November and an appearance in August 1964, along with The Kinks and Mike Berry. But this time the reviewer noted there were fewer girls outside, a handful of empty seats in the first house and that he was able to hear quite a bit of The Beatles singing above the screams.

However, he heard more than enough to confirm that The Beatles were still out on their own. "True, the most obvious signs of mass hysteria were not so evident," he wrote, "but switch on a spotlight, or let John, George, Paul or Ringo make a move, and a deafening sound certainly banished any thoughts that The Beatles are through. There were a couple of empty seats here and there in the first house, unthinkable not so long ago, but I don't think that means too much. After all, nearly four and a half thousand people paid to see them last night."

The Beatles' audience was by no means confined to teenagers and pre-teens. Mums and dads (and sometimes their mums and dads) enjoyed their tunes – and their style – but the screaming was still bad enough to have the 20- and 30-somethings sticking fingers in their ears.

There was evidence that Mary Wells, backed by Sounds Incorporated, was settling into the tour. She had suffered from audiences being unfamiliar with her songs (other than 'My Guy') on the early dates, but she put in a confident performance for the Bournemouth public, and her personality was beginning to shine through.

Enough was heard of The Rustiks, Mike Haslam and The Remo Four, plus Sounds Incorporated in their solo spot, to provide a variety of entertaining music in both houses while everyone waited for The Beatles. Tommy Quickly was replaced in Bournemouth by Scottish-born country singer and radio host Lorne Gibson whom The Beatles knew well. They had guested on his radio show *Side By Side* and he on their *Pop Go The Beatles* show. Lorne (real name Eric Brown) put in a professional performance down on the coast. The *Echo* reviewer concluded: "Lorne Gibson showed us why he doesn't mind the spot before the stars. A very fine performer, this young singer."

Saturday saw the tour heading eastwards to Suffolk for two houses at the Gaumont Cinema in Ipswich. The Gaumont's genial host David Lowe was an old friend of The Beatles from their 1963 visit on the Roy Orbison tour, but things had moved on a tad since then. If the screaming was loud the last time the Fab Four were in town it was off the scale this time – and it was like a military operation getting them in and out.

It started with a phone call to Lowe from Susan Fuller, promoter Arthur Howes' secretary. "She said, 'I have a booking for you David – and it's right out of the top drawer. The very top drawer.' I said, 'You don't mean The Beatles?' 'Yes,' she said. I phoned the chief constable and said 'Mr James, The Beatles are coming. 'Heaven help us,' he said."

They began arranging a military-style operation straight away – a good three months before the show. A crisis meeting was held in the "control room" at the Suffolk County Hall to organise how they were going to handle staging a concert by the world's most famous group at the local cinema in St Helen's Street. Lowe proposed that tickets would be sold on a first come, first served basis – meaning a full night's queuing on the pavement before the box office opened on a mercifully sunny autumn morning.

"I went down at 5am and I remember a young lad switched his radio on and 'A Hard Day's Night' was playing and I thought, well it's certainly been that. Everyone seemed quite jolly – well, apart from one middle-aged man who was looking quite hard at me with a horrible look on his face. 'There had better be tickets at the end of this Mr Lowe,' he said. He must have been queuing for his daughter. The queue went right up St Helen's Street into Woodbridge Road and joined up in Argyle Street. It was massive."

The Beatles were a little late in arriving on the night and Lowe was under pressure from a reporter who told him: "They're not coming, are they? It's another one of your publicity stunts!"

They did arrive – quietly hidden in a police car – with Epstein in tow, and the night's action began in earnest. Lowe recalled: "Brian Epstein said to me, 'David, will you look after the lads for me?' He said, 'You can be their publicity manager for the night.' Paul had been eating an apple and he threw it into the box seats where some of my family were and The Beatles accompanied us into the foyer and I said to the reporter, 'Here they are.'

"We had a reception in my office and my wife was helping with the wines. Then they were interviewed by a television reporter and even he looked self-conscious. He asked them, 'Why The Beatles?' and John, stony-faced, replied, 'Why not?'"

Covering the show for the *East Anglian Daily Times* and the *Evening Star* were photographer David Kindred and reporter Steve Wood. Kindred said: "Steve and I were both 18 and most of the staff in those days were 30-plus so there wasn't much competition to cover the show. Most of the others thought The Beatles were just a passing phase. In fact, the picture they used that I took that day they cut up and just used single column head shots of The Beatles on an inside page.

"When we arrived The Beatles were already there. There was a press call – it only lasted about 10 minutes. It was in the manager's office, which was only about 10ft square, and there were just half a dozen press people in there with The Beatles. I was a Beatles fan and I feel incredibly lucky to be able to say I met them – well, sort of – because we were in the same room, but there wasn't much meaningful conversation. They were affable, but you could tell that it was just another press meeting – another show. They were polite, but bored. They were tired.

"I took a few photographs and then they went into the inner foyer area, like a long curved lounge at the back, and did an interview with Anglia Television. I took a photo of them with some competition winners. Six or seven years ago, a chap said to me, 'You took my picture with The Beatles when I was a competition winner.' He won a toy guitar signed by The Beatles and I said, 'Wow, that must have been worth some money?' He said, 'I swapped it later that day for an Airfix kit because I didn't like The Beatles.' Goodness only knows what that would have been worth because while there must be a few autographed albums, there were no or very few autographed toy guitars. I wonder where that ended up? It probably got thrown on a skip."

Kindred went off to process his pictures and returned to watch The Beatles – watching from the back where cinema manager David Lowe used to let press pals stand when shows in the 1,800-seat cinema had sold out. In fact, once again, there were a few tickets left over, but the fans were as enthusiastic as ever.

The cinema manager has clear memories of that Beatle effect. "It was pandemonium when they came on. No sooner had the curtains opened as we announced, 'Ladies and Gentleman, the world-famous Beatles' than the scream went up and the two girls in the front row – who had been at the very front of all that queuing – promptly fainted and had to be carried to the back on stretchers. They never saw a thing. The rest of the show went well, but really there was too much screaming and shouting. It was impossible to hear what they were singing – but it was as if people didn't expect to hear them."

There was one incident that caused a headache for Lowe. Lennon had cast aside his harmonica when he finished using it at the end of a song in the first house and Lowe's 14-year-old son, thinking the Beatle had no further use for it, claimed the prize and promptly took it home. John, though, was not amused and Lowe had to arrange a taxi back to his home to retrieve it. "I phoned my wife to make sure that harmonica was in that taxi. My son had gone to sleep with his trophy – the mouth organ – under his pillow, but John, we were told, was insisting he wasn't going on without it!" One annoyed Beatle reunited with his harmonica and harmony was restored in time for the second house.

Fan Bob Lawrence (17) was the luckiest person to be there that night.

"I'd just moved to Ipswich and had failed to get a ticket. However, I played cricket for anyone who asked that year and at a match in the village of Nacton I was playing cards with other cricketers in the pavilion because it was raining. We were playing brag and I remember one of the players ran out of money during a big pot. He produced a ticket for The Beatles' show and threw that in. I won the pot and I saw The Beatles!"

It was only later that Lawrence realised the difficult position the losing card player had put himself in. "It turned out that he was a reporter with the local paper and he had been given the ticket to cover the show! The same guy is a good friend now and we played cricket together for many years."

He remembers police standing in the aisles and having to stop fans jumping on the stage. "I joined the local police two years later and worked with some of the officers who were there that night. They told me how it was quite a plan getting The Beatles in and out of the Gaumont in the police van. There may be some photographs in the museum at the Suffolk Police HQ. I certainly remember seeing some photos of the van being surrounded by fans. I also remember being deaf for several days after!"

What were The Beatles like? "I could hear quite well, given the scream-ing. I had a great seat, though – an aisle seat about eight to ten rows from the front, quite central. It must have been very difficult for the others on the show because I remember between the acts the chants of 'We want The Beatles' over and over again. I also clearly remember the four lads obviously totally enjoying themselves. It was almost as if they were looking at each other and thinking, 'Can you believe this?' Mary Wells I remember well. She was a big favourite of mine and 'My Guy' was terrific."

Photographer Kindred concluded: "You really couldn't hear anything with all the screaming. They just had those three Vox amps – no more than you'd have for a band playing a pub today. You really had no chance."

However, as ever, it was all about being there – watching history in the making and being able to look back one day and say 'I was there'. Kindred said no photographs were allowed of The Beatles onstage during their performance, so all that remains is his shots of them backstage – of Paul with his ice cream and George with a fruit juice as they coped with that interview for Anglia Television. The Beatles spent the night at the nearby Great White Horse Hotel in Tavern Street, Ipswich, where they signed autographs for fans.

The Beatles and the rest headed for London on the Sunday. The Astoria Cinema at Finsbury Park was arguably the most important pop venue on the 1960s touring circuit, a palace that boasted a dramatic proscenium arch, huge stage and 12 dressing rooms, with seating for more than 3,000 fans. The cinema staged many pop package nights in the Sixties and was often used as the big opening night venue. The national media and pop glitterati would descend on the cinema on the Seven Sisters Road in north London for a typically riotous and over-the-top start to a national tour.

It was here in 1967 that Jimi Hendrix, desperate to make the headlines, set light to his Fender Stratocaster during his short set on the first night of a UK tour with The Walker Brothers, Cat Stevens and (believe it or not) Engelbert Humperdinck. After a period as a cinema it reopened as The Rainbow in 1971 with a three-night stint by The Who, and went on to host memorable concerts by Pink Floyd, David Bowie and many other major rock acts of the era. Today it is owned by the Brazilian based United Church of the Kingdom of God (UCKG).

It was a venue The Beatles knew well. They first appeared there at the end of 1963 with 30 performances of *The Beatles Christmas Show* between Christmas Eve and January 11, 1964. This, of course, was no opening night, but every one of the 3,040 seats were sold for the one-night visit of The Beatles, Mary Wells and package, and the noise levels apparently reached new heights. There were always more well-wishers, friends and journalists for the big London gigs and the Fabs gave more time to the most important.

The following weekend's *Melody Maker* featured a one-to-one between George and Ray Coleman about success, his hopes for the future and how he felt that good old-fashioned luck had played a part in the group's progress. The headline referred to George as 'The Shrewd One' and described what had happened to them as 'Just Like Winning The Pools'.

It was a typical snatched tour interview in a busy, cramped dressing room, but George's distinct personality as the reluctant Beatle who didn't see them as stars came through. Coleman described him as affable and polite, but bewildered by their success, and George was honest to the point of bluntness about things of which he disapproved. Paul overheard him railing against some dodgy film scripts the group had been offered and "rubbishy film spectaculars with millions of names. They're awful". Paul sent out his own coded warning, saying: "That's it George. You tell him. I can see the headline now – 'Beatle Hits Out At Film Phoneys!' That's it George, you tell him."

McCartney had an in-built sense of exactly the right or wrong thing for a Beatle to say at any given moment. Among all his other talents, Paul was a PR heavyweight who rarely (if ever) let slip anything that could damage the group's reputation. He soon realised that unguarded moments of honesty from George or John could result in unwelcome headlines.

In lighter mode, George name-checked Jim Sullivan, Lonnie Donegan, Buddy Holly and Eddie Cochran as among his guitar heroes and revealed that his first guitar cost £2 10 shillings, when he was 14.

Mary was getting her share of attention, and was featured in *Melody Maker*'s Blind Date section. This wasn't a forerunner of Cilla Black's TV show, but a column in which a star was asked to offer an opinion on some of the week's new releases without being told who the performers were – though most knew anyway. John, Paul and George were in the dressing room with her, passing on a few tips about how *MM*'s Blind Date worked.

The London show was like any other, only more so. More than 3,000 fans can make a lot of noise – especially at full pitch scream. The crowd was more than happy to listen to Mary Wells and she drew warm applause for her set from those who considered it a privilege to see a Tamla Motown star in the flesh. Sounds Incorporated contained some of the industry's finest musicians and they had tailored their sound to give Mary backing that suited her soulful songs and voice. Mary generally wasn't screamed over on this tour, although all the acts at some point or other would have to endure Beatle chants while they were onstage.

The following week began with a whirlwind trip to Belfast for two houses at the famous King's Hall. The Beatles had clear memories of the riots they unwittingly caused in Ireland a year ago and they were hoping that the excitement this time would be inspired by their music and not just the mere fact of their being on Irish soil. George's fear of flying hardly helped their mood, but they landed at Aldergrove Airport on the Monday and were met by promoter Trevor Kane who ferried them to Donegall Road, where they switched cars and were given a police escort to the King's Hall.

The Irish date was included because The Beatles had already played in Scotland and Wales, but it was also an ideal excuse to pass up an invitation to make a second appearance on the Royal Command Performance, which was staged in London the same night. Paul was quoted: "Over 4,000 tickets have been sold and we couldn't let the Belfast kids down."

The Beatles were effectively locked inside their dressing room, with co-promoter John McCabe drafted in as their chaperone. Security was so tight that The Beatles saw only a handful of favoured journalists. There were piles of autograph books awaiting them, and short of much else to do they signed as many as they could as they whiled away the hours until showtime. In among them was The Royal Ulster Agricultural Society's visitors' book, containing many famous names of those who had visited the King's Hall, including kings and queens. In the rush it got flung in with the others, but McCabe made sure it wasn't lost after all four Beatles had signed it.

The boys also presented toys to volunteers which were subsequently given to Belfast orphans for Christmas. Ringo was pictured holding a toy Beatle guitar and Paul a toy gun in a posed photo for the press. They were also photographed relaxing backstage in easy chairs in a Spartan room, their feet up on a small table. This was a venue like no other. The King's Hall held just over 8,000 people – roughly four times as many as the typical cinema venues on these tours. The contract details had been tied up in time for the 16,000 tickets to go on sale a month before the shows. This was one night when security ruled before the show. No clandestine meetings with relatives – no fans or fan club secretaries ushered in for a quiet meeting with the boys – and no press conference in the glare of a battery of flashlights. There were strict instructions from The Beatles' handlers that they were not to be disturbed.

The Rustiks got the first house underway shortly after 6pm, followed by Michael Haslam and then Sounds Incorporated. Bob Bain then introduced Mary Wells to close the first half. There was a tense atmosphere building up as everyone got ready for the main course. The Remo Four and Tommy Quickly took to the stage after the interval – then it was time for The Beatles.

Magnify the usual manic reception by four as 8,000 fans went ballistic instead of the usual 2,000. There were all the usual scenes, only more manic and with many more hysterical girls to deal with. The police and stewards manned the barriers as some tried to storm the stage. It was the same 10-song set that had wowed the English crowds. John's vocal chords were at full stretch for 'Twist And Shout' and 'Money'. Ringo tried to make himself heard with 'I Wanna Be Your Man' and Paul whipped up everything still further with 'Long Tall Sally'. The six songs from *A Hard Day's Night* completed the set. Girls pulled their own hair out and many wet themselves with excitement as they screamed the place down. Audiences sat on old moveable wooden chairs, and there was precious little time for the giant clear-up and clean-up needed to get the 8.45pm show underway on time. People were queuing around the block for the second half and the staff worked a minor miracle to meet the deadline.

The screaming was every bit as manic in the second house. Most of the touring party stayed in a big hotel in the city centre, but The Beatles spent the night at the plush Culloden Hotel on the outskirts of Belfast and flew out of Aldergrove Airport the next day, never to return to Ireland.

There was some mixing work on stereo *Beatles For Sale* tracks at Abbey Road on the Wednesday, which some or all of the group may have attended, before they drove to Bedfordshire to join up with the tour party for the two shows at the Ritz Cinema in Luton. There was a spot of nifty manoeuvring to avoid an unwanted detour, an invitation to take tea in the office of the Mayor, Cllr Frank Beckett, where they would sign Luton's official autograph book. The potential dangers of the operation were quickly pointed out and it was agreed that the Mayor and his team would instead call in to see them at the Ritz. Local dignitaries often put themselves at the head of the queue to meet The Beatles, but John, Paul, George and Ringo were generally uncomfortable in such company.

At the head of the real queue were four 14-year-olds from Stevenage who took up their positions at 10am. You couldn't miss them. They were at the entrance with a huge banner containing the message 'We Love The Beatles' and just to make sure everyone noticed they displayed it proudly for a photo in the *Luton News*. Two of them walked around the back occasionally, just in case their favourites tried to slip in unnoticed. One, Marilyn Smith, of Wigram Way, Stevenage, told the newspaper: "We've got tickets and we'll stay here until the show starts."

"We've got sandwiches as well," added Celia Tully, of Gonville Cresent.

The police were out in force of course. Superintendent Stanley Cooper was in charge of the operation and he drafted in 18 specials to try to ensure a peaceful entry and exit for The Beatles. He was taking no chances. "There will be a reserve of men at the station whom I can call on should the situation get out of hand," he told *The Luton News*, adding: "The main problem is getting them out of the cinema. I have a plan worked out . . . but of course, it's a secret."

The cinema held just over 2,100 and there were no spare tickets to be had in Luton, with every one sold within two days of the box office opening. This was the day when Lyndon Johnson won the election in America, having held the post of president for almost a year following the assassination of JFK. The Beatles were able (if they were interested) to watch it on the news thanks to a television being installed in their dressing room by a local TV company.

It was a thoughtful gesture by cinema manager Len Sobley, who commented: "After all, they have got to pass the time somehow." John met up with Joe McGrath, the BBC producer responsible for *Not Only . . . But Also*, the comedy show that starred Peter Cook and Dudley Moore. Having already met Moore and expressed an interest in the show, John was invited to make a contribution and would later appear on the show with Norman Rossington, marking the first of several appearances he made on the programme.

The inevitable press interviews found The Beatles in relaxed mood following their rare day off. Photographs catch them in their dark jackets – John with a light roll neck and Ringo a dark one – along with Jimmy Savile.

Onstage, The Beatles, in their dark suits with velvet collars, put plenty of energy and enthusiasm into the performance for the excited Luton teens. In the audience was a young man called Paul Griggs who says he saw The Beatles 10 times – but never did they sound better than this night at Luton. "I kept a diary and when I look back now it says that the November 4, 1964, performance at The Ritz in Luton was one of the best. I don't know why that was. Perhaps the girls didn't scream as loud, or perhaps it was the PA, but it was one of the best shows I saw. Mary Wells was good, but to be honest it didn't matter who was on, they were just getting in the way. We knew The Beatles liked her so felt that we should, but the truth is you just wanted other people to get off so The Beatles would be on."

Also in the audience that night were Denbigh Road Infant School girl Julie Heys and her sister Susan who had been taken along by their mum Pamela. Julie, now Julie Devine, the manager at Luton Central Library, said it was her seventh birthday, and Susan's ninth birthday was the day before. Julie recalls: "It was a birthday treat for us and I was so excited to be there to see The Beatles. I was a big fan of Paul's, but the screaming was so loud that we had to go early because Susan got earache. However, I do remember that at one point, due to the noise of the screaming, John just took off his guitar, put it down and shrugged his shoulders."

Pam Frankland (17) and her friend Elaine Ferguson, both staffers at Waterlows printing factory in Dunstable, were among the excited teenagers up in the circle. Pam, now Pam Gileany, recalls: "On the date tickets went on sale I went straight from work on the bus, but because I didn't finish work until 5pm, they had nearly sold out. I managed to get two tickets in the circle, not in the front stalls as I would have wished. Nevertheless, it was a night to remember. We set off from Dunstable, where we both lived, feeling unbelievably excited. We queued from the end of the road and when we finally took our seats, we couldn't believe our luck that we were actually going to see The Beatles live.

"I don't think we heard very much of the singing, just the ear-splitting screaming! Of course I was one of the screamers, as well as crying and pulling my hair. I screamed so loud and hard that for the following few days, it hurt every time I breathed. It was over far too quickly but that evening has remained in my memory. I adored The Beatles then and still do."

John Smail (19), who lived and worked in Luton, was up in the circle that night along with his girlfriend Anne Clements, and he wasn't deterred by the extra travelling involved when the show coincided with a Barclays Bank residential course he was obliged to attend that week in London. "There was plenty of screaming going on and we could barely hear the music at times, but the Ritz had a steep balcony which gave us a very good view," he says. "I was quite impressed by The Beatles, but looking back now of course I wasn't aware that I was in the presence of a history-making group. I certainly feel privileged to have witnessed The Beatles performing live."

The Ritz building still stands proudly in Gordon Street and these days is home to both the Chicago Rock Café and Liquid Nightclub.

The show was back on the road the next day and heading up to Nottingham for two houses at the city's Odeon Cinema. The Beatles had been escaping the clutches of over-zealous fans for some considerable time by using elaborate decoy routines to fool them, but on this evening in Nottingham it was the police who were left scratching their heads. It had all been so carefully planned: rendezvous at 5pm at the roundabout junction of the A60 and A606 where The Beatles would switch from their Austin Princess to the police van to take them in by the side St James Street entrance to the cinema in Angel Row. But while the four officers sat like lemons in their six-seater van six miles away, completely unknown to them the four Beatles simply turned up at the cinema in their own chauffeur-driven car and sprinted in, just as they had done the year before.

There were fewer fans outside than the previous year, but inside, the excitement raged as ever. The *Evening Post* reported on a girl dressed in a yellow jumper and green slacks who took George's invitation literally as he sang 'I'm Happy Just To Dance With You'. The girl, out-doing her friends in the hysteria stakes, leapt to her feet and ran down the aisle ready to leap for the stage. A cinema attendant – on this night part of the security team – spotted her charge and ran from the far side to meet her head-on. He held onto the unfortunate girl until the cavalry arrived. Three policemen and a policewoman hustled the sobbing girl out of a side exit and two others were taken out for first aid after fainting.

The cinema had prepared every bit as diligently as the police. The stage was protected by a line of police, boosted by special constables and cinema staff. It worked. None of the chargers got as far as the stage. The Beatles pounded away as ever, with only a fraction of their sound reaching the ears of the few who weren't screaming until at last, still in their stage suits, they were hustled into their own car in the theatre yard. With a police car leading the way, they made their way out through St James' Street past a 200-strong crowd held back by barriers and police. The Beatles stayed at the Swan Hotel in Mansfield that night. The Odeon closed on January 28, 2001, after 68 years of entertaining the people of Nottingham.

Tour itineraries rarely followed a logical route and, having already visited Brighton and Bournemouth within the past fortnight, they headed to the south coast for the third time on the Friday for two shows at the Gaumont Cinema in Southampton. Interviews for early evening local TV news programmes were by now almost a nightly occurrence for The Beatles. In Southampton, Southern Television reporter Tony Bilbow talked with them in their dressing room for the *Day By Day* programme, which ran from 6.05pm until 6.40pm.

The show was kicked off by The Rustiks, who, not unhampered by screaming, could be heard quite clearly. Michael Haslam's dulcet tones could be heard, too, but it was difficult for him to make much of an impression. It was difficult for anybody other than The Beatles and to make things even worse it wasn't the kind of audience to appreciate his particular talents. Mary Wells, as everywhere else, closed out the first half, and had long since come to terms with the complete pointlessness of trying to make an impact as an artist supporting The Beatles. At least without having the screams to contend with, Mary was able to display her undoubted artistry and she was appreciated by the critics (and slightly older audience members). She was on good form in Southampton.

There was yet another plaudit for Mary's backers Sounds Incorporated, too. The *Southampton Echo* reporter offered them "high praise", adding: "They have bags of ability and were vigorously applauded. Perhaps that delirious day will return when people indicate pleasure by hitting their hands together. Let's hope so."

At the start of the tour everyone had been hoping that it would be some kind of launch-pad for Tommy Quickly. Epstein had invested a lot of clout, cash, and a degree of emotional support in Tommy, but it was still not happening for him. Around £25,000 was being spent on launching Quickly in the USA, but there seemed little point when even the British public was seemingly indifferent to him. There's only so much you can do and time was running out. Audiences – Southampton's included – were amused and entertained by him, but comic renderings of 'Walkin' The Dog' and 'Humpty Dumpty' were hardly going to launch him as a cool pop star.

The spotlight, as always, was only on The Beatles. The screamfest predictably got underway as soon as they set foot onstage, and it was the man at the back who appeared to be flavour of the night in Southampton. The *Echo* recorded: "The biggest roar of the evening was for Ringo and his solo spot. He could be heard – just. Certainly, The Beatles give full value for money these days. Their 20 minutes was crammed with top numbers – no hip twitching, no histrionics, no pandering to the jungle instincts of the little girls."

There were no whispering doubts about the continuing popularity of The Beatles at the Capitol Cinema in Cardiff on the Saturday. Their visit produced the biggest response for tickets in the theatre's history, with all 5,000, ranging in price from from 8s 6d to 15s, sold out almost immediately, leaving Capitol manager Bill Hall delighted with the takings. Hall's office was filled with bags of mail begging for tickets and he had no option but to send back thousands of pounds in cheques and postal orders to disappointed fans.

The queue outside the front of the cinema was headed by 15-year-old Jean Tidcombe. Jean was particularly keen as she had travelled around 10 miles into Cardiff from Brynfedw, Bedwas, on an early morning train. The fans, some wearing leather caps like John's, gathered at the front until they were moved on after about an hour. They went round to the stage door entrance where workmen took pity on them and made them flasks of tea. They weren't all girls. Brave Peter Butler (10), of Penarth, was the lone boy, praying for more male reinforcements to arrive. One queuing girl told the *South Wales Echo*: "If I don't see The Beatles I won't commit suicide, but I will probably go mad."

Rumours began circulating about when The Beatles would arrive. Some said 3pm, while others, noting their recent late arrival at Exeter, reckoned it would be just after the first house started at 6.30pm. In the event, it was around 5pm when The Beatles arrived in a Black Maria police van. By that time there was a huge crowd at the front and fans were gathering in the streets around the cinema.

The Beatles had been chauffeur driven seven miles to the car park of the Fox & Hounds at St Mellons in Brian's limousine before transferring to the Black Maria for the remainder of the journey.

There was evidence they were in good humour. As their car entered the city boundary, George was heard to ask: "Where are all the kilts then?"

They were driven through the Station Terrace entrance to the court-yard behind the cinema, some 15 yards from the stage door, where only a few fans had gathered. Meanwhile, around 100 yards away in Edward Place, police were holding back hundreds of screaming girls. George was obviously still in a playful mood as he knocked a spotlight out of a BBC cameraman's hand with a rolled paper. Neil Aspinall was less playful. Ever protective of their privacy, he told the waiting press that The Beatles would see absolutely no one. He then went into the foyer and sent off a telegram to London which read: "Arriving home 3am".

The *Echo*'s entertainments reporter Philip Walker had bagged himself a coveted spot right by the stage. It proved perfect for hearing at least something above the screams . . . but it was also right in the line of fire of jelly babies, lipsticks and other assorted debris.

The reputation of Sounds Incorporated was still growing. They were solid in their own short sets and provided skilful backing for Mary. They were versatile, too, with their sax-appeal back-line. Reporter Philip Walker, for one, was grateful for their impact. Describing the rest of the show as "mixed", he observed: "Only when Sounds Incorporated went on did the pace quicken. The Sounds have always been a fine act, fully professional and entertaining. They make a big noise sound nice." The Remo Four kicked off the second half in rocking style and they stayed on to back Tommy Quickly who put on an enthusiastic show that went down well (with the audience, if not the reporter). But it was all about that golden 25 minutes with The Beatles . . .

The screams were deafening as the curtain parted and the girls of south Wales made the most of their chance to join in the Beatles-led hysteria. They screeched, waved, cried, whistled, swooned and bounced on their chairs. Around 50 security men stood with backs to the stage preparing for the inevitable charge. The Beatles kicked off, as they always did on this tour, with a short but ripping version of 'Twist And Shout' followed by 'Money'. They ran through their nightly collection of songs from *A Hard Day's Night* to general chaotic scenes. All too soon Paul was bringing the curtain down on their set with 'Long Tall Sally'.

Philip Walker, from his privileged position, heard enough of The Beatles to be impressed. "The Beatles are a fine act," he concluded. "What could be heard of their singing sounded just like their records, which isn't always the case with pop groups." Of course, from the second row back, they would have had to take his word for it.

Cardiff successfully negotiated, there were only three more cities to visit, the first their home town for two Sunday evening houses at the Empire – their first gig in Liverpool since December 1963. They arrived a bit later than they'd hoped following a late Saturday night, a sleep-in on Sunday morning and a foggy journey up from Cardiff.

A return to Liverpool usually gave the group an opportunity to catch up with old friends and there was one familiar face who had a particularly important job. Chief Supt Harold Whalley knew John and Paul from their skiffle days back in 1957 when his son Nigel played the tea-chest bass in The Quarrymen before briefly becoming their manager. Being a sensible man, Nigel's dad had advised the young skiffle hopefuls to settle down and get proper jobs and decent haircuts. John and Paul had a laugh about old times with the Chief Supt, who was heading the operation to get them in and out safely and – evidently delighted to have been proved wrong – he pocketed an autographed picture of the group.

It is astounding how many times fans fell for the same trick. Yet again, the crowds had surged around the venue's stage door, only for the Fabs to sneak in almost unnoticed through a side door. There was absolutely no chance of smaller crowds or any empty seats for The Beatles in their home city – more than 40,000 applied for tickets for two houses holding just over 2,300 each.

The fans were out in force to welcome them home, some having waited for up to nine hours. The police were out in force, too, some on horse-back, to try to keep order on the streets. They were needed. The traffic was brought to a halt as fans charged across Lime Street for a better view when The Beatles wandered out onto the balcony to wave to them. An estimated 1,000 people had gathered on the St George's Hall side and John, Paul, George and Ringo were soon ordered inside by police who feared for the safety of fans who were clearly oblivious to the dangers of traffic in the excitement of the moment. The revellers were dangerously close to crowds paying their respects at a Remembrance Service taking place nearby, swelling the numbers on the streets even further.

The press reception included questions about how often they managed to get home and Paul revealed that it was more often than people thought. The Beatles always had an eye for a picture opportunity. One was taken on the steps of the Empire with George, seated and pretending to cower, getting a mock dousing from John, Paul and Ringo who were holding upturned fire buckets. They were also photographed with two fans who had travelled up from Leicester to be there. Another was taken of them drawing a lucky winner from a policeman's helmet in a fan competition.

Mersey Beat editor and old friend Bill Harry joined them in their dress-ing room. He kept them up to date with the progress of various Liverpool groups and they chatted about the old days. There were other old friends in the dressing room, among them Cavern club owner Ray McFall and DJ Bob Wooler, and family in the shape of Paul McCartney's father Jim plus one of John's cousins. Ringo's mum Elsie was in the audience enjoying the show, and the welcome her now famous son and his mates were receiving. Paul told Bill Harry that Mary Wells was planning to record an album of Beatles songs as a tribute to them. It came out in 1965, entitled *Love Songs To The Beatles*, featuring 12 of Lennon and McCartney's finest.

Liverpool was more than ready to again pay homage to its favourite sons. The screams went into overdrive during both sets, with Bob Bain, totally unnecessarily, stirring the pot.

Among the minority of boys in the audience, trying desperately to hear The Beatles above the screams, was Mike Gerrard, who lived in Rainford, but attended West Park Grammar School in St Helens. "I got two tickets and offered one to my best friend, Bill Morton. He lived in Wigan so he got the bus to Liverpool from there, and I got on in St Helens. I think our mums had made us some jam sandwiches or something, to take with us and eat on the bus. Very rock'n'roll.

"We had seats a few rows from the back in the stalls. It was a good show, especially seeing someone like Mary Wells. Seeing an American singer live onstage was quite something. But when The Beatles were introduced, it was mayhem. The vast majority of the audience were teenage and pre-teen girls, there weren't many boys like us, and not many adults either. The noise was deafening, this really loud screaming and shrieking.

"It was loud all the way, but when The Beatles did something like shake their heads, it was absolutely deafening. You could just about hear their instruments, but you couldn't hear the voices at all. It was hard to tell what number they were doing, but I do remember 'Twist and Shout'. You couldn't mistake the intro to that."

Mike – as someone who was there to hear the music – could comprehend the frustrations felt by John, Paul, George and Ringo. "It was easy to understand why, after a year or two, they got tired of touring. They said it was making them lousy musicians, and they often goofed around and sang the wrong lyrics, to amuse themselves, and no one in the audience could tell the difference. Looking back, you could see in those early shows that that was inevitable. Anyway, shake it up baby and it was all over. Not a dry seat in the house, I'm sure. So we got the bus back home and probably celebrated with a meat and potato pie!"

This was one night when the second house provided the most work for the 65-strong St John ambulance crew. There were just two fainters in the first house, but 22 in the second.

John had arranged to meet Bill Harry later at a secret rendezvous to try to track down an early book of John's poems. They were unsuccessful, but they were joined by John's old school pal and former Quarryman Pete Shotton when they called in to see early Beatles bass player Stuart Sutcliffe's parents. Bill Harry later revealed that they asked John to take his pick of Stuart's paintings. John selected one that Stuart had painted during their Hamburg days and promised it would get pride of place in his living room. The Beatles stayed with their families overnight before leaving for Sheffield the next day and the penultimate shows of the tour.

As for Mike Gerrard, he went on to become a distinguished travel writer, among many other things writing about The Beatles in Hamburg for the *Independent*. He married an American and they share a home in Jo-Jo's Tucson, Arizona.

This was the fifth UK tour that The Beatles had undertaken and they appeared at the Sheffield City Hall on all five. The city's top impresarios Pete and Geoff Stringfellow had pressed important flesh to ensure that Sheffield was on the itinerary, calling in at Epstein's London office earlier in the year to cement the deal. It is testament to their persuasive powers and their reputation in Sheffield that they were also given the green light to replace Bob Bain as joint compères for the night.

As the giant tour was drawing to a close there is evidence that The Beatles were in need of a rest. The strain of completing *Beatles For Sale*, finding another chart-topping single, and slogging through town after town was taking its toll.

Neil and Mal, the great protectors, were increasingly mindful that the boys preferred their own company in their dressing room. Liverpool the night before had been an exception. Security was stepped up in Sheffield and it led to some negative publicity – and some embarrassment for all parties concerned – when the Olympic long jumper Sheila Parkin was "snubbed" at the City Hall.

A lot of careful planning had gone on over several days between Roy Shepherd of the *Sheffield Star* and The Beatles' staff and it was agreed that Sheila would meet the boys backstage to present them with a Top Stars Popularity Poll award on behalf of the newspaper. However, Aspinall insisted that nobody was getting through to see The Beatles backstage. All press were barred, too, including four young men from Barnsley who were there to make tapings for hospital radio. They had arrived as agreed at 4.30pm and waited around until 9pm before discovering that they were banned, along with everyone else.

The *Star* headline 'So-Tired Beatles Give Backstage Brush-Off To Sheila Parkin' said it all. Reporter Angela Cussans was wondering if The Beatles "have got too big for their high-heeled boots". Olympian Parkin had headed back to Lady Mabel Training College in Wentworth "disappointed and furious" after finally giving up and handing the award to Aspinall to pass on to The Beatles. No Beatle came out to say thanks. Neil, saying that two Beatles were asleep, came out instead and quoted Paul as saying, "Hey, that's gear."

The whole fiasco presented a problem for Beatles' press officer Derek Taylor. He had phoned Neil from London at 7.30pm to confirm the arrangements, but Neil was insistent – nobody was getting through. Derek told the newspaper: "I can't understand why it happened. The Beatles knew of the arrangements and had agreed to them. All I can say is that this has been a desperate year for them." He said The Beatles were simply exhausted. Brian Epstein quickly smoothed things over by inviting Parkin on an expenses-paid trip to London to meet the boys.

The slog of touring was taking its toll, but some of the supporting cast had found a second wind. With their spell in the spotlight about to close they were making the most of playing to packed and excited audiences. Sounds Incorporated won yet more friends in Sheffield. Their musicianship was beyond dispute, as was the energy of the performance, and they had some good stage banter, too, when they could be heard.

Tommy Quickly played through a cold but bounced along the stage as though he hadn't a care in the world and he earned plenty of screams for his efforts. The Beatles played their sets to the backdrop of an incredible din and the lack of energy reported backstage was in evidence onstage, too. How much can you take of giving your all onstage night after night, with nobody hearing a single note? It seemed that the end of this tour just couldn't come quickly enough.

At least they had a luxury retreat . . . and a luxury means of transport. That night The Beatles were taken by helicopter to the Park Hall Residential Country Club in nearby Spinkhill, landing on the lawn in front of the building. The club later became the Park Hall Hotel but is now a private residence.

The great autumn tour of 1964 climaxed in Bristol, a city with some experience of welcoming The Beatles. As they arrived for the tour's final shows at the famous old Colston Hall, the city's *Evening Post* ran a two-page feature greeting the world's four most famous faces, and it was to be an unusual night. Upholding a long-held showbiz tradition of last night pranks, the kings of the pop world were crowned in an undignified fashion just as they were in full throttle, minutes from the end of the second house. John and Paul had slowed the pace and joined voices for 'If I Fell' when the group was suddenly bombed with bags of flour from the overhead gantries.

The *Post*'s resident 'Beatle' reporter Roger Bennett looked on amazed. "With brilliant timing, it struck from above just as The Beatles hit the last chord," he wrote. "The Beatles collapsed in fits of laughter, pointing at each other and dancing around the stage in stitches. There was flour in their hair, on their suits, in their eyebrows, in their guitars and all over Ringo's drums. Ringo turned his tom-tom upside down and banged it in a vain attempt to get rid of the flour. Paul, bent double with laughter, grabbed the mike and shouted, 'It's the last night of the tour, you see.' Then they broke into giggles again. The audience just sat roaring and shrieking with laughter until The Beatles recovered enough to launch into 'I Wanna Be Your Man'."

The Beatles may have been genuinely amused, but Colston Hall manager Ken Cowley most definitely was not. He was beside himself that there had been such a blatant breach of his security and he was desperate to find the culprits. The mystery seemed to be solved the next day when the newspaper ran a story headlined 'How We Bombed The Beatles', containing confessions from three young men and a policeman's daughter. Evidently they had managed to shin up a drainpipe at the back, run across two roofs, drop through a trapdoor into the lighting department and then wait patiently for the right moment to drop their bombshell.

Post writer Gerry Brooke has another theory, however. "The Post's chief reporter, the late Roger Bennett, used all his investigative skills on this story in the aftermath, and he found out that it was actually a stagehand who was responsible."

The Beatles knew Bennett from their previous gig at Colston Hall and had honoured him with an exclusive interview in the run-up to the shows. When they'd arrived at the venue, they'd had to run the gauntlet of screaming girls who'd had been waiting most of the day for a glimpse of them. Some of the first – Christine Bayley, Pat Galbraith, Nichola Chanin, Hilary Wiltshire, Joy Ford, Alison Dawes and Lynda Brown – were photographed in the *Post*, precious tickets in hand. One of them, however, didn't have a ticket. Hilary (13) was among 17 stowaways found hiding in a lavatory after sneaking in through a back entrance left open for cleaners. All was well until one of the girl's coughed – alerting security. As in Sheffield, no one was permitted to meet The Beatles in their Bristol dressing room, and there were to be no press interviews.

The undercard artists were enjoying their last night of a month in the spotlight. The Rustiks put in a tuneful performance and Mike Haslam's ballad singing was appreciated. Tommy Quickly, backed by The Remo Four, was enthusiastic and Mary Wells, backed as ever by Sounds Incorporated, was a very welcome guest, with 'My Guy' again the centrepiece of her performance.

But, as usual, the real reception was saved until last. The screams were a tiny bit quieter than the year before so snatches of music got through. This was put down to there being mums and dads in the audience, although heavily outnumbered by their teenage daughters. The appeal of The Beatles was getting wider. It wasn't just flour that was aimed at them either. The ever present jelly babies were hurled, along with half a dozen fluffy toys and the usual declarations of love.

The body count? Twelve girls collapsed with "emotional stress" and two more were tackled near the stage. The Beatles rattled through their 10-strong set list for each house – powering into 'Twist And Shout' and 'Money' to start, followed by the songs from *A Hard Day's Night* before Paul took the mike for the final curtain closer, one last rip into 'Long Tall Sally'.

With the tour over, The Beatles were no doubt relieved, but for others it had been a very special period in their lives. Michael Haslam died in May 2003, but his widow Eileen says he had fond memories of the tour and the other artists on it. "The tour programme spoke of his quiet charm and that was right. He was such a lovely and charming man. He had a fabulous time on that tour and he would often talk about it. He regarded it as the time of his life. He got on with everyone on that tour and thoroughly enjoyed it."

Eileen said he kept some mementoes in a scrapbook, including his first payslip from NEMS. Michael's sister Annie went on to become the singer with progressive rock outfit Renaissance in the 1970s.

Family friend David Fredericks knew Michael since the early 1970s. "Mike was a nice and easy, fun-loving guy. He wasn't flash or brash. There was no side to him. He thought The Beatles were brilliant. He was closest to John. He thought he was a really nice guy. They used to chat quite a lot. John seemed to have more time than the others. Mike's voice was sort of a cross between Elvis and Roy Orbison and he was known as The Elvis Presley of Bolton. That's how he was billed.

"The crowds never even noticed he was there. He said that one night when he was onstage he lost a tooth while he was singing and he bent down to pick it up and the music carried on. He put it back in his mouth and carried on and nobody batted an eyelid. Nobody noticed.

"Mike enjoyed the Beatles days, but he never bragged about it. He said the best thing he ever did was the song he recorded with Annie – 'Somewhere Out There' – their duet. That meant everything to him."

Annie: "I always believed Michael had an amazing untapped potential. His voice was unique. He had a wide, very powerful vocal range, and on top of that he was very handsome!

"We recorded 'Somewhere Out There' in 1994, when I was visiting him and Eileen from the States during my breast cancer recovery. I remember the day so well. It was pouring with rain. Singing with Michael helped me immensely. Our voices had a wonderful blend."

Their recording together can be heard on Annie Haslam's CD *Woman Transcending*.

Colin Manley of The Remo Four died in April 1999. He had recalled how little the fans heard when they backed Tommy Quickly. However, John Lennon regularly loaned Colin his 12-string Rickenbacker for 'Wild Side Of Life' during the tour and Colin would hand it back when their spot was over. Tony Ashton was later to replace Don Andrew in the group, with Phil Rogers switching to bass, and they enjoyed a successful stint in Hamburg. George Harrison produced them when they recorded material for his *Wonderwall* album. After they broke up Ashton and Dyke teamed up with bass player Kim Gardner and they enjoyed a chart hit with 'The Resurrection Shuffle' in 1971 as Ashton, Gardner & Dyke.

Despite all of Brian's investment in him, Tommy Quickly just couldn't achieve the big hit that would have made his career. People who remember those days on Merseyside still debate just why that was. Bad luck didn't just dog his career – he was also to sustain a serious injury in a fall from a ladder. Tommy and The Remo Four can be seen performing 'Humpty Dumpty' in the 1965 film *Pop Gear* (aka *Go Go Mania*).

Sounds Incorporated were rated as one of the top bands around by other musicians, but they never achieved the hits. They troubled the chart compilers twice, reaching number 30 with 'The Spartans' and 35 with 'Spanish Harlem', both in 1964. But they did get to accompany The Beatles again on their 1965 tour of America, including the famous Shea Stadium gig in New York in front of a world record 55,000 fans.

Sounds' drummer Tony Newman went on to drum for many of the biggest names in rock. He now lives in Las Vegas and remembers that whirlwind 1964 Beatles UK tour: "By this time, doing shows with The Beatles had become another day at the office. We'd all become used to screaming girls and the adulation of fans."

Meeting Mary Wells was something Tony and his band-mates had looked forward to. "We were all shocked how black she was. Of course, she was equally surprised how small and white we were. But it was a great pleasure to work with her and play Motown music. In fact, Paul McCartney would come to the stage every night to listen to the bass lick on 'My Guy'. You have to remember that these were unheard of grooves at the time."

Tony recalls testing the patience of Mike Haslam on one occasion. "Mike had a great voice, and this was his first tour, and so he had to be tested. I remember one night, as he was reaching the high notes in 'I Believe' we walked behind him with a 40ft ladder and dropped it on the stage with a huge clanking sound, and then apologised to him for making such a noise.

"The Remo Four were a great band, and we became good friends. Roy Dyke, the drummer, and I would talk drums all the time. He had a copy of Dave Brubeck's 'Take Five' which we studiously would listen to. Bob Bain was a great friend of Sounds Incorporated, and we did shows in Germany at the beginning of our career. He was the one who always encouraged us to go first class. A very funny man."

Mary Wells was never to reach the same heights after quitting Tamla Motown. The split proved problematic and health problems returned. She was bed-ridden for a while with tuberculosis. She was diagnosed with laryngeal cancer in 1990, the treatment for which devastated her voice, and she succumbed to the illness in July 1992 at the age of just 49.

Brian Epstein had to mark down The Rustiks as a venture that didn't pay off. They parted company in March 1966.

As for The Beatles, the end of this long slog of a tour was welcome, but life wasn't about to get easier. They were staring down the barrel of a schedule of more TV and radio work and an exhausting 20-night (two shows a night) run of their second Christmas extravaganza, this time at the Hammersmith Odeon. Rehearsals started on December 21 and the show ran from Christmas Eve until January 16, 1965, with only three days off. The Yardbirds (with Eric Clapton on guitar), Freddie & The Dreamers and Elkie Brooks were among the other performers in shows hosted by Jimmy Savile and again including comedy skits from The Beatles.

Before all that, Ringo was to spend the first 10 days of December laid up in the University College Hospital, London, having his tonsils removed.

They were to start shooting their second film in February, 1965. A European tour, featuring dates in Paris, Milan, Genoa, Rome, Nice, Madrid and Barcelona, was next, followed by their third American tour in August.

There were two more chart topping singles, 'Ticket To Ride' and 'Help!' And the *Help!* LP was yet another number one. They stopped long enough to be invested with their MBEs in October – and then they were to release their eleventh single and their sixth LP in December 1965. And what better way to ensure both were number one hits? Why, another UK tour, of course.

CHAPTER SIX

The Sixth Tour
Stepping Off The Treadmill

December 3 – December 12, 1965
Featuring The Beatles, The Moody Blues, The Paramounts,
The Koobas, Beryl Marsden, Steve Aldo, The Marionettes
Compère: Jerry Stevens

BY the end of 1965 The Beatles had been trapped on the music world's most manic merry-go-round for three years and they were more than ready to step off. The non-stop treadmill of touring, filming and recording, while also having to find time to write songs and cope with endless TV and radio appearances, press interviews and a multitude of other intrusions into their time, was taking a terrible toll on the Fab Four.

The Beatles wanted a bit of their lives back – something had to give, and that would be touring. It was a clear-cut decision, since touring had become a largely futile and increasingly fraught aspect of their lives. Onstage the screams drowned out their music and offstage – or at least on tour – they were exposed to ever more dangerous situations.

Behind the scenes, Brian Epstein and Arthur Howes considered it vital for the band not to lose this crucial link with their fans but The Beatles themselves, developing rapidly as recording artists, were determined to spend more time in the studio and much less on the road. A compromise had to be reached.

In early August it was announced that there would be no UK Beatles tour in 1965, then, within a month, the decision was reversed. Epstein and Howes had got their way, at least to a degree. When The Beatles flew back into Britain on August 31 after a 10-date two-and-a-half-week tour of America, they were adamant that any tour of the UK that year would be short. In the end they agreed to just nine dates in eight cities for a fee of £1,000 a night. It would be the usual formula of two houses a night, a joint promotion by Howes and Epstein.

Box offices across the country opened on October 31, by which time pavement queues for tickets had already gathered. The Beatles were also committed to producing another album before the end of the year and after a short break began working on writing and recording new songs. Unlike today's premier league groups, they were quick workers, with work on their sixth album commencing in mid-October and finishing mid-November. Midway through the sessions, on October 26, they visited Buckingham Palace to receive their MBEs, an award that predictably displeased a number of Colonel Blimps.

Everything fell smoothly into place. The new album, *Rubber Soul*, and single, the double A-sided 'Day Tripper'/'We Can Work It Out', was in the shops on December 3, the day the tour opened in Scotland. There was to be no speculation from the press over the odd empty seat this time with every ticket for every show snapped up well in advance. Nevertheless, there was a noticeable change in atmosphere since The Beatles had last toured the UK. While it would certainly be wrong to describe the concerts as subdued, the wildest excesses of Beatlemania were largely a thing of the past. The police now had the benefit of experience and, often on horseback, protected venues with a ring of steel, sealing off surrounding streets so that only ticket holders could get through. The Beatles and their fans had matured. There were certainly scenes of wild excitement, especially on the London dates, and plenty of screaming, but the completely manic behaviour had cooled.

There was to be another subtle change. Because The Beatles' music was developing and they were no longer simply a guitar band, there was a Vox Continental electronic organ onstage for this tour. Paul played it when he sang 'Yesterday' and John pounded away on it during Paul's nightly show-closer, 'I'm Down'. There was minimal preparation from The Beatles. Their sole rehearsal was a get-together at Neil and Mal's London flat for a few hours to run through the set and tighten up any loose bits. Was it worth more effort? They knew that nothing much would be heard above the screams.

The main support would be a young group with whom The Beatles were friendly, them having signed with NEMS three months before. The

Moody Blues originated from Birmingham but had switched their base to London in 1964 when their manager Tony Secunda secured them a residency at The Marquee. They also had a record deal with Decca and their second single, 'Go Now', was a UK number one in January 1965 and had also made the American Top 10. The band's main vocalist and guitarist, Brian Hines, had taken the stage name Denny Laine and the line-up was completed by Mike Pinder (keyboards), Ray Thomas (flute), Clint Warwick (bass) and Graeme Edge (drums). The Beatles were pleased to have them on the tour. George told a journalist: "We've always been good friends. They go down well with the kids. Their style's different to ours, but they follow the same trends."

The Paramounts hailed from Southend, and featured Gary Brooker (piano and vocals), Robin Trower (guitar), Diz Derrick (bass) and B. J. Wilson (drums). They enjoyed a minor hit with 'Poison Ivy', their explosive first single in 1963, but despite a growing reputation among other musicians, had failed to follow it up with more hits. Like The Beatles, they were on the Parlophone label and The Beatles knew and liked them. Down the line they would disband and eventually regroup as Procol Harum, best known for their psychedelic hit 'Whiter Shade Of Pale'.

The other three acts on the tour – The Koobas, Beryl Marsden and Steve Aldo – were all Liverpudlians. The Koobas (aka The Kubas) were formed in 1962 and comprised Stuart Leatherwood (guitar and vocals), Roy Morris (guitar), Keith Ellis (bass) and Tony O'Riley (drums). Like The Beatles, they were a four-piece outfit from Liverpool who were inspired by American R&B artists, but their style was markedly different from the Fabs. They had played a three-week stint at the Star Club in Hamburg in December 1963 and had built a reputation as decent performers. Epstein signed them in 1964 and secured them a recording deal with Pye. The tour was an ideal opportunity for The Koobas to plug their second single 'Take Me For A Little While', backed with 'Somewhere In The Night'.

It remains a mystery to many people in the know why Beryl Marsden (no relation to Gerry as her real name was Beryl Hogg) didn't go on to become a household name. Beryl had a big personality to go with the big voice. She was another veteran of the Liverpool beat scene. She was already singing at the Cavern when she was invited to join local favourites The Undertakers before her fifteenth birthday. She was having a whale of a time, but when they left for a Hamburg stint, Beryl was left clicking her heels in Liverpool. Not yet 16, she was too young to go. "I was counting the days until they got back, but when they did they were all leather gear and moody image and they didn't need me any more," she says.

Beryl was taken under the wing of Brian Epstein's associate Joe Flannery, and sang with many Liverpool groups, went to Hamburg at 16 and then left home for London and the hope of stardom. She had known The Beatles for years.

"They were always my favourite group," she says. "I was a bit of a tomboy – wearing trouser suits and things like that, and they were like big brothers to me. I would watch them on nights when I didn't have a gig. I didn't just see them at the Cavern. There were occasions when I saw them over the water [the Wirral] and wouldn't have the money for the ferry home and John would say, 'Get in the van, Marsy.'"

Back in 1963 Lennon told his pal *Mersey Beat* editor Bill Harry that he planned to give Beryl the McCartney-penned 'Love Of The Loved' to launch her, but Brian had put his foot down, saying he would decide who would get their songs. The song was instead handed to his protégé Cilla Black as her first single. For her part, Beryl had turned down Brian's offer to manage her, but Epstein and The Beatles had no qualms about putting her on this package. Now 18, she was plugging her latest single, 'Who You Gonna Hurt?'

Steve Aldo was a black soul singer from Liverpool who had also known The Beatles since the Cavern days and he went on to perform with some of Liverpool's finest, including Kingsize Taylor and Howie Casey. Born in 1945, he was christened Edward Bedford but Joe Flannery, when he was managing him, decided it wouldn't do and he needed a stage name. By the end of 1965 Steve shared the same manager as Beryl Marsden and The Koobas – Tony Stratton-Smith – but promoter Arthur Howes didn't put his name forward for the tour.

Aldo maintains: "When Brian and Arthur were discussing the line-up Arthur put forward the others, and Brian said, 'Where's Steve?' Arthur said, 'Well Beryl and The Koobas are signed to my agency, but Steve isn't'. And Brian said, 'But the boys [Beatles] want him on the tour' – so that's how I got to be on it."

Beryl and Steve were both living in London, Steve in a flat in Guildford Street off Russell Square at the beginning of December 1965.

There was one other group on the tour, The Marionettes, who the tour programme recorded as consisting of Gerry Kissoon, Pauline Sibblies, Elleese Drummond and Lance Ring. Formed towards the end of 1964, The Marionettes secured a place on the bill of some Brenda Lee gigs, but their debut record on Decca was largely ignored. They then switched to Parlophone and in July 1965 released a version of 'Under The Boardwalk'. Their laid-back, easy listening pop/soul style and subtle harmonies led to TV appearances, including *Ready Steady Go!* and *Discs A Go-Go*, and a radio appearance on Brian Matthews' *Saturday Club*. A 1965 summer season with Gerry & The Pacemakers, The Karl Denver Trio and Gene Vincent was followed by a package tour with The Everly Brothers, Cilla Black and Billy J. Kramer. Their latest single, 'End Of The Day', was released on November 14, shortly before the tour started.

The tour's compère was Jerry Stevens (real name Pinder), who hailed from Seagrave Avenue in Gleadless, Sheffield. Something of a showbiz all-rounder, he started out as a singer, was a good mimic and had done some acting, too. He was also a highly rated comedian. Stevens was an experienced pop compère, having been a regular on the circuit since making his bow in 1963 on a tour starring Del Shannon and Johnny Tillotson. Jerry can remember how compèring for The Beatles came his way: "I had done three weeks on Gerry's Christmas Cracker in 1964 – a week in Glasgow, Leeds and Liverpool. Brian saw the show in Liverpool and he told me at the final night party that he wanted me to compère the next Beatles tour."

Atrocious weather heralded the tour. The Beatles headed out of London in their Austin Princess in the early hours of Thursday, December 2, and bedded down at their top secret destination – the Berwick-on-Tweed Hotel – that night. They were completing the journey up to Glasgow the following morning for the two Friday houses at the Odeon Cinema when disaster struck. One of George's guitars, a £300 Gretsch Country Gentleman, which had been fastened to the boot, fell off. They immediately stopped but the guitar had been smashed to pieces by following lorries before driver Alf Bicknell could do anything about it. Mal wasn't responsible – he had already left London in the van with most of their equipment, including seven other guitars.

The usual policy of staying at a plush hotel some miles from where they were playing was abandoned due to the weather. In the circumstances, Brian decided it would be better for them to stay at the Central Hotel in the city centre, despite the obvious security worries this would create.

They arrived in the late afternoon and it proved an ideal place to stay, resembling a fortress from the outside but plush and spacious inside, and The Beatles enjoyed a steak dinner before being whisked off to the Odeon. This was their fourth visit to the Renfield Street cinema and their Scottish fans were ecstatic at the prospect. An estimated 40 coach-loads from all over the country homed-in on Glasgow to join the huge throng of locals gathering outside the cinema. Susan Fallon (18), from Falkirk, was on a trip organised by a youth club. She told *Disc Weekly* that seats on the coach and tickets for the show were snapped up as soon as word had got round. Odeon manager George Chantrey had been overwhelmed with applications from local teenagers begging for jobs as usherettes. They were all turned down, but Beatle fan Marjorie McCormish was on top of the world . . . she'd already been doing that job for a year.

Chantrey, fully aware of what was in store, took urgent measures to beef-up his 45-strong staff. The Beatles' management and the police were also determined that the excesses of previous tours would not be repeated. More than 200 police were drafted into the city centre to control the huge crowds. Every one would be needed. There were 6,000 people with tickets – and thousands more without. There were police in cars, on horses and with walkie-talkies ready to do what was necessary to maintain order.

The Beatles made their way in and the press conference got underway at 5.10pm. Responding to complaints that The Beatles were playing only nine dates, George replied: "We could go on an everlasting tour in Britain and still not please everyone."

Paul wore a wide floral tie bought from Harrods a few days before, and John pretended to blow his nose on it, provoking much laughter. "Where did he get it?" quipped John. "He's leased it from Arthur English [a comedian known for wearing wide Kipper ties]." The press conference over, The Beatles relaxed in the theatre but shouts of We Want The Beatles could be heard outside. However, the huge police presence had dampened enthusiasm. Streets were sealed off and those police on horse-back, determined that the excesses Beatlemania would not return to Glasgow, kept fans in check.

The Beatles still liked to lark about. John turned his Beatle hairstyle into a reasonable imitation of a haystack and remarked to a reporter: "It takes me hours to look this scruffy."

Compère Jerry Stevens had already checked into his digs in Glasgow and he went back there to eat before returning to the Odeon in the early evening for his night's work. He was to wish that he had stayed in the Odeon. "When I headed back, I got two blocks from the Odeon and the streets were absolutely chock-a-block with teenagers. They could have filled Hampden Park – that's how it seemed. It was dark by then and I was stuck in the throng. I was only about 200 yards away, but that was a hell of a distance – I was going to struggle to make it. I said to a policeman, 'I'm trying to get to the theatre.' 'So are this lot,' he said. 'I know, but I'm in the show,' I replied. I told him I was the compère and he said 'OK, let's go' and he managed to get me through."

While in his digs Jerry had hit on an idea for an opening night routine and it worked so well at Glasgow that he used it for the whole tour. "I knew I needed to give some serious thought to what I was going to do immediately before The Beatles came on because this would be my toughest spot of the night in terms of getting the crowd under control. Throughout the show there were two or three minutes between the acts when the stage was being prepared behind the curtain. Kit would be moved about to set up for the next one. It was the compère's job to fill those vital minutes.

"I used to do gags, but I knew in that final spot that the screams would reach a crescendo and I wouldn't have a chance. I had to think of something else. I also did imitations, so it hit me that if I went on and got the audience to join in with me as I mimicked The Beatles, that might work."

Jerry decided it would be expedient to first check with The Beatles. He made his way backstage to find them preparing for the show. "George was tuning his guitar. They were diligent. There would be three or four tuning sessions. I introduced myself and they were very friendly and I asked how long they needed me to do. They said just two or three minutes. I ran my idea past them, assuring them I wouldn't be taking the mickey but just doing a visual impersonation because it would be impossible to do gags because nobody would hear them. John said 'I know what a tough spot it is just before us, but you do whatever you want and if it works, then fine. We'll watch and let you know.'"

The Beatles had a TV set in their dressing room – it was one luxury of the 1965 tour. They also found time to record a good luck message for Radio Scotland, a new pirate station that was to launch on New Year's Eve.

The screams in the first house were subdued enough for the support artists to be heard. The Paramounts were on first, playing their own spot, and they stayed onstage as Jerry Stevens came on to introduce first Beryl Marsden and then Steve Aldo. The two singers made some new friends on this opening night. Marsden, dressed in a trouser suit, belted out some rock numbers and Aldo's bluesy soulful voice won applause. They pooled their talents on 'Mocking Bird' and their rousing finale 'Baby Baby Baby'.

Then Stevens returned to introduce The Moody Blues, who closed the first half. It wasn't just The Beatles who had trouble on the journey to Glasgow. The Moody Blues had been pulled over by the police and given a speeding ticket. But they got a great reception during their spot. 'I'll Go Crazy' went down particularly well, as did their big hit 'Go Now'. This was a good sign. Perhaps audiences would give the support acts a chance rather than simply scream over them.

The Koobas got the second half rolling, followed by The Marionettes and then it was time for Jerry Stevens to put his new routine into practice. He recalls: "When it came to it, the noise was absolutely unbelievable. I shouted, 'Who's this?' And I ran to the spot where John was to stand and took up his stance and they screamed 'John!' Then I dashed across to Paul's spot – same result – then George and Ringo. I did this several times, each one getting a bit faster, and they just screamed their names as I did so. It was almost like I was conducting a huge, screaming choir."

The audience suitably primed, The Beatles bounded onto the stage to face the usual barrage of screams, toys and jelly babies. For this tour they had a set list of 11 songs, representing a good half-hour onstage. They included both sides of their new single released that day and two songs from the new album, but the music was becoming more intricate and this proved a problem. No longer were they simply laying down a thumping beat and sticking to that through the din. 'Nowhere Man' and 'If I Needed Someone', two songs from *Rubber Soul*, featured some delicate harmonies and it was crucial that The Beatles could hear each other. There was little chance of that.

John kicked off with 'I Feel Fine' then handed the vocal spotlight to Paul for its B-side 'She's A Woman'. George sung the harmony-laden 'If I Needed Someone' before Ringo took over for his country and western flavoured 'Act Naturally', a track from their *Help!* album. A faulty guitar lead caused problems for George before they could continue and when the problem was rectified John sang 'Nowhere Man' then teamed up with Paul for 'Baby's In Black' from *Beatles For Sale*. The screams went into overdrive for 'Help!' and 'We Can Work It Out'. The limelight was then on Paul as he sang 'Yesterday', accompanying himself on the Vox Continental. The others returned for 'Day Tripper' and then it was a traditional sprint to the finish line as Paul screamed out 'I'm Down', this time with John on the electric keyboard.

Fans now found it increasingly difficult to reach The Beatles. They faced a wall of security men protecting the stage and the backstage area was equally watertight. Even Odeon manager George Chantrey could only contact the NEMS team by intercom.

Chantrey was wise to hire that extra help. The authorities might have been better organised this time, but the fainters were still out in force. The 130 first aid and ambulance workers were kept well occupied with 65 girls fainting in the first house, five of whom were taken to hospital, with 70 more in the second. Sandra Shields (17), of Pollok, was at pains to rationalise the fans' behaviour, saying: "I couldn't bear it any longer. I wanted to rush closer to the stage. I was crying so much that I couldn't see properly and I can only remember staggering into the aisle with one thought in mind – to get closer."

The sheer weight of security on this tour meant onrushing fans would not get near The Beatles, as George observed to *Disc Weekly* with a tinge of disappointment the next day: "One thing we've noticed is that although the noise from the kids is the same, the difference is that they don't get a chance to express themselves like they used to. There are too many attendants about. It's more organised mania this time. They don't get a chance to go mad."

Compère Jerry Stevens needed to get the green light for his routine. "After the first show I asked The Beatles what they thought in the dressing room and John said, 'We saw it and it's fine, keep it in, and well done' – so that's what I did for the whole tour."

The Central Hotel may have been built like a fortress, but the downside was that everyone knew they were there. Several hundred girls had to be cleared before The Beatles could leave the next day, piling into the Princess for the journey into Newcastle after sleeping late. They faced a grim trek through snow for what would be their fourth appearance at the City Hall.

They checked into the Turks Head Hotel where a couple of esteemed guests – Sir Laurence Olivier and Albert Finney – were also spending the night, but The Beatles didn't meet them. A group of Army officers were at the hotel and Moody Blue Graeme Edge – mistaking them for porters – distinguished himself by asking one of them to get him a drink. The Beatles and the Moodies set off for the City Hall in the late afternoon.

Backstage, a young local reporter by the name of Philip Norman had managed to blag his way into the inner sanctum of The Beatles' dressing room and chatted with John and Paul for half an hour before being un-ceremoniously ejected by the ever-protective Aspinall. The same Philip Norman would later write the acclaimed Beatles biography *Shout!*

The Beatles got to watch quite a bit of television that evening in a small room next to their dressing room. They saw themselves on *Thank Your Lucky Stars* miming 'We Can Work It Out' but weren't too impressed, and perhaps as a result hit on the idea of sending promo films to TV com-panies as an alternative to miming or performing in studios. Though their disappointment with *TYLS* didn't deter them from filming TV appear-ances entirely, the promo film idea would have far-reaching consequences for the music industry – not that anyone realised it at the time.

They also watched *Lost In Space* and a play called *The Paraffin Man*, but found Thunderbirds a turn-off, and before the second house had a meal and then watched *The Avengers*. That night's episode, entitled 'Dial A Deadly Number', started just after 9pm. Paul and Ringo watched from the sofa while John sat upright in a wicker chair. Across the room George shared a sofa with Moody Blue Ray Thomas. When a reporter came in, George, who made it clear he wasn't interested in the programme, went over for a chat, revealing that they still got butterflies before going onstage.

More than 50 police were on duty outside the City Hall and dozens of security men were inside with St John volunteers at the ready, but the huge casualty list of Glasgow wasn't repeated at Newcastle. Nevertheless, there was growing impatience from the audience and the other artists had to put up with occasional shouts of 'We Want The Beatles' as they performed.

Jerry Stevens did his Beatles impersonations as the real thing waited in the wings, then jogged onstage as 2,500 voices screamed as one. Sweets, cards, Gonks and autograph books rained down as John and Paul grinned widely, George plugged in his guitar and Ringo took his seat behind the drums. They warmed up with a snatch of 'Dizzy Miss Lizzy' then launched into 'I Feel Fine', keeping on the move as they did so to avoid the objects thrown from the seats. Paul stamped out the rhythm with his foot when they burst into 'She's A Woman'. George laughed as a jelly baby bounced off John's head and huge Beatle photos suddenly adorned the balcony.

George, perhaps mindful of what happened at Glasgow, nervously checked his guitar and amp before launching into 'If I Needed Someone'. It was Newcastle, but it could have been anywhere. The front rows were one mass of waving arms, scarves, LP covers and photos. George changed his guitar as they prepared for Ringo's vocal moment which, as ever, inspired an increase in the scream level.

Their hair was longer these days. John brushed his back from his eyes and announced: "Here's a number from our new LP and all that! It's 'Nowhere Man'." His few words were enough for another girl to faint with excitement. Missiles were still being thrown and George, to his annoyance, was hit. John and Paul duetted on 'Baby's In Black', with Paul swaying his Hofner violin bass in time to the music. George could barely be heard above the screams as he stepped forward to announce 'Help!' Then it was Paul's turn as he stepped forward to introduce 'We Can Work It Out'. "At this point we'd like to sing you one side of our new single, featuring John on the organ," he said. The Moody Blues, their spot done, were watching from the wings during the next number as Paul moved over to the organ and sang 'Yesterday'. Then it was 'Day Tripper' before the closing 'I'm Down', belted out to tumultuous cheers and grief all at the same time.

Excitement there was a-plenty, but it was a fair way from a riot. One girl hanging over a gallery rail was told to get back in her seat – another was told off for hanging a banner. And that was about it. The ambulance crew and nurses were on easy street.

Anne Dedman and her Peterlee Grammar Technical School pals were in the second house that night, perched up in the circle with a perfect view of the action, but too far away to hear anything above the screaming to which they were contributing. Though only 14, Anne (now Richardson and an English lecturer at East Durham College) organised their trip to see the Fab Four. "We lived in Easington, a little mining village down the coast, and I knew Mum wouldn't let me go into Newcastle for the concert unless she was sure I would be looked after. So I went to see Alfie Snowdon, who ran Snowdon's Bus Company, and he agreed to run a coach if I could fill it. I knew there would be no problem with that.

"I filled it all right and collected the money and Alfie got the concert tickets. It was so exciting for us – 14-year-old girls from a little mining village where nothing much happened. There was no way any of us stayed in our seats up in the circle. My friend Lorna Kelsey (now Lapworth) was with me and so were Marion Rogers, Janet Temperley and also Dot Smithson, who lived in nearby Blackhall.

"Of course, we couldn't hear anything. It was just deafening. I'm not exaggerating when I say that I couldn't speak for nearly three weeks because I damaged my throat. The Beatles complained that people kept screaming and their music couldn't be heard and looking back now I realise it must have been awful for them."

Anne makes the point that it was all about *seeing* The Beatles. "It took us about three days to get ready! We had these black polo neck sweaters. We vacuumed them. We would hold them out for each other so that there wasn't a mark on them. We kept washing our hair and styling it and did our nails because The Beatles were going to see us and fall in love with us so we had to be absolutely stunning."

There would be no hanging around the stage door for Anne and her friends afterwards. "As soon as the concert was over it was back on the bus. The driver was waiting for us. He had promised my mum that no harm would come to us. The whole thing was quite a celebration. Lorna's birthday was the day before the concert and when the clock passed midnight on the bus it was Dot's birthday."

The Beatles and Moody Blues kept the beat going back at the hotel, playing records, including the Isley Brothers and B. B. King, until the early hours.

For some on the bill, playing a venue like the City Hall was a new experience. Looking back, Steve Aldo recalls: "Newcastle was weird. It was a big hall – like a big Masonic hall – but with a huge, round stage and you would come up these steps and walk up to the stage in full view of the crowd. It's not so unusual now, but it was the first time I'd seen anything like that."

On Sunday The Beatles were homeward bound for two shows at the Liverpool Empire. Their return coincided with news that the Cavern club, their spiritual home and the cornerstone of the Merseybeat boom, was facing closure. The Liverpool beat groups had either moved on to better things or faded away and attendance at clubs like the Cavern was falling sharply. In addition, Liverpool City Council was insisting that new toilets and a new drainage system had to be installed at the club, but owner Ray McFall didn't have the £3,000 needed to pay for it.

Paul spotted ticketless 15-year-olds Josephine McQuaid and Susan Hall handing out Save The Cavern leaflets by the Empire's stage door and invited them in to give the news to the other Fabs. They held an immediate press conference – but hinted there would be little they could do to help.

Paul suggested the council should treat the Cavern as a tourist attraction "rather than an old warehouse". John remarked: "We don't feel we owe the Cavern anything physical. All we owe it is allegiance." All George could muster was: "We don't want to commit ourselves too much," while Ringo observed: "I think the ball is in Ray McFall's court in a way. I'll be sorry if the Cavern goes because for two years or more it was the greatest club in the whole of Britain."

The club would close the following February but then reopen under new management in July, with Prime Minister Harold Wilson and a host of celebrities in attendance. Today the site of the original club has been filled in but a new Cavern, opened in 1991, thrives a few doors down on Mathew Street and has become – as Paul suggested – a major Liverpool tourist attraction.

In December 1965 Liverpool gave The Beatles such a huge welcome at the Empire that Ringo was moved to say: "You heard them, you saw them. That's the answer to the knockers who say we are on the way out."

Liverpool, though, was following the lead of Newcastle the day before in stopping short of a riot. Police were relieved at how orderly things were outside the Empire while 5,000 teenagers queued for the two houses. Around 40,000 fans had applied for those 5,000 tickets. Inside, 24 St John Brigaders dealt with 17 fainters from the two shows. A spokesman described it as "a picnic" compared with the recent Stones and earlier Beatles performances.

Nevertheless, those who came to enjoy the music were still frustrated – as with everywhere else, all hell broke loose when the curtains opened. When the screaming kicked in and fans jumped off their seats waving programmes, pictures and scarves at their returning heroes, The Beatles battled manfully through the opening number. "Can you hear me?" Paul yelled into the microphone, but his introduction to 'She's A Woman' was drowned by several thousand shrill voices. The Beatles, in their light jackets and dark trousers, battled on, their Vox amps struggling to cut through the din.

They played exactly the same set as the previous two nights. Facing a much shorter tour than earlier marathons, The Beatles seemed to perform with greater enthusiasm and commitment this time around, perhaps intuitively sensing that this might be the last time they would ever play their songs on a Liverpool stage. It also helped that there were plenty of relatives and friends in the Empire audience, among them George's girl-friend (and soon-to-be wife) Pattie Boyd and George and Ringo's parents.

The night hadn't been without its problems. Once again, the weather was at the forefront. The north was still in the grip of winter and it again took The Beatles' Austin Princess, with its darkened windows and the latest mod cons, four hours to wend its way down from Newcastle. It was getting on for 5pm by the time they arrived and drove past the gauntlet of teens packing Lime Street. The Paramounts had kicked off the first show at 5.40pm and they stayed on to provide the backing for the energetic Beryl Marsden and Steve Aldo. They sang 'Strong Love' together with gusto and Aldo provided backing vocals for her 'Who You Gonna Hurt'.

Nerves were jangling backstage as The Moody Blues, slated to close the first half, had failed to arrive. Their car had broken down on the motor-way. The Marionettes were shifted to their spot and everyone kept their fingers crossed. The Koobas started the second half with their three numbers, including 'Stubborn Kind Of Fellow'. Liverpool's strict Sunday stage costume regulations were waived to allow The Koobas to wear their tight floral trousers.

The Moodies eventually arrived and if they were flustered, they didn't show it onstage. Going on immediately before The Beatles, they suc-ceeded in getting through their set without a single Beatles chant from the audience – quite an achievement. 'Go Now', the big hit at the start of the year, got the reception it deserved and 'Everyday' and 'Bottom Of My Heart' were also included.

Predictably, The Beatles' dressing room was invaded between the two houses. Among the visitors were comedian Jimmy Tarbuck, MP Bessie Braddock and assorted family and friends.

The second show continued in similar exuberant manner. This was typified by Paul joining The Koobas onstage, playing drums for them on a version of the Larry Williams rocker 'Dizzy Miss Lizzy'. The fans were partying too and the Empire security people were happy to let them dance in the aisles. It was a fitting farewell to Liverpool for the world's favourite pop stars.

There was an unpleasant memory for Beryl Marsden, though, who was the victim of a theft. "Someone took my lovely red velvet top. It was made for me by Tony Stratton-Smith's tailor, Alf, and I loved it. I appealed for whoever it was to give it back, but they didn't!"

The least surprising news of the day? 'We Can Work It Out'/'Day Tripper' was installed at number one in the singles charts . . . and *Rubber Soul* topped the album charts. So much for The Beatles being on the slide.

Moodies' drummer Graeme Edge had an eventful night, as he recalled in the 2007 DVD *The Moody Blues* in the *Classic Artists* series. He was trapped by a screaming pack of girls who burst through police lines and pinned him up against a fence on his way to his hotel just yards from the Empire. Luckily for him, two burly roadies spotted his plight, but not before the girls had ripped his hair, clothes and anything else they could get their hands on. His thin knitted tie was tightened to throttling levels and had to be cut off.

Safely back in the hotel and calming down with a brandy, he was staggered when the hotel doorman came in with a pile of autograph books, with pieces of his clothing and buttons etc pinned in them for him to sign. "That's what it was like being on the road with The Beatles," he said. "This is not a great life. There is much too much taken away from you. No wonder they went to India and went all weird. It's the only place they could walk down the street without people being nuts."

Ironically, The Beatles enjoyed a more dignified departure, with some opting for home comforts with their families and all looking forward to a day off the next day. The Monday had been tentatively set aside for a concert in either Leicester, Bristol or Leeds, but The Beatles declined, opting instead to spend the day relaxing with their families and looking up old friends in Liverpool.

The tour resumed on the Tuesday with two houses at the ABC Cinema in Ardwick, Manchester, but they were still dogged by bad weather.

Driver Alf Bicknell faced a journey from hell, crawling at a snail's pace through fog so thick in the Manchester suburbs that the buses had stopped running. It was all the more bizarre as the north-west had enjoyed a generally sunny day. It took around four hours to complete the 33-mile journey, with city centre traffic virtually at a standstill.

It caused enormous problems, with The Beatles finally arriving at the ABC Ardwick 12 minutes after they were due to appear. An extra interval was hastily arranged while they changed and dashed onstage. It was a nightmare for the man whose job it was to keep the crowd in good spirits.

Compère Jerry Stevens recalls: "The tour manager came to me and said the lads have left Liverpool but they're stuck on the East Lancs Road in thick fog and there's literally nothing moving – they're going to be late. It got to the interval of the first house and The Beatles hadn't arrived, and he asked me if I could do some extra time – they couldn't stop the show. Everyone was told to lengthen their acts but of course the audience was getting restless and I had to go on and explain what was happening.

"I was telling gags but as the minutes ticked by they started getting really restless. Did they believe what I was saying, or was it just a story? Also, the crowds were starting to gather in the streets outside for the second house. It was tough. An extra interval was put in and announcements were made every few minutes to calm the audience who were beginning to panic. It was quite traumatic at the time."

Pete Martin, later to make a name as a musician and entertainer in Manchester, was in the first house and looks back with pride to the night he saw The Beatles. "I've still got my ticket, framed on the wall with the programme saying 'I was there for The Beatles' last visit to Manchester.' We went to the first performance at 6.30pm and were in row M2 and we paid 10 shillings. There was plenty of screaming, of course, but I don't remember being annoyed about it. As an event, it was absolutely amazing. I was just a Joe Bloggs from Salford and here I was watching The Beatles. Just amazing. I was just in awe."

The Beatles were photographed wearing fog masks in the terrible Manchester weather that night. "It must have just been for the press," says Martin. "They only had to step a few yards from the car into the cinema. But it certainly was foggy because I had to walk to the Ardwick, which was a couple of miles away from where I was living in Salford, and then walk home again when the show was over. I was 17 at the time and working as a shipping clerk at Broome & Wellington at Minshull Street in Piccadilly. One of my work colleagues had a ticket for the show but didn't go because of the fog."

Martin was joined for the journey through the fog by his younger sister Angela (now Angela Garner) who got the tickets, and his girlfriend Anne Copple – now his ex-wife. He added: "Apart from The Beatles, I only remember The Koobas – because of the lairy, tight trousers the bass player was wearing. They were awful."

His memories of The Beatles in their black polo neck sweaters that night have survived the years. "We were all standing on the seat rests when The Beatles came on. It was the only way you could see anything because everybody was doing the same. I wore glasses and I was sharing them – passing them down the line – with Angela and Anne. I remember George playing his Epiphone Casino that night and the Vox Continental organ on the right hand side of the stage that Paul used to accompany himself on 'Yesterday'. I don't remember the other Beatles joining him on that. I know the screaming went quiet for a bit during that song. It also went quiet when they started 'Nowhere Man'. There was the E chord and then people must have thought they were going to make an announcement down the mikes. Instead, they started singing 'Nowhere Man' acapella style and you could clearly hear that before the screaming started again. I recognised 'I Feel Fine' – that was a favourite of mine. You could recognise songs because you could hear snatches while the screamers paused for breath. That's what it was like."

One important visitor was Walter Shenson, who had produced *A Hard Day's Night* and *Help!* Both films had done enormously well at the box office and there were discussions about what their next film should be. The suggestion at the time was that they should make a Western. They had been given a script based on the book *A Talent For Loving* – but there was a problem.

Lennon told reporter Alan Smith, who was covering the tour for *New Musical Express*, that Shenson was going to be disappointed. "He thinks we're still considering that film, but as far as I'm concerned, anyway, it's scrapped. The original book was great, but the script they showed us turned out lousy." George agreed and added that they were in no rush to make another film and even Ringo, who enjoyed cowboy films and felt the script gave him a good part, admitted he had gone off the idea of making a Western.

The spotlight switched to Sheffield the following day for The Beatles' seventh and final visit, and their only appearance at the Gaumont Cinema. They were at last one step ahead of the weather and had the luxury of checking into their hotel in time to relax before heading into the city centre for the two shows at the cinema at Barkers Pool. *Beatles Book* monthly fanzine photographer Leslie Bryce was on hand to capture the Fab Four enjoying a highly creative game of snooker with their friends The Moody Blues and he later pictured them about to tuck into their favourite dish of steak, egg and chips.

Gaumont manager Harry Murray had devised an unlikely way of getting The Beatles into the theatre, but it worked very well. They phoned him five minutes before they were due to arrive and he told them to come straight to the front entrance. Police and security men were gathered at the stage door when the car arrived at the front, dropped them off, and they walked straight in, in sight of the large queues but before anyone could realise what was happening.

Ringo commented: "It was unusual for us. Normally we have to hide in vans or go in through back entrances. They did not realise outside what was going on."

The TV was again a focal point in their dressing room and among other things they watched the police drama *No Hiding Place,* starring Raymond Francis as Detective Chief Supt Lockhart. It was while they were watching TV that George received the news that a gold disc of *A Hard Day's Night* had been stolen from girlfriend Pattie Boyd's flat in South Audley Street, Mayfair, the previous day. George, talking with reporters, took the opportunity to appeal for its return: "The disc isn't worth much in itself," he said, "but I feel very bad about losing it. These are the sort of things one likes to keep forever. I haven't talked to Pattie about it yet. I hope whoever took it will return it."

Sheffield turned out to be one of the noisiest shows of the short tour and all the acts had to contend with outbreaks of screaming. The Koobas' bright trousers were still getting them noticed as they bounced around the stage pounding out songs nobody could hear. This was the local gig for compère Jerry Stevens. He said it was about the loudest reception of the tour for him and for The Beatles, telling the *Sheffield Star*: "It is a big experience working with The Beatles and I have learned a lot. I said before I met them I thought they were the greatest. Now I think they are even better than I thought they were."

The Beatles had the usual missiles to dodge, but the glare of the spotlights and the sheer volume of items thrown didn't give them much of a chance. A pear drop caught Paul in the left eye, causing him to blink throughout the rest of the performance. Ringo said later: "Another half inch and Paul could have been blinded for life."

'Yesterday' quieted the screamers temporarily – perhaps because they sensed something quite different was happening on the stage. McCartney always managed to portray the melancholy of a song quite different from the rest of their set.

During the show Jerry Stevens presented them with two *Top Stars Special* awards – for being voted the most popular group by the readers of the Sheffield newspaper and for *Help!* being voted the most popular single of the year.

Looking back in 2010, Stevens recalled: "The *Sheffield Star* said they were presenting The Beatles with an award and as I was a local guy on the show could I do it? I said yeah, that would be great. They published a picture and it is one of my proudest pictures – there I am up on the stage surrounded by the four Beatles. I remember John saying to me – I'm not sure if it was that night – that it's terrible, playing your home town. He didn't really enjoy playing Liverpool, he said, because so many people knew them. A lot of people in showbiz felt like that, but I was quite surprised when he said that, though I knew exactly what he meant."

One of many who saw The Beatles inside the Gaumont that evening – but certainly didn't hear them – was 14-year-old Gleadless Valley Secondary School pupil Janet Yates, who was with her friend Linda. Janet, now Janet Drabble and still living in Sheffield, says: "We were very excited at going to see them, but all I can remember is the continuous screaming and thinking that Paul had looked at me! We were in the stalls, but really you couldn't hear anything other than the screams. When we came out, we went round to Pinstone Street where there was a narrow passage behind the Gaumont. It was filled with screaming girls looking up to a small window, believing The Beatles were there."

The site of the old Gaumont off Barkers Pool now hosts the city's Embrace nightclub.

Bad weather was back with a vengeance the next day. Fog and heavy rain delayed The Beatles to the extent that they arrived at the Birmingham Odeon on the Thursday a good 10 minutes after they were due onstage. There was at least the consolation that they were able to make their entrance unhindered as fans presumed they were already inside the New Street cinema. In fact, there were so many people around and so much traffic that people didn't even notice The Beatles arriving at the stage door. They got in to find their stage suits, polo-neck sweaters and Cuban-heeled boots all stacked neatly for them to leap onstage as quickly as possible.

Birmingham Mail photos of people queuing for tickets show a fair few boys around, but they were of course heavily outnumbered. Outside the cinema, the barricades were in place, with extra police drafted in, while inside red-capped officers from a private security firm lined the front of the stage and patrolled the aisles. The cinema, fearing the worst, had also hired additional staff. The Beatles' late arrival caused havoc backstage with The Moody Blues having to play an extended set in their home city and an extra interval put in while everyone waited nervously for the fog-hit Fabs to turn up. Predictably, the excitement built during the show and went into overdrive when The Beatles finally appeared onstage. The girls could no longer contain themselves – and the security team were struggling to contain them, too. Dozens left their seats and tried to storm the stage as security worked overtime to turn the tide. One girl in the dress circle risked life and limb as she made several attempts to stand on the ledge.

And the music? As usual, not much got through. *Birmingham Evening Mail* reviewer Fred Norris wrote: "The half-hour appearance by The Beatles was one long ear-aching, head-reeling blast. Shrieking, struggling girls were carried back to their seats. It was absolute pandemonium – some of the worst scenes I have witnessed in a theatre. If this is modern 'live' entertainment one understands why The Beatles themselves spent most of their time backstage, watching television."

There was extra pressure on everyone as the staff attempted to clear the audience from the first house so that the equally excited second house could get in. Groups of sobbing girls were still in the cinema and had to be ushered out and there was a near stampede as the others tried to get in. There were false rumours that The Beatles had to be rushed out to a nearby hotel. In reality they were settling down in their Spartan dressing room to watch television, including themselves on *Top Of The Pops*. A photo taken by the *Daily Mirror* captured The Beatles, looking the very picture of boredom.

Predictably, the second show carried on in pretty much the same manner. Buried among the screaming girls in a seat on the second row from the back up in the balcony was Solihull teenager Alan White. In the distance he saw Beatles bobbing up and down, but his ears picked up only the screams all around him. "It was pretty scary for a 16-year-old to be in the middle of all that – the girls screaming and jumping and waving their arms around," he says. "The funny thing is I was more of a Stones fan, but I got a free ticket. One of the two girls next door couldn't go so I went instead. You couldn't even make out what they were playing from where we were. The Moody Blues were a local band and I'd probably already seen them by then. They were good. We had got the bus in and it was the second show because I remember them announcing at the end that The Beatles had left so there was no point in hanging around."

Alan, who these days lives just outside Lancaster, recalled that there was no let-up, even on the journey home. "The girls were still screaming on the bus back, but it's something I'll never forget – the night I saw The Beatles."

The announcement clearly worked as The Beatles were able to leave relatively quietly out of the back door at the end. The tour was now heading down to London for high-profile shows on the Friday and Saturday. And if Beatles fans had mellowed slightly in the venues of the north and the Midlands, the roles were reversed when they played the Hammersmith Odeon on the Friday and the Finsbury Park Astoria the next night.

Maybe it is because London was letting its hair down for the weekend, but there were fantastic scenes at Hammersmith which stunned everyone, largely because The Beatles and their small entourage had become used to the sophisticated London fans giving them an enthusiastic but controlled welcome in the past. The Hammersmith Odeon was bigger than most venues – seating 3,500 – but not many of the 7,000 that night stayed in their seats. They stood on them and screamed for all their worth in scenes that harkened back to the very height of Beatlemania at the end of 1963.

Police, determined to avoid the stigma of this being the night something terrible happened, linked arms right across the front of the stalls to make sure nobody got through to the stage. It was a pretty good day for

The Beatles. In the annual *NME* readers' poll they were confirmed as Best British Group and Best World Group, and John Lennon was voted British Vocal Personality.

The Beatles were returning to the scene of previous triumphs. Jerry Stevens recalls: "I had played the Hammersmith Odeon a few times before, but never was there anything like a Beatles night. Being London, there were always more guests in their dressing room and I remember that P. J. Proby was with them for most of the evening. He had done the infamous split trousers thing and made some great recordings and was big news at the time."

Proby recalls that he very nearly didn't make it into the Odeon that night. "I was in the limo with my secretary Pat Hayley and the kids mobbed us. They were rocking the limo and swarming all over us. They thought that Pat was Jane Asher, I think that's what the problem was. I'd brought crates of beer with me and we eventually got in and we just drank and were goofing around. That's what we did when I was with The Beatles, because we hung out a lot together at the time.

"After the Odeon shows we went back to my place – I had a home in Chelsea at the time opposite the barracks – and then we went on to the Ad Lib Club, our regular. It was hard to get in and it had these great views, all over London. It was run by Alma Cogan's boyfriend."

Proby got on well with all The Beatles, but it was John that he spent the most time with. "John was married and I was going through a divorce at the time, so maybe that was part of it, but we just enjoyed goofing around together. Everything we did was slapstick. John would say stuff to people but half the time they just didn't understand his humour. I was a regular visitor at his place and Cynthia would always cook deep fried southern food for me when I was there.

"John and I would go upstairs to the top floor because that was his territory. I remember that he had this electric racing car track that pretty much covered it and he was always racing these cars. It was his floor of the house – it was all matte red and matte black – and the rest of the house was Cynthia's. John didn't really drink when I first knew him – he just had coke and a few beers. But I introduced him to Bourbon. I would go up every week and take four bottles of Bourbon."

On the Hammersmith night, PJ had not long since had a minor hit with John and Paul's 'That Means A Lot' – a song The Beatles themselves felt they couldn't do justice to. As for The Beatles, they ticked off another riotous gig.

Hammersmith had been the venue for their 1964 Christmas shows when, in a two houses a night format, they made 38 appearances between December 24, 1964 and January 16, 1965. But Christmas shows were a thing of the past now, the mere suggestion of them drawing sarcastic responses from John and George. Now known as The HMV Hammersmith Apollo, it remains one of London's important entertainment venues.

The fantastic scenes at Hammersmith were repeated at the famous Astoria on the Saturday night. A breathless George expressed his amazement to *NME*'s Alan Smith moments after leaving the stage. "This is one of the most incredible shows we've done, not just because of the audience, but because they're Londoners," he said. "This is the funny thing. It's always been the other way round – fantastic in the north, but just that little bit cool in London. It's incredible. It seems like the Beatlemania thing is happening all over again."

John was equally surprised: "What happened? Did we win a prize or something?" he asked.

Over the two nights in London the casualty count stood at more than 200 – and that was just the fainters. At Finsbury Park the girls broke through the security lines and burly security guards gave chase across the stage. There were hundreds – possibly thousands – milling around outside and the police had to erect barriers to keep the traffic moving. There was no let-up inside the cinema either. By the end of the night some of the front row stalls seats were smashed to bits in damage reminiscent of that wreaked in 1956 by the Teds when Bill Haley's *Rock Around The Clock* was being screened.

In his *NME* report Smith wrote that scenes from the two London nights rivalled the pandemonium of the height of Beatlemania two years' before. "Finsbury Park Astoria holds 3,000 people and I swear that almost every one of them has been standing on a seat. I do not really know where to begin. All I know is that this was the wildest, rip-it-up Beatles performance I have watched in over two years. Girls have been running amok on the stage. Some were hysterical and I have just seen one girl carried out, screaming and kicking, and with tears streaming down her contorted face."

The Beatles managed to find some peace between the two houses, relaxing in the sanctuary of their dressing room. Being London, many friends called in, among them Helen Shapiro, always comfortable in their company, and still with a crush on John. Lennon, though, was sharing a sofa with Walker Brothers John Maus and drummer Gary Leeds, plus Maus' pop star wife Kathy Young. Paul was sat on his own and Ringo was crouched near the sofa. Their conversation about guitars and the music scene was replaced by laughter when the BBC comedy *Get Smart* came on.

Restless George, who seemed less entranced by television than the others, wandered in and out.

Gary Leeds, looking back in 2010, remembers an awkward incident that night. "John (Maus), Kathy and I were ushered in and The Beatles said hello to the two of us, but they didn't say anything to Kathy. It wasn't until John said, 'And this is my wife Kathy' that it all changed instantly. They were very polite, how do you do and all of that, but up until that point if they didn't know you and you weren't in the loop they wouldn't talk to you."

Gary remembers them all watching *Get Smart* until somebody whispered something in John Lennon's ear. "He suddenly turned to me and said, 'Gary come with me to the toilet.' So I had to go. So we got there and I said, 'Nice toilet John' – that was my bit of humour. He said, 'Yes, yes, they're not bad.' I didn't know what to say. I said we'd better get back to the dressing room and he said, 'No, we can't go yet.' Eventually, George Harrison turned up and said, 'OK, you can come back now.' John just said there's this girl that's chasing me. It was some time after when I found out it was Helen Shapiro he was trying to keep away from."

Gary watched both houses from the wings that night, but he could be seen by some girls up in the balcony and that only caused yet more screams. "When they came on the crowds just went wild. I remember Paul singing 'Yesterday' in the spotlight and when it came to the end the curtain came down and they ran right past me out to leave and John Lennon said to me, 'See you later.' That was because he would. Because we would go on to a club later – it was probably the Speakeasy. Then the crew turned to me and said, 'Now we have another problem.' I said, 'What's that?' They said, 'Getting you out!' John Maus and Kathy were to get in a van with the instruments, but Kathy said no, she would get a taxi. So John and I went in a van with the instruments."

The Walkers could swap notes with The Beatles about what it was like to be the subject of major league adoration. "We would see each other in the clubs because we went to the same kind of places," said Gary. "I went to Paul's house at St John's Wood once and left my jacket there. We were on Brian's mailing list which is how I got to be on 'All You Need Is Love'. And after it was all done I said, 'Now it's time for the big decision . . . what club are we going to go to?'"

The Astoria housed more than 3,000 but tickets were priceless to die-hard fans and young Paul Griggs was doubly fortunate – he saw both houses. "I saw The Beatles 10 times in all and this was the only time I ever had to queue for tickets. We queued for about two hours and they weren't great seats. What made it special was that after the first show we saw Mal Evans outside and I went up to him and got his autograph. The girls were demented, as usual, but they just ignored him, but I recognised him. He was a nice guy. I was 21 at the time."

Having secured his autograph, Paul then splashed some cash to buy a seat for the second show from a tout. "It didn't cost that much. It couldn't have because I didn't have much, but it was another chance to see The Beatles."

The Beatles weren't the sole beneficiaries of the screamers. The hip London fans loved The Moody Blues and deservedly gave them a great reception for their sets.

There was no fanfare, there was no big announcement, but The Beatles' final tour of their homeland was completed the next day – Sunday, December 12, 1965 – with their two shows at the Capitol Theatre in Cardiff. They were performed to the usual backdrop of screaming and hysteria, and an incident a few minutes from the end of their second performance, reported in the newspapers, illustrated just why the group had become so sick of touring.

A man in a pink sweater somehow managed to bypass the ranks of security men in front of the stage. He made his way to the stage area and made his assault from the wings. He ran on as John was introducing 'Day Tripper' and grabbed Paul and George, wrestling with the startled Beatles for several seconds before a security man intervened and he fled as quickly as he came.

Mal, embarrassed that the man had got through, brushed it off as just something that happened now and again. No physical harm was done, and the performance was delayed for but a few seconds, but it was yet another indication of how dangerous it could be, how pointless it all was and of how little the music seemed to matter to too many people.

The massive queues spread out from the Capitol all along Queen Street and several hundred yards into Churchill Way. Two full houses meant 5,000 tickets had been sold – and theatre staff revealed they had applications for 25,000, meaning they had to return a staggering £8,000 to disappointed fans.

Despite everything The Beatles were still showing willing. They even found time to give interviews with the local press, talking to reporters from the *South Wales Argus* and the *South Wales Echo* between the two houses. Retreating from the wild scenes outside, they tucked into sausage and mash in the relative security of their dressing room and watched a Western on the TV until they were back onstage.

A look at the stats confirms that the evening was more a battleground than a concert, and involved 40 police, including 24 cadets drafted in, plus 50 bouncers and numerous female attendants pitted against 2,500 fans in each house, all of them screaming, shouting, standing on their seats and ready to storm the stage at any moment.

Nobody was bothered about the support acts, and when the curtains opened for The Beatles, Beatlemania erupted all over again, and though the screams died down briefly for 'Yesterday', little could be heard of the rest. The intricate new songs that graced *Rubber Soul* – evidence of how The Beatles were broadening their wings as songwriters and performers – were lost to the rage.

The Beatles sped out of Cardiff, escorted from the city by a white police car, and headed for London and a Christmas party at the Scotch of St James club, where they could celebrate the end of the tour. It's likely they knew they would never tour the UK again – but it would be wrong to suggest that they didn't get any enjoyment out of their final UK tour, or that it had been a salutary experience for the other performers.

Beryl Marsden says: "The Paramounts, who were backing me and Steve, were a great bunch of guys and very good musicians. The Moodies were a good bunch, too, and even though people were there to see The Beatles, they appreciated all of the other people on the show. There was no 'We Want The Beatles' while other people were onstage. It's such a long time ago now, but I remember silly things like George coming into my room and asking for an iron – as if he was going to iron his own shirt! And The Beatles would be standing in the wings while I was on and John would be saying 'Like your shirt Marsy' or 'Lend us your shirt Marsy'

"I loved their music, but they also made me laugh. They were fun. I don't think they realised how talented they were. They were always taking the piss – including out of themselves, but when you heard that sound – those great harmonies . . . They sounded great, even through some naff PA."

The following May, Beryl was to link up with a young singer called Rod Stewart, plus Mick Fleetwood and Peter Green in Shotgun Express.

Steve Aldo adds: "We had a great time, we really did. The Moody Blues were just that. They were a moody lot, but The Paramounts were a great bunch and they were great musicians, too. The Beatles – well my memory is of me and George sneaking off to a quiet room upstairs when we could for a spliff. We would be terrified that *NME* journalist Chris Hutchins would find us because he was doing these exposés about pop stars smoking stuff.

"I remember being onstage one night and I had this song 'Don't Fight It' in which I would cross my arms in front of my face. George was watching from the wings and we were both stoned. He was waving furiously at me and being stoned I hadn't cottoned on that anything was wrong. But I'd knocked the mike and it was heading for the orchestra pit. I realised and managed to catch it – but I don't know how. George was an incredibly lovely guy and really genuine. Paul was also a very nice guy. John – well he was very sarcastic – his humour always had a touch of sarcasm to it. Ringo seemed to adopt a persona like he was born to this."

Aldo says he regularly watched The Beatles perform, sometimes from the wings, sometimes standing in front of one of the exits in the auditorium. "There was so much screaming that you really wondered if the audiences could hear anything. There would be hundreds of toys thrown on the stage when The Beatles were playing. Their dressing room always seemed to be crowded and there would be people in there with disabled children. I don't know, but what can you say to a sick child? Artists wouldn't tolerate it today. They want privacy in their dressing rooms before a show so they can prepare. But The Beatles just got used to it I suppose."

Steve remembers spending a day at Brian Epstein's home over Christmas and The Beatles receiving early versions of video recorders as Christmas presents from Capitol.

Looking back at the nine dates, he sums up: "It was a great tour – a happy tour. The only thing was it didn't go on long enough. We were really tight and everyone was up for it and having a great time and then it was all over."

Jerry Stevens was another who would never forget his precious memories of being on a Beatles tour. "I had been doing pop package tours for almost three years, but I didn't do any more after that. The Beatles was the last one. I remember thinking where can you go from here? When you've done The Beatles, what next? I figured any pop tour I went on after that may have been a bit of an anti-climax, and also there were rumours that The Beatles might not do a UK pop tour again, which did turn out to be true. It had all been a wonderful experience but now I was keen to move on to other avenues in the world of show business."

Jerry opted for more sophisticated shows, often with full orchestras onstage. He appeared at the Royal Festival Hall in London with Frank Sinatra, performed with Sammy Davis Junior, did a summer show, a concert tour and a season at the London Palladium with Tom Jones, and toured with many Americans – including six tours with Johnny Mathis. Stevens, who has lived in London for 50 years, went on to star in a TV series with fellow comic Lennie Bennett in *Lennie & Jerry* in the late 1970s, but is now happily retired with a lifetime of showbiz memories.

Gary Brooker, then a key member of The Paramounts, is another with fond memories. The friendliness between them was illustrated by George Harrison hosting a party in his hotel room for The Moody Blues plus Gary and his mates in The Paramounts. "I think it was the day off so that would make it after the Liverpool night," recalls Gary. "It was great. A right laugh, and we all had dinner in George's suite."

The Paramounts were using their group van on the tour, but the fun started when the singers and groups got together. "It was like a big party," he says. "Everybody was good friends and we all mucked in together." Mucking in sometimes being the operative words . . . "It wasn't all plush hotels and home comforts. Sometimes there was nowhere to wash, and your hair would be greasy. There was this trick of carrying talc around because when you put it in your hair it absorbed the grease and you didn't look so bad. The back area at the Finsbury Park Astoria is one that stands out. There were these horrible little rooms in a dark corridor with no lights and no bathroom. The women would bring in plastic bowls with warm water and soap."

But with The Beatles about there were more laughs than frowns. "We got along with them very well. They were great – fun to be with. There was a good, sociable atmosphere. When we were setting up we would have a jam and if Paul was around he'd play along on the drums. He liked having a go on the drums. The two outstanding things were one, that the audience just screamed at them all the way through, and two, that they were captives. Their food and anything else they needed had to be brought to their room. But there was this one time in Newcastle when John put on a disguise and the two of us went out for fish and chips. We were walking around Newcastle, and when we went back John told the doorman who he was and the doorman said, 'You're not coming in, even if you're John Lennon himself!' It was nice for John. He just didn't get to do that kind of thing on these tours."

Like so many people who toured with The Beatles, Brooker took the opportunity of sampling their genius. "We would stand at the side of the stage some nights and watch them. There used to be a speaker there for the man who drew the curtains. I'm sure the audience couldn't hear much because of the screaming, but The Beatles' harmonies were magnificent – all those cascading voices. They were always very, very good."

The tours were a good way for bands like The Paramounts, who'd had a hit with 'Poison Ivy', to keep in the spotlight. "Television was important, too," says Brooker. "If you could get an appearance on *Ready Steady Go* or *Thank Your Lucky Stars*, your money went up afterwards. By the end of 1965 we had been around for a while."

The Beatles had also been around for a while. In fact, as far as touring goes, they reckoned they had been around for far too long. They had a meeting and all agreed how bored they were of being constantly on the road, of the hotels, the endless press interviews and being under siege from the moment they woke until the moment they went to sleep. Worst of all, they concluded they were going downhill as musicians because of it. They were much more interested in what they could achieve in the recording studio, if they could only get the time.

Paul later likened it to being painters who, instead of being allowed to develop, were simply going up and down the country hawking paintings they had already done.

Jerry Stevens had seen enough of The Beatles at close hand to understand their predicament. "I was being interviewed by Pete Murray on the radio one time and he asked me why do you think we don't see The

Beatles playing live any more? Well I'd seen how professional – how diligent and what perfectionists they were, doing three or four tune-ups before every show, but with the fans' non-stop screaming, if nobody would know if they were singing or playing out of tune, what was the point?

"When you think of the beautiful stuff they played and those intricate harmonies all being lost in a whirlwind of noise, it just had to be so frustrating for them. I think they must have made a decision that from now on they would just go in the studio and record their music in peace. After all, as far as touring with pop shows was concerned, they'd been there, done that, and all four of them had got millions of T-shirts."

After the final show in Cardiff, The Beatles didn't perform live again for more than four months. Their final paid gig in the UK was a 15-minute performance at the *NME* poll-winners' concert at the Empire Pool, Wembley, on Sunday, May 1, 1966, when they sang 'I Feel Fine', 'Nowhere Man', 'Day Tripper', 'If I Needed Someone' and 'I'm Down'.

If they could, they would have ended all live gigs there and then, but they had concert dates to fulfil in Germany, Japan and the Philippines, plus another tour of America. As all Beatles fans know, those 1966 trips brought more than their share of trouble – the fallout from John's "bigger than Jesus" remark, their rough treatment in Manila following the "snub" to Imelda Marcos, the death threats over their gigs at the "sacred" Budokan, the frenzied fans, George's fear of flying . . . the problems seemed to go on and on until they left the stage for the final time after the show at Candlestick Park, San Francisco, on Monday, August 29, 1966.

"That's it. I'm not a Beatle any more," George was heard to remark. He was wrong, of course. He was still very much a Beatle, and no matter how hard he tried to leave the group behind him in the eyes of the world he would remain a Beatle for the rest of his life. They all would.

At least 50 per cent of The Beatles – specifically John and George – were determined never to tour with the group again, and the other 50 per cent would have needed a long break and a significant change in format before they could have been persuaded to perform again. In the long term, however, Paul had never wanted to be the kind of musician who didn't perform for his public. He was, and remains, an entertainer and would never have been satisfied by a life tucked away in a studio. Ringo, too, liked performing and would probably have been happy to go along with the other three if they had decided to go back on the road at some point.

George, however, was sick of the Beatle circus and everything that went with it and John made his feelings clear. "They could send out four waxwork dummies," he said. "The concerts were not about music any more – just bloody tribal rites."

After the US tour of 1966 The Beatles made one final live performance together – on the roof of their Apple building in London's Savile Row, on January 29, 1969. Mal and Neil set up the instruments as of old, and The Beatles, with Billy Preston on keyboards, took up their positions, with Paul on the left, still playing his violin bass, John in the centre with a blonde Epiphone, George on the right with a Fender Telecaster, and Ringo at the back in a red waterproof jacket. Traffic was brought to a standstill as lunchtime crowds gathered on the pavement below and all the windows and roofs nearby quickly filled with West End office workers, getting a privileged view of the last ever Beatles live concert. The police tried to put a stop to it, but the combined Apple door security, and reluctance on the part of the police to actually pull the plug on such an extraordinary scene, meant that they played for 42 minutes.

They began with a rehearsal of 'Get Back', 'Don't Let Me Down', 'I've Got A Feeling', 'One After 909', 'Dig A Pony' (for this, an assistant had to kneel in front of John holding the words on a clipboard), 'God Save The Queen', 'I've Got A Feeling' (again), 'Don't Let Me Down' (again) and 'Get Back' (again). This final version of 'Get Back' was interrupted by the police and Paul ad-libbed, "You've been playing on the roofs again and you know your momma doesn't like it, she's gonna have you arrested!" At the end of the song, Maureen Starkey burst into loud applause and cheers, causing Paul to return to the microphone and acknowledge her, "Thanks, Mo!"

John ended the set, and The Beatles' live career, with the words: "I'd like to say thank you on behalf of the group and ourselves and I hope we passed the audition."

APPENDIX ONE

FULL LIST OF TOUR DATES

February 2 – March 3, 1963

Saturday, February 2:	Gaumont Cinema, Bradford
Tuesday, February 5:	Gaumont Cinema, Doncaster
Wednesday, February 6:	Granada Cinema, Bedford
Thursday, February 7:	Regal Cinema in Wakefield
Friday, February 8:	ABC Cinema, Carlisle
Saturday, February 9:	Empire Theatre, Sunderland

Tour break

Saturday, February 23:	Granada Cinema, Mansfield
Sunday, February 24:	Coventry Theatre
Tuesday, February 26:	Gaumont Cinema, Taunton
Wednesday, February 27:	Rialto Theatre, York
Thursday, February 28:	Granada Cinema, Shrewsbury
Friday, March 1:	Odeon Cinema, Southport
Saturday, March 2:	City Hall, Sheffield
Sunday, March 3:	Gaumont Cinema, Hanley

March 9 – March 31, 1963

Saturday, March 9:	Granada Cinema, East Ham
Sunday, March 10:	Hippodrome Theatre, Birmingham
Tuesday, March 12:	Granada Cinema, Bedford
Wednesday, March 13:	Rialto Theatre, York
Thursday, March 14:	Gaumont Cinema, Wolverhampton
Friday, March 15:	Colston Hall, Bristol
Saturday, March 16:	City Hall, Sheffield
Sunday, March 17:	Embassy Cinema, Peterborough
Monday, March 18:	Regal Cinema, Gloucester
Tuesday, March 19:	Regal Cinema, Cambridge

Wednesday, March 20:	ABC Cinema, Romford
Thursday, March 21:	ABC Cinema, West Croydon
Friday, March 22:	Gaumont Cinema, Doncaster
Saturday, March 23:	City Hall, Newcastle
Sunday, March 24:	Empire Theatre, Liverpool
Tuesday, March 26:	Granada Cinema, Mansfield
Wednesday, March 27:	ABC Cinema, Northampton
Thursday, March 28:	ABC Cinema, Exeter
Friday, March 29:	Odeon Cinema, Lewisham
Saturday, March 30:	Guildhall, Portsmouth
Sunday, March 31:	De Montfort Hall, Leicester

May 18 – June 9, 1963

Saturday, May 18:	Adelphi Cinema, Slough
Sunday, May 19:	Gaumont Cinema, Hanley
Monday, May 20:	Gaumont Cinema, Southampton
Wednesday, May 22:	Gaumont Cinema, Ipswich
Thursday, May 23:	Odeon Cinema, Nottingham
Friday, May 24:	Granada Cinema, Walthamstow
Saturday, May 25:	City Hall, Sheffield
Sunday, May 26:	Empire Theatre, Liverpool
Monday, May 27:	Cardiff Capitol
Tuesday, May 28:	Gaumont Cinema, Worcester
Wednesday, May 29:	Rialto Theatre, York
Thursday, May 30:	Odeon Cinema, Manchester
Friday, May 31:	Odeon Cinema, Southend
Saturday, June 1:	Granada Cinema, Tooting
Sunday, June 2:	Hippodrome, Brighton
Monday, June 3:	Granada Cinema, Woolwich
Tuesday, June 4:	Town Hall, Birmingham
Wednesday, June 5:	Odeon Cinema, Leeds
Friday, June 7:	Odeon Cinema, Glasgow
Saturday, June 8:	City Hall, Newcastle
Sunday, June 9:	King George's Hall, Blackburn

November 1 – December 13, 1963

Friday, November 1:	Odeon Cinema, Cheltenham
Saturday, November 2:	City Hall, Sheffield
Sunday, November 3:	Odeon Cinema, Leeds

Tuesday, November 5:	Adelphi Cinema, Slough
Wednesday, November 6:	ABC Cinema, Northampton
Thursday, November 7:	Adelphi Cinema, Dublin
Friday, November 8:	Ritz Cinema, Belfast
Saturday, November 9:	Granada Cinema, East Ham
Sunday, November 10:	Hippodrome, Birmingham
Wednesday, November 13:	ABC Cinema, Plymouth
Thursday, November 14:	ABC Cinema, Exeter
Friday, November 15:	Colston Hall, Bristol
Saturday, November 16:	Winter Gardens Theatre, Bournemouth
Sunday, November 17:	Coventry Theatre
Tuesday, November 19:	Gaumont Cinema, Wolverhampton
Wednesday, November 20:	ABC Cinema, Manchester
Thursday, November 21:	ABC Cinema, Carlisle
Friday, November 22:	Globe Cinema, Stockton-on-Tees
Saturday, November 23:	City Hall, Newcastle
Sunday, November 24:	ABC Cinema, Hull
Tuesday, November 26:	Regal Cinema, Cambridge
Wednesday, November 27:	Rialto Theatre, York
Thursday, November 28:	ABC Cinema, Lincoln
Friday, November 29:	ABC Cinema, Huddersfield
Saturday, November 30:	Empire Theatre, Sunderland
Sunday, December 1:	De Montfort Hall, Leicester
Tuesday, December 3:	Guildhall, Portsmouth (postponed from Tuesday, November 12)
Saturday, December 7:	Odeon Cinema, Liverpool
Sunday, December 8:	Odeon Cinema, Lewisham
Monday, December 9:	Odeon Cinema, Southend
Tuesday, December 10:	Gaumont Cinema, Doncaster
Wednesday, December 11:	Futurist Theatre, Scarborough
Thursday, December 12:	Odeon Cinema, Nottingham
Friday, December 13:	Gaumont Cinema, Southampton

October 9 – November 10, 1964

Friday, October 9:	Gaumont Cinema, Bradford
Saturday, October 10:	De Montfort Hall, Leicester
Sunday, October 11:	Odeon Cinema, Birmingham
Tuesday, October 13:	ABC Cinema, Wigan
Wednesday, October 14:	ABC Cinema, Manchester

Thursday, October 15:   Globe Cinema, Stockton-on-Tees
Friday, October 16:   ABC Cinema, Hull
Monday, October 19:   ABC Cinema, Edinburgh
Tuesday, October 20:   Caird Hall, Dundee
Wednesday, October 21:   Odeon Cinema, Glasgow
Thursday, October 22:   Odeon Cinema, Leeds
Friday, October 23:   Gaumont State Cinema, Kilburn
Saturday, October 24:   Granada Cinema, Walthamstow
Sunday, October 25:   Hippodrome, Brighton
Wednesday, October 28:   ABC Cinema, Exeter
Thursday, October 29:   ABC Cinema, Plymouth
Friday, October 30:   Gaumont Cinema, Bournemouth
Saturday, October 31:   Gaumont Cinema, Ipswich
Sunday, November 1:   Astoria Cinema, Finsbury Park
Monday, November 2:   King's Hall, Belfast
Wednesday, November 4:   Ritz Cinema, Luton
Thursday, November 5:   Odeon Cinema, Nottingham
Friday, November 6:   Gaumont Cinema, Southampton
Saturday, November 7:   Capitol Cinema, Cardiff
Sunday, November 8:   Empire Theatre, Liverpool
Monday, November 9:   City Hall, Sheffield
Tuesday, November 10:   Colston Hall, Bristol

December 3 – December 12, 1965

Friday, December 3:   Odeon Cinema, Glasgow
Saturday, December 4:   City Hall, Newcastle
Sunday, December 5:   Empire Theatre, Liverpool
Tuesday, December 7:   ABC Cinema, Manchester
Wednesday, December 8:   Gaumont Cinema, Sheffield
Thursday, December 9:   Odeon Cinema, Birmingham
Friday, December 10:   Odeon Cinema, Hammersmith
Saturday, December 11:   Astoria Cinema, Finsbury Park
Sunday, December 12:   Capitol Cinema, Cardiff

APPENDIX TWO

INTERVIEWS

1. Susan Fuller, Secretary to Arthur Howes

Susan Fuller was by the side of Arthur Howes as his operation grew from its humble beginnings promoting dances in their home town of Peterborough in the late 1950s into a huge London showbiz empire, representing the biggest names in the entertainment world. They operated from their office at 34 Greek Street in Soho, before moving into Harold Davison's offices at Eros House in Regent Street.

Howes was an orphan, born in Peterborough and brought up by his adopted parents on their farm in Yaxley. He did his National Service in the Royal Navy during which time he was introduced to Lew and Leslie Grade and Harold Davison, among others. His military service over, Howes began promoting pop shows at Peterborough's Embassy Cinema (later the ABC) where he befriended the managers – including Brian Epstein – of the bands that were beginning to pop up all over Britain in the early 1960s. He stayed in touch and remained friends with the impresarios of the day and became Leslie Grade's protégé, securing the top American artistes for UK tours.

Susan Fuller, initially his junior secretary and eventually his PA, remembers Howes as a man who was respected and admired and who inspired loyalty and affection from everyone he came into contact with in the industry.

What was Arthur like?
Well physically, he was not very tall (5ft 6in), with a widow's peak on his hairline and a birthmark on his forehead, but he was an enormous character – courteous, kind and generous, a man who would help anyone. He had a great, wicked sense of humour. He never swore. He had a beautiful, deep, well modulated voice. He was very well spoken, with immaculate

table manners. Arthur could be Mr Super Cool Sophistication . . . or a wicked devil!

He really enjoyed life. He was a flashy dresser, with a beautiful Musquash coat, a leather trench coat and a navy cashmere coat. He always looked a million dollars. He was a smoker, drank whisky and liked his steak well done. He also liked fish and chips, but loved champagne.

No one ever said a bad word about him. Arthur was loved by everyone and so generous to artistes and friends during his life.

There was no one in his league for promoting the big UK and American artistes, except Harold Davison and Lew and Leslie, who became The Grade Organisation, then later London Management. Larry Parnes also promoted package tours, of course. He was a good promoter and Kennedy Street Enterprises (who handled the Beatles/Roy Orbison/Gerry & The Pacemakers package) were good promoters also.

When Arthur wasn't hard at work, how did he relax?
He loved parties and music, particularly big band music and Latin American, but he also liked watching football and the big fights. He loved the movies – war, action and thrillers, and Bond films – and he read thrillers, adventures and spy novels.

There was another side, too. He loved boating and the River Thames and he was a brilliant gardener, and was very proud of that.

He was very successful and no doubt enjoyed the trappings of wealth.
Of course. He loved foreign travel, ski-ing and holidays in the sun. Travel was first class and he enjoyed having fast, expensive cars. Let me see, there was the cream Jaguar SK 150, a metallic blue Mark 10 Jag, a white E-Type Jag, a silver Ferrari, a blue Jensen Interceptor SHM 429F, a silver Rolls-Royce Shadow, a black Daimler limousine and a white Jag.

Home was a detached house at Wimbledon Park side, opposite Harold Davison, and he had two apartments in Torremolinos. He wore a heavy gold signet ring with the letters AH joined together and a gold Rolex watch.

What was it like for you – a young girl whose daily work involved mixing with young pop stars in the swinging 1960s?
It was very, very exciting. We would be invited to all the premieres, record company parties, concerts and press receptions to meet the stars

who we were promoting in concert. All the big artistes. There was first class travel all over the world. It was incredible in those days. We were treated like royalty.

You travelled with Arthur to the shows. Were you ever on the coach with the touring party?
I nearly always travelled with Arthur by car, in his Jag, Ferrari, or whatever he was driving at the time. He always took me backstage to meet everyone and we would buy the artistes drinks. At the end of the tours we would throw a big dinner party at the Lotus House on the Edgware Road. This was a restaurant owned by the late Johnny Koon. It was a well-known showbiz restaurant. When Johnny bought the China Garden, just off Regent Street, we took everyone there for the end-of-tour parties.

If Arthur was not going, sometimes I travelled on the coach. I was always treated with respect by the artistes, as I was Arthur's PA.

You saw The Beatles many times on tour. What were they like onstage? What did you think of them as people?
I loved their shows – the loud music, which you could never hear – the excitement, the charisma – the whole event of a Beatles concert. My personal favourite was George, a very spiritual, loving man, although I used to quite fancy John. I loved his sense of humour. They thought the world of Arthur and George even named his dog after him. Once Arthur arrived at the theatres the word would sweep through backstage as if God had appeared!

What are your memories from that "audition" night in Peterborough?
Strangely enough, my memory, along with Arthur and my mother when they were both alive, was that some of the Peterborough audience were booing, yelling 'Get Off' or 'Rubbish' etc, but we all thought the boys had great talent. I remember drinking with Eppy and Arthur afterwards and we were all confident that they had the talent to be successful.

Any outstanding memories from other gigs?
I once went to see The Beatles without Arthur and was sitting on John Lennon's knee, chatting, and the tour manager insisted I left the dressing room and virtually threw me out! Then there was the time that Liberace was at The Palladium. Arthur and I went backstage to see him and he had

the cheek to ask if he could give the bouquet that we had sent him to Cilla Black, who was there the next night!

You got to know many pop stars in those days. Who were your favourites?
The Beatles. But I also admired Cliff & The Shadows. We often met them and had drinks with them. I loved Neil Diamond, the Tamla Motown artistes – especially Stevie Wonder.

What is your over-riding memory of the tours – and of those days?
The fantastic fun we had in the Swinging Sixties. You never knew who would walk in the office, and what party we would be invited to. It would be quite normal for David Bowie to be waiting in reception, or Roger Moore would pop in. One time, Paul Anka was over and dressed as a tramp as a joke to get in to see Arthur without an appointment. We used to work hard during the day on the tours and then go out to see the shows, but we had to be back at our desks for 10am the next day.

Many times we were still smashed from the night before, and Arthur would say 'Shall we go to the China Garden for a livener?'

Tell me about tour coach driver Ron King, Johnny Sparks (another driver) and the tour manager John Clapson.
For the Helen tour, Ron was driving and John Clapson was also on the coach. John Clapson was the typical sergeant major. He began with us as a tour manager when we were in Peterborough and eventually joined the company as general manager in London and he was the premier tour manager. He was always effing and blinding. He was a very efficient man and the artistes thought the world of him. His downfall was a tour when both artistes wanted to top the bill, demanding to close the shows, have their own limousines etc. Johnny had a nervous breakdown and was never the same again.

Ron King was a Timpsons coach driver. He was a very good man and eventually joined the company as a tour manager. He had a great sense of humour. I was on the coach with The Hollies on one tour when he suddenly stood up, let go of the steering wheel, faced the coach load of artistes and proceeded to tell a joke. It was a good joke. Dangerous – but fun.

Johnny Sparks was another Timpsons driver. He used to go around the shows flogging our programmes for cash and not declare the proceeds to

Arthur. He would say to members of the public 'I'm Arthur Howes, ain't I!' He was a devil.

Have you stayed in contact with survivors from those days?
There is a small, elite showbiz crowd who knew Arthur Howes and worked for him. I try to keep in touch with them all, but many others are not alive now. Years ago, I organised a reunion for everyone who had worked with Arthur. It was a very emotional, memorable evening, held in the Coach & Horses in Greek Street, Soho, opposite our very first London office. Norman, the famous landlord, was alive and remembered us all, and was proud of our connection with The Beatles.

2. Ronnie Wells, The Viscounts

Ronnie Wells, one-third of singing group The Viscounts, got a close-up look at The Beatles just as the bandwagon started off apace early in 1963. The Viscounts had been kicking around the touring scene for a few years when they joined The Beatles on the Chris Montez and Tommy Roe package that set out on a 21-date tour of England on March 9, 1963, just six days after the Beatles' Shapiro stint had ended.

During that tiny break between the tours The Beatles recorded their third single, 'From Me To You'. 'Please Please Me' had already topped the *NME* and *Disc* charts and their popularity was rapidly rising. The Viscounts had toured with some of the rock'n'roll greats and had heard screaming before – but not on this scale.

What are your memories of how the acts went down on the tour – The Beatles in comparison with the Americans?
Well The Beatles went down extremely well – probably because they were different. They looked different and they sounded different, because nobody had that kind of two-part harmony sound. Other groups around – like us – were three-part harmonies, but they featured the two voices and it was done in such a way that it was different. It sounded bigger than what it was. The instrumentation was good and the sound they had was solid and, unlike other groups, they used to do their own songs. Not all the time, but they used to throw in one or two of their songs along the way which made it more interesting – certainly from our point of view. I'd never seen anybody do that. It wasn't done in those days. It was rock'n'roll

– it was American, therefore, everybody tried to be Americans and The Beatles were the only ones who started to do their own stuff and, yeah, they went down extremely well. But it wasn't the wild screaming stuff that happened later. It was solid.

So you could hear the songs above it all. Was it screaming or applause?
It was half and half, to be honest, and we all got our fair share of screams because we were the teenage idols of the time, if you like. We'd done a bit of TV – much more than they had. At the time we were probably better known than they were, but it didn't matter. If you were good you got a good reception, and obviously they appealed because they looked good with the haircuts and all that. They wore smart suits like we did in those days. It was the suits and the ties – Italian type suits.

Would you watch The Beatles from the wings?
Normally, we would stand in the wings, but if there was a bit of room at the back, we would sometimes nip to the back of the theatre and watch from there. They were on in the first half and we were in the second, just before Chris Montez, in fact.

What did you think of The Beatles at the time?
We'd heard a lot about them beforehand. The Vernons Girls had already told us these guys were really good and, fair enough, they were absolutely right. We were certainly impressed – very impressed. We were never in competition as such, because we were a stand-up group – today we'd be called a boy band.

It would have been nice if it was The Beatles who were backing you!
Yeah, but it was the Terry Young Six on this tour. We would have had rehearsals beforehand. We had a lot of backing groups in those days. At one time we had Tony Sheridan who had worked with The Beatles out in Germany. He had a trio – it was Tony Sheridan and three others. He was an excellent player, one of the top men of the day.

What were The Beatles like?
Very friendly. Ringo was the jack-the-lad one, cracking gags and making everybody laugh – that type of thing. John was very serious, or gave that impression, anyway. Paul was very happy-go-lucky. George was, again, a little more serious, but they all liked a laugh and a joke. Paul would invite

us into their dressing room to listen to a song because they valued opinions in those days.

And as performers and musicians?
We liked them. There's no doubt they were different. You got so used to listening to people playing American songs. We were doing them, too – everybody was. The Beatles' songs were raw, if you like, but they were refreshing in the way they were played. It was refreshing because nobody else was doing it, and perhaps because John and Paul wrote together and sung together.

Are there any incidents that stood out?
We used to stay in digs on tour – hotels, and places that were specifically for artists. At that time most towns had a theatre, and there were guest houses that had a reputation of putting up show-business people. Everybody's got stories about those sort of places. They loved show-business people, so they catered for them. And sometimes we'd stay at one of those places and sometimes a hotel because in those days there weren't that many hotels around. I can remember staying together at some place and getting up fairly early in the morning to catch the coach and The Beatles were all trudging up a hill with their gear – all moaning – and a few years later I thought, bloody hell, I bet they're not doing that now! The other thing I remember is they normally used to sit at the back of the coach and one or other of them would be strumming on a guitar.

And the Americans were on the coach, too.
I remember John Lennon having a spat with Chris Montez on the coach. I don't know what happened but one of them said something and they squared up to each other. Two people had to pull them apart. That's as near as it got really. Tempers get a bit frayed when you're working with the same people for a length of time in any job. It's bound to happen, isn't it? People don't always see eye-to-eye.

You've obviously got fond memories of this tour.
Yeah, of course. To be honest we'd done loads of those tours – Gene Vincent, Red Price, Billy Fury. Then there was the Eddie Cochran tour. They were all special in their way.

3. Vilma and Anita, The Honeys

The lovely blonde Liddell sisters, Vilma, Anita and Pearl, made up the singing group The Honeys. They never got to make a record, but they did get to tour with the stars and were Southern Television regulars and appeared on *The Benny Hill Show*, among others, in the early 1960s. On one of those TV shows the Liddell sisters teamed up with The Lana Sisters, including a young Dusty Springfield, in the back of a car as Tommy Steele sang 'Seven Little Girls (Sitting In The Back Seat)'. The Lanas and the Liddells made six, and the seventh would have been Hattie Jacques, but for her being unwell.

The Honeys also got to spend time with The Beatles at the time when John, Paul, George and Ringo were simply four more young hopefuls on the coach, looking to make a name for themselves.

The sisters were born in Portsmouth, but moved to Reading when they were four. They returned to Portsmouth in 1953 when they were teen-agers, and their father Jay, a drummer, set up Jay Liddell & The Dancetimers. The girls were encouraged to take their own first tentative steps on the musical ladder, with their dad encouraging them to mime to The Beverly Sisters and The McGuire Sisters. Soon he was encouraging them to sing and finally they were introduced to Bill Cole who taught them to harmonise, and The Honeys were born.

Here, for the first time, are the recollections of Vilma and Anita (Pearl lives in Spain and keeps in close contact with them) on touring with The Beatles in February/March 1963.

I suppose the ideal thing would be for you to say that you kept a diary back then . . .
Anita: Well I do now, but I wish I had then!
Vilma: There was such an innocence about those days. We would all be on the coach, including The Beatles, and there would be a following van with all the gear. I remember when we stopped off for that first gig in Bradford these girls were there and they asked us if we were The Beatles. I said, 'No, we're girls, and The Beatles are boys.' Nobody knew who they were.

How did you get on The Beatles' tour?
Vilma: We had been on some Arthur Howes' tours before. We did the Moss Empires. In those days you could go round the Moss Empires and work all the time. We did most of the towns in England with Adam Faith,

in between going across to Germany to do American [Army] camps. But I suppose Evelyn Taylor, Adam's agent, would have just rung up, as she would do, and said, 'You are on this tour with Helen.'

Red Price's band was backing us – they were a lovely band.

So did you head to London to join the coach?
Vilma: Yes, we'd get the train up to London and, of course, The Beatles would be on the coach with us, but their equipment would be brought behind the coach in that little van. They would pass around bits of a song they were working on and say – what do you think of this?

So you recall them on the coach working on songs?
Vilma: Oh yes. They were just across from us.
Anita: They'd also hand round what they'd written for a song and they'd ask what about this or what about that?

So what else would be going on – would the boys be playing cards, that sort of thing?
Anita: Yes, that's right. There would always be something going on, and The Beatles, they were all a good laugh.

And how did all those boys on the coach treat you?
Anita: They were fine. The whole thing for us – it was all a big laugh really. That's how it was then. But we always stuck together – the three of us together. I knew they used to take the mickey out of us. Kenny Lynch was very nice – always in his Wellington boots – he always had wellies on when he got on the coach. And the comedian, Dave Allen – he used to ruffle our hair all the time. Remember, he had half a finger missing – well he would put it up against his nose as though he was picking it! It was good fun – nothing was serious.

What of the audience reaction at shows? Did things build up during the tour?
Anita: Towards the end of the tour they were all waiting for The Beatles. I remember going to the stage door and the girls there asking is this [room] for The Beatles? As it went on they were getting more and more. By the end of the tour, they knew who The Beatles were.
Vilma: I don't think their songs had quite made that impact yet. It's something I remember with Adam more – all that screaming. It didn't start with The Beatles. My husband Chris would put his head out of that window on

an Adam Faith tour and all the girls underneath would be going "Aaagh!" We liked The Beatles' songs and we started doing them. On later tours we sang 'From Me To You' and 'She Loves You'.

So what you were witnessing with The Beatles wasn't unprecedented. You didn't think – My God what's going on here?
Both: No.
Vilma: Because at the time they weren't topping the bill. In our minds we didn't have reverence with them. It was more things that Helen Shapiro did that we would remember because they were on the bill, another boy group, but suddenly they became somebody.

And what of the reaction to Helen?
Anita: Most of the people would have gone to see her. She had a good jazzy voice – low pitched. She would have been singing her hits and she did go down very well. It was packed audiences, because that's what they were there for (to see Helen). It was a good tour really. You could hear the music.
Vilma: Helen was such a sweet girl. She was so nice.

Had you toured with Helen before?
Both: No, but we got on well, everybody did. We all went off and had a meal together, and that's with The Beatles, too.

And you got to see each other singing every night?
Vilma: Yes, we watched each other's shows. They [The Beatles] used to stand at the side of the stage – we all used to at the time – and watch the shows. I remember them standing with us once and saying they wanted to go off and get a drink – did they have to come back soon? Little things that showed they were quite green in those days, because they were new. But we liked their haircuts – they looked different.

Did you have a favourite Beatle?
Anita: We liked George a lot – nice fellow he was. John was like he was – a bit wild. Paul was just ordinary, and Ringo, he was always a bit of a laugh.

So what was appealing about George?
Anita: He was just a very nice, quiet bloke.
Vilma [to Anita]: He appealed to you!

Anita: Well they were all very nice. It was John that was the mad one really. You just weren't on his wavelength. He was a different type altogether.

Did that make you wary of him?
Anita: Not really. He was just a different type of person to anyone else.

But were they sociable? Did you socialise with them?
Vilma: Oh yes and I remember them coming into our dressing room to say goodbye when they left the tour. It was in the Potteries area, I think [Hanley]. They came in and said cheerio to us.

So you got three or four songs to sing? Which would you have done for this tour?
Anita [to Vilma]: Would we have done maybe 'The Day That The Rains Came?' Probably Everly Brothers – we always did Everly Brothers – they used to suit our harmonies, Everly Brothers songs – 'Dream'. We also used to sing 'Manana'.

So you would have sung that on this tour?
Anita: Yes. The Beatles would always be singing 'Manana' at us. After the tour finished they were in a car once and all leaned out and said 'Oi girls'. Then they sang 'Manana' at us! I'd forgotten about that – it's such a long time ago.

So you've got kick-started then, TV work and you're on tours – why didn't you make any records?
Vilma: It was very difficult at that time. Because of The Beatles, girl groups really weren't wanted too much. It became just all about the boy groups.

Did your paths cross again?
Anita: Some time after that we were walking along somewhere and they were in a car and they called out 'Manana' to us and asked, 'Where are you going today girls?'

4. Gordon Sampson, of the *Halifax Evening Courier*
To the good people of Halifax, 21-year-old Gordon Sampson was a sober suited eager young reporter for the *Halifax Evening Courier*. But Gordon was by no means a typical regional newspaper journalist, as when he wasn't reporting on the dealings of the local council or who was up

in court, he was wearing another hat . . . as a concert reviewer for *New Musical Express*.

Gordon first set eyes on The Beatles at their very first house on their very first gig on their very first national tour at the Bradford Gaumont on Saturday, February 2, 1963. By that time he was already the proud holder of an *NME* card that was in those days a passport to hobnob with the stars.

"People used to look at you when you were ushered through to the backstage area where nobody could go and wonder, 'How has he managed to do that?' But when you were a reporter for *NME* you were taken seriously and there wasn't a tour manager who wouldn't have welcomed you."

Gordon's first passport to the stars came a few years before that – when he was still a schoolboy.

"A friend of mine, Phillip Griffin from Halifax, knew Cliff Richard and Hank Marvin and he helped set up an interview with them for me. I sent it to *NME* and they printed it, and that's how I got started really. I got a taste for it and eventually ended up covering shows and stories for *NME*."

The Beatles were on their best behaviour when Gordon chatted to them between houses at Bradford and it was the first of several conversations he was to enjoy with the Fab Four.

"They appreciated my report for *NME* and the boost it had given them and they told me so shortly afterwards when I was ushered through to meet them at Sheffield City Hall. That was a bigger backstage area where the stars could all mingle together. They thanked me for the report and they all signed a picture and gave it to me. I also got them to sign my autograph book that I used to take to the shows. It might surprise some that I did that, but I was a fan.

"I wasn't in awe of The Beatles, however – or anyone for that matter. I had covered lots of pop package shows and it was always just another night – another show."

After those two early tour nights, the paths of The Beatles and Gordon were to cross a few more times and he still remembers what happened at the Leeds Odeon on June 5, 1963, on the Roy Orbison tour. By then The Beatles were big enough to have their own dressing room.

"I had been in there with them, and then John Lennon and Roy Orbison emerged from their dressing rooms at the same time and bumped into each other. It was quite comical. Roy, with his dark glasses, couldn't see very well and John of course was as blind as a bat without his glasses.

"A lot of the audience had come to see The Beatles, but they were quite spellbound by Roy. He would seem to take a while to warm up, but when he got going with 'Pretty Woman' and the rest, it was quite something.

"He never said much. He was always quiet and polite. He always called you Sir and was a gentle man. The Beatles really liked him."

They weren't the only stars on that tour.

"I remember Gerry & The Pacemakers performance that night. They were quite vibrant at the time. It was raw, exciting stuff. It had a buzz about it."

As The Beatles' fame grew during 1963, even an *NME* pass wasn't enough to get you five minutes with them.

"I did see them again after that [Bradford 1964], but by the end of 1963 those intimate moments could no longer be had. By then there was just the press conference for everyone and that was it. It wasn't the same for me. I wanted to be able to chat to them to get that exclusive on what they were planning – what was going to happen next.

"In the early days they were mild mannered and they gave sensible answers to questions. There was none of the cockiness that started to emerge later. Maybe it was the image they wanted to develop or perhaps their way of dealing with people who just asked them about their hair or how long they were going to last, rather than anything they wanted to talk about."

Gordon, who lives in Brighouse, West Yorkshire, is retired but keeps his hand in with journalism and still covers concerts "for the pure joy of it" for the *Halifax Evening Courier*.

5. Geoff Williams and Roger Greenaway, The Kestrels

The claws of The Kestrels – Geoff Williams, Roger Greenaway, Pete Gullane (later replaced by Roger Cook) and Tony Burrows – spread deep across the music world in the years after their Beatles tours. The group disbanded in 1965 but Cook and Greenaway honed their writing skills and had chart hits themselves under the recording names David and Jonathan with Lennon and McCartney's 'Michelle' and their own 'Lovers Of The World Unite' in 1966.

They went on to write many classic songs together, including 'You've Got Your Troubles', 'I'd Like To Teach The World To Sing', 'Home

Lovin' Man', 'Blame It On The Pony Express', 'Melting Pot' and 'Something's Gotten Hold of My Heart'.

Tony Burrows went on to become just about the most popular voice in pop as a studio singer in the 1970s. His voice can be heard as the lead singer on many classic songs, including 'Love Grows (Where My Rosemary Goes)' by Edison Lighthouse, he once had four top 40 singles with four groups in a space of four months, and at one saturation point he was temporarily banned from *Top Of The Pops* by the BBC for fronting four bands on the same show.

The Kestrels have reformed to some acclaim in recent years. Their occasional concerts and a CD entitled *The Kestrels, Still Flying After 50 Years* have helped to raise more than £200,000 for charities such as Cancer Research UK, The Royal British Legion and the Princess Alice Hospice in Esher, Surrey.

Tragically, Geoff Williams – The Kestrel with the memory – died while on holiday in Crete in August 2010. He was 71. Roger Greenaway says: "I'll miss him. We all will. He was the glue that held the group together for 50 years."

Geoff Williams

The famous Beatle bow, always performed with grace at the end of every number onstage, didn't happen by accident. Manager Brian Epstein insisted that his boys should display impeccable manners onstage, but it was touring buddies The Kestrels who helped them master the military precision of bowing and rising in unison.

Kestrel Geoff Williams remembers The Beatles approaching them after watching a performance on the Helen tour. "We would start the second half on the Helen tour and The Beatles had obviously been watching us because when we finished they came up to us and said how do you manage to bow like that, all so neat and tidy.

"What they didn't know is that we had all been in the Army and we were used to doing things in a military style. We'd take a step back, bow from the waist, count two, three, and then rise together. That was exactly how we did it and we taught the move to The Beatles. And whenever you saw them after that you'd see them take a step back, bow low, and two, three, and they would rise together."

Geoff also believes that it's highly possible The Beatles were inspired by

The Kestrels' suits too. "Those stage suits The Beatles used to wear, without the lapels, we used to wear all the time. Ours were grey – very smart."

Geoff is The Kestrel with the keen memory and he smiles at the famous story of Kenny Lynch's abortive song-writing session with The Beatles at the back of the coach. "Kenny wasn't impressed," he smiles, "but we all had a lot of fun. We always used to head for the back of the coach. John and Paul would be working on their songs, while George and Ringo played cards with us. Newmarket was the game we often played, for pennies and tuppences. In those days, if you won a shilling you were doing very well.

"We were pretty much on that coach together for the whole tour, although sometimes people would get a car home if we were within a short drive of where they lived."

Geoff even recalls the gig when it all started to happen for The Beatles. It was the night of Tuesday, February 26 when they played the Gaumont Cinema at Taunton. 'Please Please Me' was sitting proudly on the top of the pile.

"We had been playing to packed houses every night, but people hadn't been coming to see The Beatles . . . up until we got to Taunton. That's when it happened. Helen was off sick that night and Billie Davis had been called in to close the show. She closed the first house, but such was the reaction to The Beatles that they closed the second. It was as instant as that.

"I hadn't met Billie Davis before but to me she was just another singer, not strong enough to close the show really. She had a hit with 'Tell Him', but that was her only song. We opened the second half in the second house to warm everyone up for The Beatles. It seems like that was our place in life."

Geoff also recalls that The Beatles got quite a reception when the tour called in at Southport for the gig at the Odeon Cinema on Friday, March 1. "The press were waiting for them and so were the fans," he said. "There was quite a lot of activity inside the auditorium."

The Beatles were generous with their songs, and The Kestrels were handed 'There's A Place', a Lennon and McCartney track from the *Please Please Me* LP.

"We recorded it and it went out as a single and was doing very well," said Geoff. "It was selling about 500 copies a day but then EMI decided to put it out on a Beatles EP and that was it – everyone lost interest in ours. It just killed our record stone dead."

There was a friendly atmosphere, not just on the bus, but also in the hotels where the performers stayed together. However, security at the theatres had to be tight.

On that first tour The Beatles had the benefit of being able to perform their songs to an audience that could hear them. The screaming hadn't yet broken the sound barrier. "People listened. And it was a good sound. It was very simple, when you think, just the drums and their three guitars with small amplifiers. They even shared mikes. But that's why they were popular, because they could generate such an exciting sound from those few instruments and they could perform onstage every bit as well as they did on record.

"Some of the places were packed for both houses. It would take about a quarter of an hour to clear the place between shows and then it would all start again. The Helen Shapiro tour we did the previous autumn had not been as popular as expected, so Arthur Howes took no chances, booking not just The Beatles but Danny Williams and Kenny Lynch on to the package.

"We knew Helen pretty well by then and got on well with her. She was a young girl, very sociable and nice. We invited her to a party at (fellow Kestrel) Tony Burrows' house one night and she came. She was very pleasant."

Geoff says he never saw The Beatles with drugs – but he can't say the same for Danny Williams. "I'd noticed there used to be this strange smell coming from Danny's changing room. I'd never worked out what it was. Then one night I saw him take this stuff that he'd been hiding in a sock and he smoked it. In all innocence, I asked him why he was hiding it in his sock and he just laughed. The funny thing is when The Kestrels disbanded in 1965 I joined the police. I got promoted to sergeant and they put me in charge of the drugs squad because they reckoned that as I'd been in the music business I must know all about it!"

Then there was the night when they all ended up watching rugby on the television. "It was in Mansfield. There was a rugby international on and we managed to find a local shop that sold televisions and they let us into a back room to watch the rugby."

By the time The Kestrels toured with The Beatles again at the end of 1963 everything had changed. By now The Beatles were not only bill-toppers but they were in a stratosphere all of their own. The mass hysteria was already beginning to get them down, and it was proving troublesome for bands that toured with them, too. Troublesome is probably an understatement. "It was hell. Absolute mayhem. People wouldn't believe what went on during that tour. The Beatles were the biggest thing to ever hit this country.

"It was hell going on before them. Arthur Howes came up one day and said, 'Who's going on in the second half before The Beatles?' But everyone just sat there. It was the spot that nobody wanted. In the end he said he'd pay us double and so we did it. We'd finish our set, step back and bow and make our way off, and the place would erupt. The others used to think we went down an absolute storm, but the truth is the cheering wasn't for us. It was because they knew that as soon as we left the stage there was only one act coming on – The Beatles."

The routine would be the same. "We'd arrive about noon and then we'd not be allowed out – we'd never be able to get back in again. We'd try to get what food we could before we got locked in. The Beatles would arrive about 2.30pm and do all their media stuff, then they would be locked in as well. We used to play Scalextrics."

Geoff remembers the shock of the Kennedy assassination. "We heard the news that JFK had been shot before we went onstage at the Globe Cinema in Stockton. It wasn't until afterwards that we found out he was dead. We went back to the hotel and watched it all on the TV. People couldn't believe it. We were all stunned. We all sat there before the TV – stunned to silence. Nobody said anything. Nobody was into politics in those days, but Kennedy was a popular guy. Everyone loved him as a president. We just couldn't believe that it could happen."

Geoff admires all of the Beatles, but if he had a favourite it would be George. "He was a nice guy – down-to-earth. I'd often find myself chatting with George. Ringo was similar. There was no side to him whatsoever. Everyone knows about John. He could be nasty – very abrupt, especially on the first tour. He was prepared to say what he thought. He was a bit more guarded by the second tour. By then he knew that reporters would pick stuff up. As for Paul, I found him OK on the first tour. But by the second it appeared he may have changed a bit. It was nothing definite.

He didn't do anything to upset me, it's just that he was going out with Jane Asher by then and there was this suspicion that he thought he was better than us now."

The Kestrels also appeared with The Beatles on other occasions, including some Sunday night shows.

Geoff has few regrets about those days, but he does rue not having the gift of foresight. "When you think of the tours we did with The Beatles – all those days we were around them – and we never asked for their autographs. Just imagine if we'd got them to sign the odd programme for us what they'd be worth? I can kick myself about it now, but really it never occurred to us. We were all in it together. We were all part of the package."

But Geoff has purchased one little piece of pop history. "I bought a poster on eBay the other day of a gig we did at the Princes Theatre in Torquay. The Fourmost were on the bill too plus Lynne Perry who went on to play Ivy Tilsley in *Coronation Street*. She was a singer then. I was speaking to Roger [Greenaway] about it but none of us could remember her!"

Roger Greenaway

The songwriter Roger Greenaway now heads the international team of ASCAP (the American Society of Composers, Authors and Publishers), but in 1963 he was a member of the singing group The Kestrels.

Roger and his Kestrels songbirds were in an ideal position to chart the progress of The Beatles in that monumental year of 1963. They toured with them at the beginning of the year, when The Beatles were Fab only on Merseyside, and then again at its end, by which time the group was attracting hysteria at a level never seen before or since.

On that first tour he witnessed night after night the raw performance of the newly suited group onstage, and the reaction of the fans. He was there when the burgeoning talents of Lennon and McCartney penned one of their earliest hit songs and he saw how the mop-tops rubbed along with a bunch of entertainers, who at that time were more famous than they were.

By November, when The Kestrels toured with them again, The Beatles had done a lot of growing up. Those few months had changed their lives forever. They had achieved the domestic fame they craved, but were paying a price. By now they were under siege at every venue.

Tell me about The Red Price Band, who backed The Kestrels on the Helen tour.

Red Price was the saxophone player and Jimmy Nichol was on drums. Yes, it was the same man that drummed for The Beatles when Ringo had his tonsils out. God knows what he's doing now. Great band. We worked with Red in the studio – he had TV stuff as well.

Did you know much about The Beatles before that tour with Helen?

We didn't know much about them because nobody thought they were going to last two minutes. After 'Please Please Me', that's when it happened.

Can you remember the effect that 'Please Please Me' had?

My memory is that they closed the first half right from the beginning, but maybe my memory plays some tricks with me. I don't think they were bottom of the bill at all, even though they had that initial song that wasn't that big. By the time they started that tour they were starting to make noise. So although Geoff [Williams of The Kestrels] remembers it differently, the screaming started right from the beginning for me.

They screamed, but not as much as the second time we did it, because nobody would go on before them because of that. That first tour – I think it built. What happened is that once that record went zooming up the charts every kid in the country was aware of The Beatles. It was like an instant thing and something they have to have and have to be involved with that's cool, although the word cool wasn't used in those days.

Yeah, I remember it being almost instantaneous. If there were a few shows where they didn't scream then I don't remember them. I just remember the chaos. Wherever you were in the theatre or cinema if you had a dressing room and if it had a window and you stuck your hand out of it they would all just go berserk. If you had friends come in and see you to say hello you'd say 'watch this' – they'd go absolutely frantic. And as soon as we'd go out they'd blag anybody that was coming through the door. They'd say can you get me this from The Beatles? Can you get me that from The Beatles? Throwing books at you to get them to sign autographs. It was that crazy. So I remember that almost instantaneously. I don't remember any gigs where they were actually sat down and listened to. Helen found it almost impossible, closing the bill after they had closed the first half.

It must have been embarrassing for her actually. She was only a kid. She was very young. And to be that big and then suddenly have these four tousle haired guys come in . . . but they were girls and young girls are always going to be much more interested in guys.

And of course this is that terrible winter of 1963.
We slept on the coach. We couldn't afford digs. We'd sleep on the coach – about half a dozen of you at the back. The coach was always parked in the local bus station – if they could find a local bus station – and you'd have to get up at 5am because everything started going out. And you'd have to find a tap wherever you could just to throw some water on your face – it was that bad. Every now and then, once a week, you'd find somewhere to have a proper wash because cinemas didn't have the greatest dressing rooms in the world in those days and we were in communal dressing rooms lots of the time. That's why, you know, they shared dressing rooms with us, because cinemas didn't have dressing rooms. Old theatres maybe, but mostly those shows, those one-night stand tours, were in cinemas.

So you're on the road for a month and a lot of the time you're not even getting a bed and breakfast.
Grabbing a bite wherever you could. I have to say they were wonderful times. I don't think young people in the music industry have the excitement or the thrill and the fun that we had in those days. It was just perfect. We were making no money, and initially The Beatles weren't making any money. It took them a while before they started to make any real money. But I feel sorry for any young kids today coming into the music business now, because that's gone. Although you were getting up at 5am and washing yourself under cold taps and things like that, I don't think of that as hardship. If the kids had to do that today . . .

And that's apart from writing songs, recording them, going on the television, going on the radio.
It wasn't glamorous. It was a lot harder than people think. It was 24 hours a day and if you were lucky you may get 15 or 20 minutes onstage, but it was worth it for all that. And, we did the rocking trad shows as well, with Billy Fury and Duffy Power and people like that for Larry Parnes. We did two or three of those. It was hard, but it wasn't, because you were young

kids pioneering. Remember, we hadn't worked in a factory but we'd worked in offices attached to factories and we'd been in the army, so, it was hard, but it was a joy.

What was Helen like? How did you get on with her?
I loved Helen. She was very nice – very down-to-earth, right from the beginning. Although I think she had her first hit record when she was 13 or 14, she never, ever got big-time, big headed. And she was a very talented kid. She played a mean banjo and eventually became a great performer. She'd do the clubs and she could do an hour, two hours, singing and entertaining people. She was that good. And of course she was such a young kid but she had this low voice. It was unique. Helen sang bang in tune. She had a good voice. Jazz and blues – she could do that stuff. She should have been a lot bigger, but the reason why she wasn't bigger is because she made it when she was too young. In those days if you were that young and you had a couple of hits, it was over. You got past puberty into adulthood and it wasn't acceptable, although she still had a great career, but she should have been bigger for longer.

And on this tour you've also got Dave Allen as compère, you've got Kenny Lynch, Danny Williams. So there's a lot of talented people on that coach.
Yes it's an incredible tour when you look back at it. You're right. They do those kind of tours in America now, where you get a dozen – maybe more – big acts. You'd have a comic. Dave Allen was a comic. But he used to introduce the acts, and tell a gag in between.

How did you get on with all these guys?
I can't remember having arguments with anybody. It was fun.

As far as The Beatles are concerned, you'd heard of them before the tour, but what did you think when you met them? What were your first impressions?
I remember thinking they weren't very good. They were fun to be with. They were very friendly. They were as mesmerised as we were about everything. I didn't think they believed they were going to last two minutes. I remember Brian saying if we get a year out of this we'll be lucky. Remember, they'd played some months in Hamburg. That's a tough gig really. That's how they honed their act. Their original drummer, Pete Best, they'd let go.

There's always been this debate among Beatles fans about that.

He didn't go because he wasn't a good drummer, although George Martin will tell that story. He went because he was the best looking. There was a jealousy about it, that's what I was told, in the early days. Pete was so good looking that the girls were all going for him and so Paul and John – John in particular – didn't want that kind of competition from the guy behind. George Harrison had known Ringo from another band. He was rated as *the* drummer of all the local bands in Liverpool. Everybody thought Ringo was a great drummer because he could lay it down. So we never saw or met Pete Best but you heard them talking about him – heard the stories – but George Martin, who I know very well and he recorded us, of course – would tell the story that it was down to him eventually that they had to get rid of Pete and get Ringo in.

How did you find The Beatles – as people?

It seemed to me that the nicest one of them all – and that seemed to apply all the way through the years – was George. I got back into contact with him not long before he died. He was probably the nicest. John could be caustic and difficult, but not with people like us. He was never nasty to us. He wasn't mad about the police. He didn't like the police and of course with all the security you would be surrounded by police – police women too – who would make them [the fans] queue alongside the dressing room.

Did you get a chance to see The Beatles in action on that Helen tour?

I always watched them – I don't know if the other guys did. I've spent my life studying other people. I was the one in the group that when they went to the pictures in the afternoon I'd go round the record stores or I'd learn chords on the guitar – things like that.

You have spoken before about John and Paul's song writing, and how it influenced you . . .

It was so arrogant when I think about it now. They were doing this and I thought, 'Hang about. Kenny Lynch was right. Maybe I could do better than this. I've got to be able to write songs better than this.' And then I met a guy, oddly enough, while visiting a publisher, a guy called Barry Mason, a big writer, but he was managing a guy called Tommy Bruce we were on tour with at that time with one of the Rocking Trad shows. And

I started dabbling a bit after The Beatles. I started trying to do a few things. I didn't realise yet that it wasn't that easy to write songs. But Barry said to me, 'Do you write songs?' And I said, 'No I don't write songs.' He said, 'You're in The Kestrels, you're in the music business, you could write a song.' And he said he needed a B-side for his act, Tommy Bruce. So it was The Beatles and him who finally convinced me I should write some songs. Well I wrote the B-side, but I didn't get the B-side. He said, 'No it's too late now', but that's what started me writing, the thought that I could do better than them.

You were around the Beatles at that time. I'd imagine they were working on songs quite a lot when they weren't onstage.
Every spare moment if they had ideas, they would work on them. On the coach certainly several days they would be working on songs.

You saw them at close hand at a very special time when John and Paul were working together and not separately as they did soon after.
Maybe about the first five hits were like that. And it was during those touring times. You're right, because they did surely but slowly become separate. It kind of happened with Roger Cook and myself after a long period of time, but I know that even though some of the songs he wrote by himself and some of the songs I wrote by myself – that were hits – I know that neither he nor I would have written those songs if we weren't still a partnership. I believe this sincerely, even though they weren't sat down together as they had in the very early days to write songs together, they were influencing each other. Paul would say to himself, 'No John wouldn't like that.' He would say to himself, 'If I play this to John what might he do?' So there was that kind of influence going on. And vice versa. That's a fact in my case, and I think it applied to them as well. In fact, I've seen it happen with other teams. When they split there's no longer the quality or style and they weren't as prolific. And remember, they went to the studio to record those songs and they would have influence over each other while they were recording as well. That's where George Martin's influence would come in about the quality of the arrangements and the quality of the playing, because George would not accept second best. He'd have them there for hours until they got it right. And sometimes, as you know, they didn't always record together, but one

of them might have to stay behind and be there for hours afterwards on their own trying to do what they were doing and get it right.

Did you see them in between the Helen tour and your tour with them at the end of 1963?
I went to see them somewhere on the Roy Orbison tour shortly after the Helen tour. I can't remember why. They were probably playing some town we were in.

Your winter tour with The Beatles started on November 1, 1963.
That was the crazy tour. God, that was crazy. They didn't travel on coaches by then. They'd turn up in these big black limousines. Each town would be warned in advance. You'd have twice the number of police you'd normally see in any town – maybe four times in some places – because it got dangerous. You know when you get a couple of thousand crazy kids literally charging at you.

What were your feelings at the time?
Very quickly we realised it was not good for us. It almost destroyed us as a group. They almost had Geoff's [Williams] eye out. They were throwing things at us because we were keeping them from The Beatles. We only did 15 minutes and we'd shout and swear into the microphones. You could say anything you wanted because they'd just scream. It became awful. The first couple of nights you tried hard just to do your act and hope that they would listen to you, but no. No chance of that. They were screaming for The Beatles. And so I guess there was a building resentment that we'd been around a long time, made a lot more records than even The Beatles had at that stage – never had any success – although the closest was with John Lennon's 'There's A Place'.

How was Brian Epstein reacting to their success?
Well we still shared dressing rooms with them. I remember being in the dressing room with them once – the other Kestrels weren't there at the time – and Brian coming in and saying I've got some news for you guys. He was telling them what was going on with this and what was going on with that and by the way we're not ever going to record anybody else's songs. We're always going to record your songs from now on. And Paul said, 'Are you mad?' And he said, 'No, that's the way it's got to be from now on. Everything by The Beatles – totally self-contained.'

And Beatles' performances this time?
They improved. McCartney improved a lot. And I was quite impressed by McCartney's piano playing. He wasn't doing it onstage – but he could pick up anything and play. As they became better musicians their songs became too musical. They stopped breaking all the rules. You start thinking, 'I can't do this and I can't do that.' You start mastering your craft and as soon as you've mastered your craft you stop writing the hits.

When Roger Cook and I wrote together there was this magic spark. I've written lots of hits with other people, but I've never had that same feeling of that magic spark, and it was the same for Lennon and McCartney. When they wrote together it was just electric – magic – even though Kenny Lynch thought it was crap, of course!

Let's not forget that story. Your memories of that?
We were sat up towards the front of the coach and they were at the back. And if I remember rightly they used to write on Paul's bass or John might have the acoustic guitar. But he wrote songs with just a bass in the early days. I remember that. Now whether McCartney would agree about that – but I saw it. I thought how can he write songs on a bass? But it keeps it simple.

Looking at the second tour – what were the stress levels like?
I don't remember stress. Everybody was aware that everyone was there just to see The Beatles.

That's hard to take, isn't it?
Yes. It is hard. You're performing because you want applause. At the end of a song if people don't applaud – what did I do wrong, you know? I've got to get this right. I'm not getting this right. We had to analyse it every night and said look, this is not us. It's got nothing to do with us. We know we can do well. We've gone out on a Sunday concert with Shirley Bassey and the audience gave us a standing ovation. I would never have worked with The Beatles again after that. We just wouldn't contemplate it. They could have paid us four times the money we were on and we wouldn't have done it. It was soul destroying, and by the end of it we were drained.

Were The Beatles embarrassed about it as well?
No. I don't think they even thought about it. They were just doing their

367

own thing and you didn't see them at the end. You never saw them at the end of a show. They just went.

What were they like? Had they changed?
I don't think so. I don't remember them being any different the second time around. Even when I think now – that McCartney has managed to bring up his family, his kids, the way he has. He's done an incredible job when you think he's probably the biggest pop star that has ever lived. How he's managed it, I don't know. And he has to have a thick skin in certain situations. People say he's difficult, but I don't think he's difficult at all. But he could be tough.

Your memories of them – affable guys?
I can't remember seeing them being nasty to anybody, [laughter] other than John with the police. But he was doing it to make people laugh, or to get his own back on authority. They took it in good part. I don't remember any nastiness. It wasn't a nasty age. The whole thing was about having fun and doing something you loved and getting paid to do it – being lucky enough to do what you were born to do.

The 1960s were just incredible. Each era, especially in the music business, would claim to be the very special one, but of all the decades, the 1960s were special and it was all to do with The Beatles. Their music. They changed the world. They opened America, too. British people didn't get hits in America before them. There was the odd exception – but we copied everything from America. We didn't do anything original. The Beatles opened a market for British writers. At one stage we were getting about 25 per cent of their market – including albums and singles – and that was all pioneered by The Beatles. So I have a lot to thank them for – first of all for making me want to write and secondly for opening the biggest market in the world, for me and for lots of others. I don't think people give them enough credit for that.

6. Don Andrews, of The Remo Four
When The Beatles arrived back from Hamburg at the end of 1960 to storm the Merseybeat scene, The Remo Four were already established as one of the busiest and best paid groups – and bill-topping regulars at The Cavern. Bass player Don Andrew and lead guitarist Colin Manley had been through school – the Liverpool Institute – with Paul and George but

they were as surprised as everyone else to discover that the 'sensational group from Hamburg' included their ex-schoolmates!

The Remos soon surrendered their 'top-paid' status and appeared alongside The Beatles on dozens of occasions over the next two years, but they retained one key advantage – the phenomenal craftsmanship of lead guitarist Colin Manley, universally admired and respected by guitarists in every group on the scene, including George Harrison.

After personnel changes, they turned pro in 1962 to tour the American Army bases in France, before being signed up by Brian Epstein – primarily for their musical ability – and joining several nationwide tours promoted by Epstein and impresario Arthur Howes. They had provided backing for visiting US stars Tommy Roe and Gene Pitney, plus Cilla Black, before The Beatles/Mary Wells tour, on which they had their own spot and also backed Tommy Quickly.

Don Andrew says: "Everybody on the show – apart from The Beatles – travelled on the tour bus, including Mary Wells. The tour was a daily routine of getting to the next theatre early – then being shut inside and besieged by the non-stop screaming of girls until after the second house finished and the crowds went home.

"We enjoyed the shows – particularly working with Tommy Quickly immediately before The Beatles' spot. He was young, cheeky and a natural stage performer. He was like a baby-faced, white version of James Brown and The Beatle fans loved him. We played him on and off with the riff from James Brown's 'Think', going straight into 'I'll Go Crazy'.

"Pye Records sent a mobile recording unit to the Liverpool Empire night and recorded Tommy's spot. 'Humpty Dumpty' was released as a single, complete with a screaming audience and 'I'll Go Crazy' on the B-side."

"My memories include standing in the wings during The Beatles act and watching the jelly babies – some in full boxes – raining onto the stage, along with chocolates, dolls, letters, scarves (no knickers in those days!) and Gonks. As soon as the final curtain closed we dived onstage and scooped up armfuls of sweets.

"Backstage at the show in Glasgow, George came into our dressing room with his guitar. He played a solo he had composed for one of the forthcoming *Beatles For Sale* album tracks and asked Colin what he thought – and how he could make it better.

"Baz and Dick from Sounds Incorporated had cine cameras and filmed parts of the show from the wings. I had offered to draw cartoons of the artistes for captions and a reporter and photographer from *Jackie* were backstage at one of the shows. I still have the cutting from the magazine showing me drawing Tommy Quickly.

"Drummers are all slightly mad, but Sounds drummer Tony Newman was the ultimate nut case. You always knew when he was around and we all loved him. I was amazed recently to learn that my singer/songwriter daughter Helen – stage name Aitch McRobbie and now living in Oxfordshire, is close friends with Tony's son Rich, who plays drums for her performances!"

Don is one old touring mate who does have a programme signed by all four Beatles – and it's a unique item. "The attached programme cover was signed 'To Don' with typical 'school mate' messages: Sodoffy from John Leper. Lots of love from Geoff Harrison. From Another FAT SCHOOL-BOY – Paul McCartney."

7. Bill Covington, of The Rustiks

The Rustiks were counting their blessings when Brian Epstein, on the panel of a TV talent show, signed them to his NEMS empire in 1964. They thought all their Christmases had come at once when they released their debut single 'What A Memory Can Do' in September 1964 and then Epstein immediately booked them in as one of the support acts for The Beatles on the autumn tour.

However, the boys from the West Country were in for a rather bumpy ride.

Drummer Bill Covington says: "It was mental, wasn't it? I came from Plymouth and the band from Paignton and there we were heading up to the bright lights of London to be with the stars. It was unbelievable. But there was very much an attitude from quite a lot of people on the NEMS team that we were just country bumpkins. They couldn't work out why he would bring anybody in from the West Country. They were all northerners and there was hostility towards us. It was a sort of regional racism really. The Rustiks were not a particularly welcome part of the Brian Epstein empire."

But like it or not, The Rustiks had arrived – upping sticks from

Paignton and landing in London. "We moved into The Madison Hotel near Praed Street and that's where we stayed for about a year. In the next room to me was Denny Laine who was in The Moody Blues. Mal Evans would come to see us, and Alf Bicknell was a lovely fellow, too. Peter Brown [Brian Epstein's assistant] was a proper gent. I got legless once at a Beatles party and he rescued me and took me back to the Madison. I apologised when I saw him a couple of days later but he wasn't bothered. It's just rock'n'roll isn't it, was his response."

The Rustiks were on about £30 a week at the time – decent money in 1964, but their expenses – hotel bills etc – came out of that. Not a lot was left, but at least they had a van, equipment and top suits all bought and paid for by Brian Epstein.

Bill recalls there being a friendly atmosphere on the coach among the back-up performers, but they saw little of The Beatles who didn't travel on the tour bus.

"It just wasn't practical by then," he said. "They were having to be sneaked into the venues and they would have to dash out of a side door to escape every night before people knew anything. But they were friendly enough. Ringo was fabulous really and George was a fantastic bloke. I remember he swapped guitars with Rob from our band a couple of times."

The Rustiks had a better chance of talking with a Beatle at a nightclub after the nightly shows – but even then it was difficult. "You would have to catch their ear. We were down the pecking order. There were other guys who knew them from Liverpool or from their Hamburg days and The Beatles didn't know us. Nobody did! But we would head to the clubs with everyone on nights we were in London."

Like most of the artists who toured with The Beatles, Bill would stand in the wings when they were onstage to watch them in action.

"You couldn't really hear anything beyond the first row because the girls would be going mental. I could barely hear anything standing in the wings – maybe the odd drum beat. It was crazy really. Anybody that came out of the stage door was fair game. They would rip the clothes off your back just through association. They would knock walls down. They would go through anything and anyone."

Bill remembers Tommy Quickly as "a mad, lunatic Scouser" but decent to talk to. Mary Wells was also on the coach – but there are no memories of conversations. Age was the barrier this time. "I was only 18 and to her I was just a little kid." Mary had reached the grand old age of 21 . . .

There was little glamour on tour. Everything was on a budget. "We stayed in the cheapest B&Bs you could find. They were always counting the cost. Brian had been a small businessman and he used to keep his eye on the money. It was never a glamorous thing – it would be on to the coach, on to the next show and then out, into the digs and then off and out again the next day. That was it – the daily grind."

The Rustiks and Brian Epstein parted company in March 1966, but Bill has one other memory of a Beatle. "George would sometimes come in when we were playing the Savoy and he would pass notes up – taking the mick, that sort of thing. He'd say that we were still a pile of crap, something like that."

8. Danny Betesh

Danny Betesh of Kennedy Street Enterprises had not long started out when he signed up to promote this tour of stars in the summer of 1963.

The deal was clinched after several meetings with Brian Epstein who was delighted to get his Beatles on a national tour headlined by a top American, and Epstein was even more delighted that his as yet little-known Gerry & The Pacemakers would be included. By the time the tour was to start in the middle of May 1963 there wasn't a self-respecting teen-ager in the country who hadn't heard of The Beatles, and Gerry & The Pacemakers were chart-toppers, too.

So it was great news for Danny and his tour partners Peter Walsh (and associate Tito Burns), and they were fortunate that the American star they eventually signed was as mild mannered and completely lacking in ego as Roy Orbison, who steadfastly never whined about being upstaged by the British pop stars.

"I'm going to say what I'm sure everybody else would say about Roy," said Danny. "He was a very, very nice gentleman. He was never a moment's trouble and just rubbed along with everyone. He was a gentle-man. We toured Roy a little later on when he did top the bill – and that was a line-up that included Freddie & The Dreamers, Brian Poole & The Tremeloes and The Searchers."

Promoting The Beatles on a national tour in the days before full-on mania was a joy. "I had already had some contact with them, and I got to know them very well on this tour," says Danny. "They were full of fun. It's hard to imagine how hot they were at the time. It was ridiculous. They were already selling out just about every venue and people were queuing from 7am or 8am on the day the box offices were opening. On this tour they were still able to go out of a theatre, so there was a chance that fans would bump into them, and they signed autographs. They were very amenable, but later on it just got ridiculous."

Danny and his Kennedy Street empire are among the great survivors from those glory days. Now acting largely as promoters, the Kennedy Street Enterprises have shifted their base from Manchester to Altrincham and they are still involved with some of the biggest names in the business.

ACKNOWLEDGEMENTS

WHEN I started out on this long and winding road about three years ago I had no idea where it would lead. No one commissioned me to write this book. I couldn't even be sure that anyone would publish it. So perhaps the first of my votes of thanks should go to Omnibus Press, and in particular Managing Editor Chris Charlesworth, first for agreeing to publish the book, and secondly for his support while I was writing it.

I am one of the many millions who love the music of The Beatles, and my idea three years ago was to investigate what I saw as one of the few untold aspects of their story – what really happened on their UK tours. I wanted to recreate those heady, magical nights in towns and cities the length and breadth of Great Britain at the very height of Beatlemania, when a temporary and nowadays unimaginable madness gripped its teenage population, especially the female half.

I soon realised that it could only be done through the eyes and ears of those who were there. I set out to trace eye witnesses – the singers, musicians, and one surviving compère, from the six tours, the writers from the music papers of the day – *Disc*, *Melody Maker*, *New Musical Express* and *Record Mirror* – and the reporters and photographers whose duty it was to capture those remarkable scenes in words and pictures for regional news-papers. There were numerous others caught up in the Beatle phenom-enon: cinema managers, hotel employees, security men and, not least, hundreds of policemen whose unenviable role was to somehow maintain public order and prevent injury (or even loss of life) as Beatle visits prompted scenes of hitherto inconceivable mayhem in the nation's towns and cities.

But above all Beatlemania belonged to the fans. Most were teenagers at the time, and now many are grandparents – and grandparents who would worry themselves silly if their 13- and 14-year-old grandchildren were caught up in the kind of scenes that they themselves created and were engulfed in a couple of generations ago. This book could not have happened without the kindness of all of those fans who gave generously from their memory banks for the pure and simple joy of reliving an exceptional, unforgettable time of their lives. This book is their story. I cannot name them all here, but their stories are preserved within these covers. I thank every one of them. Finding them was a matter of rolling up my sleeves to write stories for regional papers, or to steel myself for radio appearances to repeatedly ask the same question – were you there when The Beatles came to town?

My third tactic was that 21st century godsend of the lazy journalist . . . thank you Google!

Research into what was published at the time was vital, of course, and I thank the many newspapers I have used for reference and the journalists I haven't been able to locate or who are sadly no longer with us, but whose words at the time communicated the biggest story of the day.

In addition I would like to thank former Beatles press officer Tony Barrow for allowing me to use several passages from his 2005 book *John, Paul, George, Ringo & Me, The Real Beatles Story* published by Andre Deutsch. By my side constantly through this were the great Beatles diary books *The Complete Beatles Chronicle* by Mark Lewisohn and *The Beatles – A Diary* by Barry Miles, and also Bill Harry's *The Beatles Encyclopedia*. My thanks to them and also to Terry Rawlings for his book *Then, Now and Rare: British Beat 1960–1969*, published by Omnibus, and another must-have for 1960s music fans. My thanks also to the now defunct *Beatles Book Monthly* which always carried the best information on the group.

There are a few people deserving of a special mention for their unwavering support – or put another way – for tolerating my endless questions without once succumbing to the temptation to tell me to go away. I'm thinking in particular of Susan Fuller, from the Arthur Howes organisation, the writer and BBC Radio Merseyside broadcaster Spencer Leigh, the photographer and all-round nice guy Ian Wright, and Mal Cook, another from the Arthur Howes stable. Thanks also to Arthur's son Mark Howes, and to Danny Betesh of Kennedy Street Enterprises who was there in 1963 and was still there beavering away in 2010.

Thanks also to Pete Nash of The British Beatles Fan Club, to Beatles London walks tour guide Richard Porter and to proof reader Lucy Beevor. There will inevitably be others that I have missed here – you will know who you are – so my apologies in advance and my grateful thanks to everyone involved. Thanks of course also to the four people who inspired it all – John, Paul, George and Ringo. Their music touched and changed all of our lives.

Thanks are particularly extended to my beautiful Pravina for supporting me every step of the way while I lost myself in all this for so long.

This book is dedicated to the memory of three men who are very much a part of it, but who sadly didn't live to see it published: Geoff Williams, regarded by his fellow Kestrels as the memory man of the group; Martyn Vickers, the son of the Doncaster policeman; and Derek Adams, the former Hanley journalist who had the unique distinction of having shared a fish and chip supper with The Beatles on March 3, 1963.

Martin Creasy, October 2010